*New Beacon Bible Commentary

1 & 2 THESSALONIANS
A Commentary in the Wesleyan Tradition

Terence Paige

BEACON HILL PRESS
OF KANSAS CITY

Copyright 2017 by Beacon Hill Press of Kansas City

Beacon Hill Press of Kansas City
PO Box 419527
Kansas City, MO 64141
www.BeaconHillBooks.com

ISBN 978-0-8341-2394-6

Printed in the United States of America

All rights reserved. No part of this publication may be reproduced, stored in a retrieval system, or transmitted in any form or by any means—for example, electronic, photocopy, recording—without the prior written permission of the publisher. The only exception is brief quotations in printed reviews.

Cover Design: J.R. Caines
Interior Design: Sharon Page

Unless otherwise indicated all Scripture quotations are from the *Holy Bible, New International Version*® (NIV®). Copyright © 1973, 1978, 1984, 2011 by Biblica, Inc.™ Used by permission. All rights reserved worldwide. Emphasis indicated by underlining in boldface quotations and italic in lightface quotations.

The following versions of Scripture are in the public domain:

The American Standard Version (ASV).

The King James Version of the Bible (KJV).

The following copyrighted versions of Scripture are used by permission:

The *Contemporary English Version* (CEV). Copyright © 1995 by the American Bible Society.

The Holy Bible, English Standard Version (ESV), copyright © 2001 by Crossway Bibles, a division of Good News Publishers. All rights reserved.

Good News Translation® (*Today's English Version*, Second Edition) (GNT). Copyright © 1992 American Bible Society. All rights reserved.

Holman Christian Standard Bible® (HCSB), copyright © 1999, 2000, 2002, 2009 by Holman Bible Publishers, Nashville, Tenn. All rights reserved.

The Jerusalem Bible (JB), copyright © 1966 by Darton, Longman & Todd, Ltd., and Doubleday, a division of Bantam Doubleday Dell Publishing Group, Inc.

The *Lexham English Bible* (LEB). Copyright 2012 Logos Bible Software. Lexham is a registered trademark of Logos Bible Software.

The *New American Standard Bible*® (NASB®), © copyright The Lockman Foundation 1960, 1962, 1963, 1968, 1971, 1972, 1973, 1975, 1977, 1995.

The *New English Bible* (NEB), © the Delegates of the Oxford University Press and the Syndics of the Cambridge University Press 1961, 1970.

The *NET Bible*® (NET), copyright © 1996-2006 by Biblical Studies Press, L.L.C., http://bible.org. Quoted by permission. All rights reserved.

The *New Revised Standard Version* (NRSV) of the Bible, copyright 1989 by the Division of Christian Education of the National Council of the Churches of Christ in the USA. All rights reserved. Emphasis indicated by italic.

The New Testament in Modern English (Phillips). Revised Student Edition, by J. B. Phillips, translator. Reprinted with permission of the Macmillan Publishing Company. Copyright 1958, 1960, 1972 by J. B. Phillips.

The *Revised English Bible* (REB). Copyright © 1989 by Oxford University Press and Cambridge University Press.

The *Revised Standard Version* (RSV) of the Bible, copyright 1946, 1952, 1971 by the Division of Christian Education of the National Council of the Churches of Christ in the USA. All rights reserved.

Library of Congress Cataloging-in-Publication Data

Names: Paige, Terence Peter, 1960- author.
Title: 1 & 2 Thessalonians / Terence Paige.
Other titles: First and Second Thessalonians
Description: Kansas City, MO : Beacon Hill Press of Kansas City, 2017. | Series: New Beacon Bible commentary | Includes bibliographical references.
Identifiers: LCCN 2016036849 | ISBN 9780834123946 (pbk.)
Subjects: LCSH: Bible. Thessalonians—Commentaries.
Classification: LCC BS2725.53 .P35 2017 | DDC 227/.8107—dc23 LC record available at https://lccn.loc.gov/2016036849

The Internet addresses, email addresses, and phone numbers in this book are accurate at the time of publication. They are provided as a resource. Beacon Hill Press of Kansas City does not endorse them or vouch for their content or permanence.

DEDICATION

In Memory of
RALPH MARTIN (1925-2013)
one who modeled Christ
Τοῦτο φρονεῖτε ἐν ὑμῖν ὃ καὶ ἐν Χριστῷ Ἰησοῦ (Phil 2:5)

COMMENTARY EDITORS

General Editors

Alex Varughese
    Ph.D., Drew University
    Professor of Biblical Literature
    Mount Vernon Nazarene University
    Mount Vernon, Ohio

Roger Hahn
    Ph.D., Duke University
    Dean of the Faculty
    Professor of New Testament
    Nazarene Theological Seminary
    Kansas City, Missouri

George Lyons
    Ph.D., Emory University
    Professor of New Testament
    Northwest Nazarene University
    Nampa, Idaho

Section Editors

Robert Branson
    Ph.D., Boston University
    Professor of Biblical Literature
      Emeritus
    Olivet Nazarene University
    Bourbonnais, Illinois

Alex Varughese
    Ph.D., Drew University
    Professor of Biblical Literature
    Mount Vernon Nazarene University
    Mount Vernon, Ohio

Jim Edlin
    Ph.D., Southern Baptist Theological
      Seminary
    Professor of Biblical Literature and
      Languages
    Chair, Division of Religion and
      Philosophy
    MidAmerica Nazarene University
    Olathe, Kansas

Kent Brower
    Ph.D., The University of Manchester
    Vice Principal
    Senior Lecturer in Biblical Studies
    Nazarene Theological College
    Manchester, England

George Lyons
    Ph.D., Emory University
    Professor of New Testament
    Northwest Nazarene University
    Nampa, Idaho

CONTENTS

General Editors' Preface	7
Author's Preface	9
Abbreviations	11
Bibliography	17
Table of Sidebars	28

INTRODUCTION TO FIRST AND SECOND THESSALONIANS — 29

- A. Thessalonica: The City — 29
- B. Religion in Thessalonica — 30
- C. The Founding of the Church and the Troubles at Thessalonica — 32
- D. After the Apostles Left Thessalonica — 35
- E. The Writing of 1 Thessalonians: Authorship, Date, and Integrity — 35
- F. The Literary Structure of 1 Thessalonians: The Outline, Literary Structure, and Genre of 1 Thessalonians — 36
- G. The Contents of 1 Thessalonians — 37
- H. The Writing of 2 Thessalonians: Authorship — 38
- I. The Occasion and Date of 2 Thessalonians — 40
- J. The Genre of 2 Thessalonians — 41
- K. The Contents of 2 Thessalonians — 41
- L. Theological Themes of 1 and 2 Thessalonians — 41
  1. Theological Emphases in 1 Thessalonians — 42
  2. Theological Emphases in 2 Thessalonians — 44

COMMENTARY — 47

1 THESSALONIANS — 47

- I. Greeting: 1 Thessalonians 1:1 — 47
- II. Thanksgiving: 1 Thessalonians 1:2-10 — 53
  - A. Thanksgiving for the Thessalonians' Faith, Love, and Hope (1:2-3) — 54
  - B. Assurance of the Thessalonians' Salvation (1:4-5) — 57
  - C. Thanksgiving for Lives that Demonstrate Faith, Hope, and Love (1:6-10) — 62
- III. Paul and the Thessalonians: 1 Thessalonians 2:1—3:10 — 73
  - A. The Apostles as Models of Holy Love (2:1-12) — 73
  - B. Faithful Imitation and Unfaithful Persecution (2:13-16) — 85
  - C. Separated but Not Divided (2:17—3:10) — 97

1. Separation Anxiety (2:17-20)	98
2. Why Paul Sent Timothy (3:1-5)	101
3. Timothy's Report on the Thessalonians (3:6-10)	104

IV. Second Prayer: 1 Thessalonians 3:11-13 — 109

V. Exhortations and Encouragement: 1 Thessalonians 4:1—5:11 — 117
   A. Ethical Instructions (4:1-12) — 118
      1. Introduction (4:1-2) — 120
      2. Sanctification and Sexuality (4:3-8) — 121
      3. Sanctified Love (4:9-12) — 132
   B. Encouragement from the Parousia (4:13—5:11) — 139
      1. The Dead in Christ Shall Rise (4:13-18) — 139
      2. Be Ready for the Day of the Lord (5:1-11) — 151

VI. The Community of Christ: 1 Thessalonians 5:12-24 — 163
   A. Respect Those Doing Ministry (5:12-13) — 164
   B. Caring for Difficult People (5:14-15) — 166
   C. Preserve a Life of Worship (5:16-22) — 169
   D. Paul's Pastoral Prayer (5:23-24) — 175

VII. Epistolary Closing: 1 Thessalonians 5:25-28 — 187

2 THESSALONIANS — 193

I. Greeting: 2 Thessalonians 1:1-2 — 193

II. Thanksgiving and Excursus on Divine Justice:
2 Thessalonians 1:3-12 — 195
   A. Thanksgiving (1:3-4) — 196
   B. An Excursus on Suffering and God's Justice (1:5-10) — 197
   C. Prayer (1:11-12) — 208

III. About the Parousia and the Man of Lawlessness:
2 Thessalonians 2:1-12 — 215

IV. The Thessalonians Stand in Contrast to the Deceived:
Thanksgiving, Exhortation, Prayer: 2 Thessalonians 2:13-17 — 235
   A. Paul's Confidence in Thessalonian Christians (2:13-15) — 236
   B. Prayer (2:16-17) — 239

V. Request for Prayer: 2 Thessalonians 3:1-5 — 243

VI. Exhortation: 2 Thessalonians 3:6-15 — 251

VII. Closing: 2 Thessalonians 3:16-18 — 265
   A. Prayer-Wish (3:16) — 266
   B. Autographic Conclusion (3:17) — 267
   C. Benediction (3:18) — 268

GENERAL EDITORS' PREFACE

The purpose of the New Beacon Bible Commentary is to make available to pastors and students in the twenty-first century a biblical commentary that reflects the best scholarship in the Wesleyan theological tradition. The commentary project aims to make this scholarship accessible to a wider audience to assist them in their understanding and proclamation of Scripture as God's Word.

Writers of the volumes in this series not only are scholars within the Wesleyan theological tradition and experts in their field but also have special interest in the books assigned to them. Their task is to communicate clearly the critical consensus and the full range of other credible voices who have commented on the Scriptures. Though scholarship and scholarly contribution to the understanding of the Scriptures are key concerns of this series, it is not intended as an academic dialogue within the scholarly community. Commentators of this series constantly aim to demonstrate in their work the significance of the Bible as the church's book and the contemporary relevance and application of the biblical message. The project's overall goal is to make available to the church and for her service the fruits of the labors of scholars who are committed to their Christian faith.

The *New International Version* (NIV) is the reference version of the Bible used in this series; however, the focus of exegetical study and comments is the biblical text in its original language. When the commentary uses the NIV, it is printed in bold. The text printed in bold italics is the translation of the author. Commentators also refer to other translations where the text may be difficult or ambiguous.

The structure and organization of the commentaries in this series seeks to facilitate the study of the biblical text in a systematic and methodical way. Study of each biblical book begins with an ***Introduction*** section that gives an overview of authorship, date, provenance, audience, occasion, purpose, sociological/cultural issues, textual history, literary features, hermeneutical issues, and theological themes necessary to understand the book. This section also includes a brief outline of the book and a list of general works and standard commentaries.

The commentary section for each biblical book follows the outline of the book presented in the introduction. In some volumes, readers will find section ***overviews*** of large portions of scripture with general comments on their overall literary structure and other literary features. A consistent feature of the commentary is the paragraph-by-paragraph study of biblical texts. This section has three parts: **Behind the Text**, **In the Text**, and **From the Text**.

The goal of the **Behind the Text** section is to provide the reader with all the relevant information necessary to understand the text. This includes specific historical situations reflected in the text, the literary context of the text, sociological and cultural issues, and literary features of the text.

In the Text explores what the text says, following its verse-by-verse structure. This section includes a discussion of grammatical details, word studies, and the connectedness of the text to other biblical books/passages or other parts of the book being studied (the canonical relationship). This section provides transliterations of key words in Hebrew and Greek and their literal meanings. The goal here is to explain what the author would have meant and/or what the audience would have understood as the meaning of the text. This is the largest section of the commentary.

The **From the Text** section examines the text in relation to the following areas: theological significance, intertextuality, the history of interpretation, use of the Old Testament scriptures in the New Testament, interpretation in later church history, actualization, and application.

The commentary provides **sidebars** on topics of interest that are important but not necessarily part of an explanation of the biblical text. These topics are informational items and may cover archaeological, historical, literary, cultural, and theological matters that have relevance to the biblical text. Occasionally, longer detailed discussions of special topics are included as *excursuses.*

We offer this series with our hope and prayer that readers will find it a valuable resource for their understanding of God's Word and an indispensable tool for their critical engagement with the biblical texts.

Roger Hahn, Centennial Initiative General Editor
Alex Varughese, General Editor (Old Testament)
George Lyons, General Editor (New Testament)

AUTHOR'S PREFACE

These two fascinating letters by Paul may be the earliest Christian documents still extant. That alone might give any reader reason enough to ask what they reveal about the beginnings of Christianity. My prayer is that through contemplation of these letters by Paul, readers will be led to a fresh encounter with the living Lord whose presence was so overwhelming that it transformed the lives of this apostle and a whole community of former polytheists in Macedonia.

Wrestling with the text of Scripture is both an academic and a spiritual discipline. It is academic as far as one brings discipline, thoughtfulness, and the tools of study to the text. It is spiritual in so far as one brings prayer, meditation on the text, and faith in the mystery that the living God has spoken through his human servants, and continues to speak through Scripture, to reveal his saving will and to guide people into lives of faith, love, and hope through the Son of God, in the power of the Spirit. I invite readers to join in this wrestling and decision-making, along with the whole body of Christ.

My long-suffering editor George Lyons has provided many helpful comments and insights to the work and has continued to support me despite missed deadlines. This commentary would not have been finished without the great patience and support of my wife, Tracy, who spent many weekends and evenings a "commentary widow" while I worked on it. I am also grateful to Houghton College for a sabbatical leave and to the gracious assistance of the people at the University of Buffalo library, Christ the King Seminary library, and last but not least the interlibrary loan folks at Houghton College who have supplied me with an amazing variety of material.

For whatever is of value herein, *soli Deo gloria*.

ABBREVIATIONS

With a few exceptions, these abbreviations follow those in *The SBL Handbook of Style* (Alexander 1999).

General

†	author's translation (other than Scripture)
‖	parallel
→	see the commentary at
AD	anno Domini (precedes date) (equivalent to CE)
BC	before Christ (follows date) (equivalent to BCE)
BCE	before the Common Era (equivalent to BC)
CE	Common Era (equivalent to AD)
ch	chapter
chs	chapters
ed.	edition, editor
eds.	editors
e.g.	*exempli gratia*, for example
esp.	especially
etc.	*et cetera*, and the rest
f(f).	and the following one(s)
Gk.	Greek
ibid.	*ibidem.*, at the same place
i.e.	*id est*, that is
ktl	*kai ta loipa* (Gk.: etc.)
Lat.	Latin
lit.	literally
LXX	Septuagint (the Greek OT)
MS	manuscript
MSS	manuscripts
MT	Masoretic Text (of the OT)
n.	note
n.d.	no date
n.p.	no place; no publisher; no page
nn.	notes
NT	New Testament
OT	Old Testament
Q	Qumran
repr.	reprinted
s.v.	*sub verbo*, under the word
v	verse
vv	verses

Modern English Versions of the Bible

ASV	American Standard Version
CEV	Contemporary English Version
ESV	English Standard Version
GNT	Good News Translation
HCSB	Holman Christian Standard Bible
JB	Jerusalem Bible
KJV	King James Version
LEB	Lexham English Bible
NASB	New American Standard Bible
NEB	New English Bible
NET	The NET Bible
NIV	New International Version (2011)
NRSV	New Revised Standard Version
Phillips	J. B. Phillip's New Testament
REB	Revised English Bible
RSV	Revised Standard Version

Print Conventions for Translations

Bold font   NIV (bold without quotation marks in the text under study; elsewhere in the regular font, with quotation marks and no further identification)

Bold italic font   Author's translation (without quotation marks)

Behind the Text: Literary or historical background information average readers might not know from reading the biblical text alone

In the Text: Comments on the biblical text, words, phrases, grammar, and so forth

From the Text: The use of the text by later interpreters, contemporary relevance, theological and ethical implications of the text, with particular emphasis on Wesleyan concerns

Ancient Sources

Old Testament

Gen	Genesis	Dan	Daniel	**New Testament**		
Exod	Exodus	Hos	Hosea	Matt	Matthew	
Lev	Leviticus	Joel	Joel	Mark	Mark	
Num	Numbers	Amos	Amos	Luke	Luke	
Deut	Deuteronomy	Obad	Obadiah	John	John	
Josh	Joshua	Jonah	Jonah	Acts	Acts	
Judg	Judges	Mic	Micah	Rom	Romans	
Ruth	Ruth	Nah	Nahum	1—2 Cor	1—2 Corinthians	
1—2 Sam	1—2 Samuel	Hab	Habakkuk			
1—2 Kgs	1—2 Kings	Zeph	Zephaniah	Gal	Galatians	
1—2 Chr	1—2 Chronicles	Hag	Haggai	Eph	Ephesians	
Ezra	Ezra	Zech	Zechariah	Phil	Philippians	
Neh	Nehemiah	Mal	Malachi	Col	Colossians	
Esth	Esther			1—2 Thess	1—2 Thessalonians	
Job	Job			1—2 Tim	1—2 Timothy	
Ps/Pss	Psalm/Psalms			Titus	Titus	
Prov	Proverbs			Phlm	Philemon	
Eccl	Ecclesiastes			Heb	Hebrews	
Song	Song of Songs/Song of Solomon			Jas	James	
Isa	Isaiah			1—2 Pet	1—2 Peter	
Jer	Jeremiah			1—2—3 John	1—2—3 John	
Lam	Lamentations			Jude	Jude	
Ezek	Ezekiel			Rev	Revelation	

(Note: Chapter and verse numbering in the MT and LXX often differ compared to those in English Bibles. To avoid confusion, all biblical references follow the chapter and verse numbering in English translations, even when the text in the MT and LXX is under discussion.)

Apocrypha

Bar	Baruch
Add Dan	Additions to Daniel
Pr Azar	Prayer of Azariah
Bel	Bel and the Dragon
Sg Three	Song of the Three Young Men
Sus	Susanna
1—2 Esd	1—2 Esdras
Add Esth	Additions to Esther
Ep Jer	Epistle of Jeremiah
Jdt	Judith
1—2 Macc	1—2 Maccabees
3—4 Macc	3—4 Maccabees
Pr Man	Prayer of Manasseh
Ps 151	Psalm 151
Sir	Sirach/Ecclesiasticus
Tob	Tobit
Wis	Wisdom of Solomon

OT Pseudepigrapha

Apoc. Ab.	*Apocalypse of Abraham*
Apoc. Mos.	*Apocalypse of Moses*
Apoc. Sedr.	*Apocalypse of Sedrach*

As. Mos.	Assumption of Moses
2 Bar.	2 Baruch (Syriac Apocalypse)
3 Bar.	3 Baruch (Greek Apocalypse)
4 Bar.	4 Baruch (Paraleipomena Jeremiou)
1 En.	1 Enoch (Ethiopic Apocalypse)
2 En.	2 Enoch (Slavonic Apocalypse)
3 En.	3 Enoch (Hebrew Apocalypse)
4 Ezra	4 Ezra
Jos. Asen.	Joseph and Aseneth
Jub.	Jubilees
Liv. Pro.	Lives of the Prophets
Mart. Ascen. Isa.	Martyrdom and Ascension of Isaiah
Mart. Isa.	Mart. Ascen. Isa. 1—5
Ps.-Phoc.	Pseudo-Phocylides
Pss. Sol.	Psalms of Solomon
Sib. Or.	Sibylline Oracles
T. Isaac	Testament of Isaac
T. Naph.	Testament of Naphtali
Vis. Ezra	Vision of Ezra

Qumran
1QH^a	Hodayot^a or Thanksgiving Hymns^a
1QM	Milhamah or War Scroll
1QpHab	Pesher Habakkuk
1QS	Serek Hayahad or Rule of the Community
1QSb	Rule of the Blessings
4Q161	plsa^a
4Q169	pNah
4Q174	Florilegium
4Q521	Messianic Apocalypse
CD	Cairo Genizah copy of the Damascus Document

Mishnah, Talmud, and Related Literature
Exod. Rab.	Exodus Rabbah
Gen. Rab.	Genesis Rabbah
m. ʾAbot	Mishnah ʾAbot
m. Peʾah	Mishnah Peʾah
t. Sanh.	tractate Sanhedrin

Josephus
Ant.	Jewish Antiquities
J.W.	Jewish War

Philo
Ebr.	De ebrietate (On Drunkenness)
Flacc.	In Flaccum (Against Flaccus)
Leg. 1, 2, 3	Legum allegoriae I, II, III (Allegorical Interpretation of Laws 1, 2, 3)
Legat.	Legatio ad Gaium (On the Embassy to Gaius)
Mos.	De vita Mosis (On the Life of Moses)
Prob.	Quod omnis probus liber sit (That Every Good Person Is Free)
Somn. 1, 2	De somniis I, II (On Dreams 1, 2)
Spec. 1, 2, 3, 4	De specialibus legibus I, II, III, IV (On the Special Laws 1, 2, 3, 4)
Virt.	De virtutibus (On the Virtues)

Apostolic Fathers
Barn.	Barnabas
1—2 Clem.	1—2 Clement
Did.	Didache
Herm. Mand.	Shepherd of Hermas, Mandate(s)
Herm. Sim.	Shepherd of Hermas, Similitude(s)
Herm. Vis.	Shepherd of Hermas, Vision
Ign. Eph.	Ignatius, To the Ephesians
Ign. Magn.	Ignatius, To the Magnesians
Ign. Phld.	Ignatius, To the Philadelphians

Ign. *Pol.*	Ignatius, *To Polycarp*
Ign. *Rom.*	Ignatius, *To the Romans*
Ign. *Smyrn.*	Ignatius, *To the Smyrnaeans*
Mart. *Pol.*	*Martyrdom of Polycarp*
Pol. *Phil.*	Polycarp, *To the Philippians*

New Testament Apocrypha and Pseudepigrapha

Apoc. Pet.	*Apocalypse of Peter*
Apos. Con.	*Apostolic Constitutions and Canons*
Gos. Thom.	*Gospel of Thomas*

Greek and Roman Literature

Apuleius
    Metam.   *Metamorphoses (The Golden Ass)*
Aristides
    Apol.   *Apology*
Augustus
    Res gest. divi Aug.   *Res gestae divi Augusti (Deeds of the Divine Augustus)*
Clement of Alexandria
    Strom.   *Stromata (Miscellanies)*
Demosthenes
    Fals. leg.   *De falsa legatione (False Embassy)*
Dio Chrysostom
    Alex.   *Ad Alexandrinos (Or. 32; To the People of Alexandria)*
Diodorus Siculus
    Library   *Library of History*
Diogenes Laertius
    Lives   *Lives of Eminent Philosophers*
Dionysius of Halicarnassus
    Ant. rom.   *Antiquitates romanae (Roman Antiquities)*
Epictetus
    Diatr.   *Diatribai (Dissertationes)*
Eusebius
    Hist. eccl.   *Historia ecclesiastica (Ecclesiastical History)*
Firmicus Maternus
    Err. prof. rel.   *De errore profanarum religionum (On the Error of Profane Religions)*
Gregory of Nyssa
    Or. catech. magn.   *Oration catechetica magna (Great Catechism)*
Homer
    Il.   *Ilias (Iliad)*
    Od.   *Odyssea (Odyssey)*
John Chrysostom
    Hom. 1 Thess.   *Homiliae in epistulam i ad Thessalonicenses (Homilies in 1 Thessalonians)*
    Hom. 2 Thess.   *Homiliae in epistulam ii ad Thessalonicenses (Homilies in 2 Thessalonians)*
Justin Martyr
    1 Apol.   *Apologia i (First Apology)*
    Dial.   *Dialogus cum Tryphone (Dialogue with Trypho)*
Juvenal
    Sat.   *Satirae (Satires)*
Livy (Titus Livius)
    Livy   *Ab Urbe Condita (The History of Rome)*
Lucian
    Alex.   *Alexander the False Prophet*
    Peregr.   *De morte Peregrini (The Passing of Peregrinus)*
    Philops.   *Philopseudes (The Lover of Lies)*
Martial
    Epigr.   *Epigrammata (Epigrams)*
Origen
    Cels.   *Contra Celsum*
Ovid
    Ars   *Ars amatoria*

Pausanias
    Descr.   *Graeciae description (Description of Greece)*
Plato
    Apol.   *Apologia (Apology of Socrates)*
    Crat.   *Cratylus*
    Gorg.   *Gorgias*
    Phaed.   *Phaedo*
    Phaedr.   *Phaedrus*
    Resp.   *Respublica (Republic)*
    Symp.   *Symposium*
    Tim.   *Timaeus*
Plutarch
    Adul. amic.   *Quomodo adulator ab amico internoscatur (How to Tell a Flatterer from a Friend)*
    Aem.   *Aemilius Paullus*
    Cam.   *Camillus*
    Conj. praec.   *Conjugalia Praecepta (Advice to Bride and Groom)*
    Cons. Apoll.   *Consolatio ad Apollonium (Letter of Condolence to Apollonius)*
    Cons. ux.   *Consolatio ad uxorem (Consolation to His Wife)*
    Fab.   *Fabius Maximus*
    Inim. util.   *De capienda ex inimicis utilitate (How to Profit by One's Enemies)*
    Is. Os.   *De Iside et Osiride (On Isis and Osiris)*
    Pomp.   *Pompeius (Pompey)*
    Pyth. orac.   *De Pythiae oraculis (The Oracles at Delphi No Longer Given in Verse)*
    Rom.   *Romulus*
    Tim.   *Timoleon*
Polybius
    Hist.   *Histories*
Sophocles
    El.   *Elektra*
Suetonius
    Claud.   *Divus Claudius*
    Otho   *Otho*
    Vit.   *Vitellius*
Tacitus
    Ann.   *Annales (Annals)*
Tertullian
    Apol.   *Apologeticus (Apology)*
    Res.   *De resurrectione carnis (The Resurrection of the Flesh)*
Theophilus of Antioch
    Autol.   *Ad Autolycum (To Autolycus)*
Virgil
    Aen.   *Aeneid*
    Ecl.   *Eclogae*
Xenophon
    Anab.   *Anabasis*
    Cyr.   *Cyropaedia*
    Oec.   *Oeconomicus*

Papyri

    BGU   *Aegyptische Urkunden aus den Königlichen Museen zu Berlin, Griechische Urkunden.* Vol. 2. Berlin, 1898.
    P.Eleph.   *Aegyptische Urkunden aus den Königlichen Museen in Berlin: Griechische Urkunden*, Sonderheft. *Elephantine-Papyri*, ed. O. Rubensohn. Berlin, 1907.
    P.Giss.   *Griechische Papyri im Museum des oberhessischen Geschichtsvereins zu Giessen*, ed. O. Eger, E. Kornemann, and P. M. Meyer. Leipzig-Berlin, 1910-12.
    P.Oxy.   *The Oxyrhynchus Papyri*. Graeco-Roman Memoirs. London: Egypt Exploration Society, 1898-2010.
    PSI   *Papiri greci e latini*. Pubblicazioni della Società Italiana per la ricerca dei papiri greci e latini in Egitto. Vol. 12. Florence, 1943-51.

P.Tebt.	*The Tebtunis Papyri*, Vol. I. Ed. B. P. Grenfell, A. S. Hunt, and J. G. Smyly. London: Oxford University Press, 1902.	
UPZ	*Urkunden der Ptolemäerzeit (ältere Funde)*, ed. U. Wilcken. Berlin, 1927-57.	

Secondary Sources

AB	Anchor Bible
ABD	*Anchor Bible Dictionary* (see Freedman)
ANRW	*Aufstieg und Niedergang der römischen Welt* (see Temporini)
BAGD	*A Greek-English Lexicon of the New Testament*, 2d rev. ed. (see Bauer)
BDAG	*A Greek-English Lexicon of the New Testament*, 3d rev. ed. (see Bauer)
CDC	Centers for Disease Control and Prevention
DPL	*Dictionary of Paul and His Letters* (see Hawthorne)
EDNT	*Exegetical Dictionary of the New Testament* (see Balz)
ICC	International Critical Commentary
IG	*Inscriptiones Graecae*
JSNTSup	Journal for the Study of the New Testament: Supplement Series
JSOT	*Journal for the Study of the Old Testament*
JTS	*Journal of Theological Studies*
LSJM	*Greek-English Lexicon* (see Liddell)
LSJM Supplement	*Greek-English Lexicon: Supplement* (see Liddell)
MM	*The Vocabulary of the Greek Testament* (see Moulton and Milligan)
NICNT	New International Commentary on the New Testament
NIDNTT	*New International Dictionary of New Testament Theology* (see Brown)
TDNT	*Theological Dictionary of the New Testament* (see Kittel)
WesTJ	*Wesleyan Theological Journal*
WUNT	Wissenschaftliche Untersuchungen zum Neuen Testament

Greek Transliteration

Greek	Letter	English
α	alpha	a
β	bēta	b
γ	gamma	g
γ	gamma nasal	n (before γ, κ, ξ, χ)
δ	delta	d
ε	epsilon	e
ζ	zēta	z
η	ēta	ē
θ	thēta	th
ι	iōta	i
κ	kappa	k
λ	lambda	l
μ	mu	m
ν	nu	n
ξ	xi	x
ο	omicron	o
π	pi	p
ρ	rhō	r
ρ	initial rhō	rh
σ/ς	sigma	s
τ	tau	t
υ	upsilon	y
υ	upsilon	u (in diphthongs: au, eu, ēu, ou, ui)
φ	phi	ph
χ	chi	ch
ψ	psi	ps
ω	ōmega	ō
ʽ	rough breathing	h (before initial vowels or diphthongs)

Hebrew Consonant Transliteration

Hebrew/ Aramaic	Letter	English
א	alef	ʼ
ב	bet	b
ג	gimel	g
ד	dalet	d
ה	he	h
ו	vav	v or w
ז	zayin	z
ח	khet	ḥ
ט	tet	ṭ
י	yod	y
כ/ך	kaf	k
ל	lamed	l
מ/ם	mem	m
נ/ן	nun	n
ס	samek	s
ע	ayin	ʽ
פ/ף	pe	p; f (spirant)
צ/ץ	tsade	ṣ
ק	qof	q
ר	resh	r
שׂ	sin	ś
שׁ	shin	š
ת	tav	t; th (spirant)

BIBLIOGRAPHY

Commentaries

Airhart, Arnold E. 1965. I and II Thessalonians. Pages 433-537 of vol. 9 in Beacon Bible Commentary. Kansas City: Beacon Hill Press of Kansas City.

Aland, Barbara, Kurt Aland, Johannes Karavidopoulos, Carlo M. Martini, and Bruce M. Metzger, eds. 1999. *Novum Testamentum Graece*. 27th ed. Stuttgart: Deutsche Bibelgesellschaft.

Aquinas, Thomas. 1969. *Commentary on Saint Paul's First Letter to the Thessalonians*. Translated by Michael Duffy. Albany, NY: Magi Books. HTML-formatted by Joseph Kenny, O.P. Accessed online at: http://josephkenny.joyeurs.com/CDtexts/SS1Thes.htm.

Beale, G. K. 2003. *1 & 2 Thessalonians*. IVP New Testament Commentary. Downers Grove, IL: InterVarsity.

Best, Ernest. 1986. *The First and Second Epistles to the Thessalonians*. Black's New Testament Commentary. London: Black, 1972. Repr., Peabody, MA: Hendrickson.

Bockmuehl, Markus. 1997. *A Commentary on the Epistle to the Philippians*. London: A & C Black.

Bruce, F. F. 1982. *1 & 2 Thessalonians*. Word Biblical Commentary 45. Waco, TX: Word.

Brueggemann, Walter. 1984. *The Message of the Psalms: A Theological Commentary*. Minneapolis: Augsburg.

Calvin, John. 1960a. *The Epistles of Paul the Apostle to the Romans and to the Thessalonians*. Translated by Ross MacKenzie. Grand Rapids: Eerdmans. First Latin ed., 1540.

Cranfield, C. E. B. 1975. *A Critical and Exegetical Commentary on the Epistle to the Romans*, 2 vols. International Critical Commentary. Edinburgh: T&T Clark.

Elias, Jacob. 1995. *1 & 2 Thessalonians*. Believers Church Bible Commentary. Scottsdale, PA: Herald Press.

Fee, Gordon. 1995. *Paul's Letter to the Philippians*. New International Commentary on the New Testament. Grand Rapids: Eerdmans.

———. 2009. *The First and Second Letters to the Thessalonians*. New International Commentary on the New Testament. Grand Rapids: Eerdmans.

Findlay, George G. 1904. *The Epistles of Paul the Apostle to the Thessalonians*. Cambridge Greek Testament for Schools and Colleges. Cambridge: Cambridge University Press.

Frame, James Everett. 1912. *A Critical and Exegetical Commentary on the Epistles of St. Paul to the Thessalonians*. International Critical Commentary. Edinburgh: T&T Clark.

Furnish, Victor Paul. 1984. *II Corinthians*. Anchor Bible 32A. Garden City, NY: Doubleday.

———. 2007. *1 Thessalonians, 2 Thessalonians*. Abingdon New Testament Commentaries. Nashville: Abingdon.

Gaventa, Beverly Roberts. 1998. *First and Second Thessalonians*. Interpretation. Atlanta: John Knox.

Gorday, Peter, ed. 2000. *Colossians, 1-2 Thessalonians, 1-2 Timothy, Titus, Philemon*. Ancient Christian Commentary on Scripture, vol. 9. Downers Grove, IL: InterVarsity.

Green, Gene L. 2002. *The Letters to the Thessalonians*. Pillar New Testament Commentary. Grand Rapids: Eerdmans.

Havener, Ivan. 1983. *First Thessalonians, Philippians, Philemon, Second Thessalonians, Colossians, Ephesians*. Collegeville Bible Commentary. Collegeville, MN: Liturgical Press.

Holmes, Michael William. 1998. *1 and 2 Thessalonians*. NIV Application Commentary. Grand Rapids: Zondervan.

Lightfoot, Joseph B. 1957. *Notes on the Epistles of St. Paul, Based on the Greek Text from Previously Unpublished Commentaries*. London: Macmillan, 1895. Repr., Grand Rapids: Zondervan.

Lyons, George. 2012. *Galatians: A Commentary in the Wesleyan Tradition*. New Beacon Bible Commentary. Kansas City: Beacon Hill Press of Kansas City.

Malherbe, Abraham J. 2000. *The Letters to the Thessalonians*. Anchor Bible 32B. New York: Doubleday.

Marshall, I. Howard. 1983. *1 and 2 Thessalonians*. New Century Bible Commentary. Grand Rapids: Eerdmans.

Matera, Frank. 2012. *God's Saving Grace: A Pauline Theology*. Grand Rapids: Eerdmans.

Menken, Maarten J. J. 1994. *2 Thessalonians*. London and New York: Routledge.

Milligan, George. 1908. *St. Paul's Epistles to the Thessalonians. The Greek Text, with Introduction and Notes.* London: Macmillan.
Morris, Leon. 1991. *The First and Second Epistles to the Thessalonians.* New International Commentary on the New Testament, Rev. ed. Grand Rapids: Eerdmans.
Neil, William. 1950. *The Epistle of Paul to the Thessalonians.* Moffatt New Testament Commentary. New York: Harper & Brothers.
Plummer, Alfred. 1918. *A Commentary on St. Paul's First Epistle to the Thessalonians.* London: Robert Scott Roxburghe House.
Reese, James M. 1979. *1 and 2 Thessalonians.* New Testament Message. Wilmington, DE: Glazier.
Richard, Earl. 1995. *First and Second Thessalonians.* Sacra Pagina. Collegeville, MN: Liturgical Press.
Rigaux, Béda. 1956. *Les Épitres aux Thessaloniciens.* Études bibliques. Paris: J. Gabalda.
Shogren, Gary S. 2012. *1 & 2 Thessalonians.* Zondervan Exegetical Commentary on the New Testament. Grand Rapids: Zondervan.
Theodoret of Cyrus. 2001. *Commentary on the Letters of St. Paul,* Vol. 2. Translated with introduction by Robert C. Hill. Brookline, MA: Holy Cross Orthodox Press.
Thiselton, Anthony C. 2011. *1 & 2 Thessalonians Through the Centuries.* Chichester, UK: Wiley-Blackwell.
Trilling, Wolfgang. 1972. *Untersuchungen zum zweiten Thessalonicherbrief.* Leipzig: St. Benno.
Wanamaker, Charles A. 1990. *The Epistles to the Thessalonians: A Commentary on the Greek Text.* New International Greek Testament Commentary. Grand Rapids: Eerdmans.
Ward, Ronald Arthur. 1973. *Commentary on 1 & 2 Thessalonians.* Waco, TX: Word Books.
Whiteley, Denys Edward Hugh. 1969. *Thessalonians in the Revised Standard Version.* New Clarendon Bible. Oxford: Oxford University Press.
Williams, David John. 1992. *1 and 2 Thessalonians.* New International Biblical Commentary 12. Peabody, MA: Hendrickson Publishers.
Witherington, Ben, III. 2006. *1 and 2 Thessalonians: A Socio-Rhetorical Commentary.* Grand Rapids: Eerdmans.
Woolsey, Warren M. 1997. *1 & 2 Thessalonians: A Bible Commentary in the Wesleyan Tradition.* Indianapolis: Wesleyan Publishing House.

Monographs, Articles, Other Resources

Abbott, Frank F., and Allan C. Johnson. 1926. *Municipal Administration in the Roman Empire.* New York: Russell & Russell.
Aland, Kurt, and Barbara Aland. 1989. *The Text of the New Testament,* 2d ed. Translated by E. F. Rhodes. Grand Rapids: Eerdmans.
Ancient Macedonia II: Papers Read at the Second International Symposium, Thessaloniki, 19-24 August 1973. 1983. Hidryma Meletōn Cheronēsou tou Haimou, 155. Thessaloniki: Institute for Balkan Studies.
Ancient Macedonia III: Papers Read at the Third International Symposium, Thessaloniki, 21-25 September 1977. 1983. Hidryma Meletōn Cheronēsou tou Haimou, 193. Thessaloniki: Institute for Balkan Studies.
Ancient Macedonia V: Papers Read at the Fifth International Symposium Held in Thessaloniki, October 10-15, 1989. 1993. Hidryma Meletōn Cheronēsou tou Haimou, 240. Thessaloniki: Institute for Balkan Studies.
Ancient Macedonia VI: Papers Read at the Sixth International Symposium Held in Thessaloniki, October 15-19, 1996. 1999. Hidryma Meletōn Cheronēsou tou Haimou, 272. Thessaloniki: Institute for Balkan Studies.
Archaia Makedonia: anakoinōseis kata to Prōton Diethnes Symposion en Thessalonikē, 26-29 Augoustou 1968 [Ancient Macedonia: Papers Read at the First International Symposium Held in Thessaloniki 26-29 August 1968]. 1970. Hidryma Meletōn Cheronēsou tou Haimou, 122. Edited by Vasileios Laourdas and Ch. Makaronas. Thessaloniki: Institute for Balkan Studies.
Archer, Gleason L., Jr., Paul Feinberg, Douglas Moo, Richard Reiter. 1996. *Three Views on the Rapture: Pre-, Mid-, or Post-Tribulation?* Grand Rapids: Zondervan.
Ascough, Richard S. 2003. *Paul's Macedonian Associations: The Social Context of Philippians and 1 Thessalonians.* Tübingen: Mohr Siebeck.
Aune, David E. 1983. *Prophecy in Early Christianity and the Ancient Mediterranean.* Grand Rapids: Eerdmans.
Balsdon, J. P. V. D. 1962. *Roman Women: Their History and Habits.* Westport, CT: Greenwood Publishers.

Balz, Horst. 1972. *hypnos, ktl. Theological Dictionary of the New Testament* 8:545-56.
Balz, Horst Robert, and Gerhard Schneider. 1990. *Exegetical Dictionary of the New Testament.* Translated by Virgil P. Howard and James W. Thompson. Grand Rapids: Eerdmans.
Barclay, John M. G. 1992. Thessalonica and Corinth: Social Contrasts in Pauline Christianity. *Journal for the Study of the New Testament* 47:49-74.
———. 1993. Conflict in Thessalonica. *Catholic Biblical Quarterly* 55:512-30.
Bassler, Jouette M. 1984. The Enigmatic Sign: 2 Thessalonians 1:5. *Catholic Biblical Quarterly* 46:496-510.
———. 1994. Peace in All Ways: Theology in the Thessalonian Letters: A Response to R. Jewett, E. Krentz, and E. Richard. Edited by Jouette M. Bassler. Pages 71-85 in *Pauline Theology*, Vol. 1: *Thessalonians, Philippians, Galatians, Philemon.* Philadelphia: Fortress.
Bauer, Walter. 1979. *A Greek-English Lexicon of the New Testament and Other Early Christian Literature*, 2d ed. Translated and adapted by W. F. Arndt and F. W. Gingrich. Revised by F. W. Gingrich and Frederick W. Danker. Chicago: University of Chicago Press.
Bauer, Walter, Frederick Danker, William F. Arndt, and F. W. Gingrich. 2000. *A Greek-English Lexicon of the New Testament and Other Early Christian Literature*, 3d ed. Revised and edited by F. W. Danker. Chicago: University of Chicago Press.
Baumgärtel, Friedrich, and Johannes Behm. 1965. *Kardia. Theological Dictionary of the New Testament* 3:605-14.
Beard, Mary, John North, and Simon Price, eds. 1998. *Religions of Rome.* Vol. 1: *A History.* Cambridge: Cambridge University Press.
Becker, Ulrich. 1999. Gospel, Evangelize, Evangelist. *New International Dictionary of New Testament Theology* 2:107-15.
Behm, Johannes. 1967. *Noutheteō. Theological Dictionary of the New Testament* 4:1019-22.
Bengtson, Vern, with Norella M. Putney and Susan Harris. 2013. *Families and Faith: How Religion Is Passed Down Across Generations.* New York: Oxford University Press.
Bertram, Georg. 1974. *Ōdin, ōdinō. Theological Dictionary of the New Testament* 9:667-74.
Blundell, Sue. 1995. *Women in Ancient Greece.* Cambridge, MA: Harvard University Press.
Boatwright, Mary T., Daniel J. Gargola, and Richard J. A. Talbert. 2004. *The Romans from Village to Empire.* New York: Oxford University Press.
Book of Common Prayer. 1979. New York: Church Hymnal Corporation.
Bradley, Keith. 1986. Wet-Nursing at Rome: A Study in Social Relations. Pages 201-29 in *The Family in Ancient Rome: New Perspectives.* Edited by Beryl Rawson. Ithaca, NY: Cornell University Press.
———. 1991. *Discovering the Roman Family: Studies in Roman Social History.* New York and Oxford: Oxford University Press.
Brocke, Christoph vom. 2001. *Thessaloniki: Stadt des Kassander und Gemeinde des Paulus:eine frühe christliche Gemeinde in ihrer heidnischen Umwelt.* Wissenschaftliche Untersuchungen zum Neuen Testament 2.125. Tübingen: Mohr Siebeck.
Brother Lawrence. 1600s. *The Practice of the Presence of God.*
Brown, Colin, ed. 1986. *The New International Dictionary of New Testament Theology.* 3 vols. Translated by a team of translators, with additions and revisions, from *Theologisches Begriffslexikon zum Neuen Testament.* Edited by Lothar Coenen, Erich Beyreuther, and Hans Bietenhard. Grand Rapids: Zondervan.
Bruce, F. F. 1977. *Paul: Apostle of the Heart Set Free.* Grand Rapids: Eerdmans.
Brueggemann, Walter. 1997. *Theology of the Old Testament: Testimony, Dispute, Advocacy.* Minneapolis: Fortress.
Büchsel, Friedrich. 1964. *Eidōlon. Theological Dictionary of the New Testament* 2:375-80.
Bultmann, Rudolf, and Dieter Lührmann. 1974. *epiphainō, epiphanēs, epiphaneia. Theological Dictionary of the New Testament* 9:7-10.
Burke, Trevor J. 2003. *Family Matters: A Socio-Historical Study of Kinship Metaphors in 1 Thessalonians.* London: T&T Clark International.
Burkert, Walter. 1985. *Greek Religion.* Translated by John Raffan. Cambridge, MA: Harvard University Press.
Burnett, Andrew, Michel Amandry, and Ian Carradice. 1992. *Roman Provincial Coinage*, Vol. 1: *From the Death of Caesar to the Death of Vitellius (44 BC—AD 69). Part 1: Introduction and Catalogue.* London: British Museum Press.
Calvin, John. 1960b. *Calvin: Institutes of the Christian Religion.* 2 vols. Edited by J. T. McNeill. Translated by Ford L. Battles. Philadelphia: Westminster.

Centers for Disease Control and Prevention. 2002. *Cohabitation, Marriage, Divorce, and Remarriage in the United States*. Vital and Health Statistics Series 23:22. Washington, DC: GPO.

———. 2010. *Births: Preliminary Data for 2009*. National Vital Statistics Reports 59:3, December 21. Accessed online at: http://www.cdc.gov/nchs/data/nvsr/nvsr59/nvsr59_03.pdf.

———. 2013. National Marriage and Divorce Rate Trends. Accessed online at: http://www.cdc.gov/nchs/nvss/marriage_divorce_tables.htm.

———. 2014. *Births: Preliminary Data for 2013*. National Vital Statistics Reports 63:2. Washington, DC: GPO.

Charlesworth, James H., ed. 1983-85. *The Old Testament Pseudepigrapha*, 2 vols. New York: Doubleday.

Clark, Gillian. 1993. *Women in Late Antiquity: Pagan and Christian Lifestyles*. Oxford: Clarendon.

———. 1996. Roman Women. Pages 36-55 in *Women in Antiquity*. Edited by Ian McAuslan and Peter Walcot. Oxford: Oxford University Press.

Cohen, Shaye J. D. 1987. *From the Maccabees to the Mishnah*. Philadelphia: Westminster.

Coleson, Joseph, ed. 2008. *Be Holy: God's Invitation to Understand, Declare, and Experience Holiness*. Indianapolis: Wesleyan Publishing House.

Collins, Raymond F. 1988. *Letters That Paul Did Not Write*. Wilmington, DE: Glazier.

———, ed. 1990. *The Thessalonian Correspondence*. Leuven: Leuven University Press.

Comrie, Bernard. 1976. *Aspect: An Introduction to the Study of Verbal Aspect and Related Problems*. Cambridge: Cambridge University Press.

Cooper, John. 1989. *Body, Soul, and Life Everlasting: Biblical Anthropology and the Monism-Dualism Debate*. Grand Rapids: Eerdmans.

Cooper, Laurence. 2001. Beyond the Tripartite Soul: The Dynamic Psychology of the *Republic*. *The Review of Politics* 63, 2:341-72.

Copeland, Kenneth. N.d. N.p. "What about Suffering with Christ?" Cited July 23, 2011. Accessed online at: http://www.kcm.org/real-help/article/what-about-suffering-christ.

Copeland, Warren R. 1994. *And the Poor Get Welfare: The Ethics of Poverty in the United States*. Nashville: Abingdon.

Cosmopoulos, Michael B. 1992. *Macedonia: An Introduction to Its Political History*. Winnipeg: Manitoba Studies in Classical Civilization.

Davies, W. D. 1977. *Paul and Rabbinic Judaism*, 4th ed. London: SCM Press.

Deissmann, Adolf. 1910. *Light from the Ancient East*. Translated by Lionel R. M. Strachan. New York: Hodder and Stoughton.

Delling, Gerhard. 1968. *Plērēs, ktl*. Theological Dictionary of the New Testament 6:283-311.

———. 1972. *telos*. Theological Dictionary of the New Testament 8:49-87.

deSilva, David A. 2000. *Honor, Patronage, Kinship & Purity: Unlocking New Testament Culture*. Downers Grove, IL: InterVarsity.

de Vos, Craig S. 1999. *Church and Community Conflicts: The Relationships of the Thessalonian, Corinthian, and Philippian Churches with Their Wider Civic Communities*. Society of Biblical Literature Dissertation Series 168. Atlanta: Scholars Press.

Dihle, Albert, Edmond Jacob, Eduard Lohse, Eduard Schweizer, and Karl-Wolfgang Tröger. 1974. *Psyche, ktl*. Theological Dictionary of the New Testament 9:608-60.

Dillon, John. 1977. *The Middle Platonists: 80 B.C. to A.D. 220*. Ithaca, NY: Cornell University Press.

Dodds, E. R. 1951. *The Greeks and the Irrational*. Berkeley: University of California Press.

———. 1965. *Pagan and Christian in an Age of Anxiety: Some Aspects of Religious Experience from Marcus Aurelius to Constantine*. Cambridge: Cambridge University Press.

Donfried, Karl P. 2002. *Paul, Thessalonica, and Early Christianity*. Grand Rapids: Eerdmans.

———. 2010. 1 Thessalonians. Pages 504-24 in *The Blackwell Companion to the New Testament*. Edited by David E. Aune. Chichester, UK: Wiley-Blackwell.

Donfried, Karl P., and I. Howard Marshall. 1993. *The Theology of the Shorter Pauline Letters*. Cambridge: Cambridge University Press.

Donfried, Karl P., and Johannes Beutler. 2000. *The Thessalonians Debate: Methodological Discord or Methodological Synthesis?* Grand Rapids: Eerdmans.

Du Boulay, Juliet. 1974. *Portrait of a Greek Mountain Village*. Oxford: Clarendon.

Dunn, J. D. G. 1970. *Baptism in the Holy Spirit*. London: SCM Press.

———. 1975. *Jesus and the Spirit*. Philadelphia: Westminster.

———. 1998. *The Theology of Paul the Apostle*. Grand Rapids: Eerdmans.

Dunning, H. Ray. 1988. *Grace, Faith, and Holiness: A Wesleyan Systematic Theology*. Kansas City: Beacon Hill Press of Kansas City.

Easterling, P. E., and J. V. Muir, eds. 1985. *Greek Religion and Society*. Cambridge: Cambridge University Press.
Edgar, Brian. 2002. Biblical Anthropology and the Intermediate State. *Evangelical Quarterly* 74(1):27-45; 74(2):109-21.
Edson, Charles. 1940. Macedonica. *Harvard Studies in Classical Philology* 51:125-36.
———. 1948. Cults of Thessalonica. *Harvard Theological Review* 41(3):153-204.
———, ed. 1972. *Inscriptiones Thessalonicae et Viciniae*. Vol. 10, part 2, fascicle 1 of *Inscriptiones Graecae*. Berlin: Walter De Gruyter.
Elgvin, Torleif. 2000. Belial, Beliar, Devil, Satan. Pages 153-57 in *Dictionary of New Testament Background*. Edited by Craig Evans and Stanley Porter. Downers Grove, IL: InterVarsity.
Elliger, W. *Paulus in Griechenland: Philippi, Thessaloniki, Athen, Korinth*. 1978. Stuttgarter Bibelstudien, 92/93. Stuttgart: Verlag Katholisches Bibelwerk.
Engberg-Pedersen, Troels. 1995. *Paul in His Hellenistic Context*. Minneapolis: Fortress.
Errington, Robert Malcolm. 1990. *A History of Macedonia*. Translated by Catherine Errington. Berkeley: University of California Press.
Fantham, Elaine, Helene Peet Foley, Natalie Boymel Kampen, Sarah B. Pomeroy, and H. Alan Shapiro. 1994. *Women in the Classical World: Image and Text*. New York: Oxford University Press.
Fee, Gordon. 1994. *God's Empowering Presence: The Holy Spirit in the Letters of Paul*. Peabody, MA: Hendrickson.
———. 2007. *Pauline Christology: An Exegetical-Theological Study*. Peabody, MA: Hendrickson.
Ferguson, John. 1970. *The Religions of the Roman Empire*. London: Thames & Hudson.
Fitzmyer, Joseph. 1993. *Romans*. Anchor Bible 33. New Haven: Yale University Press.
Foerster, Werner. 1964a. *Harpazō, harpagmos. Theological Dictionary of the New Testament* 1:472-74.
———. 1964b. *Daimōn. Theological Dictionary of the New Testament* 2:1-20.
Frankenmölle, H. 1990. *anaireō. Exegetical Dictionary of the New Testament* 1:81-82.
Fredrickson, David E. 2003. Passionless Sex in 1 Thessalonians 4:4-5. *Word and World* 23:23-30.
Freedman, David Noel, ed. 1992. *Anchor Bible Dictionary*. 6 vols. New York: Doubleday.
Freitas, Donna. 2013. *The End of Sex: How Hookup Culture Is Leaving a Generation Unhappy, Sexually Unfulfilled, and Confused About Intimacy*. New York: Basic Books.
Frend, W. H. C. 1984. *The Rise of Christianity*. Philadelphia: Fortress.
Friedrich, Gerhard. 1964. *euangelizomai, euangelion, proeuangelizomai, euangelistēs. Theological Dictionary of the New Testament* 2:707-37.
Frontline. Posted April 1, 2004. Ghosts of Rwanda. Written and produced by Greg Barker. Boston: WGBH Educational Foundation. Accessed online at: http://www.pbs.org/wgbh/pages/frontline/shows/ghosts/interviews/dallaire.html.
Fudge, Edward. 1984. The Final End of the Wicked. *Journal of the Evangelical Theological Society* 27:325-34.
Gamble, Harry Y. 1995. *Books and Readers in the Early Church: A History of Early Christian Texts*. New Haven: Yale University Press.
Gärtner, Burkhard. 1999. Revelation: *epiphaneia. New International Dictionary of New Testament Theology* 3:317-20.
Giblin, Charles H. 1967. *The Threat to Faith: An Exegetical and Theological Reexamination of 2 Thessalonians 2*. Rome: Pontifical Biblical Institute.
Gill, David W. J. 1994. Macedonia. Pages 397-417 in *The Book of Acts in Its Graeco-Roman Setting*. Edited by David W. J. Gill and Conrad Gempf. Grand Rapids: Eerdmans.
Gill, David W. J., and Conrad Gempf, eds. 1994. *The Book of Acts in Its First Century Setting*, Vol. 2: *The Book of Acts in Its Graeco-Roman Setting*. Grand Rapids: Eerdmans.
Goldingay, John. 2009. *Old Testament Theology*, Vol. 3: *Israel's Life*. Downers Grove, IL: IVP Academic.
Green, Joel. 2008. *Body, Soul, and Human Life: The Nature of Humanity in the Bible*. Grand Rapids: Baker Academic.
Gregory of Nyssa. *The Great Catechism*. Edited by Philip Schaff. 1892. New York: Christian Literature Publishing.
Gruen, Erich S. 1984. *The Hellenistic World and the Coming of Rome*. 2 vols. Berkeley: University of California Press.
Gupta, Nijay. 2008. An Apocalyptic Reading of Psalm 78 in 2 Thessalonians 3. *Journal for the Study of the New Testament* 31:179-94.
Hahn, Hans-Christoph. 1999. Destroy, Perish, Ruin: *apōleia, olethros. New International Dictionary of New Testament Theology* 1:462-67.

Hammond, Nicholas G. L. 1989. *The Macedonian State: Origins, Institutions, and History*. Oxford: Clarendon.

―――. 1991. *The Miracle That Was Macedonia*. London: Sidgwick and Jackson; New York: St Martin's Press.

Harder, Günther. 1968. *Ponēros, Ponēria*. Theological Dictionary of the New Testament 6:546-66.

Hardin, Justin K. 2006. Decrees and Drachmas at Thessalonica: An Illegal Assembly in Jason's House (Acts 17.1-10a). *New Testament Studies* 52:29-49.

Hardy, Lee. 1990. *The Fabric of This World: Inquiries into Calling, Career Choice, and the Design of Human Work*. Grand Rapids: Eerdmans.

Harris, William V. 1989. *Ancient Literacy*. Cambridge, MA: Harvard University Press.

Hauck, Friedrich. 1967. *Hosios*. Theological Dictionary of the New Testament 5:489-93.

Hawthorne, Gerald, Ralph P. Martin, and Daniel Reid, eds. 1994. *A Dictionary of Paul and His Letters*. Downers Grove, IL: InterVarsity.

Head, Barclay V. 1963. *A Catalogue of Greek Coins in the British Museum: Macedonia*. Edited by Reginald S. Poole. Bologna: Arnaldo Forni.

Heidland, Hans W. 1967. *Omeiromai*. Theological Dictionary of the New Testament 5:176.

Hemer, Colin J. 1989. *The Book of Acts in the Setting of Hellenistic History*. Edited by Conrad H. Gempf. Tübingen: Mohr.

Hock, Ronald F. 1980. *The Social Context of Paul's Ministry: Tentmaking and Apostleship*. Philadelphia: Fortress.

Horsley, Greg H. R. 1983. *New Documents Illustrating Early Christianity: A Review of the Greek Inscriptions and Papyri Published in 1978*. North Ryde, Australia: Macquarie University.

―――, ed. 1997. *Paul and Empire: Religion and Power in Roman Imperial Society*. Harrisburg, PA: Trinity Press.

Hughes, Frank Witt. 1989. *Early Christian Rhetoric and 2 Thessalonians*. Journal for the Study of the New Testament: Supplement Series 30. Sheffield: Sheffield Academic.

Hunt, A. S., and C. C. Edgar. 1932. *Select Papyri*. 5 vols. Loeb Classical Library. Cambridge, MA: Harvard University Press.

Hurtado, Larry. 1993. Lord. *Dictionary of Paul and His Letters* 560-69.

Jenson, Robert W. 1999. *Systematic Theology*, Vol. 2: *The Works of God*. Oxford: Oxford University Press.

Jewett, Robert. 1986. *The Thessalonian Correspondence: Pauline Rhetoric and Millenarian Piety*. Philadelphia: Fortress.

―――. 1993. Tenement Churches and Communal Meals in the Early Church: The Implications of a Form-Critical Analysis of 2 Thessalonians 3:10. *Biblical Research* 38:23-43.

Judge, E. A. 1971. The Decrees of Caesar at Thessalonica. *Reformed Theological Review* 30:1-7.

Kallet-Marx, Robert Morstein. 1995. *Hegemony to Empire: The Development of the Roman Imperium in the East from 148 to 62 B.C*. Berkeley: University of California Press.

Keener, Craig S. 2000. Kissing. Pages 628-29 in the *Dictionary of New Testament Background*. Edited by Craig A. Evans and Stanley Porter. Downers Grove, IL: InterVarsity.

Kelly, J. N. D. 1977. *Early Christian Doctrines*. 5th ed. London: Black.

Kennedy, George A. 1984. *New Testament Interpretation Through Rhetorical Criticism*. Chapel Hill: University of North Carolina Press.

Kerényi, Carl. 1976. *Dionysos: Archetypal Image of Indestructible Life*. Translated by Ralph Manheim. London: Routledge & Kegan Paul.

Keuls, Eva C. 1985. *The Reign of the Phallus: Sexual Politics in Ancient Athens*. Berkeley: University of California Press.

Kittel, Gerhard, and Gerhard Friedrich, eds. 1964-76. *Theological Dictionary of the New Testament*. 10 vols. Translated and edited by Geoffrey William Bromiley. Grand Rapids: Eerdmans.

Knox, John. 1989. *Chapters in a Life of Paul*. Rev. ed. London: SCM Press.

Koester, Helmut. 1994. Archäologie und Paulus in Thessalonike. Pages 393-404 in *Religious Propaganda and Missionary Competition in the New Testament World: Essays Honoring Dieter Georgi*. Edited by L. Bormann, K. Del Tredici, A. Standhartinger. Leiden: Brill.

Kriwaczek, Paul. 2005. *Yiddish Civilization*. New York: Alfred A. Knopf.

Ladd, George E. 1956. *The Blessed Hope: A Biblical Study of the Second Advent and the Rapture*. Grand Rapids: Eerdmans.

Lang, Friedrich. 1971. *Sainō*. Theological Dictionary of the New Testament 7:54-56.

Leisegang, Hans. 1919. *Der heilige Geist: das Wesen und Werden der mystisch-intuitiven Erkenntnis in der Philosophie und Religion der Griechen*. Leipzig and Berlin: Teubner.

Levick, Barbara. 1976. *Tiberius the Politician*. London: Thames & Hudson.
Levine, Lee I. 2000. *The Ancient Synagogue: The First Thousand Years*. New Haven: Yale University Press.
Lewis, Clive Staples. 1996. *The Great Divorce*. New York: Macmillan, 1946. Repr., New York: Simon & Schuster.
Liddell, Henry George, and Robert Scott. 1996. *A Greek-English Lexicon*. Revised and augmented by Henry Stuart Jones and Roderick McKenzie. With a revised supplement. Oxford: Clarendon.
Link, Hans-Georg. 1999. Take, Receive: *dechomai*. *New International Dictionary of New Testament Theology* 3:744-46.
Llewelyn, S. R., ed. 2002. *New Documents Illustrating Early Christianity*, Vol. 9: *A Review of the Greek Inscriptions and Papyri Published in 1986-1987*. Grand Rapids: Eerdmans.
Locke, John. 1695. *The Reasonableness of Christianity as Delivered in the Scriptures*. Repr. in: *The Reasonableness of Christianity, with A Discourse of Miracles, and part of A Third Letter Concerning Toleration*. Stanford: Stanford University Press, 1958.
Lohse, Eduard, W. von Martitz, Wilhelm Schneemelcher, and Eduard Schweizer. 1972. *huios, huiothesia*. *Theological Dictionary of the New Testament* 8:334-99.
Lüdemann, Gerd. 1984. *Paul, Apostle to the Gentiles: Studies in Chronology*. Translated by F. Stanley Jones. Minneapolis: Fortress.
Lyons, George. 1985. *Pauline Autobiography: Toward a New Understanding*. Society of Biblical Literature Dissertation Series 73. Atlanta: Scholars Press.
MacMullen, Ramsay. 1974. *Roman Social Relations: 50 B.C. to A.D. 284*. New Haven: Yale University Press.
_____. 1981. *Paganism in the Roman Empire*. New Haven: Yale University Press.
MacPherson, Dave. 1995. *The Rapture Plot*. Simpsonville, SC: Millennium III Publishers.
Maddox, Randy. 1981. The Use of the Aorist Tense in Holiness Exegesis. *Wesleyan Theological Journal* 16(2):106-18.
_____. 1994. *Responsible Grace: John Wesley's Practical Theology*. Nashville: Kingswood Books.
Malherbe, Abraham. 1970. "Gentle as a Nurse": The Cynic Background to 1 Thessalonians 2. *Novum Testamentum* 12 (1970):203-17.
_____. 1983. *Social Aspects of Early Christianity*. 2d ed., enlarged. Philadelphia: Fortress.
_____. 1987. *Paul and the Thessalonians: The Philosophical Tradition of Pastoral Care*. Philadelphia: Fortress.
_____. 1988. *Ancient Epistolary Theorists*. Atlanta: Scholars Press.
_____. 1989. *Paul and the Popular Philosophers*. Minneapolis: Fortress.
Malina, Bruce J. 1981. *The New Testament World: Insights from Cultural Anthropology*. London: SCM Press.
Marshall, I. Howard. 2004. *New Testament Theology: Many Witnesses, One Gospel*. Downers Grove, IL: IVP Academic.
Martin, Ralph P. 1964. *Worship in the Early Church*. London: Marshall, Morgan & Scott.
_____. 1981. *Reconciliation: A Study of Paul's Theology*. Atlanta: John Knox.
Maurer, Christian. 1974. *Phylē*. *Theological Dictionary of the New Testament* 9:245-50.
Meeks, Wayne A. 1983. *The First Urban Christians: The Social World of the Apostle Paul*. New Haven: Yale University Press.
Metzger, Bruce. 1994. *A Textual Commentary on the Greek New Testament*. 2d ed. Stuttgart: United Bible Societies.
The Midrash Rabbah. 1977. Vol. 1: *Genesis*. Translated with notes by H. Freedman and Maurice Simon. London, Jerusalem, New York: Soncino Press. Vol. 2: *Exodus, Leviticus*. Translated with notes by S. M. Lehrman. London, Jerusalem, New York: Soncino Press.
Millar, Fergus. 1993. *The Roman Near East, 31 BC—AD 337*. Cambridge, MA: Harvard University Press.
Mitchell, Margaret. 1989. Concerning *peri de* in 1 Corinthians. *Novum Testamentum* 21:229-56.
_____. 2004. Review of Abraham J. Malherbe, *The Letters to the Thessalonians*. *Review of Biblical Literature* 6:36-48.
Moore, George Foot. 1962. *Judaism in the First Centuries of the Christian Era: The Age of the Tannaim*. 3 vols. Repr., Cambridge, MA: Harvard University Press, 1927-30.
Moule, C. F. D. 1959. *An Idiom Book of New Testament Greek*. 2d ed. Cambridge: Cambridge University Press.
_____. 1977. *The Origin of Christology*. Cambridge: Cambridge University Press.

Moulton, James H., and George Milligan. 1972. *The Vocabulary of the Greek Testament Illustrated from the Papyri and Other Non-Literary Sources.* London: Hodder and Stoughton, 1930. Repr., Grand Rapids: Eerdmans.
Mueller, James. 1980. The Temple Scroll and the Gospel Divorce Texts. *Revue de Qumran* 10:247-56.
Murphy-O'Connor, Jerome. 1995. *Paul the Letter-Writer: His World, His Options, His Skills.* Collegeville, MN: Liturgical Press.
———. 1996. *Paul: A Critical Life.* Oxford: Oxford University Press.
Nicholl, Colin R. 2000. Michael, the Restrainer Removed (2 Thess. 2:6-7). *Journal of Theological Studies* 51:27-53.
———. 2004. *From Hope to Despair in Thessalonica: Situating 1 and 2 Thessalonians.* Society for New Testament Studies Monograph Series 126. Cambridge: Cambridge University Press.
Nock, A. D. 1933. *Conversion: The Old and the New in Religion from Alexander the Great to Augustine of Hippo.* Oxford: Clarendon.
O'Brien, Peter T. 1977. *Introductory Thanksgivings in the Letters of Paul.* Leiden: Brill.
O'Brien Wicker, Kathleen. 1975. De defectu oraculorum (Moralia 409E-438E). Pages 131-80 in Hans Dieter Betz, ed., *Plutarch's Theological Writings and Early Christian Literature.* Studia ad Corpus Hellenisticum Novi Testamenti, Vol. 3. Leiden: Brill.
Oden, Thomas. 1998. *Life in the Spirit.* Vol. 3 of *Systematic Theology.* San Francisco: HarperSanFrancisco, 1992. Repr., Peabody, MA: Prince Press.
Oepke, Albrecht. 1967. *Parousia, pareimi. Theological Dictionary of the New Testament* 5:858-71.
Oord, Thomas Jay, and Michael Lodahl. 2005. *Relational Holiness: Responding to the Call of Love.* Kansas City: Beacon Hill Press of Kansas City.
Paige, Terence. 1993. Holy Spirit. *Dictionary of Paul and His Letters* 404-13.
———. 2002. Who Believes in "Spirit"? Pneuma in Pagan Usage and Implications for the Gentile Christian Mission. *Harvard Theological Review* 95(4):417-36.
———. 2006. Body Worship. *Stonework* 3. http://stonework03.blogspot.com/2005/11/stonework-issue-3.html.
———. 2008. Holiness in the New Testament. Pages 43-56 in *Be Holy: God's Invitation to Understand, Declare, and Experience Holiness.* Edited by Joseph Coleson. Indianapolis: Wesleyan Publishing House.
Papazoglou, Fanoula. 1979. Quelques aspects de l'histoire de la province de Macédoiné. *Aufstieg und Niedergang der römischen Welt* II.7.1:302-69.
———. 1988. *Les Villes de Macedoine a L'Epoque Romaine.* Athens: Ecole française d'Athènes; Paris: Diffusion de Boccard.
Pearson, Birger. 1971. 1 Thessalonians 2:13-16: A Deutero-Pauline Interpolation. *Harvard Theological Review* 64(1):79-94.
Pillar, Edward. 2013. *Resurrection as Anti-Imperial Gospel: 1 Thessalonians 1:9b-10 in Context.* Minneapolis: Fortress.
Pinnock, Clark. 1996. *Flame of Love: A Theology of the Holy Spirit.* Downers Grove, IL: InterVarsity.
Plevnik, Josef. 1997. *Paul and the Parousia: An Exegetical and Theological Investigation.* Peabody, MA: Hendrickson.
Pomeroy, Sarah. 1975. *Goddesses, Whores, Wives, and Slaves: Women in Classical Antiquity.* New York: Schocken.
———. 1984. *Women in Hellenistic Egypt from Alexander to Cleopatra.* New York: Schocken.
———, ed. 1991. *Women's History and Ancient History.* Chapel Hill: University of North Carolina Press.
Porter, Stanley E. 1989. *Verbal Aspect in the Greek of the New Testament, with Reference to Tense and Mood.* New York: P. Lang.
———. 1999. Developments in German and French Thessalonians Research: A Survey and Critique. *Currents in Research: Biblical Studies* 7:309-34.
Powell, Charles E. 1997. The Identity of the "Restrainer" in 2 Thessalonians 2:6-7. *Bibliotheca Sacra* 154:320-32.
Price, Martin. 1974. *Coins of the Macedonians.* London: British Museum Publications.
Price, S. R. F. 1997. Rituals and Power. Pages 47-71 in *Paul and Empire: Religion and Power in Roman Imperial Society.* Edited by Richard A. Horsley. Harrisburg, PA: Trinity Press International.
Prior, Michael. 1989. *Paul the Letter-Writer and the Second Letter to Timothy.* Journal for the Study of the New Testament: Supplement Series 23. Sheffield: Sheffield Academic.
Quarles, C. L. 1997. The *Apo* of 2 Thessalonians 1:9 and the Nature of Eternal Punishment. *Westminster Theological Journal* 59:201-11.

Ramsay, William M. 1902. *St. Paul the Traveller and the Roman Citizen*. London: Hodder & Stoughton.
Rawson, Beryl, ed. 1986. *The Family in Ancient Rome: New Perspectives*. Ithaca, NY: Cornell University Press.
Reicke, Bo. 1968. *Proistēmi. Theological Dictionary of the New Testament* 6:700-703.
_____. 2001. *Re-Examining Paul's Letters: The History of the Pauline Correspondence*. Edited by David P. Moessner and Ingalisa Reicke. Harrisburg, PA: Trinity Press International.
Reid, Daniel. 1993. Triumph. *Dictionary of Paul and His Letters* 946-54.
Reid, J. S. 1913. *The Municipalities of the Roman Empire*. Cambridge: Cambridge University Press.
Richard, Earl J. 1990. Contemporary Research on 1 and 2 Thessalonians. *Biblical Theology Bulletin* 20:107-15.
Rösel, Martin. 2007. The Reading and Translation of the Divine Name in the Masoretic Tradition and the Greek Pentateuch. *Journal for the Study of the Old Testament* 31:411-28.
Rostovtzeff, Mikhail. 1957. *The Social and Economic History of the Roman Empire*. 2d ed. 3 vols. Oxford: Clarendon.
Sachar, Abram Leon. 1965. *A History of the Jews*. New York: Alfred A. Knopf.
Safrai, Zeev. 1995. Communal Functions of the Synagogue in the Land of Israel in the Rabbinic Period. Pages 181-204 in vol. 1 of *Ancient Synagogues: Historical Analysis and Archaeological Discovery*. Edited by Dan Urman and Paul V. M. Flesher. Leiden: Brill.
Sakellariou, M. B., ed. 1983. *Macedonia: 4000 Years of Greek History and Civilization*. Athens: Ekdotike Athenon.
Saller, Richard P. 1982. *Personal Patronage under the Early Empire*. Cambridge: Cambridge University Press.
Salmon, E. T. 1968. *A History of the Roman World 30 BC to AD 138*, 6th ed. London: Methuen.
_____. 1970. *Roman Colonization Under the Republic*. Ithaca, NY: Cornell University Press.
Sanders, E. P. 1977. *Paul and Palestinian Judaism*. Philadelphia: Fortress.
_____. 1983. *Paul, the Law, and the Jewish People*. Philadelphia: Fortress.
Schmithals, Walter. 1972. *Paul and the Gnostics*. Translated by John E. Steely. Nashville: Abingdon.
Schmitz, Otto, and Gustav Stählin. 1967. *Parakaleō, paraklēsis. Theological Dictionary of the New Testament* 5:773-99.
Schreiner, Thomas R. 2001. *Paul: Apostle of God's Glory in Christ*. Downers Grove, IL: InterVarsity.
Schrenk, Gottlob. 1964. *Ekdikeō, ekdikos, ekdikēsis. Theological Dictionary of the New Testament* 2:442-46.
Schubert, Paul. 1939. *Form and Function of the Pauline Thanksgivings*. Beihefte zur Zeitschrift für die neutestamentliche Wissenschaft 20. Berlin: Alfred Töpelmann.
Schweitzer, Albert. 1953. *The Mysticism of Paul the Apostle*. 2d ed. Translated by William Montgomery. London: Black.
Selter, Friedel. 1999. Exhort, Warn, Console, Rebuke: *noutheteō. New International Dictionary of New Testament Theology* 1:568-69.
Sherwin-White, Adrian N. 1939. *The Roman Citizenship*. Oxford: Clarendon.
_____. 1978. *Roman Society and Roman Law in the New Testament*. Oxford: Oxford University Press, 1963. Repr., Grand Rapids: Baker.
Smith, Jay E. 2001. 1 Thessalonians 4:4: Breaking the Impasse. *Bulletin for Biblical Research* 11:65-105.
Smyth, Herbert W. 1984. *Greek Grammar*. New York: American Book Co., 1920. Repr., Cambridge, MA: Harvard University Press.
Snyder, Howard A. 1980. *The Radical Wesley and Patterns for Church Renewal*. Downers Grove, IL: InterVarsity.
Spicq, Ceslas. 1994. *Theological Lexicon of the New Testament*. 3 vols. Translated and edited by James D. Ernest. Peabody, MA: Hendrickson.
Stählin, Gustav. 1967. *Parmutheomai. Theological Dictionary of the New Testament* 5:816-23.
_____. 1974. *Phileō, kataphileō, philēma, philos, philē, philia. Theological Dictionary of the New Testament* 9:113-71.
Stambaugh, John, and David Balch. 1986. *The New Testament in Its Social Environment*. Philadelphia: Westminster.
Stark, Rodney. 1996. *The Rise of Christianity: A Sociologist Reconsiders History*. Princeton: Princeton University Press.
Stauffer, Ethelbert. 1964. *agōn, agōnizomai. Theological Dictionary of the New Testament* 1:134-40.
Still, Todd. 1999. *Conflict at Thessalonica: A Pauline Church and Its Neighbors*. Journal for the Study of the New Testament: Supplement Series 183. Sheffield: Sheffield Academic.

Stowers, Stanley K. 1986. *Letter-Writing in Greco-Roman Antiquity*. Philadelphia: Westminster.
Strathmann, Hermann. 1967. *Martys, ktl. Theological Dictionary of the New Testament* 4:474-514.
Tafrali, O. 1913. *Topographie de Thessalonique*. Paris: Librairie Paul Geuthner.
Temporini, Hildegard, and Wolfgang Haase, eds. 1984. *Aufstieg und Niedergang der römischen Welt*. Berlin and New York: Walter de Gruyter.
Thiselton, Anthony C. 1978. Realized Eschatology at Corinth. *New Testament Studies* 24:510-26.
Trilling, Wolfgang. 1980. *Der zweite Brief an die Thessalonicher*. Neukirchen: Neukirchener-Verlag.
_____. 1987. Die beiden Briefe des Apostels Paulus an die Thessalonicher: Eine Forschungsübersicht. *Aufstieg und Niedergang der römischen Welt* II.25.4:3365-3403.
Trozzo, Lindsey M. 2012. Thessalonian Women: The Key to the 4:4 Conundrum. *Perspectives in Religious Studies* 39:39-52.
Trummer, P. 1990. *Axios. Exegetical Dictionary of the New Testament* 1:113.
UNAIDS. 2013. HIV Estimates with Uncertainty Bounds 1990—2012. UNAIDS online. Accessed online at: http://www.unaids.org/en/resources/campaigns/globalreport2013/globalreport/.
U.S. Dept. of Health, Education, and Welfare. 1950. *Vital Statistics of the United States 1950*. Vol. 1. Washington, DC: GPO.
_____. 1978. *Divorces and Divorce Rates: United States*. National Vital Statistics System Series 21 no. 29. Washington, DC: GPO. Repr., 1980.
Vacalopoulos, Apostolos E. 1963. *A History of Thessaloniki*. Translated by T. F. Carney. Thessaloniki: Institute for Balkan Studies.
Von Rad, Gerhard, G. Kittel, and W. Grundmann. 1964. *Angelos, archangelos, isangelos. Theological Dictionary of the New Testament* 1:74-87.
Walbank, F. W. 1981. *The Hellenistic World*. New Jersey: Humanities Press.
Wall, Robert. 2002. Acts. Pages 3-368 in vol. 10 of *The New Interpreter's Bible*. Edited by Leander Keck. Nashville: Abingdon.
Wallace, Daniel B. 1996. *Greek Grammar Beyond the Basics*. Grand Rapids: Zondervan.
Walters, James C. 1996. Review of *Seek the Welfare of the City: Christians as Benefactors and Citizens*, by Bruce Winter. *Journal of Biblical Literature* 115:536-38.
Watson, D. F. 2000. Greece and Macedon. Pages 421-26 in *Dictionary of New Testament Background*. Downers Grove, IL: InterVarsity.
Wengst, Klaus. 1987. *Pax Romana and the Peace of Jesus Christ*. Translated by John Bowden. London: SCM Press.
Westermann, Claus. 1981. *Praise and Lament in the Psalms*. Translated by K. R. Crim and R. N. Soulen. Atlanta: John Knox.
White, John L. 1986. *Light from Ancient Letters*. Philadelphia: Fortress.
Wiles, Gordon P. 1974. *Paul's Intercessory Prayers: The Significance of the Intercessory Prayer Passages in the Letters of St. Paul*. Cambridge: Cambridge University Press.
Willis, Wendel. 1996. Review of *Seek the Welfare of the City: Christians as Benefactors and Citizens*, by Bruce Winter. *Catholic Biblical Quarterly* 58:569-70.
Winter, Bruce. 1994. *Seek the Welfare of the City: Christians as Benefactors and Citizens*. Grand Rapids: Eerdmans.
_____. 2001. *After Paul Left Corinth: The Influence of Secular Ethics and Social Change*. Grand Rapids: Eerdmans.
Wise, Michael, Martin Abegg Jr., and Edward Cook. 1996. *The Dead Sea Scrolls: A New Translation*. San Francisco: HarperSanFrancisco.
Wiseman, James. 1999. Deus Caesar and Other Gods at Stobi. Pages 1359-69 in *Archaia Makedonia 6: Papers Read at the Sixth International Symposium Held in Thessaloniki, October 15-19, 1996*. Thessaloniki: Institute for Balkan Studies.
Witherington, Ben, III. 1990. *The Christology of Jesus*. Minneapolis: Fortress.
_____. 1994. *Paul's Narrative Thought World*. Louisville, KY: Westminster / John Knox.
Witt, Reginald E. 1970. The Egyptian Cults in Ancient Macedonia. Pages 324-33 in *Archaia Makedonia: Anakoinōseis kata to Prōton Diethnes Symposion en Thessalonikē, 26-29 Augoustou 1968* [*Ancient Macedonia: Papers read at the First International symposium held in Thessaloniki 26-29 August 1968*]. Hidryma Meletōn Cheronēsou tou Haimou, 122. Edited by Vasileios Laourdas and Ch. Makaronas. Thessaloniki: Institute for Balkan Studies.
_____. 1971. *Isis in the Graeco-Roman World*. Ithaca, NY: Cornell University Press.
Wright, N. Thomas. 1991. *The Climax of the Covenant: Christ and the Law in Pauline Theology*. Edinburgh: T&T Clark.

———. 1992. *The New Testament and the People of God.* Vol. 1 of *Christian Origins and the Question of God.* Minneapolis: Fortress.
———. 1996. *Jesus and the Victory of God.* Vol. 2 of *Christian Origins and the Question of God.* Minneapolis: Fortress.
———. 2008. *Surprised by Hope: Rethinking Heaven, the Resurrection, and the Mission of the Church.* New York: HarperOne.
Yarbrough, O. Larry. 1985. *Not Like the Gentiles: Marriage Rules in the Letters of Paul.* Atlanta: Scholars Press.
Yarbrough, Robert. 1999. Sexual Gratification in 1 Thess 4:1-8. *Trinity Journal* 20:215-32.
Zakopoulos, Athenagoras. 1975. *Plato on Man.* New York: Philosophical Library.
Ziesler, John. 1990. *Pauline Christianity,* rev. ed. New York: Oxford University Press.

TABLE OF SIDEBARS

Sidebars	Location
Map	INTRODUCTION: A.
Faith, Hope, Love	1 Thess 1:2-3
Brothers and Sisters: Why Inclusive Language?	1 Thess 1:4
What Was the Thessalonians' "Affliction"?	1 Thess 1:6
Jew against Jew	1 Thess 2:16
Shame, Honor, and Biblical Holiness	1 Thess 3:13
Beliefs about Death and the Afterlife in the Ancient World	Behind the Text for 1 Thess 4:13-18
The Rapture Theory	1 Thess 4:17
Pagan Models of Inspiration	1 Thess 5:22
Greek Verbs and Sanctification	From the Text for 1 Thess 5:12-24
The Identity of the Restrainer	2 Thess 2:6-7

INTRODUCTION TO FIRST AND SECOND THESSALONIANS

A. Thessalonica: The City

Thessalonica exists today as modern Thessaloniki in Greece, at the northwest corner of the Chalkidiki peninsula. Cassander, one of Alexander's generals, named it after his wife (a half-sister of Alexander) when he founded it in 316 BC (Vacalopoulos 1963, 5-7; Papazoglou 1988, 189-90). Its location made it an important crossroad of land and sea routes. Rome recognized this by laying the Egnatian Way through it, a road connecting the Adriatic Sea to the Hellespont.

Map

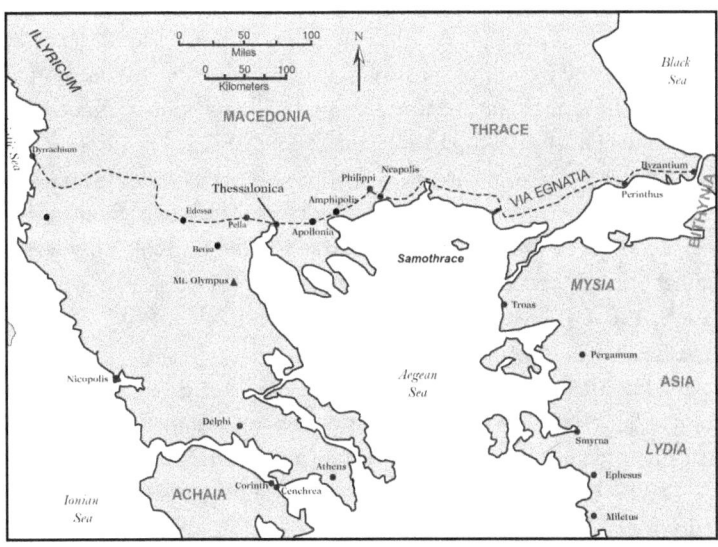

Macedonians were a hardy agrarian people—famous for horse breeders and riders, shepherds and farmers, and fierce fighters. They gave allegiance to kings rather than to cities. Though they shared the same language and ethnicity, the Greeks considered them uncultured, particularly in arts and literature (Hammond 1989, 12-13; Errington 1990, 3-4, 248-49).

When Rome defeated Philip V in 197 BC, it stripped Macedonia of its subject territories. After another war, it removed the Macedonian monarchy and divided it into four self-governing republics (168 BC). Thessalonica was the capital of one of these (see Livy 45.29; Walbank 1981, 231-39; Hammond 1991, 193-204; Boatwright 2004, 128-32).

Repeated wars and revolts against Roman rule ended Macedonia's independence and ruined it economically. Plunder and tribute from Macedonia enabled Italy to cancel direct taxes for over a century. In 148 BC Rome made Macedonia a province ruled by a proconsul (Hammond 1989, 379; Sakellariou 1983, 193; Kallet-Marx 1995, 12-29).

During the next century and a half, Thessalonica suffered more invasions from outsiders and the ravages of the Roman civil wars. The victorious Octavian granted Thessalonica the status of a "free city" in 42 BC. This exempted it from paying Roman taxes and quartering soldiers. He allowed it to govern itself by its own ancient laws and administration. It was ruled by a council of politarchs (Acts 17:6, 8), an "assembly of the people" (Gk.: *ekklēsia*), and a council (Rostovtzeff 1957, 253; Vacalopoulos 1963, 13; Sherwin-White 1939, 150-53, and 1978, 96). This may explain Paul's failure to publicize his Roman citizenship here (contrast Acts 16:35-40). He did not have the same legal advantages here as in a colony.

B. Religion in Thessalonica

Macedonians worshipped Greek deities, especially Hermes, Poseidon (god of sea and horses), Artemis (goddess of the woods and the hunt), Apollo (a sun god and patron of music and prophecy), and Athena. Roman coins from Thessalonica also feature the demigods Heracles, Pan, Nike, and the Roman god Janus (Edson 1940, 126; Head 1963, 108-14; Vacalopoulos 1963, 14).

In this culture known for drinking parties, Dionysus was a special favorite. His festivals, a kind of first-century Mardi Gras, featured drunkenness, masked figures, and a parade of a large phallic symbol. This was only one of a number of Thessalonian cults involving sexual images in worship (see Edson 1948, 160-80; Head 1963, ##3, 10-18; Blundell 1995, 168; Green 2002, 36; Keuls 1985).

Dionysian mystery rites promised an afterlife to initiates. Plutarch mentions Dionysiac rites that offered the hope of immortality of the soul, reincarnation, and an afterlife in "a better" place (*Cons. ux.* 611D-612A).

The mystery god Cabirus eventually became the patron deity of Thessalonica (Edson 1948, 190-91; Head 1963, lxiii; Price 1974, 35-36). We know nothing about the Cabiri cult's rites. The founding myth involves two brothers killing a third (Firmicus Maternus, *Err. prof. rel.*, 11).

A Serapeium devoted to the Egyptian gods Isis, Sarapis, and Osiris stood in Thessalonica. The city politarchs made offerings there (Edson 1948, 181-87; Witt 1970; Green 2002, 38). The cult of Isis was one of the most popular cults in the empire. She was acclaimed as "lord" (Gk.: *kyria*), "savior," and "Queen of heaven" (Witt 1971, 56-57, 128-29, 133-34, 264-65). An important Thessalonian inscription to her survives (Edson 1972 [= *IG* 10.2.1], #254). Some religious societies met for meals in her honor at Thessalonica. These mystery rites included stories of death, resurrection, and immortality (Witt 1971, 152-64).

Ancient religion was so embedded in everyday life that it was inseparable from "secular" affairs. Government business in Rome and its provinces always began with taking auspices (divination involving birds) and prayer. City councils paid annually for sacrifices and banquets to honor patron deities. Athletic games, music, and drama honored the gods. Shrines guarded crossroads. Wives prayed daily at the household hearth, and husbands prayed to the family's guardian spirit. There were gods for every task, every disease, every life event.

Religion so permeated life in antiquity that Gentile conversions to Christianity required a clean break from everyday routines. Conversions were not "private" decisions, for they meant withdrawing from practices that had once hallowed all areas of life. Conversions entailed unavoidable and severe social and political consequences—often including persecution.

The imperial cult thrived at Thessalonica, as it did throughout the eastern empire. Its roots go back centuries earlier to the worship of dead Macedonian kings, the goddess Roma, and the "Roman benefactors." The Thessalonians enthusiastically supported emperor worship. A priest of Augustus officiated in the city during his lifetime, and athletic competitions honored him (Hammond 1989, 26-31; Ferguson 1970, 89; Green 2002, 39; Head 1963, 108; Edson 1940, 127-29, 132-36; *IG* 10.2.1 [= Edson 1972], 31).

Scholars debate whether the worship of Roma and the emperors was a purely political act or involved religious sentiments. Probably a mixture of both was involved. Certainly cities hoped their devotion to the empire and emperors would bring them benefits. The Caesars were the ultimate patrons (Donfried 2002, 36).

Pagan notions of deity differed from ours. They might consider particularly gifted humans to have divine ancestry. Within this worldview, emperors appeared to be divine. They possessed unimaginable wealth and could field vast armies, level whole cities, drain swamps, and build massive aqueducts.

Recent scholars argue that Thessalonica's attachment to the imperial cult may have occasioned the persecution of Christians there. The gospel message employs "heavily loaded political terms" ("kingdom," "Lord," "good news"). And the claim that Jesus (not Caesar) is God's Son and Lord may have made converts appear to be disloyal to Rome (Donfried 2002, 42-43; Green 2002, 42; Pillar 2013, 3, 253-62).

Acts testifies to the existence of a Jewish community in Thessalonica. It was influential enough to incite a mob against Christians and to prompt legal action by civic authorities (Acts 17:5-7). Centuries later Judaism continued to be a strong presence there (Green 2002, 47).

C. The Founding of the Church and the Troubles at Thessalonica

Acts 17:1-10*a* narrates the visit by Paul and Silas (and Timothy) to Thessalonica. Its reliable, albeit condensed, account agrees with 1 Thessalonians on these salient points:

- They preached there after being mistreated at Philippi (1 Thess 2:2; Acts 16:20-24; 17:5).
- Most converts were Gentiles (1 Thess 1:9-10; Acts 17:4).
- The Jewish community played a role in driving Paul out (1 Thess 2:15-16; Acts 17:5).

Acts seems well informed about local details, such as Macedonia's division into districts and the designation of its leaders as politarchs (Acts 17:6; Rostovtzeff 1957, 253; Vacalopoulos 1963, 13; Sherwin-White 1978, 96).

Paul's stop in Thessalonica made good sense for both travel and mission. As an important crossroad of land and sea routes, he could expect to find supplies, information, and an audience for his preaching. He also found there something else dear to his heart: a synagogue (Acts 17:1). Paul's synagogue preaching demonstrated that the Scriptures of Israel were fulfilled in Jesus (vv 2-3).

In 1 Thess 1:9-10, Paul describes the conversion of non-Jewish Thessalonians. Consequently, some scholars dismiss Acts as contradicting Paul. Yet both sources indicate that he preached to and converted Jews *and* Gentiles. Acts emphasizes his preaching to Jews; 1 Thessalonians, his preaching to Gentiles. Acts has theological reasons for emphasizing Paul's practice of evangelizing Jews first (see Rom 1:16); it did not invent his synagogue preaching.

From Acts and 1 Thessalonians we learn of at least three different types of converts at Thessalonica:

- First, Diaspora Jews, of whom Luke says only "some" converted (Acts 17:4).
- Second, "God-fearing Greeks," Gentiles who attended synagogue out of interest in Judaism (Acts 17:4). They remained uncircumcised and did not observe many Jewish purity laws. They had limited knowledge of the OT.
- Third, Gentiles with no association to the synagogue. They "turned to God from idols" (1 Thess 1:9). This probably included the aristocratic women converts from "prominent" families of Thessalonica (Acts 17:4).

That Christianity should have an immediate appeal to elite, ruling-class women might seem surprising. But it happened often. It is understandable when one considers how women were treated in antiquity. Female babies were frequently exposed, left to die. Girls were considered a financial drain on the family, not a blessing. A married woman had no say over her husband's affairs. She could not even inherit his estate. If he beat her, the Law offered no protection. And if divorced, she had no right to any support nor even to keep her own children. Women belonged to their father or husband under Roman law. The Christian message especially appealed to women as good news: "In Christ Jesus you are all children of God through faith . . . There is neither Jew nor Greek, neither slave nor free, nor is there male and female, for you are all one in Christ Jesus" (Gal 3:26, 28).

Acts tells us that Paul preached in the synagogue on "three Sabbath days" (Acts 17:2). This may suggest that immediately afterward the apostles had to leave the city. But Paul must have been there longer, if he offered catechetical instruction to the many converts with no synagogue ties (1 Thess 1:9-10). The reminders of his message and lifestyle among them certainly imply a longer stay (1 Thess 2:5-12; 3:4; 4:1-2; 5:1-2; 2 Thess 2:5, 15; 3:6). For the Philippians to send financial support to Paul in Thessalonica "more than once" (Phil 4:16) presumes a longer stay. All this suggests a stay of between two and six months rather than three or four weeks.

Paul was forced to leave when the Jewish assault on the nascent movement resulted in the movement's loss of protection under Roman custom and law. Gentiles found it difficult to distinguish Christianity from Judaism. After all, Jewish apostles and converts formed the nucleus of what appeared to pagans as merely another synagogue. The Romans respected the ancestral customs of Jews. They treated Judaism as an officially recognized religion, even favoring it with certain exemptions from civic or military obligations regulating pagans.

So when the synagogue denounced the Christians before the politarchs, the church was declared to be separate from their *koinōn* (community). Christianity suddenly became just a strange new cult, accused of acting against "Caesar's decrees" by proclaiming Jesus as "another king" (Acts 17:7).

It is not clear *what* decrees Christians were accused of breaking. It was not refusal to worship the emperor, for in AD 50 that was not mandatory. Several possibilities exist:

1. That the apostles are charged with *maiestas* or treason (Frame 1912, 4; Plummer 1918, xvi; Neil 1950, xi) and banished from the city. But such a serious charge would have gone before the provincial governor, not a city magistrate. And if convicted, Paul and his companions would not have been allowed merely to leave town (Bruce 1982, xxiv; Hardin 2006, 32-33).
2. The "decrees" may refer to legislation by Augustus against astrology or predicting people's deaths. The prediction of Jesus' return to judge

the earth was interpreted by Paul's opponents as a prediction of a change of ruler (Judge 1971; Bruce 1982, xxiv). Local magistrates took an oath to the emperor that they would punish any activity disloyal to him (Judge 1971).

This educated guess has been popular in recent years. But the link between astrology and the charges against the apostles seems tenuous. Furthermore, this legislation apparently applied only to Rome and Italy, not to the provinces (Hardin 2006, 35-37).

3. The "decree" related to the emperors' suppression of private associations. They feared that such groups were a cover for "subversive political agendas" (Hardin 2006, 38-40). The legal charges were not against the apostles but against those who hosted the churches illegally. Paul and Silas flee, because the local Christians fear for their safety in view of the mob assembled against them (Acts 17:6-7; Hardin 2006, 38-39, 46-47).

There is evidence that such meetings were punished with fines in Rome. But the imperial rulings against voluntary associations applied only in Italy. Such associations continued to exist in the East. But the Thessalonian magistrates may have enforced what they knew the emperor wanted.

But this explanation leaves several unanswered questions: Why did Paul feel it was impossible for him to return to the city (1 Thess 2:17-18)? And why was it possible for Timothy to go back (1 Thess 3:2)? If Christian meetings were banned, how did they continue to meet in a setting where Paul's letter could be read? Were their continuing meetings the cause of the persecution mentioned in the letters? Is it possible that the Jewish charges were exaggerated rhetoric designed to inflame the civic leaders against Christians as "unpatriotic"?

If the Christian house-church meetings were deemed politically subversive, the city may have attempted to shut them down. This would result in more legal action. Anyone hostile to the movement might spy on its hosts and denounce them. This could account for Paul's angry words in 1 Thess 2:14-16. Such a situation would necessitate moving meetings from house to house, or reducing the number of people who gathered in one spot. Severe penalties could result in Christians losing their property and citizenship. They almost certainly faced troubles such as fines, informal anger, and ostracism.

Persecution may have been especially hard on the upper-class women who converted to Christianity. A freeborn male convert might also suffer. But at least he was the master of what he did in his own home. Not so for wives. They were expected to support the ancestral deities of their husbands and to reject all "foreign superstitions" (Plutarch, *Conj. praec.* 140D).

Conversion to Christianity would have required women to cease daily offerings to household gods and family deities. They would have withdrawn from the civic religious festivals, the imperial cult, and private religious associations of their husbands. This would have shamed their husbands and male relatives. Civic officials were expected to attend religious ceremonies and take turns serving as priests. A wife's nonparticipation would publicly humiliate her husband—grounds for divorce in the ancient Mediterranean world.

We can only imagine the pressure put on aristocratic women converts to abandon their faith. By choosing Christ and not honoring her husband's gods, Christian wives risked violence against themselves, abandonment by their families, humiliation, divorce, and poverty. Paul's words indicate that this risk became reality for some. Christians did not offend by proclaiming Jesus "Lord" in a polytheistic society. But insisting that he *alone* was Lord was offensive because it attacked the national gods as false (1 Thess 1:9-10).

Acts customarily emphasizes the conversion of honorable and high-status people. But it does not report the conversion of aristocratic men at Thessalonica. This suggests that no noblemen converted at first.

D. After the Apostles Left Thessalonica

When the apostles left Thessalonica and arrived at Berea, they entered a different district of Macedonia. There the Thessalonian government had no authority. Trouble from Thessalonica came from private persons connected with the synagogue (Acts 17:13).

From Berea, Paul apparently traveled along the road to Dium on the sea. From there he embarked for Athens (vv 14-15), leaving Silas and Timothy behind in Berea. He later sent Timothy back to Thessalonica "to strengthen and encourage" the church (1 Thess 3:2; see vv 1-5 and Acts 17:15). While Timothy was away, Paul moved on to Corinth (Acts 18:1-4). Timothy and Silas rejoined him in Corinth, from where he writes the Thessalonians (see v 11).

E. The Writing of I Thessalonians: Authorship, Date, and Integrity

That Paul wrote 1 Thessalonians is the unanimous opinion of virtually all contemporary NT scholars. Its authorship has not been seriously disputed since the mid-nineteenth century (Best 1986, 22-23).

Deciding when Paul wrote the letter depends on whether we trust Acts. Some scholars construct a chronology based almost entirely on Paul's letters. This allows a date as early as AD 41-43 (Knox 1989, 68; Lüdemann 1984, 224-26). Our preference for the traditional date, nearly a decade later, incorporates the Acts data.

The facts pertinent to dating 1 Thessalonians are:
1. The letter speaks of Paul's and his associates' founding mission to the city, the beginning of the church there, and the conversion of the Thessalonians as something quite recent (1:4-6; 2:1).
2. Several details fit the itinerary in Acts of Paul's first visit.

3. Other details in the letter point to the time when Paul had recently arrived in Corinth:
- He was prevented from returning to Thessalonica and had not been back (2:17-18; Acts 17:6-10).
- He had been left alone in Athens in the recent past, after sending Timothy back to Thessalonica for news (1 Thess 3:1; Acts 17:15).
- He wrote soon after Timothy returned (1 Thess 3:6; Acts 18:5).

This fits Acts' account of Paul's travel to Athens and Corinth, where he was ministering when Timothy returned.

Gallio was proconsul of Achaia from July AD 51 to July AD 52. He was in Corinth to review the case against Paul (v 12). If Paul reached Corinth roughly a year to eighteen months earlier, he must have written 1 Thessalonians in 50 (Acts 18:11-12; Jewett 1986, 60; Murphy-O'Connor 1996, 15-22; Malherbe 2000, 73; Furnish 2007, 30).

The only serious question about the letter's literary integrity is whether 2:13-16 contains a later interpolation (Bruce 1982, 48-49; Richard 1995, 119-27; Lyons 1985, 202-7 [history of the debate]; → 2:13-16). A few scholars speculatively divide the letter into several letters (Richard 1995, 29-32; Schmithals 1972, 123-218). Most, however, accept the letter as a literary unity composed by Paul.

F. The Literary Structure of I Thessalonians: The Outline, Literary Structure, and Genre of I Thessalonians

Malherbe holds that 1 Thessalonians was a paraenetic letter, in the tradition of moral philosophers. It offers Paul as a model to be imitated, gives consolation, and encourages its readers to live out their faith (Malherbe 2000, 81-86). But Malherbe has been criticized for drawing too sharp a distinction between philosophy and rhetoric, and for assuming that paraenesis is incompatible with other rhetorical styles (Mitchell 2004).

A number of scholars analyze 1 Thessalonians according to the conventions of ancient rhetoric. They classify it as an example of epideictic persuasion (e.g., Lyons 1985, 218-21; Jewett 1986, 71-72; Wanamaker 1990, 48-50; Donfried 2002, 172; Witherington 2006, 21). This is the rhetoric of praise and blame. It was used in public and political settings, including funerals and presentations of gifts to important personages.

While much good has come from the study of rhetorical conventions, it seems difficult to restrict 1 Thessalonians to a single genre. Paul adopts and modifies conventions on letter openings, closings, and prayers. He adapts familiar religious and philosophical language, giving it his own twist. An original and creative thinker, he uses rhetorical techniques as an educated person of his culture, but with no sense of obligation to conventional composition (see Donfried 2002, 171).

First Thessalonians appears to contain a mixture of rhetorical genres, both epideictic and deliberative (Furnish 2007, 21-22). It has extended praise of the Thessalonians (1:2-10; 2:13-16; 3:6-9), as well as prayers for them and reminders that they already know how to live for God (4:1, 9), befitting epideictic. Yet in epideictic the narratio section ought to praise the deeds of the Thessalonians. Instead, it presents the *apostles* as faithful models (2:1-12).

The various exhortations about life and worship in 1 Thessalonians (4:4-12; 5:1-11; 5:12-22) are typical of deliberative rhetoric. The lesson on the Parousia simultaneously reminds, corrects, and comforts (4:13-18). This might best be described as "pastoral," Paul's own mixture of deliberative and epideictic. In the ancient church, Theodoret regarded the letter as a mixture of styles (2001, 107).

This commentary emphasizes that some awareness of the social and religious situation of Paul and his audience in Thessalonica is essential for understanding the letter. For the apostle this includes the OT and Jewish literature. But it also contains things that were common knowledge to educated persons living in the Roman Empire (but unknown to most average modern readers). For the Thessalonians, this included things such as Greek and Roman religions and their social and civic life. The rhetoric of the letter presumes a symbolic universe rooted in their culture. Unless we take seriously this world "behind the text," these symbols may not communicate the same meaning to us.

G. The Contents of I Thessalonians

Following a surprisingly plain greeting (1:1), Paul moves immediately into a complex thanksgiving (vv 2-10). This mentions their lived-out faith, love, and hope in imitation of the apostles who brought them the gospel.

The letter's next, more lengthy section reviews the history of Paul's and his companions' dealings with the Thessalonians (2:1—3:10). Paul's initial visit served as a model of the Christian life he teaches, which exhibits love in hard work and holiness (2:1-12). He rejoices that the Thessalonians believed. And he consoles them that their persecution places them in the same company as the Lord Jesus and the persecuted Christians in Judea (vv 13-16).

Paul's enforced absence from the Thessalonians led him to send Timothy to visit and encourage them (2:17—3:5). He rejoices that their faith in the Lord and their strong friendship with Paul continues (3:6-10). His prayer for their strengthening in holiness (vv 11-13) closes this first part of the letter and transitions to the paraenesis (4:1—5:22).

The exhortation (or paraenetic) section of the letter begins with instructions on sanctified sexuality (4:3-8) and brotherly love (vv 9-12). It then addresses events of Christ's return: the hope of resurrection (vv 13-18) and exemption from the wrath unbelievers will face (5:1-11). This serves as one rationale for living in holiness. The other motivation is their identity as God's children (vv 5-8).

Paul appeals to the community to respect its leaders and to help its members live responsible, Christlike lives (vv 12-15). There follows a series of brief injunctions about the church's worship life (vv 16-22), a prayer (vv 23-24), and a request for prayer (v 25). The letter ends with a final greeting, a command that it be read aloud to all the assembled believers, and a closing benediction (vv 26-28).

H. The Writing of 2 Thessalonians: Authorship

The early church accepted the Pauline authorship of 2 Thessalonians without question. It is echoed in Polycarp (*Pol. Phil.* 11.3-4; Justin, *Dial.* 32.12; 110.6), quoted in Clement of Alexandria (*Strom.* 5.3), and cited often in Tertullian. It is listed in the Muratorian Canon (ca. AD 200) and was endorsed by Marcion (ca. 140; Frame 1912, 39; Green 2002, 60).

Nearly all major English commentaries defend the authenticity of 2 Thessalonians (except Gaventa 1998 and Furnish 2007). In 1801 J. E. C. Schmidt first argued that 2:1-12 was an interpolation (Trilling 1972, 161). Later in that century several rejected apostolic authorship mostly on the grounds of supposed theological differences with 1 Thessalonians (see Collins 1988, 209-10). This opinion dominated continental scholarship in the twentieth century.

The reasons given for rejecting Pauline authorship include: (*a*) the supposed literary dependence of 2 Thessalonians on 1 Thessalonians; (*b*) theological differences between the two letters; (*c*) the difference in tone between the letters; and (*d*) 2 Thessalonians' alleged use of non-Pauline style and idioms.

That 1 and 2 Thessalonians treat a number of the same issues no one doubts. Both letters touch on the suffering of believers (1 Thess 1:6; 2:14; 3:2-4; 4:13; 2 Thess 1:4-6) and the return of Christ (1 Thess 1:10; 3:13; 4:13—5:4; 5:23; 2 Thess 1:7-8, 10; 2:1, 3, 8). Both have paraenetic sections dealing with the problem of idle people (1 Thess 4:1-12; 5:12-22; 2 Thess 3:6-15). This does not prove the author of 2 Thessalonians slavishly copied Paul's letter. This is what we would expect in two letters sent to the same church in a short interval. Differences arise from issues dealt with in the first letter, which worsened and threatened to destabilize the church.

Second Thessalonians does not simply repeat 1 Thessalonians. References to Jesus' return in the opening thanksgivings of the two letters are quite different. The two thanksgivings have different foci. Attempts to show elaborate borrowings are forced and overstated (see Menken 1994, 36-38). The arguments for literary dependence cut both ways: why would a later pseudepigrapher forge a letter using the same specific issues Thessalonica had a generation earlier?

The major theological difference that aroused critics to deny Pauline authorship to 2 Thessalonians is its eschatology. They claim that in 1 Thess 5:1-5 Paul insisted that the Day of the Lord would come suddenly and unexpectedly. However, 2 Thess 2:1-12 supposedly contradicts this with a "timetable" of signs that will happen first (Schmidt in Trilling 1972, 159-61; Collins 1988, 221; Menken 1994, 28-29; Gaventa 1998, 92).

This commentary will show that such differences are generally exaggerated. The emphasis on unexpectedness in 1 Thess 5:1-3 concerns the impact of the Parousia on non-Christians, not Christians. In the Gospels, the Jesus tradition allows an unpredictable return of Messiah to coexist with signs anticipating his coming (Mark 13:4-33).

The supposedly "new" information in 2 Thess 2:1-12 is based on pre-Pauline traditions preserved in Dan 11:31, 36-37; Matt 24:4, 10-12, 15 (and parallels), and in Jewish apocalyptic literature (→ 2 Thess 2:1-12). It reminds the audience of traditions it already knows, to correct false teaching (2:2).

Trilling claims that the *sole* concern of 2 Thessalonians is eschatology, as if the only reason for the letter was 2:1-12. This is not true, as exegesis will show. Gaventa claims that 2 Thessalonians inflates "minor concerns" of the first letter and ignores "major concerns" (1998, 91). But the suffering of believers for their faith or a heresy that claims the Day of the Lord has already arrived (2:2) cannot be called minor. Even the problem with the "idle" (3:6-15) has serious implications for the church's charity and witness.

The real problem with 2 Thessalonians is not how un-Pauline it is, but its emphasis on issues distasteful to many modern interpreters. Some would rather not deal with a sacred text that celebrates Jesus as judge or predicts the eschatological punishment of non-Christians. To nineteenth-century interpreters, anything apocalyptic was simply embarrassing. We must always be wary of the temptation to label "non-Pauline" the parts of these letters we find strange or offensive, so as conveniently to dispose of them.

First Thessalonians is warm in tone, frequently referring to the audience as "brothers" Paul longs to see and is concerned about (2:17; 3:2-10). Some interpreters accuse 2 Thessalonians of being impersonal, officious, and authoritarian (Menken 1994, 30-31; Richard 1995, 23; Collins 1998, 222-23; Furnish 2007, 132). Again, it is a matter of approach to the evidence.

In the first letter Paul wrote to encourage and celebrate the persevering faith of a newly founded church. His second letter addressed a changed situation. Obstinate believers had refused to submit to his correctives (3:6-15). Others had distorted his teaching. These developments had thrown the church into confusion (2:2).

Why should ordering troublemakers with commands (3:6, 10, 12) or emphasizing Paul's teaching as authoritative tradition (2:5, 15) imply pseudepigraphy (so Collins 1988, 222-23; Menken 1994, 30-31; Richard 1995, 23-24; Furnish 2007, 132)? Galatians stresses Paul's authority far more (1:1,

11—2:10). Both Galatians and 2 Corinthians are much harder on false teachers (Gal 1:8; 5:7-12; 2 Cor 11:9). The undisputed letters of Paul contain references to authoritative tradition entrusted to the church (1 Cor 11:2, 23; 15:1-11; Gal 1:9).

Those who deny the authenticity of 2 Thessalonians regard the concluding reference to Paul's handwriting (3:17) as a clumsy attempt by a later writer to authenticate the letter (Trilling 1972, 101-8; Collins 1988, 224; Furnish 2007, 132-33). They argue that forged letters (which 3:17 and 2:2 presume) could not have come into existence so soon for the historical Paul. But 3:17*a* is identical in form to 1 Cor 16:21 and Col 4:18. The rest of Paul's remarks in 2 Thess 3:17*b* respond to the false teaching (→). His signature authenticated the manuscript as from Paul, without tampering (Malherbe 2000, 355). Proponents of the pseudepigraphy theory refuse to allow for this letter to address a Pauline church with a changed situation. Yet it fits well within the normal range of literary variation for Paul (see Malherbe 2000, 356-61, 367; Fee 2009, 239-41).

Fatal to theories of pseudonymity is the failure to provide convincing answers to these questions:

Why would a post-Pauline Christian imitate one minor letter of Paul and ignore the major themes of all the other letters, which would have been circulating by then? Why revive the problems of a Macedonian church in the mid-first century?

Second-century Christian literature indicates that sexual ethics, holiness, and marriage were major concerns then. Why are these concerns completely absent from 2 Thessalonians, even though they are in 1 Thessalonians?

Those who deny Pauline authorship claim that the writer composed 2 Thessalonians to respond to a problem with eschatology in his church. But why could Paul not be responsible for this?

Why would one writing later under Paul's name plead with his audience to pray for the apostle and his work, when they knew him to be dead (3:1-2)?

I. The Occasion and Date of 2 Thessalonians

If we presume the Pauline authorship of 2 Thessalonians, what is the order of the letters? The traditional arrangement is arbitrary, apparently based on length. A few interpreters have argued for the priority of 2 Thessalonians, because the problems of persecution and of unruly members seem to be more severe in it (and hence earlier; see 1:5-7; 2:15-17; 3:6-15; see Wanamaker 1990, 37-38). They also think Paul's remark about his signature "in all my letters" (2 Thess 3:17) makes more sense in his first letter.

On the other hand, the data of 1 Thessalonians fit a letter written soon after Paul's founding visit. He had no news of them until Timothy's recent arrival, shortly before he wrote (1 Thess 3:5). The later date of 2 Thessalonians allows time for Paul's eschatology to be altered (2:1-2) and for conflict with pagans to intensify (see 1 Pet 4:12-16).

Second Thessalonians was most likely sent from six months to a year after 1 Thessalonians (fall AD 50 to spring 51), perhaps also from Corinth. Paul wrote the letter to correct the false eschatology, to address the continuing persecution of believers (1:5-12) and the problem of able-bodied idle believers taking support from the church's common fund (3:6-15).

J. The Genre of 2 Thessalonians

Recent commentators generally agree that 2 Thessalonians is dominated by deliberative rhetoric. It attempts to persuade the audience to change their beliefs (2:1-12) and behavior (3:6-15; Jewett 1986, 81-87; Hughes 1989, 51-74; Wanamaker 1990, 46-52; Witherington 2006, 30-34; Furnish 2007, 127-28). This makes sense of 2:1-15 and 3:6-15. But the thanksgiving and prayer (1:3-12) have more the character of epideictic rhetoric. Here Paul praises the Thessalonians and condemns their persecutors. It seems that again we have a letter of mixed genre.

K. The Contents of 2 Thessalonians

A plain greeting similar to that of 1 Thess 1:1 opens this letter (2 Thess 1:1-2), followed by a thanksgiving period (vv 3-12). This mentions their faith, love, and endurance in the face of persecution (vv 3-4). It assures them that Christ will relieve them and punish their persecutors when he returns (vv 5-10). It ends with Paul's prayer that the Thessalonians may be counted worthy of the kingdom and glorify the Lord (vv 11-12). Paul deals with false teaching about the Day of the Lord. He counteracts this with a reminder that the "man of lawlessness" must first arise and deceive many (2:1-12). In contrast, Paul gives thanks for the Thessalonians who were called through the gospel and exhorts them to stand firm in his apostolic teaching (vv 13-15). He prays that God may strengthen them for "every good deed and word," concluding his thanksgiving (vv 16-17).

Paul requests prayer for his safety and the gospel's spread. He prays that the Thessalonians may know divine love and endurance (3:1-5). He urges them to deal with believers who are living irresponsibly ("idle and disruptive" [v 6]; see vv 6-15). He closes the letter with another prayer (v 16), a reference to his authenticating signature (v 17), and a benediction (v 18).

L. Theological Themes of 1 and 2 Thessalonians

One can find theological implications in virtually every sentence of the Thessalonian letters. So as not to anticipate the conclusions of the commentary, here I merely summarize some of the major theological themes and the general thrust of the letters. Of course, trying to create a theology from a single ad hoc letter is fraught with the danger of distorting or overinterpreting the evidence. It "may well obscure rather than clarify Paul's theology" (Bockmuehl 1997, 42), unless the rest of the letter corpus is also taken into account.

I. Theological Emphases in I Thessalonians

God the Father. The aspect of God emphasized above all is his love, which led him to call believers through the gospel proclamation (1:3-5; 2:12; 5:24). Monotheism is presumed: he is "the living and true God," in contrast to the false gods and their idols (1:9). God is addressed as Father (1:1, 3). The gospel presumes the story of his sending and raising his Son (1:10; 3:2). By calling it the "gospel of God," Paul emphasizes God as the originator of this salvation. He reminds readers that they can know and do God's will with the aid of the Spirit (4:1, 3, 8). This way of life is "worthy of God" (2:12), as they reflect a character befitting the God they serve (4:1; 2:4).

Christ the Lord. Jesus is called "Lord" (twenty-four times) in this letter, far more than "Christ" (ten times) or "Jesus" (sixteen times). Here the OT "day of the LORD," God's theophany of judgment and deliverance, has become the day of the Lord Jesus (5:2). He rescues those who believe the gospel from God's apocalyptic wrath on sinners (1:10; 5:9). He is the object of prayer, together with the Father (3:11) or alone (3:12-13). A benediction is issued in his name (5:28). The church exists in God the Father and the Lord Jesus Christ (1:1; 3:8). In summary, Jesus shares God's functions and honor.

Yet Paul has not totally merged the figure of Jesus with God. There is an awareness of the historical person whose story involved execution (2:15) and burial, implicit in the mention of his resurrection (1:10). He set an example that is known and imitated (1:6). It is the Lord Jesus, not the Father, who will appear at the end of the age to raise the righteous and punish the wicked (4:14-17; 5:2, 9). The vivid hope of Christians, which dominates this letter, is resurrection life shared with Jesus, the heightened continuation of the relationship already begun in this life (4:17; 5:10).

Parousia. The second coming of Jesus Christ is a major theme. It is a primary tenet of faith (1:10) and a message of comfort: the dead in Christ will be raised, and the faithful will be with him forever (4:17-18; 5:10-11). It is also an apocalyptic hour of judgment on those "in darkness" (5:3-6).

Paul appropriates the language of OT theophany and military symbolism for the Parousia: Jesus will come as victorious, conquering Lord at the head of an angelic army (3:13b; 4:16-17). Jesus appears as an imperial figure, a counterpart to the Roman emperors: he has a royal Parousia and overturns the false imperial claims of "peace and security" (5:3 NRSV; see 4:15).

Spirit. References to the Spirit are few but significant. The Spirit is at work where the gospel is preached, confirming it and bestowing God's joy on those who accept it (1:5-6). Acknowledgment of the indwelling Holy Spirit leads to obedience to God's will and sanctification (4:3, 8). This implies what is explicit elsewhere: the Spirit enables believers to live out the new existence in Christ (Rom 8:4; Gal 5:16, 22-26). And the Spirit is active in Christian worship, communicating God's will to prophets (1 Thess 5:19-20). Paul assumes that these early Christians had a vivid, existential experience of God the Spirit.

Church. Paul's view of the church shines through in this letter despite its brevity. It exists "in God the Father and the Lord Jesus Christ" (1:1). The church is composed of those who experience God's call when they hear the gospel and accept it (1:4-5; 2:12-13). They are beloved by God (1:4), and their calling entails living as people wholly devoted to him. Thus sanctified, they live to please him (2:4; 4:1-3, 7-8).

Paul repeatedly speaks of Christians as family, continuing Jesus' teaching about children of the kingdom of God (Mark 3:31-35; 10:28-30; 13:12-13). A bond of godly love unites them (1 Thess 3:6, 12; 4:9-10). Like natural families, some are responsible for spiritual oversight and some need overseeing (5:12-15).

The church is also assisted in its present service by God's Spirit (1:6; 4:8; 5:19-20), by prayer (5:17-18, 25; see 1:2; 3:10, 12-13), by the apostles' instruction (2:11-13; 3:1-4; 4:1-2, 6), and by the memory of the apostles' exemplary lives (2:1-12, 15-16). What the apostles taught and modeled is the basis for what the church came to believe (1:9-10) and learn about ethics (2:5-12; 4:2). There is a notable lack of explicit citations of scripture in 1 Thessalonians, as compared to other Pauline letters. This is evidence of Paul adapting his style for those who only recently had come out of polytheism and were unfamiliar with the LXX.

Ethics. Christian ethics are dealt with often in this letter. Paul speaks of living to "please God" (2:4; 4:1), living "worthy of God" (2:12), sanctification (4:3), and being spiritually watchful and sober (5:6, 8). The apostles' instruction communicated God's will to them, which they were to follow (2:5-12; 4:2). The Thessalonians learned this way of life comes by imitation (1:6; 2:14), because the apostles lived self-consciously as models (2:7, 10-12). The converts in turn became models for others (1:7). The Holy Spirit empowers this new way of life (4:8).

Paul notes that one aspect of the Christian life is particularly difficult: imitating the suffering of the Lord himself and other believers (1:6; 2:14-16; 3:7). But it is inevitable for those who live as God's people in a world in spiritual darkness. To help his converts face this, he takes steps to reassure and encourage them (2:18; 3:2-5; 4:13, 18; 5:11).

The God-pleasing life involves holiness, abstention from sexual immorality, honorable use of one's body, and the pursuit of love for brothers and sisters in Christ (2:10; 4:3-6, 9-10). Love entails working so as to support oneself and to present the witness of a well-ordered life (4:11-12; 5:14; see 2:9).

This letter offers a variety of examples of ethical motivation: to please God (4:1); for the benefit of oneself (4:6-8; 5:6-8); for other believers (4:6,

10; 5:12-15) and nonbelievers (4:12); and as an expression of gratitude to Christ (5:9-10).

Paul's teaching forbidding revenge is reminiscent of Jesus' (5:15). God calls Christians to pursue peace with one another (vv 13, 15, 23). This expresses their sanctification, for it embodies God's *shalom* and anticipates his eschatological peace (v 23; Bassler 1994, 82-84). The virtues of faith, hope, and love provide the context for moral instruction (1:3; 5:8).

2. Theological Emphases in 2 Thessalonians

Suffering and Reward. The present suffering of Christians for their association with God's kingdom is a major issue in 2 Thessalonians. It confirms that they have been accounted worthy by grace to be in God's kingdom (1:5). Paul honors the Thessalonians for showing faith and endurance in affliction (v 4; see Rom 8:17; 1 Thess 2:13-14). They are to view their suffering from the perspective of the end: God is just, they will be rewarded, and their persecutors will be punished (2 Thess 1:5-7).

The doctrine of resurrection is presumed in this letter rather than proclaimed. It is the church's hope to be with the Lord (2:1, 16). The saints will enjoy "relief" at Christ's coming (1:7, 10). But nonbelievers will suffer "everlasting destruction" and be forever separated from the Lord (v 9). Resurrection life will be the final culmination of what it means to be saved. Salvation is the result of God's gracious calling through the gospel and sanctifying of the saints (2:13-14).

Judgment. Paul emphasizes the role of Jesus as cosmic judge at his Parousia in order to comfort suffering saints (1:7-10). He describes Christ's coming in apocalyptic terms borrowed from the OT "day of the LORD" passages. He applies God's functions to Jesus (vv 7-8 with Isa 66:15-16; Dan 7:10; 2 Thess 1:9 with Isa 2:10). Christ's coming terminates the deceiving and destroying power of Satan and his servants on earth. Christ brings divine judgment on the church's persecutors (2 Thess 1:7-10) and on the "man of lawlessness" and his followers (2:8, 10, 12; compare Exod 15:10). Final judgment is determined by one's response to God's Messiah, as revealed in the gospel. Those who do not obey the gospel call will perish (2 Thess 1:8-9; 2:10-12).

This apocalyptic scenario is common in early Christianity (Matt 25:41-46; Mark 9:47-48; Rom 2:12; 1 Cor 1:18; 2:6; 2 Cor 2:15; 4:3; Phil 3:19; 1 Thess 5:3; Rev 20:15). Paul shows no interest in the modern question, What happens to those who have never heard the gospel? His concern is, What happens to those who hear and refuse?

Christology. This letter also emphasizes Jesus' identity as "Lord" (*kyrios*). It deliberately accords to Jesus the honorific that the LXX substituted for "Yahweh." The title is used when Jesus is grouped with God in prayer-wishes (2 Thess 1:2; 2:16), co-addressed as deity. Or one may pray to Jesus alone

(3:16). He is the source of divine grace (1:12). The title "Lord" occurs together with almost every reference to "Jesus" or "Christ" (except for 3:5).

Strangely enough, some think this is evidence of a later development away from 1 Thessalonians (Trilling 1972, 128; Donfried and Marshall 1993, 95), but see 1 Thess 3:11-13; 5:28; 1 Cor 1:1; 16:24; 2 Cor 1:1; 13:14; Phil 1:2. The confession of Jesus as Lord is foundational to participation in the new covenant community. And it predates Paul (Hurtado 1993, 562-63; Rom 10:9; 1 Cor 12:3; 16:22; see Matt 7:21; Acts 2:36).

Election. The Christian life is described as a calling that comes through the proclamation of the gospel (2 Thess 1:11; 2:14). Its goal is to save those who welcome the message, allowing them to enter into the Lord's glory (vv 13-14). God accounts people as worthy (1:5, 11) by graciously calling them (v 11). Yet those who are saved chose to believe (v 10; 2:13), while the damned refused to believe (vv 10, 12).

Paul prays for believers to persevere as Christ did (3:5). But he also commands them to stand firm in their faith and hold fast to the apostolic traditions (2:15). All this implies that there is the possibility of choosing the "power of lawlessness" at work in the world (v 7) and finding oneself aligned with evil when Christ returns.

Nevertheless, Paul is optimistic: he boldly prays that God will bring about all the good the Thessalonians long for, as God strengthens them (1:11; 2:17). As he effects his saving work in their lives, they will glorify the Lord Jesus and add to the witness of the gospel (1:12).

Believers learned from the gospel that they were beloved by the Father and Son (2:13-16). They have experienced God's grace and his Spirit, who confirms that they are God's chosen people and calls them to sanctification (vv 13, 16; compare Rom 8:9-17; 1 Cor 6:11; Gal 4:6). Believers belong to a family defined in part by fidelity to the apostolic teaching, which has the authority of the church's Lord, Jesus (2 Thess 2:15; 3:6, 10, 12).

Ethics. The only behavioral issue emphasized in 2 Thessalonians is in response to the *ataktoi*, **the irresponsible ones**. They refuse to work but receive support from the church (3:6-15), taking advantage of generous Christians. Paul asserts the moral imperative for believers to support themselves, if able. He calls for church discipline to assure that the unwilling are not enabled by others to live irresponsibly (v 10). Part of the Christian witness to the reality of God's love in the gospel is evidenced by the peace we bring into existing relationships (v 16). Other than Paul's advice concerning the irresponsible minority, there are only general references to doing good and glorifying the Lord (1:11-12; 2:17).

COMMENTARY
1 THESSALONIANS

I. GREETING: 1 THESSALONIANS 1:1

BEHIND THE TEXT

The openings of Paul's letters generally follow a standard pattern of a greeting, thanksgiving, and prayer-wish for his readers (with exceptions: 2 Corinthians has a benediction; Galatians, 1 Timothy, and Titus lack thanksgivings). Ancient letters typically named first the sender, then the recipient, and often included a wish for the recipient's health.

In most of his letters, Paul identifies himself with a title expressing his divine commission. Here it is simply "Paul, Silas and Timothy" (1:1). This is not because it is an early letter, written prior to any challenges to his authority (against Best 1986, 60; Murphy-O'Connor 1996, 26). Paul had already been in ministry for at least sixteen years. The informal greeting seems to express the intimacy Paul had with this church, as well as his humility (1 Thess 2:6b-12; so Airhart 1965, 439; Green 2002, 82).

IN THE TEXT

■ **1 Paul** always uses his Roman name in his letters. Murphy-O'Connor suggests it would have been chosen as one of the three Latin names every Roman citizen took (1996, 41-43; see Acts 16:37-38). His given name Saul we know only from Acts (9:1-25; 13:9). It was common for Jews moving in Gentile circles to adopt Gentile names in addition to their given Hebrew names (note Peter, Andrew, and Mark: Mark 3:16; Acts 12:12). Perhaps this was his way of identifying with the Gentiles God had placed under his care. "Saul" also sounded in Greek like the adjective for an effeminate gait, so **Paul** was preferable in that context.

Silas and Timothy are named as co-senders of the letter. Did Paul include them as a polite formality, because they evangelized with him and were with him in Corinth as he wrote? If so, Paul was really the sole author, speaking for all three (Best 1986, 27-28; Richard 1995, 40). Or, was the letter a cooperative effort by all three?

In 1 Thessalonians the author refers to himself in the singular in only three places (2:18; 3:5; 5:27). Elsewhere the "we"-form dominates. Most commentators interpret the "we" statements as an authorial plural, meant to express camaraderie with the readers (Malherbe 2000, 88; see also Airhart 1965, 439; Best 1986, 27-28; Wanamaker 1990, 67; Richard 1995, 40; Furnish 2007, 37; but see Lyons 1985, 179).

First and Second Thessalonians are the only Pauline letters to include a second apostle in their greetings—note the plural "apostles . . . we" in 1 Thess 2:7. Ancient papyrus letters did not normally name multiple senders in their greetings unless the letter was actually from all of them (Prior 1989, 38-39; Murphy-O'Connor 1995, 18-19).

There was good reason for Paul to seek his coworkers' aid in the creation of this letter. Paul was stretched thin in Corinth as he wrote. He was still working full time to support himself, at least until Silas and Timothy returned from Macedonia (Acts 18:3-4; → 1 Thess 2:9). Tensions with the Jewish community led to an attempt to prosecute Paul before the Roman proconsul (Acts 18:12-17). He must have been exhausted emotionally, physically, and spiritually. Besides, Silas and Timothy were well known to the audience as cofounders of the church; and Timothy had just completed a visit with them (1 Thess 3:1-2, 6). It made sense for Paul to involve his friends in the drafting of the letter (see Prior 1989, 38-39; Murphy-O'Connor 1995, 16-20; Reicke 2001, 30-32, 42, 44).

Nevertheless, the "I" statements do show Paul breaking out here and there as the senior member of the team. No doubt his voice dominates and he approved the final draft, adding his command that it be read out loud, with a benediction on his beloved Thessalonians (5:27-28). Some plurals may best be explained as authorial plurals (see 3:1). And some plurals include the Thessalonians in the discourse (3:3; 4:14). But it is a misplaced regard for Paul's authority that would balk at his sharing the task of writing a letter, when he freely praised fellow workers in the gospel (e.g., Rom 16:1-7, 21; 1 Cor 3:5-9; 16:15-16; 1 Thess 5:12-13; Reicke 2001, 30-32).

Silvanus must be the same person Acts calls **Silas**. The first form is a Latin name; the second, Greek. The NIV uses **Silas** everywhere, despite Paul's spelling. After the Jerusalem Council, Silas was sent as an emissary with Paul (Acts 15:22, 25-33). He helped evangelize Thessalonica. He was an apostle and a prophet (1 Thess 2:7; Acts 15:32).

Silas is the Greek version of the Aramaic name "Saul" for this Jewish Christian (BDAG, 923). Paul took Silas with him on his second missionary journey, perhaps as a gesture of unity between Gentile and Palestinian branches of the church (Acts 15:40; Wanamaker 1990, 69). He may have been one of the "representatives" (*apostoloi*) sent by Pauline churches to accompany their offering to Jerusalem (2 Cor 8:23; Wanamaker 1990, 69). Sometime after Paul arrived in Corinth, Silas joined him (Acts 18:5; 2 Cor 1:19).

Timothy was from Lystra in southern Galatia. He had a Jewish-Christian mother and a Greek father, who was probably pagan (Acts 16:1-3; 2 Tim 1:5). Timothy's mixed heritage proved to be the perfect preparation for bringing the gospel into the Gentile world (Wall 2002, 227). Starting as an assistant, he would become one of Paul's most trusted colleagues. He was like a son to Paul (Phil 2:22). He is mentioned as a co-sender of six letters (1 and 2 Thessalonians, 2 Corinthians, Philippians, Colossians, and Philemon).

The addressees are **the church of the Thessalonians in God the Father and the Lord Jesus Christ.** First and Second Thessalonians are the only letters to use this particular description of a church in the greeting (compare "all God's holy people in Christ Jesus" [Phil 1:1]; "God's holy people in Ephesus, the faithful in Christ Jesus" [Eph 1:1]). The word "church" never appears in the English OT. But Paul's first readers would have recognized the word "church" (*ekklēsia*) in their Greek OT.

What did this word mean, and why did early Christians choose it to describe themselves? In secular Greek, the *ekklēsia* was the assembly of male citizens gathered to do the business of a democratic city. Greeks never used the word for religious groups. That this *ekklēsia* is "in God the Father and the Lord Jesus" tells us to whom this unusual assembly owes its existence (Malherbe 2000, 102).

In the Greek OT the term *ekklēsia* was used for the "assembly" of the nation of Israel as God's people (Deut 23:2-4; 31:30; 1 Kgs 8:14; Mic 2:5). Israel gathered to hear God at Sinai on the "day of the assembly" (Deut 4:10; 9:10; 18:16; see Deut 31:12). Hence, Christians, by calling themselves "the **assembly** in God" (1 Thess 1:1; "*assembly*" of God" [Acts 20:28; 1 Cor 10:32; 11:18; 15:9]) invoked the identity of Israel as a people called to belong to God.

Their identity is established not by their ethnic heritage, but by God's call and God's covenant with them. Christians apparently understood the church to stand in continuity with ancient Israel, because they were the people of God in this age. Those who "belong to Christ . . . are Abraham's seed" (Gal 3:29).

In what sense is the church **in** God the Father and the Lord Jesus Christ? Some argue the **in** should be understood instrumentally, meaning "the assembly of the Thessalonians brought into being by God the Father and the Lord Jesus Christ" (Best 1986, 62; Richard 1995, 38; Malherbe 2000, 99). But the instrumental use of the Greek preposition *en* (**in**) usually accompanies a verb; and there is no verb in the greeting.

There are good reasons to think that Paul intended **in** as a marker of *place*, a theological metaphor, which makes God the dwelling place of Christians. It is the functional equivalent to Paul's references to being "in Christ" or in the Spirit (see Frame 1912, 70; Bruce 1982, 7). Being in God (or Christ) is the corollary to saying God indwells believers (Rom 8:1, 10; Col 1:2; 2:10; see also John 14:23; 17:21).

Believers owe their existence to God. They live inhabited by God's presence—his Spirit, thanks to the grace of the new covenant (Rom 8:9-11; 1 Cor 12:13; 1 Thess 4:8). This spatial metaphor points to Jesus' "inclusive personality," which was evidence of his divinity (Moule 1977, 47-96). Paul's greeting strikingly brackets God and the Lord Jesus together. The apostle had the highest possible view of Jesus: he shares fully in God's divine nature.

Dunn explains being in God/Christ as referring to "existential participation in the new reality brought about by Christ"—a mystical experience (1998, 400, 401; see "in Christ" and "in the Lord" in, e.g., 1 Thess 3:8; 4:1, 16; 5:12; 2 Thess 3:4; Rom 6:11; 1 Cor 1:2, 30; 9:1). This experience is alluded to in the metaphors of co-burial with Christ and being his body (Rom 6:4-5; 1 Cor 6:15; 12:12-13, 27).

That God is called **the Father** is common for Paul. Although God is occasionally called Father in the OT and Jewish literature, the title was rare. God was usually referred to by honorific titles such as the Holy One or the King of the Universe. Apparently, Jesus' constant reference to God as Father indelibly stamped the writings of his disciples.

In Paul's day, fathers were the head of the family. As such, they were to be obeyed. Nevertheless, by referring to God by this title Paul presented a more intimate image of God than was typical of Jews. He implied that believers were a fictive *family* with God as the *paterfamilias*. Hence, they call one another "brothers and sisters" (1 Thess 1:4). This concept is so important that Jesus is remembered for the radical idea that God's family may conflict with or even replace one's natural family (Mark 3:31-35; 13:12-13).

For Jesus, the title **Father** also pointed to God's love and to God's desire for the restoration of fallen humanity (Luke 11:11-13 ‖ Matt 7:9-11; Luke

15:11-32). Paul will go on in this letter to recount how he himself modeled this parental compassion for the Thessalonians (1 Thess 2:7-8, 11).

Lord (*kyrios*) is the title Christians gave to the risen Jesus (Rom 10:9; 1 Cor 12:3). Greek speakers used it of humans in positions of authority (a slave's master or a high-ranking government official). They addressed their deities as "lords" (*Hymn to Isis* [P.Oxy. 1380]; Plutarch, *Is. Os.* 367A; Apuleius, *Metam.* 11). Roman emperors—both living and dead—were addressed as "lord."

What is more relevant is that the title *kyrios* was used by Greek-speaking Jews for the God of the OT. The LXX translated God's name YHWH with *kyrios*, in line with synagogue practice. The Hebrew Scriptures address God with the Hebrew title "Lord" (*ādôn*). Several times daily Jews prayed to God as Lord, reciting Deut 6:4-5 ("Hear, O Israel: The LORD our God, the LORD is one. Love the LORD your God with all your heart and with all your soul and with all your strength"). Where English says "LORD" the Hebrew reads YHWH, and the Septuagint has *kyrios*. So to a Greek-speaking Jew like Paul, "Lord" used in prayer and religious speech was inevitably associated with God. With this usage, early Christians clearly indicated that Jesus stood "on the divine side of reality" (Marshall 1983, 49).

Christ is the Greek translation of the Hebrew title "Messiah," meaning "anointed one." It came to be used in Judaism as a title for the expected great end-time deliverer God would send to Israel. There were a variety of messianic expectations in first-century Judaism. But the most common one held that a royal messiah, a descendant of David, would restore Israel politically and defend her from her enemies.

As the **Christ**, Jesus redefined his messianic role in terms of the Suffering Servant (see Isa 52:13—53:12; Mark 8:29-31; 10:45; Luke 22:37). His disciples accepted him as Messiah, although they did not understand the full import of that until after his death and resurrection. Early Christians argued that the resurrection confirmed that Jesus was Messiah in fulfillment of prophecy (Acts 2:24-32; 1 Cor 15:20, 25, echoing Ps 110:1).

The greeting **Grace and peace** appears in every letter by Paul (1 and 2 Timothy add "mercy"). This is not identical to any greeting previously known from other ancient letters (Malherbe 2000, 100). The most familiar explanation is that Paul combines the typical greetings from Jewish and Gentile societies. Hebrew *Shalôm*, "peace," also means "hello"; and Greek *chairein* means "greetings." He substituted *charis* ("grace") for *chairein* (Best 1986, 64). Some theorize that Paul modified extant formulas in Jewish letters, such as "mercy and peace," or used the Aaronic blessing from Num 6:24-26 (*2 Bar.* 78:2; 2 Macc 1:1; Marshall 1983, 49; Malherbe 2000, 100; Fitzmyer 1993, 228).

FROM THE TEXT

Paul models humility in the greeting of this letter. The apostle to the Gentiles wrote as part of a team, respecting the work of others. Jealousy is one of the most insidious and destructive sins in the church, often masquerading as spirituality. We need to remember Jesus' request that we pray for co-workers in the harvest of potential believers (Matt 9:37-38; Luke 10:2; John 4:34-38). When others succeed in ministry, we should all rejoice.

Paul's faith infused even the conventional letter greeting: into it he has brought the special title of God as "Father," the association of Jesus with God, and the existential grounding of the church in the risen Christ and God the Father. His casual greeting alludes to two key gospel concepts: the grace God gives believers in Jesus and the peace with God this produces.

Believers are also the "assembly" called by God's grace to a new existence in Christ and in God. Like Israel in the wilderness, they are on their way to a promised land, led by their Lord.

II. THANKSGIVING: I THESSALONIANS 1:2-10

BEHIND THE TEXT

In ancient letters, thanksgivings to a deity on behalf of the recipients are rare; prayer reports, only slightly less rare (Schubert 1939, 167, 172-73; Best 1986, 65; Bruce 1982, 11; against Witherington 2006, 56). Yet most of Paul's letters (except for Galatians, 1 Timothy, and Titus) contain a thanksgiving prayer or a blessing. Further, the thanksgivings in papyrus letters, when they do occur, are extremely brief, unlike the extended, elaborate ones we see in Paul. His thanksgivings draw from the OT, early Christian preaching, and the language of worship (O'Brien 1977, 264-65). He has modified the form.

A thanksgiving starts at 1 Thess 1:2, but scholars disagree about where it ends. Some believe that one lengthy thanksgiving extends from 1:2 to 3:13 (Schubert 1939, 16-18; Best 1986, 31-34, 65; O'Brien 1977, 144; Lyons 1985, 177). This includes the thanksgiving notes of 2:13 and 3:9-10. Others argue that these three chapters are too diverse to constitute a unified whole. Occasionally, other letters have second thanksgivings (2 Thess 2:13) or prayers (Eph 3:14-21; Ign. *Pol.* 12.2; compare the doxologies in Rom 11:33-36 and 1 Pet 4:11). Most interpreters correctly identify the thanksgiving as 1 Thess 1:2-10. Here the main focus is on the *Thessalonians* and their reception of the gospel. At 2:1 the focus shifts to the *apostles*, their *ethos* and moral example.

It has been known for some time that Paul's introductory thanksgivings introduce topics to be treated subsequently in the letter (Schubert 1939, 180; O'Brien 1977, 8). They function like an *exordium* or introduction to a speech. In 1 Thessalonians the virtues of faith, love, and hope (1:3) will reappear in the issues of fidelity to God and Christ (1:9; 2:13; 3:6; 5:8); in matters of mutual love, holiness, and sexual ethics (2:8; 3:6; 4:1-10); in the hope of Jesus' return and Christians' resurrection (also 1:10; 4:13, 18; 5:10-11). Other issues anticipated are Paul's moral example (1:5), imitation (1:6-7), and suffering (1:6).

Part of this thanksgiving sounds like a rehearsal of past events (vv 5-10). It shows *how* the Thessalonians' faith, love, and hope came to expression in their lives. Reports of past events also appear in the Psalms. There, they (*a*) are a means to praise God; (*b*) remind worshippers of God's great deeds in the past, giving confidence that he will act consistently in the future; or (*c*) remind God of his deeds, urging him to respond to prayers for present needs (Westermann 1981, 55-57, 82-90; Brueggemann 1984, 55; see Pss 126; 132; 136). The thanksgiving here serves both functions (*a*) and (*b*).

The thanksgiving in 1 Thess 1:2-10 may be outlined as a chiasm (an X-shaped organization):

A. Thanksgiving for the Thessalonian Christians' faith, love, and hope (1:2-3)
   B. Thanksgiving for the assurance of their salvation (1:4-5)
A'. Thanksgiving for their lives that demonstrate faith, love, and hope (1:6-10)

IN THE TEXT

A. Thanksgiving for the Thessalonians' Faith, Love, and Hope (1:2-3)

■ 2-3 **We always thank God** (v 2) announces the beginning of Paul's thanksgiving prayer report. Paul may refer to corporate prayers offered by himself, Silas, and Timothy. He follows his own advice to "pray continually" (5:17). But this cannot mean they were on a full-time prayer vigil while they were at Corinth. We should read this as "every day when we pray, you are one of the things we thank God for." One important rhetorical and pastoral function of this letter is to reconnect with the audience and reassure them of Paul's and his colleagues' love for them.

When Paul says **all** the Thessalonians are the topic of thanks, he emphasizes that not one of the believers there is neglected in their **prayers**. They name each believer individually and aloud in God's presence (**mention you**). Paul was that rare breed, both a scholar and a "people person" familiar with the life details of his converts. The phrase translated **mention you** is used in ancient letters to let someone know they are being talked about, loved, and not forgotten. In one ancient letter, a wife writes to her absent husband:

> If you are well and everything else is going according to plan, then it is just what I have continually prayed to the gods for. Both I and the child are healthy, as are all those in the household. We are *making mention* of you always.† (Hunt and Edgar 1932, 1:97, 168 BC)

In a normal letter we might expect Paul to say "we always talk about you among ourselves." Instead the ***mentioning*** occurs in the context of prayer, **before our God and Father** (1:3), as does what they **remember**. Paul lists specific examples from his converts' lives to **remember** and be grateful to God, focusing on a triad of Christian virtues. Psalms similarly give reasons for praise and thanksgiving (Pss 32; 105; 116).

This triad of **faith, . . . love, . . . hope** appears multiple times in Paul's letters, Hebrews, 1 Peter, and early postapostolic writers (→ "Faith, Hope, Love" sidebar, below). This brief formula, which seems to summarize the Christian life, became widely used early on. It is not known where it originated. Perhaps Paul invented it as a kind of simple catechism for the Gentile Christian churches he founded. It is easy to remember and broadly summarizes the Christian worldview. The three Christian virtues replace the four virtues of pagan society advocated by Aristotle and others (courage, justice, temperance, wisdom). The latter are not bad; they are also praised in Scripture. But this sacred triad transcends them.

By **faith** Paul does not mean dogma (ideas we believe), but the *action* of belief, an attitude of trust. Faith in this sense is like what we mean when we say, "I have faith in my doctor." It is confidence that God exists and that God has our best interests at heart (see Heb 11:6). Not only is faith in God important, but so is faith in Jesus as his Son who was sent, died, and rose again for us (Rom 3:21-26; Gal 2:15-21; 4:4-5; see 1 Thess 1:10).

What is the Thessalonians' ***work*** [*ergon*] ***of faith*** (work produced by faith)? It could mean "the work faith does" or "the work that is faith" or "the work that produces faith." What Paul writes in his other letters seems to exclude the last option. But what of the other two? Some think that only "work that is faith" represents Paul's theology. But Paul can also speak of "faith *working* through love" (Gal 5:6 NRSV), and he prays in 2 Thess 2:17 that Jesus and God will "strengthen you in every good deed and word." Romans 1:5 refers to "the obedience that comes from faith." Christians were "created in Christ Jesus to do good works" (Eph 2:10).

Since this letter emphasizes that the Thessalonians became imitators of other Christians in ways people could observe and imitate, it seems best to take **work** here as more than simply believing. The NIV implies this by adding **produced by**. These works could include ministry and evangelism (1 Thess 5:12-13). They certainly involve their endurance under suffering, love for one another, and lifestyles that exhibited their trust in the living God (Best 1986,

67; Marshall 1983, 51; Wanamaker 1990, 75; Green 2002, 89). Paul emphasizes that the missionaries heard these things as evidence of their *faith*.

Next, Paul praises their **labor of love** (labor prompted by love). Labor (*kopos*) refers to work as hard physical activity that drains a person ("toil"). Like *ergon*, *kopos* can be used either of ordinary work (1 Cor 4:12; 2 Thess 3:8) or ministry (1 Cor 15:10; 1 Thess 3:8; Best 1986, 68; Green 2002, 90). Perhaps *kopos* more naturally goes with **love** because it emphasizes the difficulty and self-sacrifice that love endures to serve others.

In Jesus' teaching, **love** for God and neighbor is key to understanding God's will for us (Mark 12:28-34). His understanding of love builds on the Scriptures of Israel, in which love is a covenant quality. It means to be committed to the good of the other.

Love was so abused in the pagan world of Paul's day that when Christians translated Jesus' words into Greek, they chose a rare noun—*agapē*—and filled it with new significance. Similarly, in our day **love** is used for a wide range of things: I can love soccer, ice cream, my dog, or my wife. And popular media confuses love with "lust." But biblical **love** is about doing what is caring, just, and compassionate.

Paul writes elsewhere that "love is the fulfillment of the law" (Rom 13:10; see Gal 5:13). The highest achievement of spiritual maturity is love, because it alone will continue to be necessary in eternity (1 Cor 13:8-13). To love is to imitate the life of the Son of God, who both commanded us to love and modeled that love for us (John 13:34-35).

When Paul praises the Thessalonians for their **labor of love** he proclaims that they are actively imitating Christ as his true disciples. The **labor** Paul has in mind probably included tangible deeds of charity, shared worship, hosting traveling Christians from elsewhere, and spreading the gospel.

Hope is the last member of the triad. By putting **your endurance inspired by hope** last in the series, Paul emphasizes it as the virtue most needed in Thessalonica (compare 1 Cor 13:13). **Endurance** refers to the ability to stand firm in difficult situations. The Thessalonians had stood their ground as believers in God and in the Lord Jesus, despite being assailed by their unbelieving neighbors (1 Thess 2:14). Their **endurance** is the consequence of their **hope in our Lord Jesus Christ**.

Here **hope** does not connote wishful thinking or uncertainty, as in modern English. Biblical **hope** is about *trust in a future that God has promised and that we have not yet seen*. It is comparable to an expectant mother's anticipation of the birth of a child: it hasn't happened yet, but she is confident it will happen at the right time. Thus, **hope** is faith oriented toward the future (as 1:10; 4:14). Paul can speak of being saved in hope (Rom 8:24; see 1 Cor 15:11).

Whatever confusion the Thessalonians may have had about the future (see 1 Thess 4:13), they were confident Jesus would return and reign as messianic Lord. And they expected believers would greet him and share in the glorious fullness of the kingdom of God. This "hope of glory" (Col 1:27) strengthened their resolve to maintain their faith despite the suffering (1 Thess 1:6; see Rom 5:2-5; 8:18; 2 Cor 4:16-18).

Faith, Hope, Love

The triad of virtues—faith, hope, and love—occur repeatedly in Paul's letters. Twice they show up in 1 Thessalonians (1:3; 5:8); and in the thanksgiving for the church at Colosse (Col 1:4-5). It describes living in Christian freedom (Gal 5:5-6; compare Eph 4:2-5) or spiritual maturity (1 Cor 13:1-13). The triad is also found in Heb 6:10-12 and 1 Pet 1:21-22. These passages suggest that the triad is not simply Paul's spur-of-the-moment creation. It seems to be a widespread formula used in the early church. The triad serves as theological shorthand for all that it means to live the life of the new covenant.

We also find a few references to this triad in the church fathers of the second century (Ign. *Phld.* 11.2; Ign. *Magn.* 7.2 [AD 107]; Pol. *Phil.* 3.2-3 [AD 108]). Barnabas uses it to describe his readers as ideal disciples: "great faith and love are dwelling in you, along with the hope of his life"† (*Barn.* 1.4 [ca. AD 130-135]; see also 11.8).

As church teaching became more sophisticated, the simple triad used by the earliest Christians began to fade away, except as a memory of the strikingly beautiful and succinct 1 Cor 13:13. But it still has the power to evoke a vast vista of the Christian life in these few rich words.

Clement of Alexandria, in the last quarter of the second century AD, calls faith, hope, and love the "sacred triad." These are the three foundations of the temple of God in heaven (*Strom.* 4.7.54.1; 5.1.13.4).

Before our God and Father is a metaphor of space (not of prior time). Paul and his associates **remember** in prayer *in God's presence*. In Greek it is the last phrase of this verse. Thus, it may modify the faith-love-hope triad (so Bruce 1982, 13). But the same emphatic placement in 1 Thess 3:9 suggests that Paul refers to prayer as speech in the presence of God (Best 1986, 70; Marshall 1983, 52; Wanamaker 1990, 76; Richard 1995, 47; Malherbe 2000, 107; Green 2002, 88). Stoic philosophers also called God Father and referred to humans as his offspring. But "there were no Stoic communities of God's children called by their Father" (Malherbe 2000, 107).

B. Assurance of the Thessalonians' Salvation (1:4-5)

■ 4 Paul turns from the initial summary of their thanksgiving to what he and his coworkers **know** about the original evangelization of the city and the Thessalonians' coming to belong to God. In Greek the verb **know** is a participle dependent upon the main verb ***give thanks*** (v 2). Thus, it introduces another reason for their thanksgiving (**for**).

Paul calls the Thessalonians **brothers and sisters loved by God** (1:4). Jewish people sometimes used **brothers** for fellow Jews, emphasizing that they were part of the same nation and bound together by a common covenant that obliged them to treat one another with kindness (e.g., 1QS VI, 10, 22; CD VI, 20-21; Tob 5:10; 9:2; Philo, *Spec.* 2.79-80; Josephus, *J.W.* 2.122 and *Ant.* 10.201; and Deut 15:3; see Best 1986, 71; Wanamaker 1990, 77).

Members of some philosophical schools and mystery cults also used fictive kinship language (Malherbe 2000, 110). But this transferred sense of family becomes highly intensified in Jesus' teaching on the kingdom of God, which created havoc with his culture's understanding of family.

In some ways God's kingdom calls for a strengthened allegiance to family, as in Jesus' marriage sayings (Matt 5:31-32; 19:8-9; Mark 10:11-12; Luke 16:18). But in other ways the notion of family is radically redefined. Members of God's kingdom take precedence over one's biological family. Those who pursue the Father's will are truly family (Matt 12:48-49 ‖ Mark 3:33-35 ‖ Luke 8:21; Mark 10:28-30). Disciples may have to choose the kingdom over their natural family (Matt 10:21 ‖ Mark 13:12; Matt 10:34-39; Luke 12:51-53; 14:26; 21:16-17).

First Thessalonians uses the term **brother** more frequently than any other letter of Paul, relative to its size (fourteen times; 1 Corinthians has more occurrences, but it is three times as long; Malherbe 2000, 109-10). Perhaps Paul particularly stresses the Thessalonians' relationship to all other Christians. They belong to something larger than themselves. Their new faith ruptured their old social and familial relationships. Paraenetic letters typically emphasize personal relationships (Malherbe 2000, 125). In first-century culture family entailed responsibility to care for one another and to respect older members. Paul's family language would have brought up a well-understood network of relations and prepared his readers for the instruction that follows.

Brothers and Sisters: Why Inclusive Language?

Ancient Greek does not have genderless terms for humanity. Whenever Greeks wanted to speak about "people" in general they used the word *anthrōpos*, which can mean "man" (a male adult) or "human beings." Any description of humans in Greek must use the masculine plural to speak about humanity in general (e.g., "wise *men*"). There was no other grammatical option.

So it was with family terms as well. There is no word like the English "siblings"; Greek used "brothers" to mean *either* male relatives or *both* "brothers and sisters." Figuratively, **brothers** in the NT stands for all Christians.

This has led to a modern debate over how best to translate these terms. Some believe it is best to use male-oriented language in English, even when the context makes it clear that both men and women are meant. Many others, however—including scholars within the Wesleyan and evangelical theological communities—believe that it is more faithful to the intention of the biblical writers to make it clear in English that terms like "men" and "brothers" were intended to be *inclusive* of all humanity. This is especially important in an age in which inclusive language is becoming more the norm, and people reading Scripture without any biblical background may too easily assume that a word like "men" or "brothers" means only males.

To be a Christian is by definition to be **loved by God**, who showed his love for us by sending his Son (Rom 5:8-10). This may be what Paul means by speaking of the Thessalonians as "taught by God to love each other" (1 Thess 4:9; see Rom 5:8). God's love is closely tied to the notions of election and holiness (→ 1 Thess 4:7-10): God loves those who belong to him.

By writing of **your election** (i.e., he has chosen you), Paul reminds his audience that they belong to the people of God. The OT identifies Israel as God's chosen people (Deut 4:37; 7:6; Pss 105:6, 43; 106:5). The language of choosing emphasizes that the initiative is with God, not Israel. Hence, election is closely tied with the concepts of *grace* and of divine *love*. God pursues and saves Israel not because she deserves it but because he freely chooses to love her as a gift (Deut 4:35-38; 7:7-8; Ezek 16:1-14). And so it is with the church: election is associated with holiness because it is about being called to belong to God in a special way, to be wholly devoted to him.

The election of Israel in the OT is not an exclusive election. It is not as if no other nations could be saved. It is an election to serve God and bring knowledge of him to the rest of the world. Already in Genesis Abraham is chosen by God so that "all peoples on earth will be blessed through you" (Gen 12:3; 18:18). The prophets expected the future redemption of non-Israelite nations, who would come to worship the Creator God and become his people (Isa 19:19-25; Mic 4:1-4).

These OT ideas are clearly the basis for Paul's description of the Thessalonian Christians as "elect." Through Christ's saving work, the Abrahamic covenant applies to Gentiles also. *Gentiles* who come to faith in Jesus Christ and God the Father are "children of Abraham" (Gal 3:7-8, 26-29)—a phrase reserved for Jews!

Paul is not explicitly speaking of the election of *individuals*, but rather of *a church, a collective community* called to be the people of God. For him, election is corporate (Best 1986, 72; Marshall 1983, 53; Richard 1995, 63). To be "elect" defines one's *present condition* as a believer. The elect are those people who have responded in faith to the gospel. Election is not a guarantee of future salvation. Nor is it a license to sin without consequences. Just as in Israel, individuals could break covenant and apostatize (Lightfoot 1957, 12; Marshall 1983, 53; see Witherington 2006, 65-70). On the contrary, being God's people is "election to the service of God" (Best 1986, 72). It is an assignment, not a basis for presumption.

■ **5** The next clause may give the reason why Paul believes the Thessalonians to be elect (**because**, O'Brien 1977, 151-52; Wanamaker 1990, 78; Morris 1991,

45; Green 2002, 91; ESV, NASB, NIV, NRSV). But more likely it explains what the letter writers know about *how* their election happened: in the context of Paul's missionary preaching. This is a common Greek usage when the verb "to know" is followed by a noun and *hoti* ("epexegetical" *hoti*: "that" [Acts 16:3; Rom 13:11; 1 Cor 16:15; 1 Thess 2:1]; Lightfoot 1957, 12; Best 1986, 73; Malherbe 2000, 110). Read this way, Paul is saying, *We know . . . your election, [namely] that our gospel came to you not only in word but also in power and in the Holy Spirit and with great conviction* (1 Thess 1:4-5).

Paul's **gospel** focused on monotheistic faith, Jesus' coming, death, and resurrection on behalf of human sin, and his future return (vv 9-10; 5:9-10). In 1 Corinthians, Paul refers to these elements as the basic message all apostles preach everywhere (15:1-11, 23-24). He calls it **our gospel** (1 Thess 1:5) because the apostles were the ones who delivered it.

The Greek noun for **gospel**, *euangelion*, is the root for our word *evangelical*. It can mean "good news." Ancients used it to refer to the announcement of a military victory or other good news. It was used occasionally to refer to a ruler's birth, enthronement, or decrees (Becker 1999; Pillar sees a close association with the emperor [2013, 1-2]).

The verb form, *euangelizomai*, could be used for announcing good news, such as the "salvation"—delivering from destruction—of a city in battle. Greek speakers, familiar with the secular use of this term, would take it to indicate a significant fortunate event or decree.

The religious background to Paul's use must be sought in the LXX and in Jesus' teaching. The Gospels report that Jesus saw himself as a divine messenger of "good news" concerning the kingdom of God (Mark 1:14-15). This is anticipated in the OT. In Isaiah the verb *euangelizomai* proclaims the **good news** of God's coming reign. This will bring deliverance and restoration to some but judgment to others (Isa 40:9; 52:7; 61:1-11; Friedrich 1964, 709; Bruce 1982, 14; Wanamaker 1990, 78).

Jesus' use of the word "gospel" for his message no doubt evoked these ancient promises. Paul follows the lead of the early church in using this term to describe the great act of deliverance God achieved for humanity in Jesus' coming, death, and resurrection.

In this passage many recent commentators hold that Paul emphasizes the *preaching event* as the **gospel** he reminds them of. He stresses the power of God's miracles, the Holy Spirit's working, and that it was *not only in word*. But proclamation does not exclude its content (Wanamaker 1990, 78; Richard 1995, 48; Malherbe 2000, 110, 125; Witherington 2006, 71; Morris [1991, 45] and Green [2002, 94 n. 27] argue that it refers to content only). Paul's emphasis on his *activity* of preaching, rather than its content, is probably from the overall context rather than the term **gospel**, which implies a *word* or message.

The gospel Paul and his missionary colleagues preached to the Thessalonians was **not simply with words but also with power, with the Holy Spirit and**

deep conviction. The contrast of **words** and **power** does not belittle preaching. Paul did not suggest that only the miraculous presence of God counted or that the Spirit is better than the intellect. Rather, he emphasizes that his proclamation of the gospel was *more than* words. It was about a divine reality that erupted into the world and totally changed their lives (see Rom 1:16-17).

Paul may implicitly contrast the Christian message with that of contemporary moral philosophies or mystery cults. They would have been perceived as rivals to Christianity on questions of how to live one's life and deal with the fear of death. Traveling charlatans operated too, much like spiritual hucksters today. They promised a better life in exchange for money (humorously parodied in Lucian's *Philopseudes* [*The Lover of Lies*]; *De morte Peregrini* [*The Passing of Peregrinus*]; and *Alexander the False Prophet*).

The gospel did come in human language. Though **not simply** spoken, this is by implication the basic thing that a **gospel** is: a communication of God's saving story involving Jesus. But it is not *only words*. God's **power** lies behind it. This may refer to the presence of the **Holy Spirit**, or to miracles that occurred during his evangelism. The word **power** (*dynamis*) can mean "miracles" in the plural (Mark 6:2; 1 Cor 12:28-29; 2 Cor 12:12; Gal 3:5) and sometimes in the singular (Mark 6:5; Luke 5:17; 8:46; 9:1; Rom 15:19). Paul elsewhere refers to miracles or "signs" accompanying his mission (Rom 15:18-19; 2 Cor 12:12; Gal 3:5). Thus, it is reasonable to think Paul may also here (1 Thess 1:5). Although Paul is describing what he *knows* of the circumstances in which God chose them, one cannot avoid seeing these as evidence of God's election as well (so Theodore of Mopsuestia, in Gorday 2000, 60-61; also Green 2002, 95, 96).

The **Holy Spirit** was also present at his preaching, which led to their becoming God's chosen. In later letters Paul states that all believers are baptized into the body of Christ by the Spirit and that all who belong to Christ have the Spirit (Rom 8:9; 1 Cor 12:3, 13; Gal 3:5; see Heb 2:4). Acts points to the Spirit as evidence of Jesus' resurrection and lordship (2:33). *How* Paul or the Thessalonians knew the Spirit was present, he does not say. Was it a subjective, emotional experience of God's presence? Is this another reference to miracles? Is it an allusion to prophecy taking place, or some other spiritual gift (1 Cor 14:24-25, 39; Heb 2:4)? Whether it was one or all of these, this is fascinating evidence that the conversion of these earliest Gentile Christians was accompanied by a vivid existential experience of God's Spirit that Paul could point to (see also Gal 3:2, 5).

This experience indelibly marked their lives. The third characteristic that showed their preaching was from God and not merely human **words** was **deep conviction**. The term *plērophoria* may mean "fullness" (Delling 1968, 311; Green 2002, 96). But more likely here it means "conviction, full assurance" (LSJM, 1419; BDAG, 827). Exactly *whose* conviction Paul refers to has divided interpreters. Was it their own sentiments as preachers (Lightfoot

1957, 13; Marshall 1983, 54; Wanamaker 1990, 79; Richard 1995, 48; Malherbe 2000, 112)? Or was it the Thessalonians' conviction of the truth of the gospel as facilitated by the Spirit (Bruce 1982, 14; Witherington 2006, 71-72, n. 34), or both (Fee 2009, 35)? Perhaps the ambiguity is deliberate, as Paul again reminds of how God was present in the apostle's words and in his hearers' hearts (ibid., 36).

Paul then turns from *his* knowledge to *their* knowledge: **just as you know how we lived among you for your sake.** *Just as* (not in the NIV) compares the certainty of Paul's knowledge of what he preached and what God did during his mission, to the certainty the Thessalonians have about the apostles' lifestyle during that mission. He reminds them that it fit their gospel and provided a model to imitate. Recalling past lessons to memory and the theme of imitation fit paraenetic letters (Wanamaker 1990, 80; Richard 1995, 48; Malherbe 2000, 113; Shogren 2012, 65).

Paul *never* says, as some moderns do, "Don't look at me, just look at Jesus." On the contrary, he will dwell at length on the example he and his coworkers set (1 Thess 2:1-12). If the messengers are genuine, it supports the genuineness of God's call.

C. Thanksgiving for Lives that Demonstrate Faith, Hope, and Love (1:6-10)

■ **6** Paul here returns to the topic of his thanksgiving—his Thessalonian converts' faith, love, and hope. He dwells on the evidence from their lives that these things were active. Imitation is a major theme in Paul's ethics (1 Thess 2:9-12, 14-15; 3:12; see 1 Cor 4:6-7, 16-17; 8:13; 11:1; Gal 4:12; Phil 3:7-16, 17; 2 Thess 3:7-10; imitation of Christ: Rom 15:2-3, 7; 1 Cor 11:1; Phil 2:5-11; Col 3:13).

Just as the apostle's **gospel** was ***not in word only*** (1:5), so the *Thessalonians' faith* is not in word only. The **Lord** they imitate is Jesus, who taught by example as well as by word. The most common description of discipleship in the Gospels is Jesus' call to "follow." Paul carries on this tradition of instruction. Imitation was also important to ancient philosophical paraenesis (moral instruction). Teachers would hold up a positive example for their listeners to emulate (Stowers 1986, 94-96).

Exactly *how* did the Thessalonians imitate Jesus and Paul? They became imitators, **for** they **received the message while under great affliction, with joy from the Holy Spirit.** Their imitation consisted in their joyful acceptance of the gospel. And they followed the example of Jesus and his apostles in enduring suffering for their commitment to God.

Jesus is a model of *receiving* (not only proclaiming) the word. He received his teaching from the Father (Matt 11:27; John 7:16). He also was submissive and obedient to the Father, even when it meant suffering (Mark 10:38; 14:32-42; Luke 13:33; 22:42). Jesus warned about the painful consequences of following him (Mark 13:9-13 and parallels). "Blessed are you when people insult you, persecute you and falsely say all kinds of evil against you because of me" (Matt 5:11). This had been fulfilled in Thessalonica. There the new believers had imitated the Son: they **welcomed** God's word and were persecuted for doing so (1 Thess 3:3-4).

Affliction translates a Greek word that came to be used for trouble of various sorts (NIV: **severe suffering**). Interpretations of what Paul meant by *affliction* range from an internal emotional turmoil over a change of religion (Malherbe 2000, 127-28) to civil-sanctioned persecution (Lightfoot 1957, 14; Green 2002, 98), to the killing of Christians (Plummer 1918, 67).

What Was the Thessalonians' "Affliction"?

The Greek noun *thlipsis* is related to a verb meaning "to press." It can refer to "pressure" or "trouble" in general, including mental anguish. It might entail physical "affliction" or "persecution." In the Gospels Jesus predicts great *thlipsis* for his followers (Matt 24:21; "distress" [NIV], "suffering" [NRSV], "tribulation" [ESV, KJV]; see Mark 13:19, 24).

There is evidence that local Jewish leaders and Gentiles opposed the Christian movement and its leaders, and took action against them (Acts 17:5-9; 1 Thess 2:14-16). Thessalonica's civic leaders may have ruled that Christianity was an illegal private association and banned its meetings (→ Introduction).

In antiquity religion was "embedded" in every aspect of life, as anthropologists put it (Beard, North, and Price 1998, 1:43; → Introduction). The gospel calls for exclusive worship of the one God and Jesus as Lord. Its necessary corollary calls for forsaking idols—the gods of Macedonia and Rome (1 Thess 1:9). This meant conflict at every level: forsaking the family cult and gods of the ancestors; forsaking the gods of the city and worship of the divine emperor; withdrawing from public responsibilities that involved participating in pagan cults (see de Vos 1999, 155-70).

Becoming Christians must have meant losing honors and political power for the more aristocratic members of society. For all, saving faith meant no more celebrations with friends and family at familiar shrines and temples. How many were ostracized by family, divorced by spouses, disinherited by parents? How many paid an economic price in lost customers or lost jobs? How many were beaten by angry husbands or masters?

It is likely that these first Christians were regarded by their fellow citizens as irreligious and disrespectful of those things most sacred to the rest of their society. Whether or not we should link this "affliction" with the deaths of some community members (4:13) is unknown. It is a possibility, although Paul himself never makes that connection explicit.

The Thessalonians' reception of the gospel brought them **joy given by the Holy Spirit**. In Luke and Acts, **joy** is associated with the coming of salvation, God's kingdom, or his Messiah (Luke 1:14; 2:10; 15:5-7, 32; 19:6; Acts 8:8; 13:48). **Joy** is a result of the Spirit's presence in one's life (Rom 14:17;

15:13; Gal 5:22). Both Acts and Paul routinely associate joy with the suffering believers experience for their faith (Acts 5:41; 13:52; 2 Cor 8:1-2; Col 1:24).

Paul does not claim that suffering is good. But it can confirm that believers are God's beloved who endure hardship for their association with him. The origin of this **joy** is with the **Holy Spirit**. This indicates that its source is not in human resolve, as it was with Stoics, who encouraged their adherents to embrace fate. For Christians, joy flows from the same divine presence that brought them the gospel and now indwells them (Rom 8:15-16; Gal 4:6; 1 Thess 1:5; Paige 1993). It is a sign of hope and renewal.

■ **7** The results of their faithfulness is that they **became a model to all the believers in Macedonia and Achaia**. Paul expands on the Thessalonians' imitation of the apostles: their faith in the gospel and joy under persecution have made them, in turn, examples for others. Within these two provinces Acts mentions churches at Philippi, Berea, Athens, and Corinth (Acts 16:12-40; 17:10, 34; 18:1-17). They were associated from the time of Alexander the Great until the Roman victory of 197 BC. Under Roman rule they were separate provinces, except for two brief periods (31-27 BC and AD 15-44) that included the reign of Tiberius, not long before Paul's visit (Suetonius, *Claud.* 25.3; Tacitus, *Ann.* 1.76.4; Cosmopoulos 1992, 49-50; Gill 1994, 404).

Paul may think of certain key cities as representative of the entire province (Bruce 1982, 16). If so, Paul's remark about **all the believers** may have in mind only a few Christian communities. He would have heard reports from these communities through colleagues or travelers passing through Corinth, a major trading port. Since Thessalonica was also a trade hub joining land and sea routes, it is not surprising that news of its fledgling Christian community spread elsewhere quickly. The oddity of the Christian faith at Thessalonica and the trouble that was stirred by conversions would have made the church a topic of gossip for everyone. Paul is thankful that the gossip served a positive purpose: it witnessed to the gospel and encouraged suffering Christians elsewhere.

In militaristic societies such as ancient Macedonia and Rome, people admired courage and endurance under hardship. Persecution in Thessalonica was no exception among Christian communities in **Macedonia** (against Wanamaker 1990, 82-83; see 2 Cor 8:1-2; Phil 1:28-29).

■ **8** The Thessalonians did more than passively endure suffering. They actively evangelized, proclaiming **the Lord's message**, the story of Jesus. Paul's description in vv 8-10 suggests that their evangelism consisted in a mixture of the gospel story and the Thessalonians' own faith story being told and retold.

The verb translated **rang out** (*exēcheō*) is uncommon. It could refer to the sound of thunder (Sir 40:13), the roar of a crowd (Philo, *Flacc.* 39), the spread of a rumor (3 Macc 3:2), or the sound of a trumpet blast (John Chrysostom, *Hom. 1 Thess.* 2.1 [Homily 111.1]). It pointed to a loud sound going out in all directions (BDAG, 350; Frame 1912, 85; Richard 1995, 50).

By describing what the Thessalonians broadcast as ***the word of the Lord***, Paul echoes OT formulas for a prophet's message (Isa 1:10 LXX; Jer 2:4 LXX; see Bruce 1982, 17). But the term was readily understandable by pagans with no background in Scripture. Paul uses the phrase only here and in 2 Thess 3:1. But it occurs frequently in Acts.

After praising the effect of the Thessalonian's exemplary conversions on **Macedonia and Achaia** (vv 7-8*a*), Paul speaks of their influence **everywhere** in making known the gospel and their **faith in God** (v 8*b*). He engages in a bit of hyperbolic praise, a common feature in the exordium of speeches (compare Rom 1:8; Best 1986, 81; Kennedy 1984, 142; Malherbe 2000, 118).

Although **everywhere** is rhetorical exaggeration, it suggests that Paul has heard reports about the Thessalonians from Christian communities farther East than Macedonia and Achaia. It is an amazing achievement that the Thessalonian Christians managed within a short time not only to survive in a hostile environment but also to broadcast their faith into multiple provinces of the empire.

There is some debate over whether Paul speaks only of the spread of the Thessalonians' faith reputation (Wanamaker 1990, 83) or of their missionary activity (Malherbe 2000, 116, 130-31; Green 2002, 102). His language suggests both are involved. He refers to the spread of ***the word*** (the gospel) and of their **faith** (their response). But he also mentions what others report about them (v 9).

By saying ***your faith has gone out*** along with the gospel, Paul ties the narrative of their lives with the narrative of God's saving work in Christ, which they accepted. The two are inextricably intertwined. Normally Paul uses "faith" for the *activity* of believing. But here it seems to refer to the *content* of their belief (→ vv 9-10).

■ **9** Paul boasts that the apostles "do not need to say anything about" the Thessalonians' faith (v 8) to people from the provinces. Instead ***they themselves keep telling about us, what sort of reception we had with you***. Some Greek MSS have ***about you*** instead of ***us***. This changes the topic of the report to the Thessalonians as in v 8. The more difficult reading is preferable. This emphasizes that the Thessalonians proudly talked about the lives of the messengers who brought them the gospel.

Reception translates *eisodos*, which usually means an "entrance" (the entry to a place or the opening event), the act of accepting someone, or a visit by a person (LSJM, 496; BDAG, 294-95). Some interpreters restrict the term to the apostles' first visit to Thessalonica (Frame 1912, 87; Green 2002, 105). Others extend it to include their **reception** by the community (Bruce 1982, 17; Witherington 2006, 73). The imagery of the apostles' entrance to Thessalonica may be used by metonymy to refer to their entire stay (as in 2:1; Marshall 1983, 56; Wanamaker 1990, 84; Richard 1995, 51; Malherbe 2000, 118).

Ancient communicators considered it essential to establish with their audience their character (*ethos*) and trustworthiness in relation to their message. Paul seems to follow this precedent. So far in the thanksgiving he has reminded the Thessalonians of the manner in which his gospel was accompanied by God's presence and miraculous signs. This was evidence that the apostles were God's emissaries. And their lifestyle supported the gospel: **You know what sort of people we were when among you** (v 5).

Here he again points to their own **report** of the **reception** the community gave the apostles, believing their message. That is, the Thessalonians' faith story has spread to other cities of Macedonia and Achaia, and Paul has heard others **report** it. This anticipates the discussion of the apostles' integrity and care for the Thessalonians in 2:1-12. The Greek present tense of **keep telling** has an iterative sense (repeated action). This suggests that multiple people reported this to Paul.

Climaxing Paul's thanksgiving is the detailed report of the Thessalonians' conversion, with the content of their faith (1:9b-10). It is the result of the apostles' **reception**; and it is rhetorically intertwined with it. This is the earliest (AD 49) existing evidence of Paul's missionary preaching to Gentiles: a *narrative* that describes their conversion from idolatry. Paul does not say "you became monotheists," but **you turned to God from idols . . . to wait for his Son from heaven** (1:9b-10a). The scene comes to life before our eyes.

We can outline Paul's points about their evangelism/conversion in vv 9-10 as follows:

- You turned away from idols.
- You turned to the true and living God.
- You serve God.
- You are waiting for God's Son to return from heaven.
- God raised his Son from the dead.
- God's Son is Jesus.
- Divine wrath is coming.
- Jesus rescues us from the coming wrath.

In the Christian conception of conversion, turning *to* God always involves turning *away from* false gods and false notions of God (see Acts 17:23-29; Rom 1:18-25; 1 Cor 8:4-6; 10:14; Col 1:13-14; 1 Pet 1:18-21). Technically, **idols** refers to statues or other objects representing deity. In Jewish usage it came to include the fabricated gods these idols represented (Büchsel 1964, 377-78; Best 1986, 82). The LXX gave the term a negative slant, emphasizing the unreality of pagan gods.

In the polytheism of Mediterranean societies, there was no need for conversion from one god to another. People worshipped multiple gods without conflict. New deities or cults were simply added on to the preexisting multitude (Nock 1933). But Paul reports that they left their old gods. This was a radical alteration of their thinking about deities and religions. Worship was now to be seen like a monogamous marriage, with one exclusive loyalty (see 2 Cor 11:2; Eph 5:25-32). Paul's description assumes that most of his Thessalonian converts were Gentiles from pagan backgrounds (Wanamaker 1990, 85; Green 2002, 107-8).

The God Paul proclaimed was **living and true**. He was unique, in contrast to the pseudogods they abandoned. In the OT and Judaism the false gods of the Gentiles and their idols are mercilessly attacked as dead and useless, unable to save Israel from mortal perils or from God's wrath (Deut 4:28; Isa 2:17-21; 44:9-11, 19-20; 57:13; Jer 10:14-15; Ezek 6:4-6; Bel 1:3-5; 3 Macc 4:16; *Apoc. Ab.* 1-5). The Creator, by contrast, is not only alive but also the source of all life. Hence, God is aptly called "living" (Num 14:21, 28; Deut 5:26; 32:40; Pss 42:2; 84:2; Jer 10:10; *Jos. Asen.* 11:10-11; Best 1986, 82; Green 2002, 108). To attribute his life-giving to idols is the grossest error, and a chief source of the woes of human society (Hos 2:5-9; Acts 14:15-17; Rom 1:21-23).

As the only God and Maker of the reality we inhabit, he is by definition **true**. This is the case in the Hebrew sense of that term: what God says is utterly reliable; he can be trusted. But it is equally true in the Greek sense: there is an ultimate reality who exists as this God; other alleged gods do not exist. All other gods of society are false gods, including the goddess Roma and the supposedly divine emperors (see Tob 14:6; Bar 4:7; 1 Cor 10:19-21). Paul was totally opposed to the deadly religious pluralism of pagan society, which killed the soul.

"Turn" (*epistrephō*) was a familiar term from the Greek OT. In the LXX it translated the Hebrew *šub* ("turn" or "return"; LXX: Isa 6:10; Jer 18:8; Ezek 14:6; Sir 5:7; 17:25; Bar 2:30; 4:28). In the NT "repentance" refers to turning to faith in the Lord Jesus, whether by Jews accepting him as Messiah (Acts 3:19; 2 Cor 3:16) or by pagans converting to Christianity (Acts 14:15; 26:17-18). It vividly suggests a change of life, not simply remorse.

The purpose of their conversion is **to serve . . . God** (v 9). The LXX often used **serve** as an equivalent for worship (Exod 23:33 LXX; Deut 28:64 LXX; Mal 3:14, 18 LXX; Tob 14:8; Sir 2:1). Yet the old covenant held the expectation that worship extend to everyday conduct. Thus, it included serving God with justice, mercy, and love for neighbor (Exod 20:1-17; Lev 19:9-18; Isa 1:17; Mic 6:8). Likewise, the new covenant calls people to a renewed existence characterized by love for God and neighbor (→ 1 Thess 1:2-3; see Rom 13:8-10; Gal 5:13-14). That the Thessalonians *served* God emphasizes the genuineness of their faith and love.

■ **10** The final element of Paul's preaching and the Thessalonians' response is eschatological: they now **wait for** God's **Son from heaven**. This is the only reference to Jesus as God's **Son** in either 1 or 2 Thessalonians. The Son of God title has its origins in Jewish messianic hopes. It could be a way of referring to Israel (Exod 4:22; Hos 11:1); then to Israel's king as the supreme representative of the nation, special caretaker and dispenser of justice under God, appointed by the Almighty himself (2 Sam 7:14; Pss 2:7; 89:26-27). By Jesus' day, Jewish groups could call Messiah "Son of God." His coming would bring in supernatural victory over all sinners (and Gentiles), worldwide rule, and inaugurate an era of peace and justice that would restore Israel's religious purity and political sovereignty (Wright 1996, 481-86; Dunn 1998, 197 n. 78; *Pss. Sol.* 17:21-51; 1QSb V; 4Q161 I; 4Q174 III). His reign was often pictured in supernatural terms and was sometimes associated with the resurrection of the dead (*2 Bar.* 30, 72-73; 4Q521).

This was the context, but not the boundaries, of Jesus' self-understanding. Jesus used the title of himself, and referred to God as "my Father" (Matt 12:50; 18:10, 35; Mark 13:32 and parallels; 14:36). He saw his relationship to God as intimate and completely unique: he alone "knew" the Father and revealed him (Matt 11:25-27 || Luke 10:22). He called people into God's kingdom. He shared divine prerogatives with the Father, such as his authority over sickness, nature, and demonic oppression; his extending forgiveness and grace; his coming end-time judgment of souls and granting life for the age to come (e.g., Matt 25:31-46; Mark 2:5-12; 6:37-44 and parallels; 8:38 and parallel; John 5:21-29). He inaugurated the new covenant (Matt 26:26-29 || Mark 14:22-25 || Luke 22:17-20). Jesus' resurrection granted the apostles insight into the true nature of his divine sonship: it was unlike anything Judaism had anticipated (John 2:22; Rom 1:3). Their old wineskins were unable to adequately contain this category (see Witherington 1990, 215-33, 275-77).

Paul frequently associates Jesus' identity as **Son** of God with his being sent to suffer and die for humanity's sins (Rom 5:10; 8:3, 32; Gal 2:20; 4:4-5; Dunn 1998, 224-25; Fee 2007, 40). In 1 Thess 1:10 the **Son** . . . **rescues** believers from **the coming** eschatological **wrath** of God, by his death (see 5:9-10). But Paul also used this title to describe Jesus' exalted status at the Father's right hand after the resurrection (Rom 1:3-4; Col 1:13-14).

The anticipated coming of Christ adopts and adapts the twofold sense of the OT apocalyptic expectation of the "day of the LORD." The day would bring God's judgment on the unbelieving, wicked nations. But it would also mean salvation for those faithful to Yahweh and his covenant (Isa 2:11-21; 13:6-13; Joel 2:28-32; Amos 5:18-24; → 1 Thess 4:15-16; 5:2).

Old Testament teaching about the day was incorporated by Jesus into his teaching on the kingdom of God and his return. Jesus in multiple sayings and parables identified himself as the divine Judge. This was Yahweh's role in the OT. The early church accepted that teaching, as here, in speaking of Christ coming **from heaven**. It does not refer to a compass direction. Paul insists that Jesus will exercise the authority and power of God the Father.

The theme of divine judgment is clear in the final reference to **Jesus** rescuing believers **from the coming wrath**. Nothing here supports the popular view that the **wrath** believers are rescued from refers to the so-called great tribulation.

Wrath is often misunderstood or misrepresented in modern society as simply God's bad temper, as if he had an anger management problem. This explains why some regard the idea as unworthy of Christian theology. But **wrath** refers to God's role as cosmic Judge. He is the ultimate guarantor of justice. The lament psalms call on God to intervene against injustice and punish the psalmists' enemies. They presume God cares about the world and is opposed to evil. As the Creator, this is a responsibility for which he alone is qualified. Biblical writers see no conflict between his love and his justice (Ps 33:5). One could say that God's **wrath** is his "indignation against injustice, cruelty and corruption, which is an essential element of goodness and love in a world in which moral evil is present" (Cranfield 1975, 109).

Paul's emphasis here however, as with the letter as a whole, is not on God's **wrath**. It is on the deliverance effected by God's **Son. Jesus . . . rescues us from the coming wrath**. Believers are delivered from facing God's retributive justice for their sin (Rom 3:10, 23; Gal 3:10, 13). Instead, they receive God's mercy.

Paul had also proclaimed to them that God **raised from the dead** his **Son**. The Thessalonians heard the passion story as part of the gospel (1 Thess 2:15). He describes this as the gospel he delivered to the Corinthians shortly after leaving Thessalonica (1 Cor 15:1-8). There is no gospel without Christ's death "for our sins" and his resurrection (1 Cor 15:3-4).

Jesus preceded the Thessalonians in experiencing death and resurrection. And he will be the means of their resurrection because of their faith in him (1 Thess 4:16-17; see 1 Cor 15:49). Here Paul anticipates his discussion of their anxieties about death and Jesus' return at 1 Thess 4:13-18. The Savior is identified as both **Jesus** and God's **Son** (1:10). Paul holds together both his human and his divine natures.

The new lives of believers are eschatologically oriented. They are framed by the great end-times events: the coming, death, and resurrection of the **Son** in the past and the hope of deliverance at his appearance in the future.

By this time (dead) Caesars had begun to be worshipped, and living emperors were dubbed "son of god" on Roman coins. Temples devoted to the deified emperors had sprung up across the East (→ Introduction). It would be hard to avoid the implied comparison between the two "sons" addressed as Lord, the "peace" they offered, and their different uses of power (Phil 2:6; see Pillar 2013, ch 7). To a citizen of the empire, insisting that Jesus was the Son of *the living and true God* implied that the "divine" Caesars are dead and false. And that he returns **from heaven** emphasizes the majesty and supremacy of his divine authority over all other supposed rulers. Nevertheless, we must be careful not to suppose that this title was adopted or promoted *primarily* as an anti-imperial tactic. The Christians' veneration of Jesus equally challenged all pagan religious systems and some philosophy as well. Their understanding of him goes back to Jesus' own use of the Son of God title in the context of his life, death, resurrection, and commissioning of the apostles (Gal 1:1, 15-16).

FROM THE TEXT

Paul's opening thanksgiving anticipates all of the significant points of the entire letter. We reserve some comments for Paul's fuller developments later in the letter. But a few things can be said about the theological and practical significance of the thanksgiving.

Faith, love, and hope still communicate the essentials of Christianity. But the church must carefully define these terms in ways faithful to Scripture:

- *Faith* is confidence in God (not ourselves, fate, or a program). Those with Christian faith believe that God exists and that he is worthy of worship and obedience. Christian faith believes Jesus of Nazareth is the Messiah and Lord, God's Son. He truly lived, died, and rose again for us. He redeemed us from sin and will return for us.
- *Love* is the *agapē* type of love, directed to both God and neighbor. It must not be confused with either sentimentality or eroticism. "The commandments . . . are summed up in this one command: 'Love your neighbor as yourself.' Love does no harm to a neighbor. Therefore love is the fulfillment of the law" (Rom 13:9-10). Real love is hard work (1 Thess 1:3) but brings the Spirit's joy (v 6).
- *Hope* is the confidence that God will ultimately triumph and will cause us to triumph with him. Hope trusts fully that the future is in God's loving care. He will triumph with his Son, and believers will participate in his future, even beyond death.

Seldom in history have these three virtues been more needed than now. As I write, threats of ecological or nuclear disasters hang over humanity. The globe seems no less prone to warfare and genocide than in 1939. The West—Europe, North America, and Australia—are swiftly moving in a post-Christian direction, embracing moral relativism. Those who believe, live, and proclaim Christ are beginning to appear just as bizarre to their societies as did the Thessalonians in theirs. Will we turn from our cultural idols to give ultimate allegiance to the true and living God alone? It still demands courage for Christians to proclaim faith, love, and hope.

The *Holy Spirit* is essential to evangelism, salvation, and Christian living. So it is not surprising that he plays a prominent role in Paul's thought. The thanksgiving alludes to the Spirit as God's presence the Thessalonians know from experience (1 Thess 1:5-6). He is no less essential today.

Imitation is still important for Christian discipleship and ethics. Both Jesus and Paul self-consciously set examples for disciples to imitate. And imitation is exactly how the Thessalonians witness to the gospel themselves (v 7). These disciples in turn became teachers and evangelists. Imitation is a statement not only of acceptance but also of solidarity with the body of Christ. Christians today must realize that the call to faith is a call to *follow Christ* and those who embody his example. Will we have the moral courage to recapture the power of Christianity for ourselves and for the sake of the watching world? This calls for choosing imitation of Christ in the particulars of our lives as we express our faith and love. Only that will convince non-Christians that our faith is real.

Holy living has always been an emphasis of Wesleyan theology. Salvation entails both right belief and right living for God—as John puts it, to love "with actions and in truth" (1 John 3:18). Christian obedience is the result of the activity of God's grace and his Spirit in believers' lives. It demonstrates that they truly belong to God, that they are called to live as his holy people.

In other words, believers are called to be *sanctified*. Paul's thanksgiving praises the Thessalonians for lives that exhibit sanctification, although the term is not used until 1 Thess 4:3 (→). Our society is rightly skeptical of people who claim to belong to God or to speak for God. The term "sanctification" seems archaic and unattractive to many Christians. Even some Wesleyans are put off by memories of the legalisms of more than half a century ago in denominations and independent churches that called themselves holiness churches. Others have accepted a popular distortion of Reformed theology that is actually "easy believism." The church desperately needs to recapture the beauty and power of sanctified living. It is about making faith, hope, and love real. It is about imitating our Lord.

Communication is always directed to a particular culture, yet the communication of the gospel is not determined by that culture. Paul's letters imitate letter forms that are familiar to his audience. Yet he expands and reshapes those literary forms to suit his purpose, as with the thanksgivings and prayers. In his description of the Thessalonians' conversion, there is not one word that requires knowledge of the OT (1:9-10). Everything he wrote could be understood by a non-Jewish, first-century audience. Yet observant readers will see how deeply his description is rooted in OT theology, in Jesus' teaching, and in early Christian preaching. Paul was a remarkably skillful cross-cultural communicator.

Today, we face a challenge no less daunting: our culture was once familiar with biblical terms and ideas. But these truths have become increasingly archaic-sounding, distant, and misunderstood by society outside of church culture. Even worse, some biblical-sounding phrases (like "born again," "have faith") have been adopted in secular culture and given transformed meanings. So we cannot simply use such terms unless we are prepared to explain them.

We need to think carefully about what unchurched people do or do not understand, and make concerted efforts to communicate the gospel faithfully in terms they comprehend. A friend of mine was in Germany in the mid-1990s playing baseball for the Haar Disciples. At one of their games, fans of the opposing team held up a huge banner with the words "John 3:16" on it. Curious, at the inning break he sent his wife over to investigate who these Christians were. As it turned out, the people were not Christians at all. They had no clue what "John 3:16" meant. They had just seen Americans hold up this sign on sports programs and figured it was some bizarre tradition, perhaps referring to a lost boy named John! If we don't explain ourselves in everyday terms and stop assuming people understand theological basics, we will end up with audiences just as confused as those Germans.

Gratitude may be the most obvious lesson from this section, although the most easily overlooked. Paul reminds us to be grateful to God for his Son and his saving work. We need to be grateful for those believers who came before us. Their living, witnessing, and teaching made our salvation possible. We need gratitude for God's continuing work in his church. It has been well said that gratitude is the beginning of all worship.

III. PAUL AND THE THESSALONIANS: I THESSALONIANS 2:1—3:10

A. The Apostles as Models of Holy Love (2:1-12)

BEHIND THE TEXT

Just what Paul intends to accomplish with this section is debated by contemporary scholars. Older commentaries assume that 2:1-12 is *apologetic*, Paul's defense against attacks on his integrity. They may come from outside the church (e.g., Frame 1912, 90; Airhart 1965, 450; Best 1986, 16; Kennedy 1984, 142-43) or from critics inside (Jewett 1986, 102-4, 177). Or Paul may be defending himself against possible future misunderstandings (Green 2002, 111-12, 114).

Newer rhetorical studies have proposed that 2:1—3:10 is a narratio of a paraenetic letter in which Paul offers himself as a moral example (Wanamaker 1990, 90-91). Similarly, it is considered an "epideictic *narration*." As part of a larger praise section (1:4—3:10), Paul here commends both himself and the Thessalonians (Witherington 2006, 26-27, 78).

The apologetic interpretation was attacked by Malherbe (1970; 2000, 152-56) and Lyons (1985, 177-201). Both argue that 2:1-12 is not a reply to opponents. These autobiographical remarks are to be understood within a rhetorical tradition in which the author holds himself up as an example to be imitated by his audience. Paul offers himself as a model of one who struggles, endures suffering, sincerely seeks to please God, and cares for his converts (Malherbe 1970; 1987, 48, 52-60; 2000, 154-56; also Stowers 1986, 25-26; Wanamaker 1990, 90-91). This anticipates his ethical teaching later in the letter (4:1—5:24; Lyons 1985, 61, 65-67, 182-84, 218-19, 226). This (paraenetic) type of moral instruction has similarities to the style used by Hellenistic philosophers, who also contrast their ideal behavior to bad behavior and motives (Malherbe 2000, 154-56).

If, in fact, Paul offers his life as an example to emulate, then this is deliberative rhetoric, with the goal in mind that the audience should be encouraged to *live in the manner recommended* (as Kennedy 1984, 36, 142).

IN THE TEXT

After praising the Thessalonians for becoming examples to others, Paul turns to the apostles' example. He invites the Thessalonians to remember the visit of himself, Silas, and Timothy. He offers this as a witness to the apostles' character (2:1). Similar appeals occur in 1 Cor 9:12, 15-23; 2 Cor 6:3-10. First Thessalonians' frequent reminders of the founding visit draw author and readers together as they relive past events in their imaginations. The evangelists' lives demonstrated what it means to please God (1 Thess 2:4) and "to live lives worthy of God" (v 12).

In the ancient world, praising oneself was generally considered to be in bad taste because of the arrogance it exhibited. It was, however, excused if an author:

- responded to charges at a trial
- had been wronged and was seeking justice
- praised the audience along with himself
- was accused of shameful behavior and explained how he had, in fact, acted honorably
- transferred the praise from himself to the virtues themselves
- mentions humiliating circumstances such as minor failures or low birth or
- narrates hardships that he endured because of his good character (Lyons 1985, 57-58)

Several of these conditions clearly apply to Paul here: he refers to his shameful treatment at Philippi, enduring hardship at Thessalonica, and praises the Thessalonians.

In addition, the moral philosophers held up themselves as examples, which Paul does here (→ Behind the Text above). These issues come up again later in the letter:
- not having "impure motives" (in 2:3 and 4:7)
- "love" (in 2:8 and 3:12; 4:9; 5:13)
- "work" (in 2:9 and 4:11)
- being "blameless" (in 2:10 and 5:23)
- "encouraging" (in 2:12 and 4:18; 5:11; see Malherbe 2000, 156)

■ 1 Paul opens the new topic by reminding the Thessalonians that the apostles' **visit . . . was not without results**. **Visit** translates the same Greek word rendered "reception" in 1:9 (*eisodon*) and refers to the same event. **Not without results** translates *kenos* (lit. *empty*). Later, Paul admits that he had feared his work in their behalf might become "useless" (*kenos*): what if "the tempter" had led them astray through their hardships (1 Thess 3:5)? In other letters Paul uses similar expressions to speak about his ministry not being *kenos*: it was not empty of God's grace; genuine conversions to enduring faith in Christ had come about in response to his preaching (1 Cor 15:10; Gal 2:2; Phil 2:16). His encounter with the Thessalonians was not a waste of time.

You yourselves know, Paul reminds them that they are witnesses to the apostles, repeating the theme of 1:5-6, 9. Because their visit was "not in word only, but also in power and in the Holy Spirit" (v 5 NRSV), it resulted in their faith.

Brothers and sisters: the fictive kinship language, frequent in this letter (→ 1:4), strengthens Paul's appeal to their mutual experience and knowledge as God's family (→ "Why Inclusive Language?" sidebar at 1 Thess 1:4).

■ 2 In the second half of the Greek sentence that began in v 1, Paul presents what his visit achieved: it was not "nothing," *but* the bold proclamation of the gospel despite suffering. The missionary party had previously **suffered and been treated outrageously in Philippi**. This experience had included public humiliation and imprisonment for preaching the gospel (Acts 16:16-24). Despite this, **with the help of our God** they **dared to tell** the Thessalonians the **gospel**. **Dared** (*eparrēsiasametha*) and **opposition** speak of the risks Paul and his friends took at Thessalonica also, and of the courage they showed. Greek culture admired courage as one of its chief virtues.

Parrēsia, "boldness" (a cognate of the verb **dared**), expressed the Hellenistic ideal of speaking the truth courageously, even when it was unpopular or dangerous. One of Socrates' students rejected a paid position under Pericles, saying, "I will not give away my free speech [*parrēsia*]"† (Diogenes Laertius, *Lives* 2.123). The Cynic philosopher Diogenes described *parrēsia* as the most beautiful thing in the world (ibid., 6.69.1). The gospel is proclaimed with *parrēsia* in Acts and in Paul (Acts 2:29; 4:13, 29, 31; 13:46; 28:31; Eph 6:19, 20; Phil 1:20; 1 Tim 3:13; Phlm 8; compare *1 Clem.* 34.4; 35.1). The founding fathers of the United States of America, who read the classics, transmitted this virtue in the right to "freedom of the press" in the First Amendment to the Constitution.

Unlike the classical ideal of freedom of speech, Paul was not pursuing an abstract notion of truth. God was the energizing source and reason for his mission (**with the help of our God**). It was **to tell** the Thessalonians the **gospel**. Thus, Paul's courage arose from the divine commission that "entrusted [him] with the gospel" (1 Thess 2:4).

Paul's Spirit-inspired speech shone out all the more courageously in the **great struggle** (*agōn*) he faced (v 2). The translation **opposition** (most modern versions) suggests an allusion to the events narrated in Acts 17. But the term generally refers to the experience of **struggle**, with or without opponents. Greeks used it to refer to athletic contests, psychological-spiritual struggles, or even the effort to live a philosophic life (Col 2:1; 1 Tim 6:12; 2 Tim 4:7; see 1 Cor 9:25; Col 4:12; LSJM, 18-19; Stauffer 1964, 135; Best 1986, 92; Malherbe 2000, 137-38). Greek-speaking Jews characterized martyrdom due to faithfulness to God's law as an *agōn* (4 Macc 11:20; 17:11).

Paul struggled amid hostile circumstances to proclaim the gospel (1 Thess 1:6; 2:2, 15-16). His evangelistic party faced mundane struggles too, such as working to support themselves in a strange city (v 9), giving pastoral care on an individual basis (vv 7, 11-12; compare Col 1:28-29), and living as models of holiness by God's power (1 Thess 2:10).

■ **3** The apostles braved persecution and hardship **because** (for) they were impelled by the consciousness that they had been "entrusted" (v 4) with a divine commission. The King of kings had sent them out with good news for his entire realm.

Paul describes the character of God's envoys in a series of contrasting negative and positive statements. And he invites the Thessalonians to testify to the truth of his claims (2:1, 5). Three abstract nouns describe what did *not* motivate their preaching: **error** (*planē*), **uncleanness** (*akatharsia*), and **deceit** (*dolos*). Ancient writers used these terms to describe sophists. These dishonest, itinerate philosophical charlatans swindled followers with flattering, clever speech. They enriched themselves at the expense of the gullible, then moved on.

Contrasting himself to such frauds, Paul denies that he deceived the Thessalonians or was deluded himself (Malherbe 2000, 139-40). The word **motives** has no Greek equivalent here but helps capture the force of the term **uncleanness**. Paul often uses it to refer to sexual immorality (Rom 1:24; 2 Cor 12:21; Gal 5:19; 1 Thess 4:7). But here it probably applies to moral evil in general (Rom 6:19; Eph 4:19). In 1 Thess 2:5-6, Paul's concern is deception, greed, and vainglory, not sexual misconduct (Best 1986, 93-94; Malherbe 2000, 140; Green 2002, 118-19; Furnish 2007, 54).

The word translated **appeal** is *paraklēsis*. It can mean encouragement or comfort (as in Rom 15:4-5; 2 Cor 1:3-7; 2 Thess 2:16; Phlm 7). But here it refers to Paul's evangelistic efforts directed toward the Thessalonians (→ 1 Thess 2:1-2). So here **appeal** has the sense of "exhortation." It emphasizes the apostles' caring approach (2:7-8; Schmitz and Stählin 1967, 5:795; BDAG, 765; Best 1986, 92-93; Malherbe 2000, 138-39).

■ **4** The apostles did not lack a moral compass. They spoke **as those approved by God** from their credible character (v 4). The verb **approved** (*dokimazō*) identifies something or someone that has been tested and found to meet appropriate standards. **Tests** is clearly the sense it has the second time it occurs in this sentence. If it has this sense here, Paul's point seems to be that the apostles were called to be evangelists *because* God had tested and found them worthy (Green 2002, 120). But for Paul it was not a personal achievement; it was God's gracious call that made him worthy (1 Cor 15:9-10; Gal 1:13-16).

In the passive voice, *dokimazō* also means **approved**—fit for some task. If God appointed him an apostle, then he is by definition **approved** for duty! His approval means that he is **entrusted with the gospel**. This emphasizes the great honor and responsibility God bestowed on the missionaries to act as his ambassadors.

This basis for Paul's confidence was unlike that of the popular philosophers who were self-approved by their philosophic introspection or were merely deceiving swindlers (Malherbe 2000, 141). Paul's claim echoes the OT prophets' appeal to the Lord who sent them and validated their message (Jer 1:4-10; Amos 7:14-15). Those God calls, he qualifies and equips to fulfill their assigned task.

Paul asserts that what he and his colleagues **speak** corresponds to their holy calling and solemn trust. They preach the **gospel to please . . . God,** not to flatter their human audience. This required bold truth-telling and faithful living. His refusal to **please people** means that he would not accommodate or compromise the gospel to make it more appealing. He did not employ "flattery" (v 5) as a persuasive tactic, as swindlers did.

Not trying to please people does not contradict biblical exhortations to serve others (e.g., Mark 10:43; Gal 5:13). Christian service seeks the best interests of others, as measured by God's will. Thus, we cannot simplemindedly do whatever pleases others. As his ultimate character witness, Paul appeals to the conviction that God examines even people's thoughts (**our hearts;** "God is our witness" [v 5]). Only God could vouch for Paul's motives. But Paul was confident God would.

When modern readers hear the word "heart," they tend to think of it as the seat of emotions or commitment. But in Scripture, the heart was the seat of *all* intellectual activity and inner resolve: thinking, remembering, loyalty, love, and so forth (e.g., Deut 6:5; Ps 10:6, 11 [ESV, NRSV]; 14:1; 28:7; 36:10; 58:2; Baumgärtel and Behm 1965, 605-13; BDAG, 508-9). It is "the total inner person, the real self" (Malherbe 2000, 141-42). *All* that goes on in Paul's mind is open to God, and he would welcome God to bear witness to his sincerity.

■ **5 Flattery** is insincere and unwarranted praise, usually intended to manipulate others. The ancients loathed it. Because flatterers seek to gain something dishonestly, it is associated with the **greed** that drives it. To flatter is the opposite of speaking the truth boldly (v 2); its words do not honestly communicate love. It creates false impressions and, if believed, leaves hearers weaker, not stronger. **Flattery** is the enemy of true friendship. For these reasons, Paul refused to use it.

For a second time Paul refers to God's knowledge of his sincerity: **God is his witness** (v 5; see v 4*b*). Although the formula may seem strange today, in the ancient world it was common for people to solemnly invoke their god to show their truthfulness, fearing that God would punish any who swore falsely (Exod 20:7). In the final analysis, God alone is qualified to judge one's inner motives.

■ **6a** Last in his description of his motives, Paul denies ***seeking glory from people***. This could be one result of living ***like those pleasing people*** (1 Thess 2:4). **Glory** in this context refers to human honor, fame, or **praise**. Social status and honor were extremely important to people of the Roman Empire. They left monuments behind them by the thousands, boasting of their service to the gods and their cities. Some cities even voted to erect monuments to famous philosophers and teachers.

Paul deliberately renounces interest in human honor. To seek it was to play a social game inconsistent with his pursuit of Christ (2:9; 2 Cor 11:7-9; see Phil 3:4-11). He follows Jesus' teaching by focusing on *God's* approval. Similarly, Greek culture valued as ideal philosophers those who renounced the pursuit of reputation and wealth so as to speak the unvarnished truth (Malherbe 2000, 143; Dio Chrysostom, *Alex.* 11).

■ **6b-7a** Paul reminds the Thessalonians of the behavior of his missionary party while they were with them. Their lives validated the purity of their motives. This made them examples of holy, loving living (1 Thess 2:7-12).

As apostles of Christ the evangelists **could have asserted** their **authority** (v 6; v 7 in Greek), but they refused. **Asserted . . . authority** translates an idiomatic phrase, *en barei*. Since *baros* can mean **burden**, some interpreters take it to refer to the apostles' right to receive offerings (see KJV: "we might have been burdensome"). This coheres with his claim that he "worked . . . in order not to be a burden to anyone" (v 9; John Chrysostom, *Hom. 1 Thess.* 3.1; Theodoret of Cyrus; Bruce 1982, 30-31; Williams 1992, 40; Witherington 2006, 80). Beyond the literal meaning ***weight***, the word *baros* also refers metaphorically to **authority** or ***importance***, as in the English idiom to "throw one's weight around" (BDAG, 167). Here the idiom is not to "be *a* burden" (v 9) but to ***be <u>with</u>*** [*en*] ***authority***.

Paul and his colleagues refused to assert their *status* as spokesmen for God in a harsh, overbearing manner. Such was the typical pattern of contemporary teachers and aristocrats (Frame 1912, 99; Marshall 1983, 68; Wanamaker 1990, 99; Malherbe 2000, 134; Green 2002, 125; Furnish 2007, 56).

This translation provides a better rhetorical contrast with Paul's assertion that the apostles were like **young children** (v 7) in their midst.

Instead of making demands on them, ***we became babes among you***. The NT Greek MSS are divided between reading ***gentle*** (*ēpioi*) and ***babes*** (young children [*nēpioi*]). Some consider ***gentle*** the easier reading, fitting the image of a nurse, and contrasting with being "a burden" (v 9).

The majority of commentators and English versions favor "gentle" (Best 1986, 101; the minority opinion in Metzger 1994, 561-62; Marshall 1983, 70; Wanamaker 1990, 100; Malherbe 2000, 145-46; Witherington 2006, 61; HCSB, NASB, NEB, NRSV, RSV).

Nevertheless, the earliest and best Greek MSS read ***babes***. So do the earliest translations into Latin, Sahidic, Bohairic, and Ethiopic, and several church fathers. It is precisely the oddness of the reading ***babes*** that suggests it was original, and only later "corrected" by a well-meaning scribe (Frame 1912, 100-101; Green 2002, 126-27; Fee 2009, 65-71; Shogren 2012, 99-103). Furthermore, *ēpios* is rare in Paul (only here and in 2 Tim 2:24). He typically prefers a different word for "gentle" (*epieikēs*: Phil 4:5; 1 Tim 3:3; Titus 3:2; and the cognate noun in 2 Cor 10:1), or uses various terms for "meek" to convey the idea (e.g., 1 Cor 4:21; Gal 5:23; 6:1; Col 3:12).

We cannot reject a reading simply because the rhetoric does not appear to progress consistently. Rhetoric has its own reasons that are not always logical. Compare Gal 4:19 or the sharp shifts at 1 Thess 2:8-11 from Paul as wet nurse to father (Lightfoot 1957, 24; Shogren 2012, 101-2). ***Babes*** makes a nice contrast to the previous characterization of the behavior of sophist hucksters. ***Babes*** cannot throw their weight around, care nothing for reputation, and have not yet learned to deceive.

Some argue that in Pauline usage ***babes*** is always pejorative. But the image can be neutral (1 Cor 13:11) or even positive in 1 Cor 14:20 (the verb; Fee 2009, 71). Paul may have in mind how Jesus used children as a metaphor for those believers who are lowly and unassuming. He praised God the Father for revealing the mysteries of the kingdom to "babes" (*nēpioi* [Matt 11:25 ‖ Luke 10:21]) and taught that his disciples would have to become like little children to enter the kingdom of God (Matt 18:3; 19:14 ‖ Mark 10:14). By comparing themselves to ***babes***, Paul stressed the apostles' innocence, harmlessness, and sincerity.

■ **7b-8** *As when a wet nurse cares for her own children, so we cared so deeply for you that we resolved to share with you not only the gospel of God but our lives as well, because you had become dearly loved*. Here Paul shifts to another household metaphor to express the affectionate care of God's messengers for their converts. Although the sudden shift from helpless babe to caregiver seems unexpected, the idea of children probably led him from the one thought to the next. The NIV makes better sense of the Greek text by starting a new sentence here at v *7b* than some other versions (as Fee 2009, 66-68, 74-75).

Paul uses a rare feminine image for the apostles. Like **babes**, it is another assertion of how they rejected the temptation to abuse power and superior knowledge and instead became meek, humble, and loving servants of the community.

Nurses were proverbial in the ancient world for their gentleness and doting care. The word **cares** (*thalpō*) can be used of a mother bird warming her eggs or of a caregiver nursing a sick person back to health (Malherbe 2000, 146). This is an apt metaphor for the apostles' spiritual guidance and pastoral care.

In the ancient world it was common for upper-class families to employ wet nurses to care for their children. It was a matter for special remark on an aristocratic woman's tombstone if she was "both mother and nurse" (Bradley 1986, 216; 1991, 16). Wet nurses usually came from family slaves or hired freedwomen.

Some commentators treat **nurse** as equivalent to **mother** (Lightfoot 1957, 25; Marshall 1983, 71; Best 1986, 101). But given the social context of the church, this word may have been meant as a special encouragement to the aristocratic women who had converted (Acts 17:4). Paul deliberately does not say "like a *mother* with her own children," for this class of Christians would not normally nurse their own children. To say this might have been taken as a subtle criticism.

Malherbe argues that the nurse metaphor here is borrowed from discussions of the ideal Cynic philosopher. This person knew how to balance the roughness of correction with the gentleness of a nurse caring for an injured child. Yet Malherbe's own evidence suggests that "nurse" is *not* an unambiguously positive symbol. On the contrary, philosophers often pictured nurses as dim-witted flatterers who spoiled their charges, or worse, encouraged immorality! And there are no explicit comparisons of philosophers to nurses, only general lessons (Malherbe 1970, 214; citing Plutarch, *Adul. amic.* 69B-C).

Paul's metaphor clearly picks up on the common household experience of women and the positive stereotype of nurses as loving, gentle, and devoted. John Chrysostom says, "A nurse does not flatter to get glory, does she? She doesn't ask the tiny children for money or possessions; isn't harsh or crude with them, is she?" (*Hom. 1 Thess.* 2.3; compare 1 Thess 2:6).

Cared so deeply (*homeiromai* [v 8]; **loved**) translates a rare term. Some ancient sources suggest it means to "yearn for" deeply (Job 3:21 LXX; see pagan examples in MM, 447; Heidland 1967, 176). John Chrysostom interpreted it as "strongly desire" (*Hom. 1 Thess.* 2.3). The verb "may describe a nurse's cooing over her charges" (Malherbe 2000, 147; see MM, 447).

When Paul says that the missionaries shared **not only the gospel**, he did not belittle the saving message, as if spiritual teaching were inferior to material aid. He highlights how, like a loving **wet nurse**, they were wholly devoted to the Thessalonians. The team would **share** even their **lives** with them. In vv 8-9 he describes their sacrifices; in vv 11-12, their parental love.

In the Hellenistic world it was a sign of great affection to declare others one's *friends* (*philoi*, "loved ones"). Paul goes further: he calls them *agapētoi*, **dearly loved**, using the word for love inspired by Jesus' teaching (Mark 12:31; John 13:34).

■ **9** Paul addresses the entire community as members of his family (→ 1 Thess 1:4). He refers to his own working life at Thessalonica with the same term—**toil** (*kopos*)—he used to praise the Thessalonians in 1:3, adding **hardship** for emphasis. The missionaries' lives had been difficult because (*a*) they voluntarily took up manual labor, which people of his social status avoided; and (*b*) their bivocational work required a significant amount of time—their trade and their ministry. It occupied them well beyond the normal workday. We can also speculate from his other letters and comparative social history that (*c*) he did not make much money at either assignment (see 1 Cor 4:9-13; 2 Cor 6:4-10; 11:27-29).

Acts indicates that Paul was a "tentmaker" (Acts 18:1-3). Earlier scholars thought this involved making tents from *cilicium*, goat's-hair wool. Most now favor the view that Paul was a leather-worker, since tents were normally made of leather in his day (supported by patristic comments; see Hock 1980, 20-21).

Since Paul was an itinerant lacking the capital to set up a new shop everywhere he went, he probably sought out local artisans to work with, as he did at Corinth. Such artisans often lived in a house where the ground floor was their shop. Jason may have had a shop where Paul plied his trade (Acts 17:5).

The typical working day was from sunrise to sunset. Few artisans made more than a poor living (Hock 1980, 31-32, 34). But Paul asserts that he worked during the **night and day**, going beyond what most did. He apparently scheduled worship meetings outside the daylight hours, when poor working people would be free to attend.

We should not imagine that Paul's evangelistic and pastoral work was all done outside his shop. Research has shown that workshops were often places for social gatherings: customers came and went, visitors stopped by to get out of the rain or trade gossip, and philosophers might even appear in a workshop to converse and teach (Hock 1980, 86 n. 118, 38-41; Malherbe 1989, 69; 2000, 161).

Being a manual laborer of any sort in Paul's day—even a skilled artisan—carried a social stigma. Most people in the Greco-Roman world considered such work demeaning and slave-like (Hock 1980, 35-36). Many Jews shared this same attitude: Ben Sirach thought those who labored could never attain wisdom and were doomed to obscurity (Sir 38:24—39:11).

Paul apparently came from a socially elite Jewish family of local prestige, who were Roman citizens. He was a man of moderate wealth, with advanced education, multilingual, and familiar with both Jewish and Greek literature. When 1 Thess 2:9 is read in light of Paul's remarks to the Corinthians (1 Cor

4:12; 9:1-14, 19; 2 Cor 11:7, 23, 27), it seems clear that Paul did not regard the life of manual labor as normal for himself. He had to lower himself to do work that his society—even his own converts—despised.

Paul was physically exhausted by his duties at Thessalonica (compare 1 Thess 2:8-9; 1 Cor 4:11-12; 2 Cor 11:27-28; 12:15). He mentions this, not to gain their sympathy, but to remind them of the genuineness of his care for them. His example of industry anticipates his call for the Thessalonians to work and be financially independent (4:11-12).

Paul worked sacrificially with one purpose in mind: **in order not to be a burden to anyone while we preached the gospel of God to you** (see 2 Cor 11:7-8; 12:13). Paul's usual policy was not to accept finances from his churches so as "to win as many as possible" and avoid hindering the gospel (1 Cor 9:12, 18-19; see 2 Cor 11:9). It is clear that a cynical urban crowd would be quick to suspect that a freeloading preacher was a scam.

Although his churches included some wealthy people, many of his converts were poor, particularly in Macedonia (1 Cor 1:26-28; 2 Cor 8:1-2). He apparently did not want people to think the church expected a fee of them, as other private associations did. Paul accepted gifts from the Philippians on several occasions (2 Cor 11:9; Phil 4:16). But we don't know why he made an exception in their case. It was, however, their voluntary action and not Paul's demand that made them "partners" in his gospel mission (Phil 1:5, 7; 4:10, 15-16).

■ **10** It seems uncharacteristic for Paul to speak of his life as **holy, righteous and blameless**. His motto was that Christians should boast in the Lord and not in themselves (1 Cor 1:31). But Paul is not boasting here. This is not about his autonomous achievement, nor is he seeking to increase his status.

His purpose here is *paraenetic* (→ Behind the Text for 2:1-12), moral instruction (Lyons 1985, 185; Malherbe 1970; 2000, 161-62). Paul holds up his example for the Thessalonians to imitate, reminding them that he *lived* what he *taught*. What he points out about himself matches what he will later exhort his audience to do: to love one another (1 Thess 3:12; 4:9); to work hard and support themselves (4:11-12; 5:14); to pursue holiness with God and with other people (3:13; 4:1-8).

Holy (Gk.: *hosiōs*, only here in the NT) describes one living devoutly, seeking to please God alone. **Righteous** (*dikaiōs*) is related to a common biblical term for one who lives justly. **Holy** and **righteous** are often paired in Greek, describing the behavior of people who fulfill the spectrum of all that is expected of them by God and human society (see Plato, *Gorg.* 507B; Lightfoot 1957, 27; MM, 460; BDAG, 728; Malherbe 2000, 150).

Blameless emphasizes that they did nothing deserving reproach or legal action in the eyes of society—he is not speaking of eschatological judgment. Paul calls on his audience's memory as his **witnesses** along with **God** that he and his colleagues lived the gospel (what was "preached" [v 9]), especially **among** those **who believed**.

■ **11** Paul turns to another family metaphor, a **father**, to describe his work among his Thessalonian converts. Parents in ancient households had the task of being moral educators (see Prov 23:22; Tob 4:3-19; Sir 3:1-11). Ideally, fathers were patient and did not lose their tempers (see 1 Tim 3:3-4; Titus 1:7). Paul uses the **father** metaphor elsewhere to describe his apostolic task of leading people to faith in God (1 Cor 4:15; Phlm 10). With parental concern, Paul dealt individually with **each** convert (1 Thess 2:11), correcting or "encouraging" them as needed (v 12). He was not satisfied merely to lecture them in groups or to speak in vague generalities. In Greek culture philosophers also compared themselves to fathers. However, the *goal* of Paul's care for his charges differed from the philosophers (Malherbe 1989, 47-48, 54; 2000, 150-51).

■ **12** Paul uses three participles to characterize his fatherly role on behalf of the Thessalonians: **encouraging, comforting and urging**. It is difficult to draw a sharp distinction between the first two Greek terms: **encouraging** (from *parakaleō*) and **comforting** (from *paramytheomai*).

Parakaleō is frequent in Paul, used for "exhorting" people to practice a certain type of behavior, "requesting" something, "encouraging," or "comforting" (see BDAG, 765; Schmitz and Stählin 1967, 5:774-78, 793-99). Paul considered the ability to encourage others a spiritual gift (Rom 12:6, 8) associated with prophecy (1 Cor 14:31; see 14:3). Here it describes Paul's apostolic-pastoral ministry to the Thessalonians.

Secular Greek used **comfort** (*paramytheomai*) to describe the consolation one gives those mourning a death. Although Paul mentions deaths at 4:13, there is no other evidence that anyone in the Christian community died while he was in Thessalonica. Thus, he seems to refer to the **comfort** he gave them in the social hardships they faced as a result of their conversions to the Christian faith. He gave them more than sympathy; he offered them hope in Christ that sustained them in dark days (Stählin 1967, 5:821; Spicq 1994, 30-34; Malherbe 2000, 152).

The apostles also gave themselves to **urging** their converts **to live lives worthy of God**. In this, the Thessalonians were to imitate what they had seen in the apostles. Paul does not believe God's grace leads to human complacency. Instead, it motivates and enables those who receive it to have a new existence in which they may choose actions and thoughts that honor God (see, e.g., Rom 6:6-7, 11, 12-14; 8:1-4; 12:1-2; Gal 5:13-14, 16, 22-23).

In other contexts **urging** (*marturomai*) has the sense ***testifying*** (BDAG, 619). Perhaps this serves as a verbal echo of Paul's insistence that he communicated what he lived: his words and his deeds were consistent. He practiced what he preached.

To invite believers to **live lives worthy of God** is not to deny grace. Paul does not say they needed to *become worthy* of God and earn his favor. **Worthy** means "suitable to." God expects his people to live consistently with **God, who calls** them **into his kingdom and glory**. Such a life echoes God's character of righteousness, love, and grace (as with Paul [vv 10-11]). To live out the possibilities of grace is to anticipate in the present the shape of **kingdom** living that will characterize relationships when God renews the entire universe at the end.

The demand to live **worthy of God, who calls you into his kingdom** reminds the Thessalonians that this God has already called and claimed them, already offered them a place in his **kingdom**, already given his Son to save them, already promised them resurrection life. In other words, the call to righteous living is a *response to the preexisting grace of God*. In much the same way, in the OT God gave the Law to those he had already brought "out of Egypt, out of the land of slavery" (Exod 20:2).

The **kingdom** of God was at the center of Jesus' teaching, according to the Synoptic Gospels (see Mark 1:14-15; Luke 9:1-2). **Kingdom** designates not a place but the righteous *rule* of God, which he will ultimately and finally manifest in history with the end-time events associated with Christ's coming—the judgment of humanity, the resurrection of the dead, and the restoration of the cosmos (Rom 2:5; 8:18-23; 14:10; 1 Cor 4:5; 15:22-26; 2 Cor 5:4, 10; 1 Thess 4:13—5:11; compare Matt 7:21-23; 8:11-13; 13:36-43; Mark 10:23-31; Luke 22:15-18; Rev 11:15; 12:10).

Scholars debate whether God's **glory** here is to be equated with or distinguished from his **kingdom**. If it is part of a hendiadys construction, they collectively describe one comprehensive reality, as "heavens and earth" describe all of creation. But it is possible that the calling to **glory** refers to the resurrection and glorification of the saints. Ancient Mediterranean people were enormously concerned with honor, as some today crave fame or notoriety. They would have immediately grasped the concept of living in a way befitting their new status. To do so honored their Christian "family" and their divine patron. And ultimately, it would result in their being recognized by all as God's true people.

FROM THE TEXT

This passage speaks about the need for Christians to live with integrity. It is of the utmost importance that our character matches our message, echoing the selfless love of the Savior. Paul's hard work and bold truth-telling demonstrated this. Our society is increasingly skeptical of religious claims, doubtful of God's existence or ability to change people. In this situation the most powerful evangelistic tools Christians possess are their own transformed lives, which testify to God's truth and power. Integrity can wear down skepticism and give hope to the hopeless.

One area of integrity in particular need of examination is the use of authority by Christians. Paul deliberately foregoes his right to financial support. He rejects the typical high-handed behavior of aristocrats and philosophers. He chooses to pursue, instead, an authority like that of a father, who educates and counsels his children (1 Thess 2:11-12).

Are there leadership practices in our society that are inconsistent with the gospel? Can we bring a servant attitude to our interactions with people over whom we exercise authority? It does not compromise the truth to be kind.

On the other hand, Paul warns us of the opposite danger of people-pleasing (2:3-6; Gal 1:10). Some ministries buy popularity with flattery that avoids confronting sin. Whether liberal or conservative, their message is tailored to the audience, minimizing any demands on people's lives. Even ordinary believers are tempted to gain acceptance with family, friends, and coworkers by speaking only about God's blessings, while remaining silent about God's call for righteousness, which is at the core of the gospel. For some people, society's approval is as addictive as a drug; but in the end it does not validate them as persons, nor does it ensure God's approval. Christians must love others enough to tell them the truth.

Indirectly this section of the letter also emphasizes the goodness of work. Paul's society considered manual labor demeaning. Yet his embrace of such labor showed that it does not, in fact, lower a person's spiritual status or worth to God.

Finally, the passage suggests that there is a link between God's calling, gratitude, and ethics (1 Thess 2:12). If we were to ask of this letter the famous question posed in Rom 6:1—*Why not continue in sin?*, the answer would be: because God has graciously called you into his kingdom, empowered you to live changed lives, and offered you eternal glory! He deserves better (compare 4:8; 5:6-10).

B. Faithful Imitation and Unfaithful Persecution (2:13-16)

BEHIND THE TEXT

First Thessalonians 2:13-16 begins as a brief second thanksgiving in praising the Thessalonians (vv 13-14). It encompasses Paul's comment heaping blame on the behavior of the opponents of the gospel, particularly Jewish ones (vv 15-16). The first half repeats themes from the first thanksgiving: faith, welcoming the gospel, imitation, and suffering (→ 1 Thess 1:2-6). The second half contrasts each of these faith steps with the negative behavior of their opponents, who invite God's wrath.

The discussion employs this rhetorical means to extend to the Thessalonians the same positive role the apostles had just finished giving themselves. The Thessalonians lived out their faith and imitated their apostolic teachers. As a result they endured persecution. They are the new generation of witnesses.

This section serves several rhetorical functions:
- Paul recognizes their faith and suffering to encourage and comfort them (2:12).

- Paul shifts the focus from himself to his audience, lest the letter seem overbalanced with self-praise.
- Paul emphasizes the Thessalonians' solidarity with the earliest Christians of Judea. They belong to something bigger than their small, struggling community (note 1:7-8; 4:10). They are part of the new covenant community composed of all God's people everywhere.
- By reciting their shared enemies and experiences of persecution, Paul emphasizes their bond of friendship (see Fee 1995, 4-6). This anticipates his explanation of why he could not encourage them in person (in 2:17-18).
- Paul's discussion of God's wrath weaves the community's experience with the synagogue into the continuing history of God's dealings with Israel. This helps make sense of what is otherwise inexplicable: why certain Jews rejected their own Messiah and mistreated those who adored him.
- Paul affirms that the Thessalonians' suffering is not punishment for unwitting offenses.

This section has several issues that have led some scholars to label part or all of it as a non-Pauline interpolation:

- It contains a second thanksgiving, unusual for Paul.
- Its harsh sentiments about Jews seem un-Pauline. He condemns all Jews as displeasing God and takes satisfaction in "the wrath of God" (v 16) that has befallen them. How may this be reconciled with his condemnation of retaliation (5:15) and exhortation to "bless those who persecute you" (Rom 12:14; see vv 17-21)?
- The assertion that God's wrath has come upon Paul's Jewish opponents "at last" (1 Thess 2:16) seems to some to contradict his hope for Israel's eventual salvation expressed in Rom 9—11.
- Finally, if this wrath refers to the historical fall of Jerusalem (AD 70), Paul could not have written it (so Pearson 1971; Bruce 1982, 48-49; Richard 1995, 119-27; for a fuller list of interpolation advocates see Wanamaker 1990, 29-33; Green 2002, 143 n. 127).

On the other hand, there are good reasons to believe this passage is genuinely by Paul:

- There is no textual evidence of an interpolation: all surviving Greek manuscripts include vv 13-16.
- The objections that it is too harsh or anti-Jewish could equally be raised against other passages in Paul, which are sharply critical of Jews or Judaizers (2 Cor 11:3-5, 13-14; Gal 5:12; Phil 3:2; see Phil 3:7-8)! In Rom 2:1—3:20 he appeals to Scripture to argue that all Jews are as much under God's wrath as are Gentile sinners. Paul was not one to speak delicately of his opponents.

- Using hyperbole in attacking common enemies was a well-known rhetorical strategy expected in ancient speeches and letters (see Malherbe 2000, 179; Witherington 2006, 25, 82-83, 88-89).
- Paul draws on an OT prophetic tradition, which accused Israel of acting like God's enemies, incurring his wrath (see Isa 1:21-23; Jer 7:9-11, 23-29; Hos 4:1-9; Amos 2:4-8, 11-16). In particular, 1 Thess 2:15 ("killed . . . the prophets") echoes the charge in 1 Kgs 19:10, 14. A similar critique is found in Jesus' sayings, including the charge of killing prophets (Matt 23:34, 37; Luke 11:47-51; 13:34). Some Jews had repeatedly attempted to frustrate Paul's mission to Gentiles. He responds in prophetic fashion (Donfried and Marshall 1993, 69-70).
- Although it is unusual for Paul to offer a thanksgiving report outside his introductions, his letters have great variation and individuality. They follow no single contemporary standard, but represent a mixture of Hellenistic letter types (Schubert 1939, 174-75). There is a second thanksgiving at 2 Thess 2:13-14, and Galatians has no thanksgiving at all. Other kinds of prayer reports occur later in the bodies of some letters (Rom 15:5-6, 13; 1 Thess 3:11-13; Eph 3:13, 14-19), not to mention concluding prayer-wishes.

Far from being an interpolation, 1 Thess 2:13-16 is intimately related to its context and the letter's themes. It shows that the apostles' ministry was "not a failure" (v 1 GNT), for the Thessalonians accepted the gospel (v 13). The evidence of their acceptance—and that they are God's "chosen" (1:4)—is their endurance of suffering in imitation of Jesus and other Christians (2:14-16). Paul's awareness of this made him especially anxious to send Timothy to encourage them (2:17—3:5).

Other instances of Jews employing harsh, even vitriolic language against fellow Jews suggests that 2:13-16 is best understood as an example of intra-Jewish polemic (→ "Jew against Jew" sidebar at 1 Thess 2:16). The problem with 2:16c is a matter for exegesis (→ In the Text for 1 Thess 2:13-16, below). Perhaps the most pressing problem is how Christians should appropriate it today, in our post-holocaust situation (→ From the Text for 1 Thess 2:13-16, below).

IN THE TEXT

■ **13** Paul thanks God for the Thessalonians' spiritual insight that allowed them to recognize his message was from the one true God. Their genuine faith led directly to their suffering at the hands of their fellow Macedonians, which explains Paul's digression in 2:14-16. This repeats a pattern seen in the introductory thanksgiving: preaching, positive response, suffering like other Christians (1:5-6). This complex of events is evidence that the apostle's visit was "not a failure" (2:1 GNT). Paul elsewhere similarly connects saving faith with suffering, as did the teaching of Jesus (Matt 5:10-12; Mark 13:9-13; Luke

6:22-23, 26; John 15:18-21; Phil 1:29-30; 1 Thess 3:3-4; probably presupposed in Rom 12:14, 17-19).

The second thanksgiving reinforces the personal, familial atmosphere of the letter. Thanksgivings occur almost exclusively in private, personal letters in antiquity (Schubert 1939, 170). Family language is common throughout this letter. That Paul and his friends **thank God continually** echoes the "always" of 1:2: The missionaries did not forget their converts after they moved on.

The first **and** links this thought to Paul's description of his pastoral care in 2:11-12. **Because** (*dia touto*, *for this reason*) explains why they give thanks. It points to the Thessalonians' favorable reception of the gospel as **the word of God**.

The pronoun **we** is emphatic in Greek. Scholars disagree as to whether **also** (*kai*) modifies **thank** ("as well as care for you we thank God" [Malherbe 2000, 165]) or **we** ("we, along with you Thessalonians, thank God"). If the latter is correct, their shared thanks may have been in response to a letter from them (Frame 1912, 106) or Timothy's verbal report of their gratitude (3:6; so Bruce 1982, 44). Perhaps it has only a weakened sense ("we for our part," so Best 1986, 110; see Moule 1959, 167; Marshall 1983, 77).

Paul describes how they **received the word of God**, using a verb that is applied to the passing on of traditions from teacher to student (*paralambanō* as in 1 Cor 11:23; 15:1, 3; Gal 1:12; Phil 4:9; Col 2:6; 1 Thess 4:1; 2 Thess 3:6; BDAG, 768; Link 1999). When he wrote, there were no written Gospels yet. What they **received** they only **heard** from Paul and his associates (1 Thess 2:13) in the drama of live communication. Oral teaching was necessary because the majority of people in antiquity were illiterate (Harris 1989). Even Paul's letters were heard in his churches as someone read them aloud (Col 4:16; 1 Thess 5:27; 1 Tim 4:13). This "heard word" also underlines how personal Paul's teaching was, whether in his workshop or after hours.

Paul strengthens his statement by adding that they **accepted** the gospel **not as a human word, but as it actually is, the word of God.** That is, they did not believe it was made up by its bearers (1 Thess 2:3-5). God is the one who planned the gospel, who carried it out through the agency of his Son (Gal 4:4-5; Eph 3:9; Col 1:25-27). God called and commissioned Paul and his associates to proclaim this message (Acts 9:3-6, 15-16; 26:13-18; 1 Cor 15:8, 11; Gal 1:1, 11-12, 15-16). And God stands behind the message as it is preached, strengthening his messengers and convincing its hearers of its truth by his Spirit (1 Cor 2:3-5, 10; 2 Cor 5:18, 20; 1 Thess 1:6).

On this basis Paul calls his preaching **the word of God**. He implicitly contrasts the saints' response of faith with the rejection of the gospel and its messengers by others (2:14-16). **You accepted** (*edexasthe*, from *dechomai*) emphasizes the Thessalonians' deliberate decision to welcome the gospel. There may be an echo of Jesus' comment on the parable of the sower (Mark 4:13-20):

some people merely *receive* the gospel but fall away when persecution (*thlipsis*) comes. Others *accept* (*paradechontai*) the word when they hear it and bear fruit.

Paul claims that the gospel's divine character appears in that **the word of God** is **at work in you who believe**. In Greek it is ambiguous as to whether the **word** or **God** is **at work** in believers. If Paul intended the former, he may have thought of God's word, active in creation and in prophecy: it has the divine power to accomplish what it announces (e.g., Ps 33:6; Isa 37:21-22, 29; 40:8; 55:11; Hos 6:5; Amos 4:1-3). If he intended the latter, his thought parallels Phil 2:13. Regardless, the net effect is the same.

■ **14** Earlier Paul had praised the Thessalonians' imitation of himself and of the Lord Jesus (1:6). Now he adds that their faithfulness was also demonstrated in the way they **became imitators of God's churches in Judea**.

Perhaps Paul mentions **Judea** to connect his converts with their roots in the earliest Christianity. They also experienced political opposition (Acts 4:1-22; 5:17-18, 26-28, 40) and violent persecution (Acts 8:1; 1 Cor 15:9; Gal 1:13; Phil 3:6; Jas 2:6-7). Paul reminds his first hearers that they are part of a movement that had already spread across half the Roman Empire. Their story is the continuation of the story that began centuries earlier with Abraham (Gal 3:6-9, 26-29).

It seems odd that the first Christians' opponents are called **Jews.** All the Judean Christians were Jews. Thus, 1 Thess 2:15*a* makes sense only as a restrictive clause delimiting Paul's statement in v 14. Not all Jews were opposed to Paul and the gospel. He criticizes only those Jews "who killed the Lord Jesus . . . and also drove us out" (v 15; Malherbe 2000, 169; Fee 2009, 95-96). Paul's usage here is comparable to the Fourth Gospel's use of the "Jews" to designate the Jewish leaders who opposed Jesus, although Jesus and his disciples were equally Jewish. It may also suggest that the parting of the ways between church and synagogue was already well underway in Thessalonica before it became final everywhere.

This is the only instance in Paul's letters where he explicitly speaks of believers imitating other churches; elsewhere they imitate Christ or Paul. But the idea is implicit when Paul speaks of churches in one place being an example to churches elsewhere (2 Cor 8:1-6; 9:2; 1 Thess 1:7-8; Malherbe 2000, 167).

The **churches in Judea** are further described as **in Christ Jesus**. The word **church** (*ekklēsia*) at this date could be a synonym for "synagogue" or could denote Greek civic assemblies (→ 1 Thess 1:1; Frame 1912, 109; Morris 1991, 82-83). Hence, **in Christ** distinguishes these Christian groups from other assemblies of believers in the God of Israel. **In Christ** not only signals their allegiance to the Messiah but also indicates the presence of Christ's Spirit among them, who facilitates their connection to the risen Christ (see Rom 8:9-10; Gal 3:14; 4:6).

That the Thessalonians **suffered from** their **own people** is now put into the context of the greater story of God's faithful people. It is not a story of failure, but of faithfulness and courage. Paul's comparison of these recent converts with the first Christians **in Judea** implies that the Thessalonians were model disciples.

Does **own people** have an ethnic meaning ("fellow Macedonians"), or local ("people who live where you do"—including Jews)? The Greek word *symphyletēs* is related to the word for **tribe** (*phylē*). But by the first century this term was widely used in a political sense, for divisions of a city (Maurer 1974, 245-46). Different words were used for ethnic groups (such as *ethnos* or *genos*). The parallel with the Judean Christians suggests that the main point is that the believers' **own people** turned on them. It does not necessarily exclude Jews, but it would refer mainly to other Macedonians.

■ **15** The suffering of the Thessalonian Christians is compared to the sufferings of Jesus and his apostles caused by the Jewish leaders. They **killed the Lord Jesus and the prophets and also drove us out**.

The prophets could refer either to Christian leaders or to the OT prophets. A strong literary tradition suggests OT prophets are meant (see 1 Kgs 19:10-14 [cited in Rom 11:3]; 2 Chr 36:15-16; Neh 9:26; *Jub.* 1:12; *Mart. Isa.* 5:11-12; *Liv. Pro.* 6:1—7:2; *Exod. Rab.* 31:16). Jesus appeals to this tradition (Matt 23:29-37; Mark 12:1-9; Luke 11:47-51; 13:34), as does Stephen (in Acts 7:51-52).

The early church added Jesus' name to the list of martyrs. He was the ultimate divinely commissioned Messenger, sent by God but rejected, although he was **the Lord** (1 Thess 2:15). The Romans physically executed Jesus, but the earliest Jewish Christians put the blame for arranging his death on the Jewish leaders (Matt 26:57-66; 27:1-2, 12, 20-23; Mark 15:1-4; John 11:47-50; 18:28-31; 19:12-16).

As part of this pattern of rejection, the apostles came with the gospel to Thessalonica, but the Jews **drove** them **out** of the city with the assistance of civic authorities. The verb **drove . . . out** (*ekdiōkō*) could also mean **persecuted**. But "to expel" is more likely in light of Paul's reference to being prevented "from speaking to the Gentiles" (1 Thess 2:16).

To **displease God** (v 15) is more serious than the English translation may indicate. For Paul, to "please God" summarizes the apex of human life (2 Cor 5:9; 1 Thess 4:1). Its opposite is pleasing the flesh or humans (Rom 8:8; Gal 1:10; Best 1986, 117). Paul's Jewish opponents—and their historical forebearers—**displease God** by rejecting and persecuting his messengers, above all the Lord Jesus.

■ **16** Paul hyperbolically charges his Jewish opponents with being **against all people** (v 15). His reason is that they drive the gospel out of the synagogues ("drove us out") and hinder the messianic hope from being preached to Gentiles. Paul believed that Gentiles as well as Jews needed to hear about Jesus and God's mercy through him to be saved (1:9-10). Other Jews believed that Paul was promoting a false Messiah and attacking the Law (Acts 21:27-

28; Rom 3:8; 6:1; 7:7). Paul naturally understands them as seeking **to keep him from speaking to the Gentiles so that they may be saved**. His opponents should have *loved their* (Gentile) *neighbors*, according to the commandment and shared with them the knowledge of the kingdom and salvation. Instead, when Paul brought God's word, some Jewish leaders used exclusion from the synagogue, legal action, and violence to undermine his ministry in Thessalonica and Berea. They unsuccessfully attempted this at Corinth also (Acts 17:13; 18:12-17).

Paul's accusations against his Jewish opponents is not the anti-Judaism found in Gentile authors (against Pearson 1971; Richard 1995, 121; → "Jew against Jew" sidebar, below). "Pagan criticism [of Jews] was social; Paul's is theological" (Malherbe 2000, 170). The entire section revolves around the *human response to the gospel* and its messengers, contrasting believers with their opposition (see Donfried and Marshall 1993, 69-70).

The result (*eis to*, "so as to") of the Jewish opposition to the proclamation of the gospel is that such people **always heap up their sins to the limit**. Theirs is the ultimate act of rebellion: they use their power to prevent others from knowing God.

Paul's language echoes (and reverses) Genesis' charge against the Gentiles who occupied the land promised to Israel: their sin "has not yet reached its full measure" (Gen 15:16). Similarly, Daniel claimed that the Hellenistic monarchies' sins were being completed (Dan 8:23). And in 2 Macc 6:14 Gentiles will be punished when "they have reached the full measure of their sins" (NRSV). Ironically, here *Jews* stand in the place of *Gentiles*, unwittingly preparing their own judgment.

The wrath of God has come upon them at last. This is the most difficult sentence of this letter. A superficial reading of it seems contrary to what we know historically: the Jews have not been wiped out by divine wrath. And it seems to contradict Paul's theology elsewhere: he remains optimistic that God's grace will eventually win Israel over (Rom 11:11-32). Scholars debate the meaning of nearly every word of this sentence.

The major options for understanding how **wrath . . . has come** are:

(*a*) The word **wrath** refers to some recent historical event(s) interpreted theologically as divine judgment. Several events have been suggested (Pearson 1971, 82-83, n. 22; Bruce 1982, 49; Witherington 2006, 86-87):

- the expulsion of Jews from Rome under Claudius in AD 49 (Suetonius, *Claud.* 25)
- the great Judean famine of AD 46-47 (Acts 11:28; Josephus, *Ant.* 20.51, 101)
- a massacre in Jerusalem in AD 49 following violence by Jewish zealots or nationalists (Josephus, *J.W.* 2.224-227)
- the insurrection of Theudas, ca. AD 44-46 (Acts 5:36; Josephus, *Ant.* 20.98)

- the destruction of Jerusalem in AD 70. This is possible only if Paul did not write 1 Thess 2:16—a view we reject (→ Behind the Text for 2:13-16, above).

The attraction of the final option is the full temporal weight it assigns the past tense (aorist) of the verb **has come** (*ephthasen*) and the expression **at last**. But **wrath** is an apocalyptic and eschatological (end-times) concept. In the two other places in this letter where it is mentioned (1:10; 5:9) it is linked with Jesus' *Parousia* and the final judgment of unrepentant sinners.

(*b*) **Has come** *may* be a proleptic aorist, referring to God's future **wrath** (his final judgment), as if it were already accomplished, emphasizing its certainty (Frame 1912, 113-14; Morris 1991, 85). Yet nothing in this sentence or its context suggests that Paul is speaking prophetically.

(*c*) The verb *ephthasen* may be interpreted to mean **has drawn near** (but not arrived). The language is similar to Jesus' words about the kingdom in Matt 12:28 ‖ Luke 11:20: God's **wrath** is about to overtake Jewish unbelievers in the present. Paul claims elsewhere that God hardened unrepentant sinners and handed them over to the power of darkness (e.g., Rom 1:18-32; Best 1986, 120; Marshall 1983, 80-81; Wanamaker 1990, 117).

The fierceness of the opposition to Christians and the Christian gospel from certain Jewish leaders proved to Paul that they stand under **wrath**. The present and eschatological meanings of **wrath** are connected: if opponents remain in darkness (1 Thess 5:4-5), their ultimate condemnation will be only the continuation of their present antagonism to God. But the era of grace lingers.

What does the expression **at last** (*eis telos*) mean? The Greek preposition *eis* usually means "toward" or "up to." And *telos* can mean "a goal," "the end," or "the completion of some activity." The phrase has been taken to mean:

(*a*) **Finally,** at last, as in Luke 18:5; *Barn.* 4.7; *Herm. Mand.* 12.2.3; *Herm. Sim.* 8.6.4; 8.8.5; 9.14.12 (Best 1986, 121). The *Shepherd of Hermas* is filled with eschatological references to the ultimate fate of souls. This makes it an interesting parallel to Paul's concern here.

But the gospel never sees God's wrath as irrevocable. If it is translated *finally*, it must mean that "at last, after all their sinning" God's patience is exhausted and the long-awaited wrath has come. It could not mean that an irrevocable wrath, with no chance of repentance, has befallen all Israel.

(*b*) **Until the end**, as in Matt 10:22; 24:13; Mark 13:13; Josephus, *Ant.* 19.96; Epictetus, *Diatr.* 1.7.17; Ign. *Eph.* 14.2; *Herm. Sim.* 8.8.2; 8.8.5; 8.9.3 (Wanamaker 1990, 117-18; Malherbe 2000, 171, 178-79). Advocates of this understanding of *eis telos* believe this durative sense is more optimistic than reading *a* above: wrath only abides *until* some end time, then is lifted. Yet it could still imply that repentance and conversion are impossible for Jews until some unspecified end time. This has the same theological problem as reading *a*.

(*c*) **Completely**, as in Amos 9:8 LXX; John 13:1 (NIV 1984); Josephus, *Ant.* 1.98.7; *Barn.* 10.5; 19.11; *Herm. Vis.* 3.10.5; *Herm. Sim.* 6.2.3; Justin, *1*

Apol. 44 (Delling 1972, 56; Marshall 1983, 81). This intensive sense would mean that the Jewish leaders had brought upon themselves God's wrathful condemnation "completely," not only after killing their Messiah but in addition seeking to prevent the gospel of salvation from reaching other nations. This is the preferred meaning.

If we read 1 Thess 2:15-16 as a restrictive clause, these words are not a condemnation of ethnic Jews in general. Nor can they be taken as an announcement of irrevocable ethnic guilt. They pronounce judgment on Israel's leaders who opposed God instead of listening to him. As such, it resembles many Hebrew prophetic texts (e.g., Isa 1:10-15, 24-26; Jer 7:17-19; 32:31-32; Hos 5:10; Amos 6:1-8). Those judgment oracles did not mean there was no more repentance for God's people, nor an end to Israel and God's plans for her. Just so, in this age the same is true.

It is not enough to inquire about how to translate these words, if we are to understand and apply the text today. We must ask: *Why* did Paul speak like this?

First, Paul had personally experienced Jewish hostility to the gospel virtually everywhere he preached. He had been the object of slander, violence, and legal action in cities in Anatolia, Macedonia, and Greece.

Second, the rhetoric of the text cannot be ignored. Hyperbole and harsh language against one's enemies were expected in polemic (Wanamaker 1990, 118; Witherington 2006, 87-89). Jesus used similarly harsh language ("whitewashed tombs" [Matt 23:27; see Luke 11:44]; "vipers" [Matt 23:33]) and hyperbole (Matt 5:29-30; Mark 10:25). In fact, Paul's rhetoric is softer than that found in some inter-Jewish disputes. Surviving literature includes calls for hatred of fellow Jews as God's enemies and prayers for divine vengeance against them (Malherbe 2000, 177-79; → "Jew against Jew" sidebar, below). We might compare the political rhetoric in Northern Ireland: the harshest criticisms are leveled by one Ulsterman against another. Paul's language is that of an *insider*, under attack from his own people, and trying to distinguish the true "Israel" from the false.

Third, this section contributes to Paul's purpose of encouraging the Thessalonians (1 Thess 3:2; 4:18; 5:11). Like the rhetoric of Revelation, it asserts that God's retributive justice is still operating in a fallen world and that he rewards faithfulness. The Thessalonians are contrasted with their persecutors: they have faith, endurance, and honor; their enemies have dishonor and wrath (Witherington 2006, 25, 83).

These same themes recur in 5:1-10. The passage also serves as a bridge, anticipating the issue of Paul's inability to return (in 2:15, 17-18). We should recall that this is the voice of a persecuted and powerless first-century minority. Paul is not calling for human vengeance on Jews in our day, nor should it ever be used for that end.

Paul sees his mission to the Gentiles as an eschatological event, coming at the final stage in salvation history and delivering believers from wrath (1:10; 5:9). Those who oppose this mission are blocking God's message of life and are deserving recipients of wrath (Malherbe 2000, 170).

Jew against Jew

Is it really possible that Paul the Jew could have written 1 Thess 2:14-16? Some scholars find it too acerbic and characteristic of Gentile anti-Semitism. Did non-Christian Jews really react so violently against Jewish followers of Jesus? In our post-holocaust age, it is difficult to assess this dispassionately. This subject needs to be approached as a *historical* question about the past.

Numerous reports of religiously motivated violence by Jews against other Jewish groups can be found from the Persian era onward. The rhetoric Jews use in this literature against opponents, both Jewish and Gentile, is far more extreme than anything Paul wrote here.

During the fifth century BC, one early instance of Jewish violence against deviant Jewish behavior involves Nehemiah. He had Jews beaten for marrying foreigners, demanding they swear an oath not to allow their children to marry non-Jews (Neh 13:23-25). Ezra insisted that Jewish men in mixed marriages divorce their wives and banish them with their half-Jewish offspring (Ezra 10:10-11).

The army that Judas Maccabeus organized in the mid-second century BC "struck down sinners in their anger and renegades in their wrath" (1 Macc 2:44 NRSV). That is, they *killed* Jews who had abandoned strict law-keeping in order to fit in with Hellenistic society (also see vv 23-26). The Maccabees forcefully circumcised uncircumcised Jewish boys (v 46). A generation later the Jewish Hasmonean ruler John Hyrcanus I (135-104 BC) coerced conquered Idumeans to convert to Judaism and be circumcised (Josephus, *Ant.* 13.257-258).

During the reign of the Hasmonean queen Alexandra (76-67 BC), the Pharisees used their influence with her to have their opponents banished or imprisoned (Josephus, *J.W.* 1.110-111). The rabbis tell of an angry mob murdering a Sadducean high priest for following a non-Pharisaic cultic procedure (Cohen 1987, 156).

Josephus narrates a deadly debate that occurred before Ptolemy Philadelphus (308-246 BC). Parties representing the temple in Jerusalem and the Samaritan temple at Mount Gerizim each laid their case before the king, asking him to decide which temple was legitimate—and to execute the losers (the Samaritans lost; Josephus, *Ant.* 13.3.4). That both parties agreed in advance to the death of the loser shows the astonishing extent of the religious zealotry of some Jews. Perhaps its closest contemporary parallels may be seen among radical Islamists.

The Dead Sea Scrolls contain more extreme rhetoric about opponents than Paul's letters. The community's instructor is charged "to teach them . . . to hate all the Children of Darkness, each commensurate with his guilt and the vengeance due him from God" (1QS I, 9-10; Wise, Abegg, and Cook 1996). The Levites are instructed to curse all those "foreordained to Belial" (Satan) with merciless damnation and burning in hell. In a reversal of the Aaronic blessing, they are to say, "May [God] lift up his furious countenance upon you for vengeance"

(1QS II, 5-10; compare 1QS IV, 11-14). The Qumran community branded all Jews who refused to listen to the Teacher of Righteousness "traitors to the New Covenant" (1QpHab II, 1-3, 6-7; VIII, 8; X, 9).

The anonymous authors of the Qumran literature and the Pseudepigrapha exult in God's future judgment on the wicked, including Jews (in 1QS V, 19; 1QpHab X, 3-5, 12-13; 4Q174 IV, 1-2; and *1 En.* 62:10-12; 84:6). Compared to such polemics, 1 Thess 2:16 sounds restrained.

Paul never taught that Christians should hate their enemies nor take vengeance on unbelieving Jews. Quite the opposite, he ordered them to overcome evil with good (Rom 12:14, 17, 19-21; 1 Thess 5:15).

FROM THE TEXT

Jewish-Christian relations. Reading 1 Thess 2:13-15 today, in the dark shadow cast by the holocaust, is difficult. Preaching it is even more so. Too many "Christians" have justified violence against Jews by appealing to excerpts from Scripture such as this. Some have claimed that Jews deserve every kind of mistreatment and even death for rejecting their Messiah.

How then can Christians use in public a text that says the Jews "killed the Lord Jesus and the prophets" and "displease God"? It would seem only to inflame the smoking coals of anti-Semitism. Abram Sachar summarizes the Jewish view of Jesus:

> Jews have known little of him and have wished to know less. Throughout their long history he was not, to them, the Prince of Peace, the harbinger of goodwill. In his name every conceivable outrage was perpetrated on the despised and cursed race that gave him life. When the crusaders set fire to Jewish villages, plundered Jewish homes, and outraged Jewish daughters, it was in the shadow of the cross they bore. (1965, 124-25)

Fruitful proclamation of this passage must begin with reference to its historical context and rhetorical function. Historically, first-century Christians were a tiny, persecuted religious minority, with no political power to oppress anyone. This passage is not the voice of the persecutor, but of the persecuted. Paul, his associates, and their Thessalonian converts had experienced judicial attacks, physical violence, and numerous unspecified social and political problems inflicted by both Jews and Gentiles. Paul was not condemning the Jewish race; he and his coworkers were Jewish, as was Jesus, and all the earliest Judean Christians he praised in 2:14.

Rhetorically, the purpose of the passage is not to characterize or curse Jews in general. It does not teach "racial guilt." To blame Jews today for what happened to Jesus in AD 30 makes as much sense as persecuting people of Norwegian descent for what the Vikings did to Europe in the tenth century.

The purpose of this passage is to *praise* the Thessalonians for their genuine faith in the gospel, to *comfort* persecuted people, and to *blame* their mutual enemies.

First Thessalonians 2:13-16 does not call for retribution against Jews. Instead, it makes a judgment about the historical actions of *some* Jews (and Macedonians). It contrasts their unbelieving assault on Jesus, his followers, and the gospel with the faith of Christians.

Because of this we can say to our Jewish neighbor with full confidence: God loves you; and God has reconciled you to himself through Messiah Jesus, if you will only accept it (Rom 1:16; 5:10; 2 Cor 5:14-21).

It would be perverse to use 1 Thess 2:13-16 to inspire Christians today to act with the same sort of violence early Christians experienced. In that case, we would be as blind to God's will as Paul's opponents were. Today's church in the West is no longer a persecuted minority.

Persecuted vs. persecutors. This passage could far better serve as an occasion to ask ourselves: What are *we* prepared to endure in order to welcome God's word into our lives and become imitators of Christ? We may never face what Paul's churches faced, but would we risk being humiliated before coworkers? Would we remain faithful if our Christian profession meant economic hardship or the loss of a promotion?

God's truth. Once again 1 Thessalonians highlights the contrast between a merely "human" word and the true word of God proclaimed about Jesus in the gospel (vv 2-6). This is a word that brings life. Therefore, it is worth suffering and sacrificing for. Believers are called to recognize and "welcome" God's truth today (v 13). Some non-Christians may consider the gospel just another "power game" to get people to follow some leader. But Christians have come to understand that there is such a thing as transcendent truth. This true word is the Creator's gift of love. The same God the Thessalonians served continues today to be "at work in you who believe" (v 13) by his Spirit.

Faith and suffering. This passage can serve as a good starting point for discussions about faith and suffering, even in the West. Some varieties of North American Christianity associate faith with material and political success. Yet 1 Thessalonians clearly indicates that suffering is a sign that believers are authentic disciples, imitators of the earliest Christians.

What happens when we apply this insight to Christian experience today? Are we willing to speak positively about a faith that perseveres in the midst of suffering? Do Christians still believe that God loves those who suffer for his name? That union with Christ, and imitation of Christ, might include receiving hostility? In the church universal people of faith still experience opposition—often, sadly, from their own families and neighbors, and even from people who claim to be Christian believers of another denomination. Are we prepared to consider our unity with these persecuted, suffering members of the larger body of Christ? We need to tell the church that suffering for Christ is not shameful.

Suffering always raises questions about God's justice and love. Even strong believers may ask: Why did God let this happen to us if we really have the truth and he loves us? Why does he not stop these sinful people? This text reminds us that no one really "gets away" with evil. In fact, those who continually strive to harm God's people or to silence the gospel are the ones who should be worried, not their victims. No matter what their ethnicity or religious profession, persecutors live under God's wrath. Unless they repent, it is *their* lot we should dread, not suffering.

C. Separated but Not Divided (2:17—3:10)

BEHIND THE TEXT

In this section Paul returns to the motif of his parental care for the Thessalonians, and how it was expressed despite an enforced absence. He and his colleagues felt like parents who had lost a child when torn away (2:17). Paul expressed his concern by sending a proxy, Timothy.

The narration of events that the Thessalonians experienced, including Timothy's visit, raises the question: Why is Paul telling them what they already know (see 2:1, 2, 5, 9, 10-11)? It is in the character of a letter seeking to maintain a relationship that authors review things they have in common with their audience. Paul used this technique earlier, for paraenesis and encouragement (2:1-12; also 1:5-6). Now 2:17—3:10 uses narration for the purpose of reassuring the Thessalonians that Paul's absence was involuntary and that their friendship remained strong.

This section tells us there must have been at least two additional visits to Thessalonica after Paul left: one by Timothy (3:2) and another one to deliver this letter after his return.

The evangelists' movements after leaving Thessalonica appear at first to differ from the Acts account. Acts says nothing about Timothy being sent back to Thessalonica. It tells us that all three went to Berea, then Paul alone took the coastal road down to Athens, escorted by some of the Berean Christians (Acts 17:13-15). He sent a message with them for Timothy and Silas to join him as soon as possible.

Acts gives the impression that Paul does not see his colleagues again until after he left Athens and came to Corinth (Acts 18:5). First Thessalonians, on the other hand, seems to say that Paul sent Timothy *from Athens* to Thessalonica and says nothing about Silas' movements. As Paul writes from Corinth sometime later, Timothy has "just now come" (1 Thess 3:6) with news of his visit to Macedonia.

I discussed the relationship between Acts and 1 Thessalonians in the Introduction (→). Acts does not give a comprehensive history. Luke passes over

Paul's special assignment for Timothy as irrelevant to his purpose. Acts mentions only one instance of a letter-carrying mission: that from the apostolic council (Acts 15:22-30).

Both accounts, however, agree that after Paul left Thessalonica, and before he came to Corinth, he was left alone in Athens. Both agree that Timothy joined Paul in Corinth. We can presume that Silas rejoined Paul there, since he is named in the greeting (1 Thess 1:1). Acts similarly says nothing about Silas' whereabouts. We are left with questions that neither Acts nor Paul address: Did Timothy visit Athens in the meantime? Did both Paul's associates, in response to his request (Acts 17:15), go to Athens, where Paul gave them the assignments they fulfilled? Timothy was sent back to Thessalonica to give pastoral care and counsel (1 Thess 3:2). We can only guess where Paul sent Silas—somewhere else in Macedonia, perhaps Berea or Philippi? For Paul this was clearly a sacrifice, because he would have preferred to have had their company and aid. He delayed sending them on their respective missions until he "could stand" being uninformed about the well-being of the Thessalonians "no longer" (v 1).

IN THE TEXT

1. Separation Anxiety (2:17-20)

In 2:17-20 Paul continues the parental metaphor to speak of his continuing care for the Thessalonian church. He longed to return personally to the church, which was "orphaned" by his enforced absence. Paul did not skip town willingly, nor forget them once gone.

■ **17 We were orphaned by being separated** translates the verb *aporphanizō*. It can be used either of children orphaned or of *parents* bereaved of their children (Wanamaker 1990, 120; "made orphans" [NRSV]). It continues the father-children metaphor of vv 11-12, with great feeling. As at 1:2-3 Paul assures the Thessalonians that he continues to remember them and cares deeply about them.

That separation does not affect friends' affection or unity is a common theme in ancient friendly letters (Malherbe 2000, 180, 181). We have a saying about fair-weather friends: "Out of sight, out of mind." Paul's friendship meant their separation is the opposite: merely **in person, not in thought** (lit. *not in heart*; → 2:4).

Paul and his companions were away only **a short time** when **out of** their **intense longing** they **made every effort to see** the Thessalonian believers again. They did not give up but exerted themselves to find a way back again, despite the risks of political trouble or renewed hostilities.

The Greek phrase translated **made every effort** contains a comparative adjective (*perissoterōs*, lit. **far more, exceedingly**). One way to read the text is that Paul's enforced separation roused his desire to return **even more** than if he had left on his own (Lightfoot 1957, 37; Marshall 1983, 85). Some interpreters treat the comparative as having superlative force: "we tried ***our hardest*** to see you" (Frame 1912, 119; Wanamaker 1990, 121; Morris 1991, 87 n. 4; BDAG, 806).

Paul's efforts came from his ***great desire*** (intense longing) to see them. Although ***desire*** (*epithymia*) is often used in a negative sense in Paul (Rom 7:7; Gal 5:24; Col 3:5), it is not always. Here and at Phil 1:23 it can signify healthy desires. Paul is effusive throughout this letter about his feelings for the Thessalonian believers: longing for them (1 Thess 2:8, 17; 3:6), love (2:8), friendship (3:6), paternal and maternal affection (2:7, 11), joy over their spiritual growth and courage (3:7-9).

■ **18** Paul's attempts to make a return visit to Thessalonica were thwarted. **We wanted to come** repeats and reinforces the message that Paul's party loved the Thessalonians. Their separation was unavoidable (as 2:17).

Paul begins the account with the first-person plural that dominates the letter (**we wanted to come**). But then he suddenly breaks out with an interjection in the singular: **certainly I, Paul, did, again and again**. Paul was clearly the dominant voice directing the letter. He is not distinguishing his view as different from the others but is emphasizing his personal efforts to see them.

He tried repeatedly to get to Thessalonica, but **Satan blocked** their **way**. What exactly happened, and how Paul knew it was Satan, he does not say. Was it an illness, like Paul's thorn in the flesh (2 Cor 12:7; Marshall 1983, 86; Wanamaker 1990, 122)? Or is it a reference to certain Thessalonians keeping watch over the city to prevent his return (see Acts 17:5-7)? Ironically, the apostles were accused of threatening the public order, but it is their accusers who stirred up the city to evil.

Paul may understand **Satan** as the sinister force behind the Thessalonian politarchs who forced the apostles out and kept Paul from returning (Ramsay 1902, 230-31; Bruce 1982, 55). That supernatural evil may drive secular rulers to persecute God's people and blind the pagan world to the one true God is an idea found in Jewish apocalyptic and Christian literature (Dan 10:13, 20; Luke 22:53; Rev 12:13-17). Jewish literature attributes human evil in a general sense, especially idolatry and violence, to the influence of malevolent spirits (*1 En.* 54:4-6; 65:6; *Jub.* 11:4-5). The community that produced the Dead Sea Scrolls spoke of Jews who were unfaithful to the Law as "sons of darkness" and an army of Belial (1QM XIII, 11; see Elgvin 2000). Paul believes supernatural evil seeks to hinder God's will from being accomplished in many ways (Furnish 2007, 75).

■ **19-20** Paul reinforces how much the Thessalonians mean to him, by adding that they are a source of his personal pride and future expectations. This continues the rhetorical task of reassuring the Thessalonian community of his ongoing friendship and commitment to them despite his failure to return.

He asks a rhetorical question that invites his audience to supply the obvious answer, yes: **What is our hope, our joy . . . Is it not you?** (v 19). To be perfectly clear, Paul answers his question in v 20: **Indeed, you are our glory and joy**. Because no answer was necessary, it was all the more emphatic.

The significance the Thessalonians hold is placed in an eschatological context: it will come to its apex **in the presence of our Lord Jesus when he comes**. Paul's rhetoric draws them into Jesus' return, when the ultimate value of all things will be weighed. In that awesome setting, the apostle says, "You will be my reason to feel joy and pride in the Lord's presence." It needs no special explanation that one person can say that another person is a source of great joy. But Paul is not merely saying the Thessalonians are a joy to him as friends. The **crown** that is paired with **hope and joy** suggests the idea of final reward; and that it is given **in the presence of our Lord Jesus when he comes** suggests the "final accounting" he knows he will face before the Lord concerning his ministry (1 Cor 3:10-15; 4:3-5; 2 Cor 5:9-10). That the Thessalonian Christians have been saved by faith in Jesus, that they have turned to the one true God, and that they will be raised when Christ returns (1 Thess 1:9-10; 4:16-17; 5:9-10) are grounds for hope and joy about the future.

They are his **hope** because he looks forward to the future knowing he will be reunited with them in the Lord's presence forever. His service to the Lord has not been in vain (1 Thess 2:1).

The Thessalonians are his ***crown of boasting*** (NIV: **crown in which we will glory**). This Hebraism means a crown that gives one reason to boast. We associate a **crown** with royalty or beauty pageants. In Paul's day a victorious athlete received a **crown** (see Phil 4:1; 2 Tim 2:5; 4:8). Athletic games were held all over Greece, Macedonia, and Asia Minor and were enormously popular and prestigious. Crowns were commonly made of celery, laurel, or oak leaves.

Paul's letters often use athletic imagery to describe the Christian life, alluding to the struggle, honor, and rewards of such competitions (see 1 Cor 9:24-27; Phil 1:27; 2:16; 3:12-14; 4:3; 1 Tim 4:7; 2 Tim 4:7-8). A modern equivalent might be: "You are my gold medal, my claim to fame when Jesus returns." Paul writes to the Romans that the only thing he will boast about is "what Christ has accomplished through me *in leading the Gentiles to obey God* by what I have said and done" (Rom 15:18). The **crown** metaphor suggests that the salvation and spiritual vigor of his Thessalonian converts somehow validated his ministry (compare 2 Cor 3:1-3). They give him a sense of accomplishment.

Paul expects to **glory** in the Thessalonians **in the presence of our Lord Jesus when he comes** (*en tēi parousiai autou*, ***at his coming***). This is almost certainly the earliest use of the term *parousia* in Paul's letters (six times in 1 and 2 Thessalonians). *Parousia* generally means "presence" or "arrival."

Parousia became a technical term in the Hellenistic and Roman eras for the visit of kings to a city (MM, 497; Oepke 1967, 860; Spicq 1994, 3:53-55). These visits were marked by the city spending lavishly on sacrifices, banquets, athletic competitions, new buildings, and monuments all in honor of the ruler

(→ 1 Thess 4:15). Jesus' return is like a royal visit, and Paul is like an athlete who has competed in the games to honor and entertain the king. His "victory" and **glory** is that he brings along with him to the kingdom those friends who give him **joy**.

2. Why Paul Sent Timothy (3:1-5)

Since Paul found it impossible to come, he sent Timothy as his best option. This further stresses to the Thessalonians how deep their mutual devotion is. Timothy's visit was to encourage them—what Paul would do if he could (3:2-3). He was to gather news and report back to Paul (v 6). Previously, Paul praised them for their steadfast faith (1:6-8; 2:13-14). Now he shows his fatherly worry over their spiritual condition in the face of persecution (3:3, 5).

■ **1-2** When Paul's efforts to reach the Thessalonians failed, and he **could stand it no longer,** he decided to take a different course of action. The verb *stegō* here means "to endure" and also "to keep silent" (BDAG, 942).

Paul may have chosen this verb for its subtle double entendre, which alludes to the legal action taken against the Christian host Jason and the apostles (Acts 17:8-9). The politarchs' ruling was designed to prevent the apostles from returning to communicate personally with anyone in the city. They could no longer teach in the city, nor lead the now illegal house meetings of the Christians (→ Introduction). But Paul cannot willingly remain silenced and cut off from them.

Paul apparently decided while **in Athens** (v 1; see Acts 17:14-15) to send **Timothy** back to Thessalonica (1 Thess 3:2). This left him alone. The **we** in this section again raises the question, "which 'we'"? Some find it an epistolary **we** (= Paul himself). Perhaps this is what Paul means here: note the strange expression "*we decided to be left . . . alone* [plural in Greek]." Up to this point in his ministry Paul has always worked as part of a team. Solitariness was a significant sacrifice for him. Acts fails to mention Timothy's visit to Athens (on Paul's trip to **Athens**, how it correlates with his coworkers' movements, and the evidence of Acts, → Behind the Text for 1 Thess 2:17—3:10, above, and → Introduction).

Why did Paul send **Timothy**? Why did he think Timothy would succeed in returning to the church when he and Silas could not? And why didn't **Timothy** get into trouble? We can only speculate, although scripture gives a few clues. Timothy was undoubtedly careful in how he approached the city and spoke with Christians. But there must be more here. When Timothy was asked to join Paul and Silas, he was a very young man. Note the allusions to his youth over a decade later (1 Tim 4:12; 2 Tim 2:22). Commentators surmise that he was a third evangelist from the start. But Acts merely says that Paul had Timothy *to go along with him* (Acts 16:3).

Timothy was perhaps merely a personal assistant for Paul and Silas (compare John Mark, a "helper" [*hypēretēs* (Acts 13:5); LSJM, 1872; Bruce 1977,

214]). Modern Westerners prefer appliances to employing people. But the ancient world had no electricity or gas; no appliances or running water. Servants were common for doing basic tasks, and often invaluable (compare Onesimus in Phlm 11, 13). This may explain how Timothy escaped the civic authorities' notice when the apostles fell into trouble: they thought of him as a servant of low status and inconsequential (he is not imprisoned at Philippi [Acts 16:19, 25]). He may not have been directly involved in evangelism or teaching at that stage. As a "nobody," he could slip into the city later unnoticed. Furthermore, Timothy was half-Greek (Acts 16:1). This meant he probably looked and spoke like a native Greek and would blend in more easily in the Hellenistic culture of Macedonia. Paul, on the other hand, was an ethnic Jew, born in Cilicia but who had resided in Jerusalem for years (Acts 22:2-3; Gal 1:13-14; Phil 3:4-6). As an oriental who spoke Greek with an accent (1 Cor 2:1, 3; 2 Cor 10:10), he could not be inconspicuous. Silas, similarly, was an Aramaic-speaking, Jewish Christian from Palestine (Acts 15:22). The Pastoral Epistles may hint that Timothy was not as forceful a personality as Paul (1 Tim 4:11-16; 6:12, 20; 2 Tim 1:6-8). If true, this would add to his ability to get around Thessalonica unnoticed.

This trip to Thessalonica may have been Timothy's first independent gospel-ministry assignment. Thus, Paul must explain to the church why he sent his servant! This desperate measure turned into the beginning of a lifelong ministry for Timothy and a great blessing for the church.

3:1-2

Paul urges the Thessalonians to respect Timothy as more than a servant. He is **our brother and a coworker of God in the gospel of Christ** (1 Thess 3:2). **Brother** speaks of his Christian faith, his closeness to Paul, and his unity with the Thessalonians. We expect Paul to add "*our* coworker." Instead, he says **coworker of God**. The expression was odd enough to lead several scribes to try to "fix" the sentence. Many manuscripts read "servant (*diakonos*) of God"; some, just "coworker" (omitting "God"). The Byzantine text combines all of these: "minister of God, and our fellowlabourer" (KJV). But "coworker of God" is probably original, as unlikely to have been invented by a scribe (Metzger 1994, 563; Best 1986, 132; Bruce 1982, 61; Malherbe 2000, 191).

The force of the expression is ambiguous in Greek: it could mean "he and God both work." That is, God is at work by his Spirit in Timothy's ministry. But it could mean that God sent Timothy on his behalf to work with Paul and Silas (Green 2002, 159-60). The balanced sentence parts (<u>our</u> **brother**, <u>God's</u> **coworker**) suggest the first meaning (compare 1 Cor 3:9; Frame 1912, 126-27; Best 1986, 132; Marshall 1983, 91; Malherbe 2000, 191; most recent commentators).

The boldness of this imagery indicates Paul's belief that Christians actively participate with God as partners in the work of bringing the message of redemption to the world. Of course, Christians are not equal partners with God. Nevertheless, they serve a vital role by God's grace.

Paul describes Timothy's responsibilities as *in the gospel of Christ* (NIV: spreading the gospel of Christ). This should be understood as more than evangelism. The call to live and work in the gospel implies that Timothy pursued the same lifestyle Paul had described in 1 Thess 2:7-12 (see 2 Cor 5:17; Phil 1:27). Here, Timothy's mission was to give pastoral care, in words echoing Paul's ministry: to **strengthen and encourage** the Thessalonians **in** the **faith** (1 Thess 3:2). **Strengthen** has the sense of making something steady and firm from something that was shaky. It is used in the NT for establishing the faith of people at risk of apostasy because of persecution (Green 2002, 160).

Encourage can signify giving of counsel and advice, exhorting someone to take a course of action (2:12). In this letter it also carries the sense of bringing comfort to the distressed, which is what Timothy does here to prevent the church from being "unsettled by these trials" (v 3; 4:18; 5:11, 14; → 1 Thess 2:12).

■ **3** Paul was clearly worried about how the Thessalonians would do without his pastoral leadership as they faced severe **trials**. This was why Timothy's mission in pastoral care was required, lest these new Christians be **unsettled** by their persecution.

Unsettled comes from a verb that, oddly enough, was used for a dog wagging its tail (*sainō*). Here it means *agitated* or emotionally distraught (Diogenes Laertius, *Lives* 8.41; Lang 1971) by their troubles (not Paul's; against Malherbe 2000, 197). Choosing the right path had resulted in trouble rather than blessing; their own families had rejected them; those they considered God's messengers had been defamed as politically dangerous troublemakers; Jesus had not returned to rescue them. For all these reasons, their hearts were **unsettled**.

Paul reminds them that he had never sugarcoated the gospel to them. He had been honest about the likely consequences of choosing God. Christians are **destined** for **trials**—not just the ordinary hardships of life, such as sickness and money troubles. **Trials** refers to persecution of various sorts that particularly befalls Christians. The Greek term *thlipsis* (→ 1 Thess 1:6) refers to "affliction" broadly. This includes everything from name-calling and social ostracism to physical violence. The root term refers to being pressured or squeezed. It reinforces the mental distress God's saints may experience.

Destined does not refer to the predestination of individuals; it is about the common fate of Christians. They **know** this from Paul's prior teaching (which Timothy reinforced). Jesus had taught that those with faith in God who follow him would face persecution (Matt 5:11-12, 44; 10:17-23; 24:9-10; Mark 13:9-13; John 15:18-21). Paul's understanding was influenced by the suffering of the prophets in Israel's history and Jewish expectations that a time of suffering would precede the coming of Messiah. Early Christians taught that suffering for Christ prior to the Parousia was *normal* and should be expected (Rom 8:17; Phil 3:10-11; 2 Tim 3:12).

■ **4** No matter how many times we might be told of persecution, few of us blithely take persecution as par for the course. This is why the apostles **kept telling** the Thessalonians they **would be persecuted** (v 4). Again Paul reminds them of his repeated teaching **when** he and his companions were with them (see 1:9-10; 2:13). It was unpleasant, but **it turned out that way**, so Paul's reminder of his teaching reminds them that it is reliable. As long as people's minds are blinded, and they respond with guilt, anger, and rejection of God's truth, **trials** are to be expected by the faithful.

■ **5** Paul expected society would be unkind to his new Christian converts in Thessalonica. He could not endure being cut off from them; he was anxious to **find out about** their **faith**. Paul mentions again the feelings that led to sending Timothy: **I could stand it no longer** (as 3:1).

Timothy's mission was to ascertain whether Paul's fears had been realized—that persecution had led them to apostasy (as in Jesus' parable in Mark 4:16-17). This seems to be the meaning of his fear that **the tempter had tempted you and that our labors might have been in vain**. **The tempter** is, of course, Satan.

Paul's **work** would have been **in vain** ("useless," *for nothing*, *eis kenon*) if his recent converts were lost in the end. The Synoptic Gospels report that Satan's temptation of Jesus was to avoid hardships—to make food miraculously, to presume on God's miraculous protection, and to achieve worldly rule without pain by bowing down to the devil (Matt 4:1-11 || Luke 4:1-13). When Peter similarly urged Jesus to reject the path of suffering, Jesus identified this as the voice of Satan (Mark 8:31-33 and parallels). The journey of faith often requires the path of suffering.

3. Timothy's Report on the Thessalonians (3:6-10)

■ **6** Paul now expresses his delight that his worst fears were unfounded and that the Thessalonians' **faith** triumphed in adversity. They have not given in to social pressure, coercion, or violence. And though hardship often makes people's **love** dim, this has not happened either. The community has remained loyal to each other as well as to Christ. This is the second time Paul expresses his admiration for how their virtues endured by grace (see 1:3, 6-7). His praise is meant to encourage them.

Is it significant that Paul omits praise of their *hope* here? Some think not, since Paul had mentioned it at 1:3 (Furnish 2007, 79). But the letter subsequently implies that they were disturbed by the deaths of some in their community (4:13). Paul's rhetoric suggests that they needed reassurance that there was still hope for the dead in Christ to have a future life in Messiah's kingdom (4:14-18). So this may be a subtle and gentle reminder that Timothy's report indicated a shortcoming. That they were "lacking" something is one reason Paul gives for desiring to visit (3:10).

The **good news** that the Thessalonians had persevered despite their suffering was **brought** to Paul by **Timothy**. He has **just** returned from his assigned mission to Thessalonica (vv 2, 6). The verb **brought good news** translates *euangelizō*, usually meaning "preach the gospel" in the NT. Here, it has its more ordinary sense of "bring good news."

Paul fails to say *where* he is when **Timothy** returns. The letter seems to suggest that: (*a*) Paul had recently founded the church (e.g., 1:5-10; 2:1-12); (*b*) it has been a relatively short time since he left the church (2:17); (*c*) he has visited Athens since he left (3:1); and (*d*) Timothy has rejoined him (3:6). Evidence from Acts leads us to conclude that Paul is in Corinth (Acts 18:5; → Introduction, The Writing of 1 Thessalonians).

Paul stresses his excitement at hearing from the Thessalonians by noting he wrote this letter in response to the news Timothy had brought **just now**. Timothy reports that the Thessalonian believers **always have pleasant memories** (*mneian*) of the apostles, echoing the Greek of Paul's prayer report in 1:2 (→ 1:2-3). Both continue to remember each other, just as both **long to see** one another. This powerful language emphasizes that their friendship has thrived in tragedy and hardship. One might expect such language of remembering and longing in a family letter (UPZ 1.59; PSI 12.1261.10, 21; BGU 2.632).

■ **7** Paul writes to encourage the Thessalonians, yet he reports that *he* is **encouraged about** them **because of** their **faith**. He specifically mentions their **faith**, because now he knows his work is not "in vain" (v 5).

He again stresses their mutuality: both apostles and Thessalonians experienced **persecution** (*thlipsis*; see 1:6; 3:3) and **distress**. And both sides comfort one another. Paul writes to the Corinthians that God uses those who are afflicted to comfort others who are afflicted (2 Cor 1:3-5). God's grace is poured out on wounded humanity in order to be shared and multiplied. Paul does not specify the nature of his troubles, or even whether he is alluding to past events at Thessalonica, his present situation, or likely both (see Acts 18:5-17; 1 Cor 2:3).

■ **8 For now we really live**, Paul exclaims, showing his relief and joy that his Thessalonian converts **are standing firm in the Lord**. That they were **standing firm** confirms their steadfast faith in God and his gospel, not yielding to pressures (1 Cor 16:13; Phil 1:27; 4:1). As parents feel themselves emotionally bound up with the success or failure of their children, so Paul felt everything his converts experienced. He could describe his agony on behalf of errant converts as birth pains (Gal 4:19).

■ **9** Here it is the opposite: the Thessalonians' triumph makes it impossible for Paul to **thank God enough . . . in return for** all the joy he felt at the "good news" Timothy delivered (v 6). He credits God as the one responsible for their success in their struggles, anticipating their needs, and responding with the Spirit's help in their hour of trial. Paul describes his **joy** as being **in the presence of our God**, referring to his prayer experience.

■ **10** Paul immediately reminds the Thessalonians that he and his companions **pray** for them **night and day** (see 1:2; 2:13). This is his greatest delight:

the salvation and continuing spiritual strength of a human life (2:19-20; compare Luke 2:10; 10:20; 15:10).

Paul's prayer is to **see you again and supply what is lacking in your faith**. He had been forced out of Thessalonica, was opposed by both Jewish and Gentile community leaders, had a court order barring him from the city limits, and believed Satan was opposing his return. This is a bold prayer indeed! Paul is nothing if not ambitious in the Lord. He believes that God can triumph under even the most adverse circumstances.

But this prayer also suggests that, based on Timothy's report, there were issues they still needed to address, growth that needed to happen. To **lack** suggests their understanding or experience is *incomplete*. There is no hint that they had fallen victim to some false teaching. Undoubtedly, the writing of this letter is itself a first effort to address **what is lacking** and strengthen their **faith**.

Did Paul ever return to Thessalonica? Both Acts and Paul's letters tell us that he returned to Macedonia at least two more times. Although the city is not named, his travel route would almost certainly have taken him straight through Thessalonica, along the Via Egnatia (Acts 20:1-5; 2 Cor 2:13; 8:1-6; 9:2). The last visit was just before his fateful, final trip to Jerusalem.

FROM THE TEXT

Paul's blunt warnings to his Thessalonian converts about the hardships of the Christian life contrast starkly with much of what passes for popular Christianity today. Some Christian websites and television programs teach that Jesus' death guarantees believers worldly success. Prosperity preachers promise that faith in God will provide financial success, happy marriages, better jobs, new cars, and so forth. One group on the web calls itself the "wealthy place." Another writer goes so far as to claim "the only suffering for a believer is the spiritual discomfort brought by resisting the pressures of the flesh, not a physical or mental suffering" (Copeland n.d., n.p.). Who can blame people for flocking to such teaching? Who would not want their lives to be better, and wish for God's help?

The problem with such teaching is that it ultimately betrays the poor it is supposed to serve. What about those who do *not* get wealthier or recover from illness? Does God love them less than other Christians? What about those whose lived-out commitment to Jesus Christ makes *more* trouble for them with family members or old friends? What of those who are denied promotions or fired from their jobs *because* they refuse to go along with immoral policies? In some parts of the world commitment to Jesus may even cost believers their lives. If we measure God's love by wealth, then we would have to say God loves the most corrupt and violent people of the world more than his saints, for they are often the ones who prosper most. Measuring spirituality by success may lead us off the path of God-worship and onto the detour of materialism and money-worship (1 Tim 6:9-10).

What would Christian teaching look like if we took seriously Paul's—and Jesus'—statement that believers should expect ill-treatment as normal? Would this turn away people from our churches? Would it spoil evangelistic campaigns? Or would it lay a more solid foundation for Christians to bear their suffering? Being prepared to expect hardship is one key to facing it with courage and overcoming it in faith.

We owe God's people the truth, which is nourishment for their hurting souls. Those who experience suffering for Christ have become imitators of their Lord. They are *faithful* disciples, not failures. The triumph of Christian faith is not measurable by material means. Victory comes in the act of saying yes to God even in the darkness. Faithfulness to Christ in the face of suffering is a *greater* act of devotion to God, and a greater personal victory, than when suffering is absent.

This section demonstrates how important *Christian fellowship* was to these first Christians in enduring suffering. Timothy's report emphasized their faith and love (1 Thess 1:3; 3:6; 4:9). Their concern for one another—in addition to their faith in God—played a major role in this community's ability to withstand outside pressure and maintain itself. Paul modeled this concern while with them, and continues his care even while away.

Prayer is equally important: Paul prayed for the community (1:2-3; 3:11-13) and will call on them to "pray continually" for him (5:17). Prayer is vital to finding God's grace and strength in trials. And not just request prayer (though that is here too [3:10]). Thanksgiving, rejoicing, and other fundamental elements of worship (v 9) are essential nourishment for the soul. They are spiritual offerings to God, who is worthy of them.

It is important to note that for Paul suffering is not a goal. It is not something we should seek to boost our spiritual status. Suffering is simply a door believers must pass through with their Lord. On the far side of that door is resurrection, reunion with loved ones, and the eternal triumph of God on our behalf. This is the essential content of what Paul calls "hope" (1 Cor 15:51-54; 1 Thess 1:3; 4:14-17).

IV. SECOND PRAYER: 1 THESSALONIANS 3:11-13

BEHIND THE TEXT

Paul was a praying Christian. Although it may be rhetorical hyperbole when he says that he prays "night and day" (1 Thess 3:10), "constantly" and "always" (1 Cor 1:4; Col 1:3; 1 Thess 1:2-3; 2 Thess 1:3, 11; 2:13; Phlm 4), it is not far from the literal truth.

So, when we suddenly find this prayer report in the middle of the letter body, it genuinely reflects Paul's mind. This prayer is not the end of a long thanksgiving (1 Thess 1:2 to 3:13) but is a separate second prayer (→ Introduction). Attempts to analyze this using ancient conventions of rhetoric or epistle writing need to be moderated with the realization that Paul's compositions are ad hoc and creative. To insist that he must conform to formal structural ideals is like forcing round pegs into square holes: they simply do not fit.

This prayer appears to be a spontaneous response to Timothy's report about the church: gratitude for their perseverance tempered by concern for their need for spiritual strengthening. The apostle longs for God to bring an end to his separation from the Thessalonians and to fulfill his desire to see them again. It also serves as an apt transition to the next topic, which is about holy living (4:1-12).

IN THE TEXT

■ **11** In English, **may** followed by an infinitive verb translates a Greek verb form that has no English equivalent—the optative mood. The optative indicates a prayer-wish. It is like saying, "I would really like—and I ask in prayer—that **God** will **clear the way** and 'make your love increase'" (vv 11-12). The optative mood was becoming rare in the Greek of Paul's day. So this prayer language may well have sounded old-fashioned and formal.

The use of possessive pronouns (**our**) with God is very ancient. It expresses belonging and commitment. Exodus has God declare to Israel, "I am the Lord *your* God," showing that he has already committed to his people (Exod 6:7; 20:2; Jer 7:23). God is *for them*; the proper response is to call him "my God" (e.g., Exod 15:2; Pss 7:1; 18:2, 6, 21; Isa 25:1), or "our God" (Deut 6:4, 20-25; Pss 18:31; 48:14; Mic 4:5).

Paul often calls God **Father** in his letters (as did Jesus; → 1 Thess 1:1). But this title occurs more frequently in 1 and 2 Thessalonians than in most of the other letters in the Pauline corpus (only Ephesians and Philemon use it comparatively more frequently). This reflects the apostle's family imagery for the church and its relationship to God in this letter. **Himself** is the emphatic first word of the prayer in Greek. It may echo an older prayer form from the synagogue and church (Best 1986, 146; Wiles 1974, 30). It lends intensity to the prayer, asking for God's personal response (Marshall 1983, 99).

It is especially striking how this prayer joins together God the Father **and our Lord Jesus**: Paul prays to *both!* Underlining this further is the fact that **clear the way** is a *singular* verb in Greek, despite the plural subject (God and Jesus). As the prayer proceeds, Paul addresses **Jesus** alone (v 12).

While Christians may take this for granted today, this was an astonishing and revolutionary thought for a Jew such as Paul: Messiah is somehow one with God. Messiah can answer prayer. Paul never explains exactly *how* **Jesus** and **God** are joined or why they share the same divine honors, titles (**Lord**), and functions (answering prayer, judging; → v 13). Unfolding the christological implications of this language would occupy the church for several centuries after this letter.

What should especially impress modern readers is the offhanded way in which Paul addresses Jesus as **Lord** in prayer (a common cultic title for deities in the Hellenistic world) and brackets him with **God**. In other words, Paul just assumes he and his readers agree on this already, as do the other apostles and

Christians in Palestine (1 Cor 15:11; Gal 2:1-3, 6-9; compare Matt 28:17-20). There is no controversy or argument here.

God is traditionally addressed as **Lord** in Jewish prayer, and—though only rarely, as the Christian era approaches—as **Father**. That Paul divides up these titles and gives one to Jesus is further proof that he thinks of Jesus as sharing in God's divine attributes. The prayer extends from 1 Thess 3:11 to 3:13 as one sentence in Greek. The content of the prayer can be outlined by tracing the four main verbs: **clear the way, make . . . increase, make . . . overflow,** and **strengthen** (vv 11-13).

The first petition is on behalf of Paul and his companions. It repeats his expressed desire (2:17) and previous prayers (3:10). He prays that God and Jesus may **clear the way for us to come to you**. The verb *kateuthynō* literally means "make straight," "guide," or "direct." It employs the imagery of God walking ahead of the apostle on the way back to Thessalonica, leading the way and clearing aside obstacles.

■ **12** The second petition is directed to **the Lord** Jesus alone, although Paul must still think of him acting in concert with the Father. The prayer is for the Thessalonians to have an intensive growth of Christian **love** (*agapē*).

The two verbs **increase and overflow** (v 12) are synonyms. **Increase** (*pleonazō*) emphasizes growth in size or quantity. **Overflow** (*perisseuō*) signals having more than enough, "abundance." Together the terms say that Paul wants an experience of divine **love** to flood their lives in a way that surpasses all they have previously known, and to overflow to people around them.

Loving **each other** has fellow Christians in mind, while **everyone else** means non-Christians. Paul is thinking of Jesus' teaching that his disciples were to be known for their love, even of their enemies (Matt 5:43-48; Luke 10:29-37; John 13:34-35; 15:12, 17). **Love** for **each other** is essential for the community to maintain cohesion and have spiritual growth. **Love** for others is essential for the gospel's witness.

Because of the harsh treatment they were receiving, they will require God's gracious and powerful aid to love in this way. Paul affirms that he and his companions have already experienced this divine love for the Thessalonians, and prays that their experience may be similar (**just as ours does for you**). The apostles again serve as models for the Thessalonians (as at 1 Thess 1:6; 2:8-10, 14). Note Paul's pastoral appreciation for his converts' progress: he does not pray that they will begin to love but that the love they already practice may **increase**.

■ **13** The final petition calls on the Lord to ***establish your hearts as blameless in holiness.*** Paul treats Christian sanctification as an act of God's grace. The heart (→ 2:17) signifies all the inner life of the self. It is not meant to contrast with the outer self, as if physical behavior need not be holy. Rather, it points to the center of human decision-making, thinking, and passions.

To **establish** (*stērizō*; NIV: **strengthen**) means to set something up permanently or to fix it in place so it does not move or fall. In this case it is the inner self that is to be established as **blameless in holiness**. The outer behavior should naturally follow.

Shame, Honor, and Biblical Holiness

Ancient Mediterranean societies—Greek, Roman, Syrian, Jewish—were all what anthropologists call "shame-honor societies." People's *reputations* were more important than their *consciences*. The outward appearance of a life—to family and society—determines the moral evaluation of behavior by individuals. Groups determine whether individuals have kept honor, gained more honor, or lost it (have been shamed) based on observation and consensus (Du Boulay 1974, 81-84; deSilva 2000, 35-42).

Consequently, people's honor in society is partly based on how they control their external appearance and reputation. (Honor is also ascribed through the accidents of birth and social status or through the bestowal of honors such as citizenship [de Silva 2000, 28-29].) They avoid being caught doing things that would bring shame and do things that would enhance their public honor (and get noticed).

Of course, this system can foster the dangerous tendency to think that appearance is all that matters. But the kind of holiness Paul prays to be established in the Thessalonians is not merely a facade to impress people while leaving the interior rotten (a practice Jesus condemned: Matt 6:1-4, 5-6, 16-18; 23:5-7, 25-28; Luke 11:43-44). Believers' "hearts" will be constituted "blameless" (without shame) with God, by his grace. A transformation of thought, will, and personality: the total person. Paul suggests his readers be encouraged by the fact that the only honor that matters in the end is the honor that God bestows. And he bestows that honor on his beloved, those who believe in the Son, who possess the Spirit, and who have consecrated their lives to him.

The perspective in this prayer is eschatological: the ultimate condition of believers on the Day of the Lord, the day **when our Lord Jesus comes** (*parousia*). The language of appearing **in the presence of our God** at Jesus' Parousia is probably intended to evoke the imagery of judgment day (one aspect of the Day of the Lord). The prayer is that, already before that day comes, the Lord Jesus will have firmly established believers **blameless** as innocent before the heavenly court. They will have been built into the firm foundation that has been laid once and for all, Jesus Christ, whom the apostles proclaimed (1 Cor 3:10-11).

What is perhaps a bit odd in this context is that Paul writes to people who already have faith in God and in Jesus (1 Thess 1:9-10). Are they not already justified? Why would Paul need to pray this? One reason is that he envisions not their present need of salvation but their ultimate state of perfection brought about by Jesus.

Another answer is that in Greek the clause about establishing them **blameless** is the *result* of being given superabundant "love" (v 12). Verse 13 is part of the same purpose clause begun in v 12 (introduced by *eis to*, **in order to establish**). So the prayer requests that God might give his divine love to the believing community for this *purpose*: **to establish** them **blameless in holiness**. To help them maintain their faith in troubled times, Paul prays that God's love overflow in them until the end, until they meet Jesus in his perfection and he meets them in theirs.

This condition is further described as **in holiness**, a rare word (*hagiōsynē*) describing the condition or state of being holy. It reminds us that Paul calls Christians "saints" (lit. "holy ones"; see Rom 1:7; 1 Cor 1:2; Phil 1:1).

Holiness is used in the Greek OT only of God. Here, it probably should be understood to refer to the **holiness** of believers (against Richard 1995, 176-77). This is a condition in which they belong completely to God and reflect his character because of the overflowing love he has given them (→ 1 Thess 4:1-8).

This will happen **in the presence of our God and Father, *at the return of our Lord Jesus*** (3:13). The language repeats almost exactly that of 2:19 (→ 2:19-20). The essential difference is that both God and Jesus are mentioned here. The Parousia (**return**) of Jesus is the NT equivalent for the OT Day of the Lord. It is an apocalyptic and eschatological (end-times) concept involving salvation and judgment.

The prayer to *establish* the Thessalonians **blameless** has reference not only to the present but also to their final accounting before God. Paul desires that God grace their inner selves—mind, will, emotion—with his transforming and sanctifying love in such a way that on that day they will greet the returning Christ unafraid and with joy as their Savior. Here emerges a third reason for this prayer: the Thessalonian believers who are being *dishonored* by their society hear that God's work in their lives will lead to ultimate *honor*.

Who are the **holy ones** Paul says will come **with** Jesus at his return? Scholars propose three possible answers. We will consider the evidence for and against each of these.

First, elsewhere in Paul's letters this word (*hagioi*) always refers to Christians as **saints**. Some understand Paul to mean that Jesus will return with dead believers who have previously gone to heaven. This idea is often linked with the theory that the church on earth will be "raptured"—that is, miraculously transported away to heaven—some time prior to Jesus' return, to wait out a period of divine punishment and final signs of judgment given to the earth.

But if *saints* refers to the Christian dead plus those who were raptured alive (as in pretribulationism), then the sentence does not fit with what Paul says later: only when Jesus comes will Christians, both dead and alive, rise to *meet* him (not to come with him; → 4:15-17).

Furthermore, if believers have already gone to meet Jesus before his Parousia, then they will have had to appear blameless before him *then*. Yet here Paul implies Jesus' coming **with all his holy ones** is the moment before which the Thessalonians will need to be **blameless in holiness**. Only then will they finally experience his unveiled presence.

Second, by **holy ones** here Paul may recall OT images of a theophany: God appears in the company of his angelic army. "When God reveals himself, for deliverance or for judgment, he is regularly attended by his angels" (Bruce 1982, 73). "Holy one" (*hagios*) sometimes refers to a divine being or angel in the OT (Job 5:1; 15:15; Ps 89:5, 7; Dan 8:13).

Zechariah 14:5 prophesies a Day of the Lord when "the LORD my God will come, and all the *holy ones* with him." Many believe Paul alludes to this passage here. The idea of an appearance of God accompanied by a heavenly army—either in the past at Sinai or in a future judgment day—is not uncommon in OT thought (see Deut 33:2; Ps 68:17; Dan 7:10).

These OT apocalyptic images were developed in later Jewish literature. In *1 En.* 1:9, the author asserts: "Behold [God] will arrive with ten million of the holy ones in order to execute judgment upon all" (Charlesworth 1983-85, 1:13-14). The NT similarly uses the imagery of angels attending Jesus at the Parousia / judgment day (Matt 13:41; 25:31; Mark 8:38; 13:27; see Best 1986, 152-53; Bruce 1982, 73-74; Malherbe 2000, 214). Interpreting **holy ones** in this way avoids conflict with 1 Thess 4:15-17 and is the view of most commentators.

Third, an option seldom taken is that **with all his holy ones** does not modify the noun *parousia* ("coming"). Instead, it describes the circumstances of the verb **strengthen**: Paul prays that God may sanctify the Thessalonian believers *along with all of his saints*.

If this were his intention, Paul would once again be using the language of unity and shared experiences to help foster these Christians' sense of solidarity with the church universal, the body of Christ (→ 1:6-7; 2:14; 3:6-7; 4:15-18).

On this reading, the prayer looks forward to a reunion of all God's people from every age. Together they will experience perfection. The phrase **with all his holy ones** might seem too distant from **establish** to modify it, but this is not a problem for Greek with its flexible word order. The greatest challenge to this view is the apparent allusion to Zech 14:5. This favors the second view.

FROM THE TEXT

This prayer stands out in its vivid combination of tradition and creativity. Paul offers here a richness of theological perspective aimed at a specific human situation. It offers a model for pastoral care and liturgical function.

Paul has confidence in God's ability to intervene not only in the human heart (1 Thess 3:12) but even in the current affairs of human life, such as illness and politics (v 11).

The christological implications of this prayer are massive: Paul places Jesus of Nazareth alongside God as the object of prayer. Even more, he makes a prayer petition to Jesus as Lord alone (vv 12-13). Such prayer clearly shows Paul thinks of Jesus as somehow sharing in deity, confirming our impressions of Paul's earlier comments (→ 1:1, 2-3, 10).

In what is likely the earliest surviving Christian literature, the church's preaching (the kerygma) has already assigned Jesus the OT role of God in the expectation of the Day of the Lord. *Jesus* makes the eschatological theophany. It is he who will arrive at the end of days with the cosmic army of "holy ones" to inaugurate the world's judgment (3:13). It is *Jesus* whose decision "rescues us from . . . wrath" (1:10) and graces us to participate in God's holiness.

Another important theme this prayer raises is the causal link between love and holiness. This link is something John Wesley particularly emphasized. He described Christian sanctification as perfection *in love*. Without love, efforts to display spirituality through orthodox teaching, sound thinking, modest dress, or circumspect behavior are doomed to futility and emptiness (1 Cor 13:1-3).

If holiness is a combination of being devoted to God and reflecting God's character, then love is the fundamental medium of carrying out both of those. Love is the basis of right relationship toward God (Deut 6:4-5; Mark 12:28-31; John 14:23). And love is the fulfillment of the Law's requirements toward one's neighbor (Mark 12:31; Rom 13:9-10).

Today, unfortunately, the term "holiness" sounds archaic at best in our society. It evokes images of ladies in black with hair bound up in buns. It provokes memories of microethical preoccupation with legalistic regulations forbidding playing cards, Sunday sports, movies, and more. To those outside the church, holiness often equates to hypocrisy and hatred of humanity, the direct opposite of its true meaning.

The church needs to recapture the biblical dynamic of holiness in a way that is intelligible today. We can start with Paul's prayer, which recognizes that holiness is a *result of the growth of God's love in us*. It shows itself as universal love—for Christians and non-Christians alike (1 Thess 3:13).

Directing this petition for love to Jesus (3:12) may also remind us of that love we are called to imitate, as in the Christ-hymn of Philippians (Phil 2:5-11). Jesus himself led the way in demonstrating what holy love is like.

V. EXHORTATIONS AND ENCOURAGEMENT: I THESSALONIANS 4:1—5:11

The exhortation segment (4:1—5:11) is the part of the letter most formally like ancient paraenesis (or moral instruction). It is often identified as the paraenetic section, although earlier sections also contribute to the paraenetic purpose of the letter. It addresses three major areas: (1) living in holiness and love, to please God (4:3-12); (2) the return of Christ and its consequences for humanity (4:13—5:11); and (3) advice on worshipping and working together (5:12-22).

The first half of the letter prepared the way for Paul's paraenesis. He repeatedly emphasized their shared faith, shared sufferings, and shared opponents (1:6; 2:8, 13-16; 3:1-3, 7). They are family in Christ. It is out of this shared existence in Christ that Paul gives his paraenesis. He prefers appealing to them or inviting them to reason from the gospel, rather than commanding them (4:1, 7, 10, 14; 5:12, 14). The friendly character of this letter is further reinforced by Paul insisting he is only reminding them of what they already know, or are already doing (4:1-2, 9-10; 5:1).

The second half of the letter is anticipated by Paul's prayer to "supply what is lacking in your faith" (3:10). Paul's rhetoric is mostly positive and encouraging. Just as he previously praised the Thessalonians for their model faith, now he asks them to change by doing **even more** of what they are already doing (4:10; 5:11). Nevertheless, there are clearly areas where Paul is concerned about them. They need to think carefully about what they have learned and continue to apply it in faith, because they still encounter troubles and temptations of various sorts (4:9-10, 13; 5:12-14). And they continue to need encouragement and guidance in finding out "how to live" so as "to please God" (4:1).

A. Ethical Instructions (4:1-12)

BEHIND THE TEXT

The first area of instruction Paul pursues is about the Christian's holiness as it relates to the body and sexuality (4:3-8). This is followed by a word about brotherly love (vv 9-10) and exhortations to "lead a quiet life" and support oneself (vv 11-12). Verses 9-12 should be seen as a single unit with the theme of *philadelphia*, "brotherly love."

Is the admonition to *philadelphia* and responsible living a continuation of the previous discussion of sanctification and avoiding sexual immorality (vv 3-8)? Paul's exhortation to "please God" (v 1) stands as a rubric over all of vv 1-12. Another possibility is that God's will of *sanctification* (v 3) is meant to cover all of the admonitions in vv 3-12.

After a brief introduction that relates Paul's instructions to God's will and the authority of the Lord Jesus (vv 1-2), Paul discusses their sanctification (vv 3-8). This subsection is marked out with an inclusio (a literary device where the same word or phrase brackets the start and finish of a section). It begins with **your sanctification** (*hagiasmos* [v 3]) and ends with **the Holy** [*hagios*] **Spirit in you** (v 8). The practical outworking of this sanctification is in self-control in sexuality. Why the focus on this issue? Jews regarded sexual sin as typical of pagans, often naming it in connection with their idolatry (see Rom 1:18-27; Wis 14:12, 22-27; *Jub.* 9:15; 20:6-10; 25:1-3; *3 Bar.* 8:4-5; 13; *Mart. Isa.* 2:4-5). In this case the stereotype has a basis in fact.

Greco-Macedonian life, literature, religion, and social events were sexualized to an enormous extent. And their understanding of what was sexually appropriate behavior was quite different from that of Judaism and Christianity. Gentiles considered it acceptable behavior for a man to engage in sex with prostitutes, foreign women, and their slave girls. Mistresses were common. None of this counted as "adultery" (though judging by some ancient marriage contracts that forbade the husband from having children via a mistress, some wives objected to it nevertheless! P.Tebt. 1.104.14-27; P.Eleph. 1.8-9). Prostitution was taxed by the Roman government as a business. Even the aristocratic philosopher Plutarch took this situation for granted when he wrote to his daughter about marriage (*Conj. praec.* 16/140B). It was generally only when a man became involved with the wife of a free man that the behavior was condemned as adultery. A double standard applied, though: pagans would not tolerate their wives philandering with a slave or male prostitute (on ancient marriage, gender roles, and sexual practices: Pomeroy 1975; Pomeroy 1984; Clark 1993; Clark 1996, 36-55; Fantham et al. 1994; Blundell 1995). Contrast this with the advice in Prov 5:15-20; 7:1-27: it is wisdom for a man to remain faithful to one wife, and foolish to have liaisons with any other woman.

In addition, many religious and social events in Greek and Macedonian cities involved drinking and sex in one way or another. Temples were often used for celebrations that combined sacrifices with banqueting and entertainment afterward. Men held banquets without their wives, hiring "flute girls" and prostitutes for entertainment (Balsdon 1962, 201; Winter 2001, 82-85). Such parties are frequently pictured on Greek vases. A number of Greek and Roman cults had ceremonies or holy objects with explicit sexual symbolism and which at times encouraged sexual wantonness. One of the most popular of these throughout Macedonia was the cult of Dionysus (Sakellariou 1983, 205). As the god of wine, his festivals were often a sort of Greek Mardi Gras, including lewd processions with men carrying enormous false phalloi (Burkert 1985, 290-92; Kerényi 1976, 131, 136; Donfried 2002, 23-24). Drinking cups from classical to imperial times are commonly found everywhere having inscriptions to Dionysus or Dionysiac scenes. Phallic symbolism seems also to have been part of the cults of Cabirus (Thessalonica's patron deity in the first century) and Serapis, also found in the city (Edson 1948, 201; Donfried 2002, 25-26; and Green 2002, 35-36, 43-46 for other examples of sexually charged cults). And as Christian apologists were later to point out, many Greek myths involved the gods committing adultery with each other or with humans. Although some philosophers gave embarrassed allegorical meaning to these traditions, many ordinary pagans simply took encouragement from these stories for their own liberties.

This day-to-day cultural situation stirs Paul's concern that the Thessalonian believers avoid adultery and be different from their society. Paul goes even beyond the ethics of the popular philosophers, which he is aware of (Malherbe 1987; Malherbe 2000, 96). He insists that the totality of the Christian life be set in the context of *sanctification*: believers are devoted to the Lord and called to live in a way that befits the Holy Spirit given to them (1 Thess 4:3, 7-8).

IN THE TEXT

1. Introduction (4:1-2)

■ 1 The paraenesis or exhortation begins with a strong plea for the Thessalonians to push themselves to go beyond what they have already achieved in living according to the apostolic teaching.

As for what remains (*loipon,* As for other matters) sometimes introduces the conclusion of a letter (2 Cor 13:11; Gal 6:17; Eph 6:10; Phil 4:8), but not always. It can occur well before the end (Phil 3:1; 2 Thess 3:1). Some commentators think it has the inferential sense, **and so** (Moule 1959, 161, 207; Malherbe 2000, 218; Furnish 2007, 87). There is another conjunction here that also means **therefore** (*oun,* not translated in the NIV); it never occurs with *loipon* when it closes a letter. The sense seems to be "therefore what follows in the letter is based on what we have rehearsed of our mutual faith and friendship, and flows out of my prayer that God strengthen you."

We ask you and urge you. The repetition of synonyms gives an urgency to the tone. A similar formula was used in letters from Hellenistic monarchs politely "requesting" that a town do something (Best 1986, 154-55). These letters used the same term, **urge** (Gk.: *parakaleō*), which often introduces Paul's ethical exhortations (Rom 12:1; 1 Cor 1:10; 4:16; Eph 4:1; 1 Thess 2:12; 4:10; 5:14; 2 Thess 3:12; Phlm 9; compare 1 Pet 2:11; 5:1; → 1 Thess 3:1-2). *Parakaleō* has many meanings, but together with **ask** it intensifies the sense of exhorting others to follow a certain course. Paul exhorts them **in the Lord Jesus**, where **in** is used for **by means of** (compare Rom 5:10, "*through* his life" [lit. "in"]; Col 1:16, "*by* him all things were created" [CEV, ESV, HCSB, KJV, NASB]). Paul appeals to the authority of the risen Jesus. It is **the Lord** who is the source of the church's norms and its new ethical existence, which flows out of its saving relationship with God in Christ.

Paul's request in Greek is interrupted by two subordinate clauses that appeal to the Thessalonians' prior knowledge and present obedience. The basic sentence is: **we ask you and urge you . . . to do this more and more.** What they are to do . . . more of (see 3:12) is **to live in order to please God.** The church was given the apostles' authoritative teaching as their guide for this: **just as you received from us** (on **receive** as a term for passing on authoritative tradition, → 1 Thess 2:13). The NIV makes explicit the cultural implications of the verb: **we instructed you.** Paul's original teaching encompassed how Christians were to live.

To **please God** is to seek to embody his will in our lives by faith. Sometimes in the OT where the Hebrew said "walk with God," the LXX translated it **please God** (Gen 5:22, 24; 6:9; 17:1; Ps 116:8-9; see Wis. 4:10; Heb. 11:5). The Jewish translators clearly understood **please God** as a "functional equivalent," meaning **live one's life** devoted to the Creator. These ideas are found together in Col 1:10, where Paul prays for believers to have wisdom to "live a life [lit. 'walk'] worthy of the Lord and please him in every way." And in Rom 12:1 Paul urges believers to think of their physical lives as "a living sacrifice, holy and *pleasing* to God."

■ **2** Paul reminds them of the apostolic **instructions** (*parangelias* [v 2]) that the evangelists **gave** the Thessalonians. *Parangelias* is often translated **orders** and implies they come from someone with authority (Best 1986, 157; Green 2002, 186; compare Acts 5:28; 16:24; 1 Tim 1:18; used in Hellenistic Egypt for a "summons" to appear in court [MM, 480-81]; see Spicq 1994, 3:10). Although the letter is a friendly one, Paul can move smoothly between writing as an encouraging brother and writing as an apostle whose word carries the weight of the Lord who sent him.

It is typical of ancient moral instruction to remind the audience of what they already **know**, particularly among friends (Malherbe 2000, 219, 221-22). This compliments their knowledge and establishes common ground between speaker and audience. Paul also praises them for the faithfulness they have already shown ("as in fact you are living" [1 Thess 4:1]).

Paul appealed to them "in the Lord Jesus" to please God (v 1); then he says his **instructions** had been given to them ***through the Lord Jesus*** (v 2). ***Through*** could mean ***through*** Jesus' own words, his teaching repeated to them (Best 1986, 157-58; Wanamaker 1990, 149). Or Paul could be speaking as apostle **by the authority of** the risen Lord (Green 2002, 186; see Rom 15:30; 1 Cor 1:10). Although we don't want to rule out that traditions from Jesus' earthly ministry were used by the apostle, the best sense fitting with the letter seems to be the second one. The risen Lord has sent Paul and authorizes his teaching.

2. Sanctification and Sexuality (4:3-8)

■ **3** It is God's will that you should be sanctified. **God's will** is known to them from the apostle's "instructions" (v 2). **Will** refers to what someone wishes to happen. Because it is **God's** it is not optional for believers. Knowing **God's will** is necessary to please him (v 1). And God's desire that believers **be sanctified** entails sexual purity, says Paul.

Earlier the apostle prayed that God strengthen their hearts *in holiness* (3:13). Now he encourages their ***sanctification***, the process or result of being made holy (Paul's Greek uses the noun *hagiasmos* rather than the verb in 4:3). This involves being wholly devoted to God; belonging to him thanks to the life, death, and resurrection of Jesus Christ. In the OT, holiness defined Israel as a distinctive people in covenant with one God only, and different from all other nations. "Israel belongs to God and it must behave in light of that" (Goldingay 2009, 608). Israel is called to imitate God's holiness, which is concerned with purity and justice (Lev 19:2; 20:7, 26; Brueggemann 1997, 289-90). So Israel's holiness comes out of its covenantal *relationship* with God expressed in lifestyle (Coleson 2008, 30).

The same holds true for holiness in the NT, only the relationship with God is intensified especially by two things: the sacrifice of Christ on our behalf and God indwelling all believers through the Holy Spirit (4:8; Paige 2008, 43-56; Fee 1994, 827-45, 880-81). Holiness also involves imitation of God's character (Exod 19:5-6; Rom 6:19, 22; Eph 5:1-3). Hence, it is associated with a certain kind of ethical life, although ethics alone cannot be equated with holiness. The preceding prayer (1 Thess 3:12-13) also suggests that *love* is necessary to becoming holy, and an exhortation to love follows this call to holiness (4:9-10). This makes sense, since Christ taught that love was the key to understanding and fulfilling all the commandments and to imitating God (Matt 5:44-45, 48; 22:34-40; Mark 12:28-31; also Paul, Rom 13:9-10).

The specific manifestation of their **sanctification** Paul focuses on is that **you should avoid sexual immorality** (*apechesthai . . . tēs porneias*). This was one of the provisions of the Jerusalem Council's decree concerning Gentile converts and was also traditional Jewish teaching (Acts 15:20, 29). Paul and his companions very likely delivered this along with other elementary instruction to the new church (16:4; 1 Thess 4:1-2, 6*b*; Green 2002, 190). *Porneia* refers in Paul and other NT writers to any type of sexual behavior outside the bounds of heterosexual marriage (MM, 529; BDAG, 854). It can be used where the specific sin is adultery (Matt 5:32; 19:9), an incestuous marriage (1 Cor 5:1), consorting with prostitutes (1 Cor 6:13), or any sexual sin generally (Acts 15:20; 2 Cor 12:21; perhaps 1 Cor 6:18). In 1 Cor 6:19-20 Paul holds that believers' experience of the *Holy* Spirit exhibits that they belong to God and consequently should remain sexually pure: "your **body is a temple** of the Holy Spirit . . . You are not your own; you were bought at a price. Therefore honor God with your **body**."

Modern readers may wonder why Paul seems to limit **sanctification** to sexual purity. The answer is, holiness *is* much broader than sexuality for Paul (Rom 7:12; 12:1; 2 Cor 6:6; Col 3:12). But he is writing a pastoral letter, not a manual of ethics. The intention is to address urgent needs of *this* church in its specific situation. And in the culture of Thessalonica, extramarital sex was epidemic (→ Behind the Text for 1 Thess 4:1-12, above). Avoiding *porneia* is important because bodies are integral elements of who human beings are. Spirituality is not just a mental thing (Deut 6:4-5; Mark 12:29-31; Rom 12:1-2; 1 Cor 6:19-20).

■ **4-5** The next clause elaborates on how believers keep "God's will" avoiding "sexual immorality" (1 Thess 4:3). Its meaning is somewhat obscure because of Paul's unusual language. Literally it sounds like: **[that] each of you know to acquire his own vessel in holiness and honor** (v 4). **Vessel** is *skeuos*, which can mean a "thing" or "possession"; a "vessel, pot, or other container"; or an "instrument" in everyday usage. Three possible meanings have been proposed for it here.

(*a*) It refers to the human **body**, particularly in its sexual aspect. Paul is saying people must practice self-control over their own bodies and avoid sexual immorality (Tertullian, *Res.* 16; John Chrysostom, *Hom. 1 Thess.* 5; Lightfoot 1957, 54; Bruce 1982, 83; Richard 1995, 198; Green 2002, 192-94; Shogren 2012, 161-64). In favor of this are a number of places elsewhere where the term *skeuos* is used for persons or their bodies: Acts 9:15; Rom 9:22-23; 2 Cor 4:7; 2 Tim 2:21; 1 Pet 3:7.

(*b*) **Vessel** is a circumlocution for male genitals (Wanamaker 1990, 152; Yarbrough 1999; Smith 2001, 92, 103-5; Fee 2009, 147-50; Donfried 2010, 507), or both male and female genitalia (Trozzo 2012; though she allows it could be **body** also). This could be an extended sense from the use of ***vessel*** for **body**; or, more likely, a euphemistic use of *skeuos* as "thing" or "equipment" (BDAG, 927-28; LSJM, 1607). It fits the sexual context. And (some say) it explains why Paul used the obscure word "vessel" instead of common words for "body," as well as his unusual use of the verb *ktasthai*. He was making a euphemism. But it is a rare use of the term. It is claimed that *skeuos* for "male member" is found at 1 Sam 21:5 (a story about David's men keeping their "vessels . . . holy" [KJV] in order to eat sacred bread at a sanctuary). But the Hebrew text is more easily read this way than the Greek of the LXX. The LXX paraphrases, omits any mention of "vessels" for the soldiers, reassigns the vessels (or "instruments") to David, and the purpose is not clear. It might refer to his soldiers or the condition of the camp as easily as to genitals. This definition also assumes that at 1 Thess 4:4-5 Paul addresses only male Christians, which is questionable.

(*c*) **Vessel** refers to a wife. It refers to a wife at 1 Pet 3:7, as the "weaker vessel" (KJV; by implication the husband is a "vessel" also, like the meaning "person"). In rabbinic Hebrew the term "vessel" (*kĕlî*) could refer to a wife, and in addition other terms for containers were used as metaphors for a wife in the OT and Jewish literature (Yarbrough 1985, 72-73; Prov 5:15-18). This interpretation also fits with the normal meaning of the verb ***acquire*** (*ktasthai*): to gain possession of something one does not have (BDAG, 572; LSJM, 1001; Malherbe 2000, 226-27).

Until recent years, the meaning "wife" had the strongest linguistic support, though not the most obvious choice of metaphor. As noted, ***acquire*** (*ktasthai*) in classical and Hellenistic Greek only meant to "possess" something in the perfect tense; otherwise it always meant to *gain* possession of something. And Paul uses it in the present tense. One can ***acquire*** a wife, but not one's own body. This verb is used for acquiring a wife in the LXX, Apocrypha, and Greek literature (see Ruth 4:10 LXX; Sir 36:29; Frame 1912, 150; Yarbrough 1985, 70-72). Translating the phrase *to heautou skeuos ktasthai* as **control your own body** (NIV and NRSV; "his body" [NEB, Phillips, REB]; "his own body" [ESV, HCSB]) gives the present tense a meaning normally only found in the perfect. Further, it assumes the extremely rare meaning **control** (1 Thess 4:4) rather than "possess."

Also in favor of (*c*) is the similar rabbinic metaphor mentioned above, employing the Hebrew "vessel" for a woman or a wife. This background cannot be too easily dismissed by saying Paul's audience was not Jewish. For non-Jewish Greek and Latin writers do use the metaphor of containers for women, denoting their "passive" role in reproduction (Fredrickson 2003). **Vessel** for "wife" seems to be related to the 1 Pet 3:7 usage, as well as other biblical metaphors for wives employing containers. And there are parallels between 1 Thess 4:3-6 and 1 Cor 7:2, where Paul urges embracing the benefits of legitimate marriage partly to avoid *porneia* (Furnish 2007, 89-90). Finally, **wife** seems to fit with the instructions to avoid "sexual immorality" (1 Thess 4:3), to not wrong a brother "in this matter" (via adultery [v 6]), and the concern for honor (v 4).

On the other hand, a number of serious objections have been raised against option *c*. Paul could easily have said *wife* if that is what he meant. Why the obtuse language? In other instances where Greek writers used *ktaomai* for "acquire a wife," the word for "wife" (*gynē*) is always used, not *vessel*. And to refer to a *wife* as a *vessel* might imply a low view of women as merely sexual instruments, not typical of Paul (Milligan 1908, 49; Wanamaker 1990, 152; Richard 1995, 198). The 1 Pet 3:7 passage is not conclusive either, since the sense—the wife as the *weaker* vessel—implies that *skeuos* refers to both husband and wife and so simply means "person" or even "body."

Option *c* also makes for unexpected and jarring transitions. The letter up to this point has addressed the church as a whole. Would Paul move from encouraging everyone toward love and holiness (1 Thess 3:11-13; 4:1-3) to suddenly address only unmarried adult males, and without any indication he is changing his audience (vv 4-8)? And then switch back again to general advice without a transition (v 9)? When Paul gives such specific advice, he usually makes it clear that his attention has shifted (1 Cor 7:3-5, 8-9; Gal 5:3; 1 Thess 5:14; 2 Thess 3:11-12). Since marriage was the norm, we would expect unmarried adult males to be a minority in the church. And how could Paul teach here that everyone (**each of you**) should be married, contrary to his advice in 1 Cor 7:8 (Fee 2009, 148)? Finally, Smith (2001) has shown that occasionally in later Hellenistic Greek the verb *ktasthai* may have the perfect meaning ("possess") in nonperfect tenses. This makes the other two options viable translations.

In light of the above, the meaning **body** fits the literary and linguistic context better. The use of *vessel* to designate persons generally is well known in pagan, Jewish, and early Christian Greek literature, particularly when people are viewed as servants or "instruments" of another (LSJM, 1607; *TDNT* 7:358-60). See examples above under (*a*), and Polybius, *Hist.* 13.5.7; Jer 51:34 (28:34 LXX); 50:25 (27:25 LXX); Hos 8:8 LXX; Wis 15:7; *T. Naph.* 8:6;

Apoc. Mos. 16:5; Acts 9:15; Rom 9:22-23; 2 Tim 2:21. Christian and Jewish writers can use *skeuos* in an extended sense to indicate a person's physical body, often seen over against the interior self (soul or spirit). This metaphor is aided by the image of a pot as a container: 1 Pet 3:7; *Herm. Mand.* 5.1.2; *Barn.* 11.9; 21.8 (the body is "the good vessel"); 7.3 (Christ's body was "the vessel of the Spirit"); *Apoc. Sedr.* 11:5, 10. In between is Paul's use in 2 Cor 4:7, referring to the apostles as "jars [*skeuesin*] of clay." This image combines the ideas of the apostle as God's "instrument"; the *mortality* of the body as clay (Gen 2:7); and the *lowliness* of the apostle as a servant (clay containers were used for common cookware and storage; see Isa 29:16; 64:8; Jer 18:6).

Why would Paul not simply say "control your *body*" (*sōma*)? Paul's choice of the words **vessel** and **control** emphasizes that the body is subject to believers' will, to be employed for good or evil. The body is the *instrument* (one meaning of *skeuos*) of the mind and soul. In sanctification Christians are enabled by God's grace to be emancipated from slavery to the body's passions; they are slaves of God and his righteousness (Rom 6:6-7, 12-14).

It makes more sense that Paul would give a general exhortation to *all* of the Thessalonians concerning the use of their bodies here, not just unmarried men, since he is speaking of God's will for everyone's sanctification (1 Thess 4:3; see 3:13). Paul's exhortation may even be seen as including women and their bodies also (Trozzo 2012, 44-51).

Under this reading, the verb *ktasthai* has the perfect meaning **possess**. The sense seems to be akin to the English idiom "get a hold on yourself." They are to "take possession of" their bodies and passions; in other words, act as owners of themselves, not victims of passion. Ancient moral philosophy often viewed the passions, particularly those tied more closely to the body, as a wild and irrational element within the soul, chaining it to the body and making humans more savage and corruptible. The body itself was seen as a hindrance to the rational, godlike philosophic life that the soul should enjoy (→ "Beliefs about Death and the Afterlife in the Ancient World" sidebar at Behind the Text for 1 Thess 4:13-18, below). Although Paul may use similar language at times, he does not hold the body to be evil or against God's perfect will. It is part of his creation, and in God's plan the body is included in Christ's redemption (Rom 12:1; 1 Cor 6:13, 19-20). But it must be consciously submitted to the grace of God to avoid remaining part of the old broken order that resists and subverts the will of the Father who made it.

So Paul wants the Thessalonians not to be driven by their bodies (**vessels**) and passions but to master them and direct them to a godly use (*ktasthai* in the participle form can also mean "owner" of a slave or an animal: Isa 1:3 LXX; Philo, *Virt.* 98; *Legat.* 155; *Prob.* 149). Hence, several translators and commentators have understood *ktasthai* in 1 Thess 4:4 as **control** (ESV, HCSB, NIV, NRSV).

What does it mean for Christians to *possess* their own bodies **in a way that is holy and honorable** and **not in passionate lust** (4:4-5)? As already suggested, it expounds on the injunction "avoid sexual immorality" (v 3). Hence, the contrast with pagans (v 5); and it is the "matter" concerning which "no one should wrong" a fellow Christian (v 6).

The relationship to God is expressed by the first term describing the **way** believers **control** the **body: holy.** In Greek this is actually the same word translated "sanctified" in v 3 (*hagiasmos*). Clearly, holiness is not only "positional" for Paul (that is, legal or fictive) but is meant to have physical and social implications as well. Otherwise it could not be said to apply to the body as one's "vessel" used for God.

The concern for ***honor***, the second term describing control of the body, tells us that sanctification has a relationship to family and society. To receive ***honor*** requires conduct that one's social group will perceive as the most noble, upright, courageous, selfless, generous, and loyal (to family, friends, and the city/state). In regard to sexuality, Christians are called on to meet and surpass pagan standards of honor. One could say this is related to loving one's neighbor, as well as being a witness of the gospel to society. In theory, if not in practice, in Paul's day general norms would have preserved the virginity of girls before marriage and forbade adultery, at least for free people. And Mediterranean societies in general counseled women to dress and behave modestly in public. We find some of these ideals written into ancient marriage contracts (Pomeroy 1984, 97-98; P.Giss. 1.2; P.Tebt. 1.104.27-30).

Paul's idea of honor is not limited to society's standards, however. For believers should be guided by what God the Father considers **honorable** (4:4, 7-8; compare Rom 2:10; 12:2; 1 Cor 4:3-4). All belong to the God who purchased us at Christ's expense (1 Cor 6:19-20).

Verse 5 of 1 Thess 4 may allude to the tenth commandment, "You shall not covet your neighbor's wife" (Exod 20:17), for the LXX translates "covet" with the verb *epithymeō*, related to *epithymia*, **passion** (1 Thess 4:5). Taking someone else's wife is not allowed (as v 6 makes clear). In any case, the plain reference seems to be to sensuality that is out of control (Furnish 2007, 91), and so it has passed the bounds of what is honorable or holy. They are not to let the **passionate lust** that can arise from the **body** drive their behavior, **like the pagans** around them do. Here Paul sounds surprisingly like the moral philosophers, who also warned against being swamped by the passions and sought to train people to follow reason instead. However, Paul's analysis and solution are somewhat different, for the **body** is not a negative thing per se. And the solution is not mere reason, but relationship with God, love, and supernatural endowment with grace and the Spirit (3:13; 4:8; 2 Thess 2:16).

Christians are contrasted with **the pagans** [lit. "nations," or **Gentiles** (*ta ethnē*)], **who do not know God** (v 5). Ironically, most of the Thessalonian audience for this letter *were* ethnically **Gentiles**. Gentile was synonymous with "idolater" for Jews, because the other peoples did not know the one true Creator God (Ps 79:6; Isa 2:2-3; Mic 5:15; Jdt 4:12; 1 Macc 1:11-15, 43; 3:45, 48; 2 Macc 6:4). Turning away from God to idols causes a fundamental distortion in the human character, leading to sins of every sort. It leads to serious errors in moral judgment (Ps 106:36-39; Ezek 20:13-16; Wis 14:12-29; Rom 1:18-32), as with **passion.** Paul assumes that these Christians are different now from their family roots (see 1 Cor 1:23; Eph 4:17). They are a new people in Christ (2 Cor 5:17), a new community that worships the true and living God (1 Thess 1:9).

■ **6** Furthermore, to highlight how serious the consequences are of *not* following God's will for keeping one's body holy, Paul goes on to first speak about the injustice sexual immorality brings against others. They need to think about the consequences of their deeds for the other person involved. That is the way of love. Paul just spoke about using their bodies in an honorable way; here he points out that the effects of sexual immorality on the partner are dishonorable. He bans this injustice, and only then adds a warning about consequences for the perpetrator.

Some commentators have thought this verse marks a departure into a new topic because some of the terms (**in this matter, take advantage**) sound like a business or legal matter (see Malherbe 2000, 231-32, for references). However, v 7 indicates the topic is still about sexual purity and holiness. And the terms can be used more broadly. Paul may deliberately play on the business-sounding metaphors for the rhetorical effect he desires: to equate sexual behavior, which the Gentiles thought of as neutral, with financial fraud and greed—things that even the Gentiles abhorred.

Is v 6 directed at an actual case (**this matter**) in the church involving two families, reported to Paul by Timothy? While this is possible, Paul's rhetoric more likely suggests a strong exhortation and reminder to the community at large, in view of the fact that this could become a problem at any time.

The text builds on Paul's general admonition to the church, and **this matter** refers not to an individual case, but to the matter under discussion, namely *porneia* or sexual immorality. Also, Paul does not seek to argue his case, nor does he clearly refer to the church's misbehavior, as at 1 Cor 5:1; 6:1-6, 12-20; Col 2:16, 20-23; 1 Thess 5:14; 2 Thess 3:6-12. In fact, he has affirmed that they *are* pleasing God (1 Thess 4:2) and that he is teaching them to remind and strengthen them. This issue must have been a constant worry for Paul nevertheless, since Christian men and women mingled in private homes for worship. The intimate setting, the sense of community and affection, could easily have led to illicit relationships forming, especially given the lax cultural practices (Green 2002, 197). Such sin not only would wound the individual's relationship with God but also would endanger the church's peace and cohesion, not to mention its reputation with outsiders.

After his exhortation to self-control and abstention from sexual immorality, Paul adds **and that in this matter no one should wrong or take advantage of a brother or sister**. In Greek it continues the previous sentence with a verb in the infinitive. Most commentators and translations take it as parallel to v 4 ("It is God's will that you should be sanctified: that you should avoid sexual immorality . . . [that] no one should wrong or take advantage . . ."). It is possible, however, to read this as an infinitive expressing *purpose* (while normally this would be in the Greek genitive case, there are examples of it in the accusative, as here: Phil 2:13; 1 Thess 3:3; 2 Esd 6:8; Smyth 1984, 453, §2034e; Frame 1912, 146, 151-52; Bruce 1982, 81). Read this way, the sentence would tell us that the *goal* of living a holy life different from the world, abstaining from sexual sin, is to avoid selfish exploitation of the other: **so that no one should wrong or take advantage of a brother or sister.**

Brother (*adelphos*) refers to a fellow Christian. Paul could be speaking of a hypothetical **brother** who is a husband, wronged by a Christian who has defiled his wife. It is **wrong** because this behavior transgresses (*hyperbainein*) the divine order of marriage and sexual purity God has established. Adultery by the wife was also standard grounds for divorce in the ancient world. It was considered an attack on the honor of the husband and the extended family on both sides. The **wrong** would be especially egregious if it led to the wife divorcing her husband to take another man, allowable under Roman law. How does adultery **take advantage** of the husband? The verb *pleonektein* (**defraud, exploit**) suggests he is "cheated" of something, which could include his exclusive rights to his wife's affection, his honor, and the certainty that their children are his offspring. This may be true even if the object of sin is an unmarried woman and the **brother** harmed is her fiancé (Best 1986, 166).

If Paul used **brother** (*adelphos*) as a generic singular noun, like our word "sibling" (**brother or sister** [NIV, NRSV]), then the text may also be heard as condemning someone who takes **advantage** of a woman who is his **sister** in Christ by seducing her and using her sexually apart from marriage. To do so is to treat another human being as an object to be used rather than a person to be loved. In either case, the offender is acting like "the pagans" driven by "lust" (v 5), instead of acting like Christ's redeemed people.

While normally Jewish and Christian writers use metaphors and idioms for sexuality that are related to *cleanliness*, here Paul takes imagery from the realm of financial fraud. **Take advantage** of (*pleonektein*) implies the activity is due to greed (*pleonexia*) as well as fraud. Some people will not be satisfied with a normal marriage and the enjoyment of relations between husband and wife that God has provided. They must have more, betraying spouses and using people.

As noted earlier, Paul's unusual language here may be an attempt to help his Gentile audience make a cultural shift and understand how serious sexual sin is, by comparing it to things they already were serious about: greed and fraud. *Hyperbainein* occurs only once in the NT, and *pleonektein* occurs only five times (here and four times in 2 Corinthians). Using persons sexually outside marriage—even if it is consensual—is to "cheat" them for the sake of lust, a form of greed (compare Eph 4:19; and close association at Mark 7:22; Col 3:5). For the apostle Paul, all sex outside God's ordained order is sexual abuse of another person.

Paul reminds them how serious a matter sexual integrity is to their Savior: **the Lord will punish all those who commit such sins** (v 6b). Whether or not those involved in adultery admit it is wrong, the **Lord** abhors it. It is an offense to his divine order for the goodness of marriage. The **Lord** here is Jesus, as is Paul's normal usage. It may be an allusion to Ps 94:1 LXX, but the idea of God as Judge and Avenger is so generalized in Judaism it is hard to tell. Either way, Paul assigns to Jesus a role traditionally held by God.

The theme of sexual sin as *injustice* is continued in Paul's term describing the Lord: *ekdikos* (lit. **dispenser of justice** or **avenger** [NIV: **will punish**]). Paul does not specify whether the punishment is something present (as in Rom 1:18) or is a reference to the future judgment on the Day of the Lord. Either way, the warning is that sin has serious consequences. Believers should not treat sin lightly because of grace.

All these admonitions come by way of reminder, for Paul **told** them **and warned** them **before**. The apostles' fundamental instructions must have included some basic morals. They did not need a problem to arise before addressing this topic. The apostolic decree shows a concern for sexual immorality; and its association with idolatry and Gentiles would have also made teaching on it natural (→ v 3 above).

■ **7-8** Paul concludes this exhortation with three more reasons why Christians should take holy living seriously: (1) it is the nature of our calling from God (v 7); (2) to reject this demand is tantamount to rejecting God himself (v 8a); and (3) holiness is the corollary to having the indwelling Holy Spirit (v 8b).

Paul uses contrast to highlight the character of God's **call** into the kingdom (v 7). Negatively, it was **not . . . to be impure** (*akatharsia*), meaning **uncleanness** in a moral sense (2:3). Here it specifically refers to sexual corruption. Instead, God's call is **in holiness** (*en hagiasmō*). As seen earlier, Greek *en* can show a location ("in") or means ("by"). It may indicate the *state* into which Christians are brought by God's calling (Frame 1912, 154; Best 1986, 168); or the *manner* of that calling: "he called us in a way that involves sanctification" (Marshall 1983, 113). God's calling through the gospel is a **holy** call because it comes from a holy God who offers relationship with him as his own people (Lev 19:2; 1 Cor 1:2; 1 Pet 1:2, 15-16). And it calls people *into* **holiness**: in the new saving relationship with God it is natural and necessary that his people reflect God's character. And that character is radically out of line with the sexual freedom of Gentile society. God's salvation is about redeeming the whole person, body and soul. In this sentence we see God as the initiator of holiness as an integral part of his saving and healing grace. Although in popular thought holiness is often perceived as unloving, for Paul the truth is the opposite. True holiness leads to the love of God—real, unselfish love—for one another (1 Thess 4:9-10).

To stress the seriousness of this ethic, Paul emphasizes that it is not simply a human-made custom. Whoever **rejects** God's call for holiness in their marriage and sexual lives **does not reject a human being but God** (v 8a). It is not human imagination or socialization that created this ethic. It comes from God the Creator and Redeemer.

Finally, lest his exhortation end on a harsh note of condemnation, Paul adds a note of promise wrapped in the final reason for living to please God. The God who calls us to holiness and commands us to live in purity is also **the very God who gives you his Holy Spirit** (v 8b). The argument implied here is that since the Spirit who indwells Christians is holy, those who have the Spirit should be characterized by ethical purity. It assumes that all Christians have the gift of the Spirit (Rom 8:9-10; 1 Cor 12:13). In a similar case at 1 Cor 6:19-20, Paul argues that prostitution is inconsistent with Christian existence because "your body is a temple of the Holy Spirit within you, whom you have from God" (ESV).

Elsewhere in his letters Paul makes it clear that the Spirit within believers opposes the sinful nature and produces the fruit of love and righteousness in believers' lives (Rom 5:5; 8:2-6, 12-14; 14:17; 1 Cor 6:11; Gal 5:16-17, 22-25; compare Ezek 36:25-27; Paige 1993). This is one of the Spirit's main functions: to lead and shape believers in the image of God's Son. So the *motivation* for holy living is simultaneously a *promise* of God's blessed presence and divine assistance to become what he has called us to be. Thus the church is empowered to carry forward in this age the charge given to Israel of old: "Be holy because I, the LORD your God, am holy" (Lev 19:2).

FROM THE TEXT

Just as Paul's churches had to combat pagan society's casual attitude toward sex, so in our day the church faces the ideology of the sexual revolution that pervades our society. This philosophy claims that sex is not a moral issue, only a private preference. All sexual ethics, it claims, are mere human constructs, culturally relative. It has become an unassailable principle for many that there are almost no limits to what one can do, or who one can do it with. We are told the word of God no longer applies to modern people. Sex is detached from marriage and childbearing. Sex has become an ersatz deity, the means to freedom and self-actualization. It is perhaps the most popular form of idolatry of the twenty-first century. Like hawkers of patent medicines, magazines in every grocery aisle promote sex tips and suggest that the customers who practice them will save their relationships and have a happy life. Yet the promises that the sexual revolution is making cannot be fulfilled, and its effects are disastrous.

Though people desire stable relationships, they are becoming less and less tenable as society imbibes the values of the sexual revolution. In 1930, there was a divorce for every 5.75 marriages; in 1965, one for every 4.24 marriages; by 2011, one for every 1.9 marriages. And though people still live together without marriage, these relationships end more frequently than marriages do (U.S. Dept. of Health, Education, and Welfare 1950, 72; U.S. Dept. of Health, Education, and Welfare 1978, 23; CDC 2013, 16, 18). And the effects on our children are catastrophic. Four percent of births in 1950 were to unmarried mothers; in 2013, it was 41 percent (U.S. Dept. of Health, Education, and Welfare 1950, 93; CDC 2014, 6). We are raising a generation of children who do not know a stable home with both biological parents in a committed relationship. The cumulative effects of this for children often include poverty, educational problems, self-esteem and social adjustment problems, an increased chance of failed marriages, and an increased likelihood for trouble with the law.

And what reader needs to be reminded of the dark legacy of the sexual revolution's naïveté, the prevalence of debilitating and deadly STDs? In the past quarter century, AIDS alone has killed more Americans than died fighting in all foreign wars from World War I through the Iraq war (UNAIDS 2013). Even for the many who escape physical harm, there is evidence that playing at a callous attitude toward sex can leave serious emotional scars. In a recent study of college students, it was shown that many on both secular and religious campuses are deeply unhappy with the cultural pressure to have casual sex without commitments, experiencing "sadness and even despair about hooking up" (Freitas 2013, 12). What they truly crave is emotional intimacy and commitment, but what they find is only humiliation (ibid., 34-36). The truth of Paul's words about not allowing lust to lead us to "wrong or take advantage of" (1 Thess 4:6) another has taken on haunting new meanings in this age.

Paul challenges us to bravely live counter-cultural lives, knowing that doing so is not only to live *for God* but also to live *for our neighbor*. Though the Christian sexual ethic may be pictured as narrow and critical of others, the truth is the opposite: it is in fact the most loving thing one can do for one's brother and sister. God still calls believers today to a holy life, devoted to him (1 Thess 4:3, 7). And one important way this still manifests itself is in our sexual lives. God calls believers to reject the ideology of the sexual revolution, which exploits persons.

God has made sanctification possible for believers by the gift of the indwelling Holy Spirit, who marks believers as sacred to God (v 8; compare 1 Cor 6:19-20). In this passage, Paul shows us that salvation includes our body and not just the "soul" or the mind. God desires to redeem our sexual relationships, which are also part of his good creation, and have their proper sphere. We are not to operate like animals, driven blindly by instinct; nor like those who refuse to recognize the goodness of the boundaries God has set to "passions."

Our guideline is God's revealed will through his word, the teaching of his prophets, apostles, and above all his Son. These agree that a loving (heterosexual) marriage is the honorable, right, and healthy sphere in God's sight for human sexuality—for those who are not called to celibacy. Even if many believers may have fallen short in the past, what matters here, as with other errors, is what we decide to do from now on, to serve our Lord with gratitude, in humble dependence on his forgiveness and grace (1 John 1:9; Eph 2:1-10; 4:32—5:2; 1 Thess 1:9).

Christians need to be unashamed about reclaiming the notion of sanctification for today, for it is about the beautiful, restorative healing of human persons that the gospel announces to us and God's grace makes possible. It is about finding what it is to cherish honor with God and love of God. "I am with you always, to the very end of the age" was our Lord's promise at his resurrection (Matt 28:20). The good news is about a relationship; the presence of God the Father, Son, and Holy Spirit with us to strengthen and transform us.

3. Sanctified Love (4:9-12)

BEHIND THE TEXT

Some think the phrase "now about" (*peri de* [4:9]) implies Paul is responding to a letter from the Thessalonians (see 1 Cor 7:1; Frame 1912, 157; Green 2002, 202; Malherbe [cautiously] 2000, 243); or to oral questions they gave Timothy (Bruce 1982, 89; Wanamaker 1990, 159). *Peri de* may simply introduce a new topic in a letter and does not always reflect a prior inquiry (Mitchell 1989). It makes sense that the comments on "love for one another" (1 Thess 4:9) connect with the exhortations of vv 11-12 and respond to Timothy's report. The Thessalonians may have been puzzled as to how far God's command to love required them to support believers who would not work. So vv 9-12 are a single paragraph with the theme of Christian love worked out in the community. It continues the theme begun at vv 1-3*a*, that of living to please God as his sanctified people.

The injunctions of vv 11-12 appear to be Paul's first attempt to deal with a problem that would worsen. He addresses it again at 5:14, then more sternly in 2 Thess 3:6-15. In both letters Paul urges Christians to work and support themselves and to live a "quiet" life, and it is apparent from 1 Thess 5:14 and in 2 Thess 3:11 that some are not doing this. Paul also is concerned that their behavior will tarnish the church's witness to outsiders. The latter passage makes it clear that those not working are being fed and supported by other Christians. This explains Paul's reference to his own example of working "in order not to be a burden to anyone" (1 Thess 2:9), and why he urges them to "not be dependent on anybody" (4:12).

It is difficult to know exactly *why* some Thessalonian believers did not work, for Paul never mentions this directly. The most popular explanation in the twentieth century was that eschatology was the problem: some in the church believed Jesus' return was so imminent that ordinary matters of life were irrelevant and they abandoned work (Frame 1912, 160; Best 1986, 175-77; Bruce 1982, 92; Marshall 1983, 117). Another theory is that some believed the millennium had already dawned and normal social structures, including work, did not apply to them (Jewett 1986, 168-78).

It is true that already in the early church some proclaimed an imminent return of Christ, leading to social disruption (Eusebius, *Hist. eccl.* 5.18; Bruce 1982, 90). However, ideas of a millenarian movement appeal to historical examples that are post-Christian and based on later developments in Christian millennial thinking or in Jewish messianic thought. There are no reliable examples of pre-Christian "millenarian radicalism" that might have fanned such thought in Paul's day. Another objection is that Paul nowhere in 1 or 2 Thessalonians explicitly links the matters of work or social disruption to eschatology; this is an inference from the presence of both issues in the same letter.

Another theory is that some abandoned work to evangelize, leading to two problems: with Christians, they want to be supported; with outsiders, they are making themselves obnoxious by attacking their morals and religion and by not working (Barclay 1993; Still 1999, 246-50; Furnish 2007, 98; Malherbe 1987, 99-101; anticipated in Best 1986, 175). This abused the love of Christians and brought down trouble on the church, two things Paul seeks to correct here.

Recently it has been proposed that the institution of patronage is behind the problems in 1 Thess 4:11-12 and 2 Thess 3:6-15. Paul is urging Christians to withdraw from patron-client relations, which allowed some Christians to live off their patron without working, and also involved them in city politics (Winter 1994, 41-60; Green 2002, 208-13; Witherington 2006, 118, 122-23). Patrons typically gave clients a daily food ration and political or other favors that their wealth and status afforded. Clients boosted the status of patrons by supporting them in court, in elections, and lending any other help needed. Paul calls on the Christian clients to follow his example and become independent, able to support themselves and also to benefit others in need (Winter 1994, 48-49).

Although patronage operated everywhere, this theory depends on at least two questionable presumptions. First, patronage did not entail the full financial support of every client. Most of the examples for this come from the superwealthy patrons of Rome, whose full support of a few artists, writers, or "friends" was not typical. The Roman satirist Martial warns a reader against expecting an easy living in Rome, saying "barely three or four" have managed to make it by courting the rich (*Epigr.* 3.38). And Juvenal mocks the rich man's generosity toward his lesser clients, who get nothing more than a dinner every few months, and a wretched one at that (*Sat.* 5.19-23; also 1.127-138). There were many kinds of exchanges of services and favors that characterized the patronage relationship, but full financial support is rare (Saller 1982, 1, 7-40).

Second, to be a client of a rich man one would have to be a citizen of sufficient social status or family connections to deserve notice. Patrons did not normally support lower-class people, unless the client was a freedman, a former slave of the patron. In the few cases where someone received something close to full support, the client would be a high-status person, although poorer than the benefactor. But the Thessalonian Christians appear to be mostly from the lower working classes. Paul expects them all to work and regards some people's indolence as unnatural, implying their status as manual laborers of various sorts. He reports the poverty of the Macedonians to Corinth (2 Cor 8:1-4).

And if Christians of Thessalonica were attached to prominent patrons, why is the church persecuted? For one of the primary benefits of a patron is political alliance and protection. However, it is unimaginable that a pagan patron would continue to support a Christian who had renounced the gods of society. This position was not only highly offensive but would politically endanger the patron as well. For all these reasons, it is highly unlikely that patronage is an issue in the work stoppage.

Acts does report that some aristocratic women became converts (Acts 17:4), but we have no evidence that their husbands converted. Without the backing of their husbands, it is doubtful they could behave as patrons of other Christians very effectively—certainly not supporting individuals by themselves, though these women may well have contributed to the common fund.

The simplest explanation for the problem addressed here and in 2 Thess 3:6-15 is that it is an abuse of the church's common fund for charity. Charity to the poor was a well-established religious obligation in Judaism, going back to pentateuchal legislation (Exod 23:10-11; Deut 15:7-11) and the prophets (Isa 58:6-9; Amos 5:11-15). Jewish teachers called almsgiving *tsedākāh*, "righteousness," and Jesus commended it to his followers (Matt 6:2-4). Judaism regarded almsgiving as the distinguishing mark of a righteous person. It was held to be a substitute for sacrifice and to gain God's favor (Tob 4:6-11, 16-17; 12:8-10; Sir 7:10; 29:8-13; 35:3-4; *Sib. Or.* 2:80; *2 En.* 63; Ps.-Phoc. 22-29). Those who refuse to help the poor face particular torment in hell (*Vis. Ezra* 27-32; compare Luke 16:19-31). There were regular methods of distributing alms to the needy and widows on a weekly basis within Jewish communities. The Mishnah tells of the highly respected almoners who had charge of the poor fund, "collected by two and distributed by three [men]" once a week in the village (*m. Pe'ah* 8:7).

The apostles taught the early church the vital importance of giving to the needy, and they seem to have immediately established formal institutions like those in synagogues or villages for handling distributions to the poor (Acts

6:1-6; 20:35; 1 Cor 16:1-3; Gal 2:10; 1 Tim 5:9-10; James 1:26-27; 2:14-17; 1 John 3:17-18). It is safe to assume that such a practice had begun at Thessalonica among the Christians also, but for some unknown reason was being abused (against Ascough, who doubts Jewish influence in Macedonia or on church organization there and understands the church as modeled on a Hellenistic voluntary association [2003, 176-90, 202]).

Possibly some claimed support so that they could preach the gospel, citing the precedent of other apostles. Some members may have believed that love required the church to support any who asked, as Jesus commanded, even if they were able to work (Matt 5:42; Luke 6:30; 1 Thess 4:9-10; Malherbe 2000, 243). Some ambivalence over how to apply Jesus' words also occurs in the *Didache* (*Did.* 1.5-6).

IN THE TEXT

■ **9** While denying the **need to write** to them about **love for one another** (*philadelphia*, also **brotherly love**), Paul, in fact, does write about it. This way he can raise an ethical issue in a gentler way by asking them to *continue* their behavior (a paraenetic technique: Wanamaker 1990, 159). Verse 9 contains a textual variant: some Greek manuscripts read "*you* have no need to write to you"; others, "*we* have no need to write to you"; and a few, "*you* have no need that *you be written to*." The first is most likely the original because the others are efforts to correct it. The sentence is an example of ellipsis, where the complete thought would be: "you have no need [for us] to write to you" (see ellipses at Rom 5:15; 1 Cor 15:13).

Philadelphia is usually used in secular Greek of love for biological siblings. The Stoic Epictetus spoke of slave and master as "kinsmen" and "brothers by nature" because both were conceived by Zeus (*Diatr.* 1.13.3-4; see also 3.22.81-82; 3.22.96). Paul depends on Jesus' teaching that the community of people who did God's will were his family (Mark 3:34-35; 10:29-30). This new family of faith supported Christians when they experienced alienation from their natural families and from society (Green 2002, 203).

The reason the Thessalonians do not need to be instructed is because they **have been taught by God to love each other** (1 Thess 4:9) and are actively showing this love to other Christians "throughout Macedonia" (v 10). **Taught by God** echoes the language of Isa 54:3 (see John 6:45) but reflects also the prophecy of Jer 31:31-34, that someday God would inaugurate a new covenant, renew his people, and write his law on their hearts. Its realization in the present means the church is an eschatological community, a sign of God's work. Paul may also be opposing the claim of philosophers to be "self-taught" (Malherbe 2000, 244). **Taught by God** refers in the first place to the gospel and all it entails, including the new way of life (2:13; Malherbe 2000, 244). For the apostles believed that God had sent Jesus as Messiah, and the saving story about him, in fulfillment of Scripture, was all a gift from the Father. Believers also have the indwelling Holy

Spirit who teaches them (Rom 8:15-16; 1 Cor 2:9-13; 12:7-8; compare Phil 2:13; 1 John 2:20-21; Barn. 21.6; Frame 1912, 158).

The **love** that they learned about in the gospel, and that the Holy Spirit grew in their hearts (Rom 5:5), is a central facet of Jesus' teaching. To love one another is Jesus' command to his disciples and the key to understanding God's will (Matt 5:43-48; 22:34-40; Mark 12:28-31; Luke 6:27-36; John 13:34-35; → 1 Thess 1:2-3). This idea is not new to Jesus; "Love your neighbor as yourself" is found in Lev 19:18, and the idea if not the verb is present amid the OT's ethics, its call for compassion toward the needy, and the demand for justice. We could say, though, that Jesus *embodies* what a life of perfect love looks like for the first time ever. His living, teaching, healings, death, and resurrection all give a fulsomeness and significance to the word that goes beyond what was known before. Paul continues Jesus' emphasis on love as the central dynamic of Christian living and ethical decision-making (Rom 14:15; 1 Cor 8:1; 13:1-3, 13; Gal 5:6).

■ **10** Paul praises the Thessalonians for already enacting God's love: they "love each other," and **all of God's family throughout Macedonia** (1 Thess 4:9*b*, 10*a*; see 1:7-8). Hardship has not restricted their attention to themselves, but they show godly love and concern for other believers in their province.

How could they have loved **all** other Christians in **Macedonia**? Of course there is some rhetorical force to the **all** (not "you have *met* every believer" but "you have shown that you love *all* Macedonian Christians, wherever they may be, by your behavior"). It is early enough in the history of the evangelization of the province that it was possible for "all" the Christian communities—probably still a limited number—to keep in touch with each other. It may be that the Thessalonian church hosted Christian visitors from elsewhere, for it was a natural trade hub for both land and sea routes. There is evidence that some Christian teachers and prophets traveled from church to church exercising their ministry, and these would have found a ready host among the Thessalonians (Luke 22:35-36; Acts 8:4-8, 26-40; 3 John 3-8; *Did.* 11-13). The Thessalonians may have sent out their own evangelists to other cities. Another way of showing love was through offerings of money, food, or other support for Christians in need. Paul praises the Macedonian churches in general for their generosity (2 Cor 8:1-6).

Paul's second ethical exhortation begins with **we urge you** (1 Thess 4:10) followed in quick succession by four requests:

Do so more and more (v 10)
"Make it your ambition to lead a quiet life" (v 11*a*)
"Mind your own business" (v 11*b*)
"Work with your hands" (v 11*b*)

We urge you translates one of Paul's favorite verbs in exhortation (*parakaleō*, fifty-four times in Paul's letters; see 2:12). Paul's message is not that they need to show love but that they go beyond what they have done so far (4:10*b*). This acknowledges their spiritual progress while encouraging them to expand on it. **Do so more and more** translates the verb *perisseuō* (lit. "to abound"), which is used for the third time in the letter (3:12; 4:1). He urges them to do this as **brothers and sisters**, echoing the theme of ***brotherly love*** (v 9).

Do the three injunctions that follow this one specify exactly how ***brotherly love*** is to be pursued in the community? If so, this would make sense of the purpose to "not be dependent on anybody" (v 12): namely, love does not take advantage of another when one can support oneself. But the reference to gaining the "respect of outsiders" (v 12) seems to have a very different purpose in mind. That is the community's reputation in a shame-honor culture and the impact it will have on the spread of the gospel. Perhaps it would be a mistake to expect too strict a logic here. Paul may simply be speaking with multiple purposes simultaneously, as we do in conversation. And after all, the love Christians are called to show one another as disciples of Jesus does have both an "internal" reference (care for one another) and an "external" reference (witness to those not yet in the kingdom: see John 13:35).

■ 11 Some interpreters infer from the next injunction **make it your ambition to lead a quiet life**, to **mind your own business**, that Paul meant to discourage the Thessalonians from engaging in politics on behalf of one's patron (Green 2002, 210; → Behind the Text for 1 Thess 4:9-12, above). The first verb, *philotimeomai*, normally means ambition for public honors and offices (e.g., Best 1986, 174; Malherbe 2000, 247). And politics is the opposite of being **quiet** and minding one's **own business**. As noted above, though, most of the Thessalonian Christians were not of the wealth or class to seek public offices, nor is it likely they were supported by patrons. Is this a call to keep a low profile and avoid undue attention from the authorities (Wanamaker 1990, 162-63)? It may be that some of these poor urban Christians are tempted to seize the city's attention and have their demands heard in the same manner that their opponents had: by raising a crowd and storming through the streets (Acts 17:5-7). Scenes such as we associate today with populist demonstrations in middle-eastern countries are exactly the sort of mob politics that the Romans feared. And sometimes it worked, at least temporarily. But Paul does not want Christians to manipulate the system that way. Not only is it not peaceful, but it would risk provoking the authorities to bring in military force to restore order (Acts 19:39-41; Josephus, *Ant.* 18.3.2, §§60-62).

It is probably best to take **mind your own business** together with **work with your hands.** Christians must be responsible for themselves and not neglect their own families (1 Tim 5:8). This is part of living out Christ's love. **Mind your own business** is not intended to suppress evangelism (against Best 1986, 175; Barclay 1993, 522). That their evangelism was partly the cause for the hostility they experienced is believable. But Paul could hardly think that evangelism itself was a problem, since (*a*) this was his calling, and (*b*) he praises them for their witness (1:8; 2:2, 9) and that they lived in a way society perceived as not "respectable" or calm (4:11, 12).

The problem was the failure of some to attend to their own families and their household **business**. These are the "idle and disruptive" of 5:14. Some of these will not listen and will require a second admonition (2 Thess 3:6-15). Paul's words here do not mean that *manual labor* is somehow better than any other kind of work. Rather, the presumption seems to be that his converts are all from a class of people who do manual work for a living (in a broad sense—including skilled labor). And the sense is, "you should desire to be supported by *your own* work (not someone else's)." Although from a wealthier family, Paul also did this sort of work during his mission there, pulling his own weight and setting them an example (Acts 18:2-3; 2 Cor 11:23, 27; 1 Thess 2:8-9; 2 Thess 3:7-10).

■ 12 The life of calm, responsible care for one's home is a witness to **outsiders** (1 Thess 4:12). Paul recognizes that there is a certain area of overlap of interests between the ideals of society (that which non-Christians find ***respectable*** [*euschēmonōs*]) and the restoration that the gospel of Christ brings. Although to **win the respect** of non-Christians is not the prime motive in ethics, it is still an important consideration for the witness of the gospel, since Christians do not live solely for themselves. Paul constantly reminds us in this letter that witness to the gospel is what disciples do with their whole lives, not just their words. Apparently for Paul the life of holiness and love also carries a certain *dignitas*.

The point of working is to **not be dependent on anybody** financially. Literally, the text reads ***that you might have need of no one/nothing*** (the Greek is ambiguous). The implication is that if they fail to "work" and attend to their "own business" (v 11), they must have their needs met by someone else, namely the church. Some were already failing in this regard (the "idle and disruptive" [5:14; 2 Thess 3:6, 11]). They had taken advantage of the church's common fund for charity (→ Behind the Text for 1 Thess 4:9-12, above), and abused people's goodwill. This was relief money that ought to have gone to those who were truly in need: widows, orphans, the sick. If they show themselves to be responsible, they will be exercising love to the Christian family, and it will smooth the way for the gospel to be heard.

FROM THE TEXT

Paul realizes that the spiritual life is a journey in relationship with God and with one another in which we do not stand still. Having the love of Christ is not like having a possession such as a car. This gift from God is like a plant that must be tended. So it is no insult to say even to the most mature Christians: "Love one another *even more!*" Every day brings new challenges and opportunities to practice being the family of Christ.

We are not without help in this task. Like these ancient Christians, contemporary believers are also taught by God how to love rightly: through holy

Scripture, through the example of Christ's life and death for us, through the Spirit God sends to those with faith in Christ, and through the example of godly believers.

This text reminds us that loving God and his Son must involve loving the church (1 Thess 4:9-10). Many moderns have a deep-seated distrust of organized religion. They prefer the pursuit of a solitary, mystical, and eclectic spirituality (Bengtson 2013, 51-53). But the NT knows nothing of solitary faith. To love Jesus is to love his people. They may not be perfect; they may need correction or exhortation (4:11-12; 5:11, 14-22); but so do you. It is *God's* church (1 Cor 1:2; 10:32; Gal 1:13; 2 Thess 1:4; etc.), the body of Christ, part of his plan (1 Cor 12:12-27; Eph 4:11-16; Col 1:24-27). To love and fellowship with the wider body of Christ is part of what it means to believe in the God who revealed himself to us in Jesus Christ.

Finally, we can take away from this scripture that *spirituality encompasses, and grows with, the Christian's earthly family and work*. It was an important emphasis of the Reformers that the Christian's calling includes the duties of being a spouse, a parent, and one's secular job. These tasks Luther also called "fruits of the Spirit," to be carried out as part of what it means to love our neighbor in supplying the community's needs (Hardy 1990, 46-47). One does not become more spiritual by abandoning work or family (a mistake some Corinthians made: 1 Cor 7:3-5, 8-14, 28). Christ's people are called to be responsible for themselves and care for their dependents as God cares for them.

Calvin emphasized work as a mode of discipleship, a spiritual duty to carry out what God has assigned us. There we learn the lessons of faithfulness, humility, and moderation. "In following your proper calling, no work will be so mean and sordid as not to have a splendour and value in the eye of God" (Calvin 1960b, 3.10.6). Our work becomes a place of service to Christ, a way to love neighbor, and a means to witness to the gospel.

B. Encouragement from the Parousia (4:13—5:11)

1. The Dead in Christ Shall Rise (4:13-18)

BEHIND THE TEXT

Structure. The new section is clearly identified as a change in topic. Paul begins with the issue that disturbed them: Christians who have died. He quickly moves to a discussion of the return of Christ (Parousia) from different angles:

1. Christ's return will bring the salvation/resurrection of believers (4:13-18).
    a. How the dead in Christ will fare (vv 13-16).
    b. How Christians who are still alive will fare (v 17).

  c. Call to comfort one another (v 18).
2. Christ's return as "the day of the Lord" will bring judgment (5:1-11).
  a. How the Parousia will arrive as judgment on those "in darkness" (vv 1-3).
  b. Paul's assurance and exhortation to the readers that they are destined to experience the Parousia differently:
    (1) as salvation (vv 4-5), and
    (2) they need to live so as to be prepared for Christ's return (vv 6-10).
  c. Call to comfort one another (5:11).

  The entirety of 4:13—5:11 clearly hangs together around the common topic of the one Parousia of Christ.

  The occasion. Apart from the deaths of some believers (4:13), it is not entirely clear what so disturbed the Thessalonians that Paul had to write. Had they imagined Christians would not die? Had they not heard of the resurrection of the dead? Both seem hard to imagine. Did the deaths challenge a belief that all Christians would live to see Jesus return? Did their grieving create a faith crisis that caused them to doubt their earlier doctrinal lessons? Or, if the deaths were due to persecution, was the church disturbed that the Lord allowed this? All we can say is that the letter was somehow prompted by the death of Christians and, perhaps, by the fear that the dead would miss Jesus' return (vv 15-16 [→]).

Beliefs about Death and the Afterlife in the Ancient World

  There was no single pagan conception of the afterlife in antiquity. One inscription often found on tombstones implies that nothing was expected: "I was not, I was, I am not, I care not" (Ferguson 1970, 136).

  Some Stoics believed the soul lingered for a short time after death, but eventually decomposed (Epictetus, *Diatr.* 2.1.17; 3.13.15; Diogenes Laertius, *Lives* 7.156). A view going back to Homer was that the souls of ordinary mortals had a dim existence in the world of shades (*Hadēs*). Only a lucky few made it to the Isles of the Blessed, where they were deified, like Hercules (Burkert 1985, 195-98; Homer, *Od.* 11.489-91). Platonists believed human souls were immortal by nature. Souls preexisted their bodies; after people died, their souls would be reincarnated again until they lived well enough to leave the body behind forever (Plato, *Resp.* 611A; *Phaedr.* 245C-246A; *Tim.* 41A-D, 42E-43A; Dillon 1977, 291, 326-27, 377; Zakopoulos 1975, 77-84h).

  The mystery religions offered popular "shortcuts" to a blessed afterlife. They promised an intimate union with the deity and special postmortem favors. One of these, known to have been popular in Thessalonica, was the cult of Dionysus (Burkert 1985, 276, 290-95; Kerényi 1976, 137-38; Edson 1948, 160-79). Others probably included the Samothracian mysteries, the rites of the Cabiri, and the Isis-Osiris cult (Edson 1948, 181-201; Donfried 2010, 4-5).

The Christian belief in resurrection from the dead was different from all these pagan conceptions. It involved *both* belief in an afterlife for the soul *and* a future body. This appeared odd to educated pagans. Just how odd can be seen from Celsus' comment that the Christians' belief in a resurrection proved they were "gross, impure, and bent upon revolting without any reason from the common belief" (Origen, *Cels.* 8.49).

IN THE TEXT

■ **13** Paul has shifted topics, turning here to the fate of Christians who have died. The matter seems so important and receives such extended comment that it must be in response to Timothy's recent visit. Had the Thessalonians sent a question back with Timothy? We don't know why some died. Were their deaths brought on by violence against the Christians (1:6; 2:14; so Still 1999, 216; Witherington 2006, 140; Donfried 2010, 8)?

Again Paul opens the new topic by appealing to his converts as his **brothers and sisters** (*adelphoi*), reminding them of their shared status in Jesus' family. The term *adelphos* occurs 19 times in 1 Thessalonians—about one-seventh of all its occurrences in Paul's letters (19 of 133) despite its brevity (less than one-twentieth of the total words in all the letters).

We do not want you to be uninformed (v 13*a*) is another way of saying "we want you to know." Paul elsewhere uses this phrase to introduce new material and to draw his readers' attention sharply to what follows (Rom 11:25; 1 Cor 10:1; 12:1; Malherbe 2000, 262). Paul seems to be correcting something that is causing the Thessalonians to **grieve like the rest of mankind, who have no hope** (v 13*b*; Witherington 2006, 130).

Some think Paul's initial teaching in Thessalonica had omitted adequate mention of the resurrection, due to his forced departure (Williams 1992, 81; Marshall 1983, 120-22). But this seems unlikely; the resurrection was central to his gospel (1 Cor 15:13-14). And Paul must have been teaching in Thessalonica longer than the three weeks Acts mentions (→ Introduction).

Plevnik thought Paul taught the Thessalonians only that they would be "caught up" when Christ returned (as v 17). They wrongly assumed everyone would still be alive then, and they feared dead Christians could not participate in the Parousia nor be taken into heaven (Plevnik 1997, 68-69, 96-97; Wanamaker 1990, 166). His argument has failed to persuade most commentators.

It seems more likely that Paul here only elaborates on the significance of what he had taught previously (Malherbe 2000, 262; Green 2002, 215-17). This is how "[we] do not want you to be ignorant" is used in 1 Cor 10:1.

Paul had evangelized for over fifteen years, and death was not a new problem. He had almost certainly given the Thessalonians standard teaching on death, resurrection, and the afterlife with the gospel. This is implied in his references to the future experience of God's "glory," rewards at Jesus' return (2:12, 19; 3:13), and rescue from "wrath" (1:10).

Paul's emphasis on the dead being raised "first" (v 16) and joining Christ together with living believers suggests the Thessalonians believed their dead would be disadvantaged somehow at the Parousia, not participating in the glorious events of Christ's return and his messianic kingdom (so Frame 1912, 163; Malherbe 2000, 261, 275, 284; Furnish 2007, 102; → v 15). This is the only place in Paul's letters that emphasis is made.

Perhaps the Thessalonians' problem was psychological. They believed that the Lord's return was imminent—as Paul did—and had not fully reckoned with the possibility of believers dying. The shock of loved ones' deaths threw them into profound grief, so that they failed to appreciate God's promises. In this scenario, their problem would be similar to that faced by some Christians even today. Paul's solution is pastoral: he calls on them to **comfort one another**, not "instruct one another" (see v 18; for other theories, see Wanamaker 1990, 164-66; Richard 1995, 231-32; Green 2002, 213-15).

Sleep (*koimaomai*) is a common euphemism for death found in the OT (Gen 47:30; Deut 31:16; Job 14:12; 21:26; Dan 12:2). The same euphemism appears in later Jewish literature (Sir 48:11 LXX; 2 Macc 12:45), Greek and Roman literature, and epitaphs (Homer, *Il.* 11.241; Sophocles, *El.* 509; Plutarch, *Cons. Apoll.* 107D-F; see also Balz 1972, 548-49; LSJM, 967; Malherbe 2000, 263-64, 281). Hence, the NIV adds **in death** to make the metaphor explicit.

It is impossible to tell whether Christian use of the metaphor came from Jesus' teaching (as Witherington 2006, 131) or common usage. For Christians, however, **sleep** implied waking again. Resurrection was a basic notion within early Christian teaching from the beginning (Mark 12:24-27; Acts 4:2; 1 Cor 15:3-11). Interestingly, Paul never softens Jesus' death by calling it sleep. The stark reality of the Lord's death is paraded as God's paradoxical victory (Rom 3:23-25; 1 Cor 1:23-25; Gal 2:20*b*-21; 1 Thess 5:10).

Paul insisted that if the Thessalonians reflected on what they already knew (1:10), they could face death with hope. By this means they would not **grieve like the rest of** humanity. Paul does not say Christians will not grieve. But the loss of one who is "in Christ" is tempered by the **hope** of resurrection life. Nor is Paul saying pagans did not believe in an afterlife; some did (→ Behind the Text for 1 Thess 4:13-18, above). But he considered the Son of God's incarnation, death, and resurrection the only sure ground for future **hope**. Other gods cannot cause one to stand blameless before God the Father in the resurrection (Rom 4:25; 6:3-5; Phil 3:8-11; Col 3:3-4; 1 Thess 5:9-10). Without Christ there is **no hope** for the rest, those outside the believing community.

■ **14** Paul begins his consolation to the Thessalonians with a reminder of the basic Christian creed, from which he then draws an inference. **We believe that Jesus died and rose again.** This comes from the earliest form of the gospel (compare Acts 2:23-24; 1 Cor 15:3-4; 1 Pet 1:3). The Thessalonians must have recognized it belonged to Paul's preaching, and their own preaching of the gospel too (1 Thess 1:8, 10; 2:15). Jesus' death and resurrection were the foundation of God's saving act in history; these events made available God's forgiveness to humanity and the salvation of the lost (5:10; see Rom 3:21-26; 5:8-10).

The believers' hope is based not only on God's promise but also on the demonstration of resurrection in a historic event: **Jesus died and rose again**. Their future is foreshadowed in the Messiah's triumph over death. This is similar to how the OT looks back to the mighty deeds of God in the past for confidence about the future (Deut 26:5-11; Pss 44:1-8; 77:11-20).

In Greek, 1 Thess 4:14 begins with *if* [*ei*] **we believe Jesus died and rose**. But this conditional sentence does not imply any doubt. Here *ei* has the force of *since*. Paul assumes Jesus' resurrection in order to argue that **God will bring with Jesus** Christians who have fallen asleep in him (i.e., *died*). This second statement is introduced with *so*, showing the logical connection between Jesus' resurrection and that of believers. What God has done for Messiah must also be a certainty for Messiah's people, who are one with him. Note the prepositions: **asleep in him** (v 14*b*) and "the dead *in* Christ" (v 16). Paul held to the corporate identity of Messiah and his people, as when he later refers to Christ as the Christian's new Adam (1 Cor 15:20-23, 44-49; compare Rom 5:18-19; Eph 2:6). So Paul urges the Thessalonians to have confidence that their dead will share Jesus' life.

The second half of the conditional sentence (the apodosis), its conclusion, contains an ellipsis. To make sense of this we probably need to repeat the verb believe: *since we believe Jesus died and rose, so [we believe] also God will bring those who have fallen asleep through Jesus with him.*

But there are some uncertainties about the meaning of the result clause. **With Jesus** modifies **God will bring**; but does *through Jesus* also go with **bring** (Malherbe 2000, 266; Furnish 2007, 102)? Or does *through* [*dia*; NIV: in] *Jesus* describe how some **have fallen asleep**? That is, they died as faithful Christians (Moule 1959, 57; Bruce 1982, 98; Richard 1995, 226; Green 2002, 221)? The latter view seems most likely, making it a variation of Paul's "in Christ" expression (Frame 1912, 169; Witherington 2006, 133). This yields a more balanced sentence that has poetic quality (Lightfoot 1957, 64; Best 1986, 88; Bruce 1982, 97):

if we believe that

A	B
Jesus died	*and rose*

so also [we believe]

A'	B'
those having fallen asleep through Jesus	*God will bring with Jesus*

Finally, *where* will **God ... bring** the resurrected **with Jesus?** Paul doesn't specify. He says only that the resurrection happens when Jesus descends in his Parousia (v 16), so that believers will be "with him" (5:10; see 4:17). But where is he? Some think 4:17 suggests heaven. Others note that the imagery of Jesus' return suggests a triumphant coming to earth to claim and renew it. Paul emphasizes that believers join Christ in the fullness and glory of the kingdom, not the direction of their travel.

■ **15** Paul reinforces the resurrection of believers as guaranteed by **the Lord's word**. What is the source of this **word**? Paul could refer to a teaching of the earthly Jesus. But vv 15-17 have no exact matches in Jesus' sayings preserved in the Gospels. Yet much of what Paul says parallels eschatological material in the gospels, especially in Matt 24. Other parts sound like Paul's commentary, such as here, **We who are still alive, who are left until the coming of the Lord**.

Perhaps Paul is quoting an *unknown* saying of Jesus, which no canonical Gospel includes (compare Acts 20:35; Morris 1991, 140-41). While possible, this is difficult to prove.

Another solution makes it a Christian word of prophecy from the risen Jesus, perhaps directly through Paul himself (compare 2 Cor 12:9; Aune 1983, 253-56; Malherbe 2000, 268). The way Paul introduces 1 Thess 4:15-17 with the phrase ***by the word of the Lord*** (*en logō kyriou*) is similar to the formula introducing prophecy in the OT (1 Kgs 13:1, 2, 5; 20:35). But the early church tended to identify prophetic messages as a word of the *Spirit* rather than a word from the *Lord Jesus* (Acts 13:2; 20:22-23; 21:11; 1 Cor 12:3; 1 Tim 4:1; 1 John 4:1; compare Ignatius, *Phld.* 7.2). Exceptions are reported as personal visions rather than prophecy to the community (Acts 18:9-10; 23:11; 2 Cor 12:8-9; except for Revelation; but note "in the Spirit" in Rev 1:10).

In the NT, the formula ***the word of the Lord*** is not used for prophecy but designates either the gospel (Acts 13:49; 15:35-36; 19:10; 1 Thess 1:8; 2 Thess 3:1) or Jesus' teachings passed on through the church (Acts 11:16; 20:35; Green 2002, 221). There is nothing essentially new in 1 Thess 4:15-17 that would require a prophecy. Everything can be found in Jesus' teaching, the OT, and standard Jewish apocalyptic ideas.

By the word of the Lord is best understood as a declaration that Paul's message is based upon the teaching of the Lord Jesus himself, but not a direct quotation. This is a natural reading of the Greek preposition *en* (***by means of***). Paul was probably aware of a number of Jesus' eschatological sayings. From these, and from his knowledge of the OT, he appears to have synthesized an answer for the Thessalonians (see Rigaux 1956, 539-51; Wanamaker 1990, 171; Witherington 2006, 135-36). It is also identical to the manner in which he uses Jesus' teaching at 1 Cor 7:10 and 9:14 (direct dependence without direct quotations; see Beale 2003, 137).

Paul begins the teaching from the **Lord** by asserting emphatically that ***we who are alive, who survive until the coming,*** will certainly not precede the

Christian dead. **Certainly not** is a strong negative in Greek. Paul asserts that the dead in Christ are not disadvantaged; the living will not **precede** (*phthanō*) them into the kingdom. *Phthanō* means **come before** or not "have advantage over" (LSJM, 1926-27; Green 2002, 223). The whole church, dead and living, will be reunited alive under its Lord (1 Thess 4:16-17).

Paul addresses the fear that the Christian dead will not participate in the Parousia and subsequent events (→ Behind the Text for 1 Thess 4:13-18, above). Some works of Second Temple Judaism expected the Messiah's coming to inaugurate his worldwide rule *only* with those who would then be living. After this messianic age, the resurrection and final judgment occur (*4 Ezra* 7:26-44; *2 Bar.* 29:2-8; 30:1-3). Did these ideas affect the Thessalonians?

The clarifying reference to those alive at Jesus' Parousia as **we who survive** uses a verb (*perileipō*) that often describes the survivors of a battle (Polybius, *Hist.* 3.64.8; 5.50.9; Diodorus Siculus, *Library* 13.67.7; 14.75.2; 17.111.3; Dionysius of Halicarnassus, *Ant. rom.* 5.44.4), or some other disaster (Polybius, *Hist.* 6.5.7; Diodorus Siculus, *Library* 5.58.5); or the survivors of a colony (Diodorus Siculus, *Library* 5.9.3-4; Dionysius of Halicarnassus, *Ant. rom.* 1.45.3).

Paul implies that the future will be like the past: it will involve struggle and suffering for the faith. Believers alive when Jesus returns are like the brave survivors of a beleaguered army or colonists holding out in hostile territory. Jesus had cautioned his disciples to be prepared for maltreatment (Matt 5:10-12; 10:16-25; Mark 13:9-13; Luke 6:22; John 15:18-21), as had Paul (1 Thess 3:3-4). They realized what fallen human nature can lead people to do. Yet the church will continue to have a witness on earth until the Lord comes.

The **coming** of Jesus the church anticipates is his Parousia. This term was used to describe the manifestation of a deity to worshippers (such as Asclepius' appearance to heal in a dream). Josephus borrowed this term to describe God's **coming** to help Israel in OT times (*Ant.* 3.80, 203; 9.55; Bruce 1982, 57; Spicq 1994, 3:53-55). It could also simply mean "arrival" or "presence" (1 Cor 16:17; 2 Cor 10:10; Phil 1:26), but the latter do not quite fit the apocalyptic context here.

Parousia also described an official visit by royalty to a city. This usage seems closest to its use here. On such a visit, the city would send out a representative deputation to greet the VIP on the road and escort him back to the city. This welcoming reception was called *apantēsis* ("meet" in v 17).

Cities celebrated these visits with lavish spending to honor the ruler (→ 1 Thess 2:19-20). When Nero visited Greece in AD 66-67, Corinth struck a coin to honor the occasion. Its legend read *adventus Augusti*, "coming of Augustus" (Lat. *adventus* = Gk. *parousia*; Head 1963, plate 18; Burnett et al. 1992, 250). Later Hadrian minted *adventus* coins in gold.

Even common coins with the emperor's likeness on them bore the inscription *divi filius*, "son of a god," because the emperors claimed descent from the goddess Venus and from deified emperors. The poet Virgil poetically describes the coming of Augustus as a "dear child of gods," as effecting cosmic shaking and renewal (*Ecl.* IV).

It cannot be an accident that Paul chose *parousia* to describe the upcoming "visit" of Jesus as messianic King, Son of God, and Judge. Nor can the Thessalonians have missed the symbolism. This "royal theology" portrays Jesus as the true emperor who is to be worshipped. His "visit" will be more splendid and terrifying than that of any earthly ruler (1 Thess 4:15-17; 5:2-3; Green 2002, 155).

Paul's description of the Lord's return is loaded with military language, only some of which is apparent in English: **survivors** (4:15, 17); "command," "trumpet," the "archangel" who is associated with God's armies (v 16); and the **looting** of living saints by God (v 17)—all evoke a sense of cosmic battle.

In addition, the language is reminiscent of scenes associated with the OT Day of the Lord. Christ's descent evokes Daniel's judgment scene (Dan 7:10, 13-14); the explicit mention of the "day of the Lord" (1 Thess 5:2-3); and the theme of God's "wrath" (v 9). Jesus descends as YHWH in a Parousia to his world, where he will both deliver and judge. Paul seems self-consciously to oppose Jesus to Caesar, affirming Jesus as the authentic coming *imperator* of the world.

Some commentators are uncomfortable with Paul assuming that he may be alive when Jesus returns. There is no need to be. Jesus himself had said, "About that day or hour no one knows" (Mark 13:32). Paul was only living up to the revelation that was given him, and as far as he knew when he wrote this, he would be alive at the Parousia. Later on, he was not so sure (2 Cor 1:8-9; Phil 1:23-24; 2:17; 2 Tim 4:6-8). Yet Christ's promise to return is still certain.

■ **16** It is **the Lord himself** who returns: the same Jesus who had come as weak and meek servant will return in glory and power (compare Rom 1:4; Heb 2:9). Paul says Jesus will **come down from heaven**. This event is sometimes obscured by debates about whether the church is meeting him "in the air" and returning to heaven or to earth (v 17). Whether or not those debates are called for, Paul's primary interest is to show Jesus as the victorious emperor who arrives to claim his territory. The language is apocalyptic. Nevertheless, it must be taken seriously to describe a real arrival or manifestation of the Son of God in an earthshaking manner (compare Wright 2008, 129).

Jesus' descent is heralded with three sonic signs (or possibly three views of one sign). The **loud command** is probably best understood as the order for the dead to rise (compare John 5:25-29). The **archangel** whose **voice** sounds here represents a commander of God's angelic army. The title **archangel** occurs elsewhere in Scripture only in Jude 9, where he is identified with Michael.

The angel of the Lord was believed to protect Israel, commanding angelic armies (unnamed in Josh 5:14; "Michael" in Dan 10:13; 12:1). At Qumran, angelic armies fight with the saints against the wicked at the end time

(1QHᵃ XII, 3-8; XVII, 6-8). In Rev 19:14 they accompany Jesus' Parousia in judgment. Judaism's speculation about the various orders and roles of angels is unmentioned in the NT. Many Jews assumed the chief angels enjoyed privileged access to the divine glory in heaven (*2 En.* 20:1; Von Rad et al. 1964, 87; Moore 1962, 1:402-4, 410).

It is odd that Paul mentions no army or weapon, only the **voice** (*phonē*) of the archangel. In a similar scene, Rev 18:2 refers to an angel who descends from heaven and shouts "with a mighty *voice* [*phonē*]" announcing the fall of Babylon. The **voice** here may announce the coming judgment (1 Thess 5:2-3). Or it may issue the order to gather up the living saints (4:17; Matt 24:31).

The **trumpet . . . of God** is associated with theophanies in the OT and later Jewish literature (Exod 19:16-19; Zech 9:14; *Apoc. Mos.* 22:1; *Apoc. Ab.* 21). Trumpets in war were to signal troop movements or to terrify the enemy (Plutarch, *Cam.* 23.6; *Tim.* 27.10; *Aem.* 33.1). The Day of the Lord, like war, is "a day of trumpet and battle cry against the fortified cities" (Zeph 1:16; see Joel 2:1; Zech 9:14; Rev 8:2, 6-13; 9:1, 13; 11:15; compare 2 Esd 6:23). Paul may echo the synoptic saying about the Son of Man returning in glory and sending out his angels "with a loud trumpet call" to gather God's elect (Matt 24:31 || Mark 13:27).

As the Lord Jesus appears in his divine splendor accompanied by his angelic armies, the **first** result is that **the dead in Christ will rise** (1 Thess 4:16*b*). This information seems clearly directed at the anxieties of the church (→ v 13). Paul emphasizes that dead believers will rise **first**; they are not neglected. Those who were **in Christ** by faith during their lifetimes remain in him, though they are **dead**. They will be raised just as he was raised (Rom 5:18; 6:5; 1 Cor 15:48-49).

Pagans in NT times found the notion of resurrection puzzling or revolting (Plutarch, *Rom.* 28.10; → Behind the Text for 1 Thess 4:13-18, above). Those who believed in any afterlife viewed postmortem existence as a flight of the soul away from the body. For Plato, the body was the soul's prison, preventing it from gaining union with divinity after death (*Phaed.* 81B-C, 82D-E).

Modern Christians seldom appreciate what a clash of cultures this particular issue created. When the Jewish author Josephus described Pharisaic views of the afterlife, he equivocated, making it sound as if they believed in the immortality of the soul (*Ant.* 18.14) or reincarnation (*J.W.* 2.163). These views were much more amenable to the Roman intelligentsia. But Paul shows no such embarrassment. Boldly he asserts that salvation in Christ comprehends both body and soul.

■ **17** Paul picks up the thread begun at v 15. He describes what will happen to the ***living who survive*** (NIV: we who are still alive) to the time of the Parousia. There is a climax in two reunions: that of living Christians with the "dead in Christ" (v 16) and of Christians of all ages brought together **to meet**

the Lord in the air. This leads to the climactic statement of the entire subsection: **and so we will be with the Lord forever.** This serves as the source of Paul's consolation to the Thessalonians: With this hope, they should "encourage one another" (v 18).

The mixture of military and theophany language continues as Paul paints the scene. **Clouds** are a common symbol of the divine presence or glory. God led Israel out of Egypt with a cloud (Exod 13:21-22); God descended upon Sinai with his glory in a cloud, and Moses entered one to speak with him (19:9, 16; 24:15-18). A cloud represented the glory of God descending upon the tabernacle (33:9-10; 40:34-38). Exodus motifs may appear here—the rescue, resurrection, and gathering of the saints is the final exodus. Rescued Christians will be carried ***in clouds*** in the final exodus, to a meeting with **the Lord in the air.** For other uses of cloud imagery, see Isa 4:5; 19:1; Ezek 1:4; Dan 7:13; Matt 24:30 ‖ Mark 13:26 ‖ Luke 21:27.

Paul describes the manner in which the saints ***will be seized*** (NIV: **caught up**) in language suggesting a victorious army plundering a city. The verb *harpazō* means to take something violently: it is used for soldiers looting goods (Xenophon, *Anab.* 1.2.27; *Cyr.* 7.2.5), seizing an enemy position (Xenophon, *Anab.* 4.6.11), or for *robbery* or *snatching* something violently (Judg 21:21, 23; Lev 6:4 [5:23 LXX]; Job 24:2; Ps 10:9 [9:30 LXX]; Hos 5:14; see John 10:12).

Elsewhere, this verb describes a visionary's transport into God's presence (2 Cor 12:2, 4; *1 En.* 39:3; 52:1; *2 En.* 3:1; see Foerster 1964a, 472; Richard 1995, 246). But Paul is not describing a visionary encounter here. Some interpreters suggest a parallel to the "rapture" of Enoch to heaven or to the supernatural transport of a saint (e.g., Philip in Acts 8:39).

Paul probably meant readers to hear overtones of these events here, since all are instances of God transporting his people. But the OT never uses this verb of Enoch (but see Wis 4:11). Military language and imagery clearly dominate 1 Thess 4:13-17 and cannot be ignored. The OT presentation of Yahweh as divine warrior fighting on Israel's behalf has a new leading figure—Jesus (Reid 1993, 952). Paul pictures his return as a military rescue. **Living** Christians ***will be seized*** out of the clutches of the power of darkness by Christ's mighty army.

Popular American evangelical teaching sees in this text evidence for a "secret rapture" of the church during the end times (→ "The Rapture Theory" sidebar, below). It is portrayed as a Star Trek style transportation to heaven. A closer cultural parallel might involve British S.A.S. soldiers or American Rangers descending on a terrorist compound to *snatch* hostages held there. This is God's version of "shock and awe." It is not secret. And there is no indication whatsoever in this text that this event is separate from Christ's return or the general judgment on the world (4:16; 5:2, 4-10).

The Rapture Theory

The most popular interpretation of the end times among North American evangelicals, and those reached by their missions, involves a "secret rapture." This theory interprets texts in Matthew, Thessalonians, and Revelation as teaching that the church must be supernaturally taken from earth up to heaven *prior* to Christ's second coming and before the antichrist can appear in the end times (→ 2 Thess 2:3). Then, these dispensationalist interpreters assert, will follow an era of unprecedented evil and deception of humanity, and finally the public return of Jesus to earth in glory.

This doctrine was first published in 1830 by Edward Irving in England. From there John Nelson Darby spread it to the Brethren Church in England and took it to America in 1859-1874. It was popularized at prophecy conferences and made it into the Scofield Reference Bible and the faculties of many conservative Bible colleges and seminaries (Ladd 1956, 39, 43-45; MacPherson 1995, 3, 6, 9-10; Reiter, in Archer et al. 1996, 12-34).

Many came to identify this pretribulation rapture theory with the defense of historic Christian orthodoxy that conservative groups were mounting in the early twentieth century. But, in fact, the historic church had never heard of a pretribulation rapture. The fathers of the early church expected the church to suffer and remain on earth awaiting Christ's glorious return (Ladd 1956, 20-31; Kelly 1977, 459-69).

Today evangelicals hold divided opinions on the rapture and the millennium. Belief in a pretribulation rapture is less often seen as a test of orthodoxy. In the past quarter century many evangelical commentaries on the Thessalonian epistles explicitly reject the theory (Morris 1991, 145; Williams 1992, 68, 127; Green 2002, 227-29; Beale 2003, 136; Witherington 2006, 137) or offer interpretations that are at variance with it (Bruce 1982; Marshall 1983, 125; Wanamaker 1990, 145). None of the Wesleyan denominations mention the rapture in their statements of faith, nor do they take any official position on the millennium.

At Qumran the Essenes looked forward to a great end-time battle and wrote about it in the *War Scroll* (1QM). They thought they would participate in a vengeful extermination of God's enemies as they fought Joshua-style through the nations, aided by angels (1QM XI, 8-11; 1QM XV, 6-13; 1QM XV, 3—XVIII, 8).

But there is nothing like that here in 1 Thessalonians or anywhere else in the NT. The surviving Christians who witness the day of the Lord's coming do not fight. On the contrary, they need to be rescued, *snatched* up by Christ. Paul's entire emphasis is upon Jesus doing everything, acting with God's authority in commanding the angelic armies (4:16-17). The Parousia echoes the Exodus, in which Israel passively observes while God fights for her (Exod 14:24-31; 15:21).

The purpose of this **snatching** is to have a **meeting with the Lord in the air** (*eis apantēsin tou kyriou*). In antiquity an *apantēsis* was the official greeting a city offered when a king or VIP made a *parousia*. A welcoming party of civic leaders would go out and escort the royal guest back for the final few miles (see Bruce 1982, 102; Richard 1995, 247; Witherington 2006, 138-39; 1 Sam 13:10 LXX; 30:21; 2 Sam 19:24; Jdt 5:4; Matt 25:6).

The citizens of Ascalon formed an *apantēsis* for Jonathan the Hasmonean, bringing gifts (Josephus, *Ant.* 13.101). And the high priest of Jerusalem led an escort to welcome Alexander the Great at his *parousia*, to ward off his wrath at the city (Josephus, *Ant.* 11.327-329).

Some interpreters object that the *meeting* at 1 Thess 4:17 is missing too many elements to be a royal welcoming: there is no escort back to the city and no mention of where they go after meeting (Malherbe 2000, 277). Some argue that God brings the saints not back to earth (their "city" in the metaphor), but on up to heaven (Wanamaker 1990, 175-76). No lavish preparations for a visiting emperor are made.

However, it may be a mistake to look for too much precision in the use of metaphor here. This is not a diagram to the end times. It is more like an impressionist painting. Paul deliberately plays with multiple images from the eschatological traditions of Scripture and from Jesus: it is like exodus; like Messiah coming to his land as glorious, triumphant king; like Yahweh as cosmic warrior who overthrows evil human powers once and for all; and like Jesus as the Son of Man to whom the Father has given the power of resurrection life. They are *all* here.

■ **18** Paul concludes this subsection by pointing to the purpose of this instruction. The Thessalonians are to **encourage one another with these words**, namely, with the knowledge that Christ's return for them and for the faithful dead is certain.

FROM THE TEXT

The Christian's glorious hope. Death is one of the severest tests of faith for Christians in any age. Grief may draw believers into a dark hole that opens unanswerable questions. Paul reminds us that death has this stranglehold on our lives only if we have *no hope*. Christians trust in a Lord who has already experienced death and resurrection on our behalf, showing the promise of what is to come (Rom 6:5; 1 Cor 15:47-49; compare 1 John 3:2).

Whenever we recite the Apostles' Creed, "I believe . . . in Jesus Christ, who . . . rose again from the dead," we are at the same time making a statement of faith about *ourselves*. Christ cannot be separated from his people.

"The Lord himself will come down" (1 Thess 4:16) and disrupt the normal cosmic order that there is no return from death and decay. This heralds Jesus claiming his full lordship over the cosmos and his triumph over sin and death on behalf of believers. Like an emperor laying claim to rebel territory, Jesus commands Death to give up its captives. There is no power or reality—human, demonic, or natural forces; not even the annihilation of our physical selves!—that can stand between the Son of God and those he summons on that day (Rom 8:31-39). This implies that God's church will never lack a presence on earth of those who are still alive until Jesus returns with his angelic armies to begin the great judgment day.

Genesis opened with a series of commands from God that called creation into being. The culmination of creation was the making of humans in his image. Here in 1 Thessalonians Paul pictures the end of human history with the Lord's command for the resurrection bodies of the saints to materialize (1 Thess 4:16-17). The ultimate healing of the world's brokenness will be complete.

Not a rapture text, but a with-Jesus text. Some think this text proves that the church will have a secret rapture *prior* to Jesus' return, to wait out a time of tribulation on earth until Jesus returns to earth for judgment (→ "The Rapture Theory" sidebar, above). There is no evidence for this. Paul envisions only one return of Christ, and it echoes scenes in Daniel, in Jewish apocalyptic texts, and in Jesus' teaching. It will bring life for some and judgment for others (5:2-4, 9).

Paul seems curiously unconcerned about *where* resurrected believers will go (earth? heaven?), or *how* or *when*. It is enough to know that "we will be *with the Lord* forever" (4:17). That gives meaning to life, hope, and assurance of a personal, covenantal relationship with God that will endure into eternity. That means victory for the persecuted saints and reunion with all who have trusted in God.

Many modern preachers and writers seem to think it necessary to convince people that the Scriptures precisely predict everything Paul simply passes over. They decode for their audience when Jesus will come, who the antichrist will be, and where the saints go. These ponderous apocalyptic schemes shift the center of gravity *away* from the Father and the Son. The focus becomes the clever details of the end-times plan itself.

On the opposite extreme, some Christians have come to doubt that there is any afterlife at all, thinking the idea of resurrection is just a myth. Both of these approaches fail to come to grips with the awesome significance of the simple promise that we will *live with him* (5:10; 4:17). God is the Creator of all life. Surely he can fulfill his promise. To live with this marvelous, wise, and loving triune God—Father, Son, and Holy Spirit—is the supreme joy and fullness of life we can anticipate.

2. Be Ready for the Day of the Lord (5:1-11)

BEHIND THE TEXT

The structure of 4:13—5:11 was discussed in Behind the Text for 4:13-18. This section carries on Paul's reminders and exhortations concerning the Parousia. The "now . . . about" (5:1) suggests a new aspect, not an entirely new topic. It does not necessarily imply Paul is answering a Thessalonian question; he may respond to issues Timothy perceived when he was there. These could be the issues that would grow into major problems the second letter had to address (2 Thess 2:1-12). Most of this section is overshadowed by the theme of judgment, either endured by those who live in darkness (5:2-4) or escaped by those who, through faith in Christ, receive salvation from God (5:4-11).

IN THE TEXT

■ 1 Modern readers should remember that chapter breaks are a late addition to the text. The previous section's theme continues. When Paul says, **Now, brothers and sisters, about times and dates**, he refers to the timing of Jesus' Parousia ("now about" [*peri de*] elsewhere sometimes introduces new topics).

The words **times and dates** (*chronōn* and *kairōn*) are nearly synonymous (see Wis 8:8). Together they signify the season when the end would draw near and the Lord would return (Bruce 1982, 108; Wanamaker 1990, 178; Malherbe 2000, 288-89; but see Witherington 2006, 144-45). Daniel declared that God had power over *times and dates* (Dan 2:21).

Apocalyptic literature generally sought to lay out the divine plan of history with signs marking key events or eras (Furnish 2007, 107). But Paul discourages speculation about timing, as had Jesus (Mark 13:32-33; Acts 1:7). The only "signs" given here are that "the day" (1 Thess 5:2) has already broken upon the world. When Paul does give something like a preliminary sign in 2 Thess 2:3-4, it is not to encourage speculation but to counteract an overrealized eschatology.

There is no **need to write to you** about this, because it was part of the original gospel they received. He praises them by implying they have been faithful to the apostles' teaching, and there is nothing new to add (see 1:8).

■ 2 They **know very well** how **the day of the Lord will come**—unexpectedly and in an overwhelming display of divine power. **Very well** (*akribōs*; "carefully" at Luke 1:3) may be ironic: you know *precisely* that no one can know the hour.

The **day of the Lord** is an ancient theme used by the OT prophets. It is the time when God will visit the earth in power and glory. Judgment will come on the nations and retribution to the wicked, even among the elect of Israel (Isa 2:10-22; 24:21-23; Joel 2; Amos 5:18-24; Mic 2:4). This negative aspect could be described as "the terror of the Lord" (Isa 2:10 ESV, HCSB, NASB, NRSV), a day of "wrath and fierce anger" (Isa 13:9). But the **day** will be good news for the faithful, who expect to witness God's merciful restoration of his people, of Zion, and even of the earth itself. Worldwide peace and justice will arise under the reign of God and his Messiah (Isa 25:6-9; Hos 2:14-23; Amos 9:11-15; Obad 17-21; Mic 4:1-3, 6-8). Hence, the **day of the Lord** was always a two-edged thing, bringing both salvation and judgment.

The previous subsection (1 Thess 4:13-18) spoke of that day's salvation aspect; 5:2-3 speaks about judgment. **Day** here means not a twenty-four-hour period but a saving event. In the OT the Lord who brings in this day is Yahweh, the God of Israel. Paul, under the inspiration of the Holy Spirit, modifies this, making Jesus the **Lord** who acts with the authority of God to inaugurate this **day** (see 4:14-16; 1:1, 6, 10; compare Matt 24:36, 42).

This day **will come like a thief in the night**. The NT is the first place we find this simile for the Day of the Lord. The thief image is always negative, associated with stealing, breaking into homes, and violence (Job 24:14-16; Joel 2:9; Matt 6:19-20; Luke 12:33). "The thief comes . . . to steal and kill and destroy" (John 10:10, 8; see Luke 10:30). The image can also suggest the unexpectedness and shock of a thief's break-in, as with Jesus' warning that his return would be "at an hour when you do not expect him" (Matt 24:43-44 || Luke 12:39-40). Paul must have known of this when he wrote the Thessalonians. Second Peter 3:10 and Rev 3:3*b*; 16:15—all judgment texts—also compare Jesus' return to the coming of a thief.

Paul indicates that the effect of the coming **like a thief** (1 Thess 5:2) is "destruction" (v 3; compare 2 Pet 3:10). The metaphor is meant to indicate not only unpredictability and suddenness but also the *judgment* associated with Jesus' return—like getting mugged. Paul goes out of his way to assure his readers that Jesus *will not come for Christians* **like a thief,** only for those in the "darkness" of unbelief and unrighteousness (v 4). This terrifying encounter with Jesus will strip them of all they value, including their lives. Jesus is *not* coming for his *church* like a thief in the night.

■ **3** The complacent take unfounded comfort in a slogan that prevails just prior to the Lord's return: **peace and safety. They** must be non-Christians, for their fate is **destruction**. Believers do not encounter the Parousia this way (vv 4-5, 8-10). These are the counterpart to the survivors of 4:15, 17.

Some have seen in this slogan an attack on false prophets of peace within the church (compare Jer 6:14; Ezek 13:10; Malherbe 2000, 292). More likely Paul is attacking the attitude of the non-Christian world, in its contentment with the status quo and indifference to coming judgment (Marshall 1983, 134; Wanamaker 1990, 180; Richard 1995, 251).

Recent research has focused on the striking similarity of **peace and safety** to the rhetoric of the Pax Romana, the "Roman Peace" brought to the world through conquest. The Roman Senate had even consecrated an altar to Pax Augusta ("Augustus' peace"). Rome saw itself as the giver of law and order to the Mediterranean (Augustus, *Res gest. divi Aug.* 13; Virgil, *Aen.* 1.291-296; Wengst 1987, 7-10, 19-26; Green 2002, 233; Witherington 2006, 146-47; Furnish 2007, 108).

Rome was honored in inscriptions at Thessalonica and was worshiped as the goddess Roma along with her Caesars (Edson 1940, 127, 132-36; Papazoglou 1979, 307; Gill 1994, 403). The might of the empire was truly stunning. Its armies had subdued every power along the Mediterranean basin. Its engineers drained swamps, built roads, and brought water in aqueducts to cities from distant lakes. Its power to create "security" (ESV, HCSB, NET, NRSV) must have seemed irresistible in the first century. Yet that was an illusion. Neither Rome's legions nor its gold were trustworthy idols. Though people foolishly relied on them, this would lead them to ruin (5:3).

For those who make this mistake **destruction will come on them suddenly, as labor pains on a pregnant woman, and they will not escape.** They rejected the only ultimate security, trust in the living God and his Son. A number of terms here differ from Paul's usual speech: **Safety** (*asphaleia*) and **suddenly** (*aiphnidios*) occur only here; and **peace** is used in a secular way.

These differences may be due to Paul's dependence on oral traditions of Jesus' teachings (compare Matt 24:37-44; Luke 17:26-30; 21:34-36). The same themes appear in end-times passages in the Synoptic Gospels: the world's false security; the coming of the Day of the Lord "suddenly" (Luke 21:34); and that day is like a thief breaking in (Matt 24:43; Luke 12:39). The lesson is the same here as in the Jesus traditions: disciples must be alert (Matt 24:42; Luke 21:34, 36; 1 Thess 5:6; → 1 Thess 4:13-17).

Some have tried to give 5:3 a timeless, proverbial (gnomic) sense: "whenever (anyone) says 'Peace and security'. . ." (Best 1986, 207-8; Richard 1995, 250-51). But Greek *hotan* here means simply ***when***, as in the sayings in Paul's Jesus source.

What is the nature of the **destruction** that befalls the wicked? It is the opposite of the saints' deliverance in 4:16-17. In the OT (LXX) both the noun *olethros* and verb *olothreuō* express the destruction resulting from God's wrath, often through warfare that ravages lands and kills people (1 Kgs 13:34; Jer 5:6; 48:3, 8; Ezek 6:14; 14:16; Hag 2:22). It can simply refer to the "destruction" (death) of human life (Jdt 11:15; Wis 1:12-14; Sir 39:30; 2 Macc 13:5-6; 3 Macc 6:30, 34).

Wisdom 18:13 (NRSV) speaks of the Egyptians acknowledging that the Israelites were God's son "when their firstborn *were destroyed*" (*epi tō . . . olethrō*) in the Exodus (→ 1 Thess 5:3). Jesus' return is like a second Exodus: believers are "children of the light" (5:5; see Gal 3:26) as the Israelites were "children of God." Divine judgment falls as *olethros* on those "in darkness" at the second coming, as on "idolaters" at the Exodus.

Did Paul think of **destruction** as the instant death of the wicked, as in warfare? *Olethros* is used just four times in the NT. Once Paul refers to the nonliteral destruction of the "flesh"—the rebellious, sinful nature (1 Cor 5:5). The other three instances refer to the judgment of the end times (1 Thess 5:3; 2 Thess 1:9; 1 Tim 6:9). There always seems to be a transcendent quality to this **destruction** (BDAG, 702). Unlike the apocryphal literature, Paul does not go into elaborate details on the fate of the wicked.

In 2 Thess 1:9, *olethros* describes the fate of the wicked, suggesting eternal punishment (→). Paul applies the term's associations with the punishment of the wicked in this life to the outworking of God's wrath. It becomes a metaphor for an end-times reality transcending earthly descriptions, not annihilation.

The **destruction** is as inescapable as it was unforeseen—like **labor pains on a pregnant woman**. The image of birth labor, universal to human cultures, tells of the woe felt by those who realize too late that they have made choices that assure their doom.

Those who live in contempt of God's merciful call to repentance in the gospel will find a day of reckoning. Once labor pains begin, there is no stopping them. Just so, **they will not escape** from the coming judgment (compare Isa 13:6-8; 26:17; Jer 6:22-25; 22:20-23; *1 En.* 62:4). Jesus used similar imagery—"the beginning of birth pains"—to describe the era preceding his return (Matt 24:8; Mark 13:8; compare 1QH^a III, 7-10; Bertram 1974, 671-72). The danger of childbirth to women in antiquity lends an additional somber note to the metaphor (Fee 2009, 190 n. 31). Some think Paul's words refer to the onset of "messianic woes," but the context points to the abrupt arrival of judgment (Best 1986, 208; Richard 1995, 251; Malherbe 2000, 293).

The prediction of judgment on the wicked promises consolation to the church. Like certain psalms and most apocalyptic literature, Paul's words tell an audience suffering from injustice that God will eventually bring justice. His justice guarantees that the current world will not always endure. Paul's message is not addressed to unbelievers, as if it were to frighten. It is for believers, to strengthen them in the face of mistreatment by persecutors. He does not authorize retaliating (5:15). The certainty of judgment urges compassion for outsiders, making sharing *the word of the Lord* all the more urgent (1:8).

■ **4** Although Paul warns of coming judgment, he reassures his hearers that it does not apply to them. They **are not in darkness so that this day should surprise** them **like a thief**. Paul again refers to them as **brothers and sisters** (*adelphoi*) to emphasize their inclusion in God's family. On **thief** as a judgment image → 1 Thess 5:2.

Darkness indicates a state of alienation from God, suggesting both ignorance of God (inability to see him) and willful evil (because criminals favor the night; compare John 3:19; 8:12; 12:35, 46; Acts 26:18; Rom 1:21; 13:12; 1 Pet 2:9; 1 John 1:5-6; 2:8-11). The OT similarly associated **darkness** with evil (Job 30:26; Prov 2:13; Isa 5:20) and folly (Eccles 2:13). **Darkness** was a cover for criminal activity (Ps 11:2; Ezek 8:12). It could also evoke thoughts of the grave (Job 10:21-22; Ps 88:6, 12), and so represents divine wrath (1 Sam 2:9; Job 12:23-25; Isa 47:5; Joel 2:2; Amos 5:18, 20). Throughout 1 Thess 5:4-10, Paul develops the imagery of day and night, light and dark.

■ **5** In contrast with those "in darkness" (v 4), Christians will welcome Jesus' return as **children of the light and children of the day**. Colossians 1:13 claims that believers are "rescued . . . from the dominion of darkness." So Jesus' return cannot be "thief-like" for them. God is the light of Israel (2 Sam 22:28-29; Ps 27:1; Isa 60:19-20; *1 En.* 41:8; 58:5; *4 Ezra* 14:20). So the OT associated **light** with his Torah, wisdom, and righteousness (Pss 43:3; 119:105; Prov 4:18). Members of the Qumran community called themselves "sons of light" (1QS I, 9-11; III, 13-26; 1QM I, 1, 3). The Gospels report that Jesus also gave this title to his disciples (Luke 16:8; John 12:36, compare Matt 5:14). This probably inspired Paul's use of the expression here.

The Greek term *huioi* (**sons / children**) refers to both genders. Jews described someone as a "son of" something to indicate that person is associated with or characterized by that thing (Moule 1959, 174-75; BDAG, 1025). "Sons of God are those who do things pleasing to God; so also sons of day and sons of light, those who do the works of light" (John Chrysostom, *Hom. 1 Thess.* 9.3). Jesus bestows the right to become God's children on those who believe in him (John 1:12). The **children of light and of the day** are people who belong to God and to his future.

Day here may point to "the day of the Lord" (v 2), but only in its saving aspect. Perhaps, in connection with the light metaphor, Paul suggests that "the day of the Lord" will bring the dawning of a new **day**, God's new creation (see Rom 13:12; Phil 1:6, 10; 2:16; 2 Tim 1:12; 4:8). **Light** evokes daybreak and God's presence, or the saving enlightenment that relationship with him brings (see 2 Cor 4:4-6; 6:14; Col 1:12; 1 Tim 6:1; Jas 1:17; 1 Pet 2:9; 1 John 1:5-6).

We do not belong to the night or to the darkness reinforces the previous point by contrast. Paul switches here to the first-person plural (**we**), identifying with his audience. The opposites of **light** and **day** are **darkness** and **night**. Both **darkness** and **night** evoke evil, death, alienation from God (→ 1 Thess 5:4; see Rom 1:21; 2:19; 13:11-13; 2 Cor 4:6; 6:14; Eph 5:8; Col 1:12-13), and the judgment awaiting the wicked (see Amos 5:18-20; Wanamaker 1990, 183).

■ **6** Paul calls on his converts to reject the behaviors associated with **night**—sleeping and the excesses of Greek drinking parties (vv 6-7). Sleep is what **others** do (*loipoi*, → 4:13).

The verb **asleep** in vv 6-7 and 10 (*katheudōmen*; contrast *koimaō* in 4:13-15) refers metaphorically to a failure to use good judgment. Epictetus complained that when it comes to using the mind to avoid evil, "we yawn and *sleep* and erroneously accept any and every external impression" (*Diatr.* 1.20.10-11; compare 2.20.10; Demosthenes, *Fals. leg.* 303; Plutarch, *Pomp.* 15.2.6). For Paul, to be asleep is to fail to use the faculties God has given us to live wisely and reverently before him.

The antithesis of sleeping is to **be awake and sober**. **Be awake** (*grēgorōmen*) means to be spiritually and morally aware (1 Pet 5:8; Rev 3:2-3; "stay alert" [NET]). The same imagery appears in eschatological passages in the Gospels. Paul probably alludes to the traditions behind these in 4:15-17 and 5:2-3.

Jesus warned his disciples to "be alert" and ready for his unpredictable return (Mark 13:34-37; Matt 24:42-44; Luke 12:35-40). The synoptic passages cite the unknown hour of his coming as the reason for alertness. Here

Paul grounds his imperatives on believers' new Christian identity: "You are all children of the light," . . . ***therefore*** . . . **let us be awake and sober** (vv 5-6).

The verb *nēphō* literally means **be sober**, but here it refers metaphorically to making sound judgments, being sensible and self-controlled (compare 2 Tim 4:5; 1 Pet 1:13; 5:8; Diogenes Laertius, *Lives* 10.132; Philo, *Ebr.* 166; BDAG, 672). The Thessalonians lived in a cultural context marked by drinking parties, banqueting, and religious festivals that encouraged excess. So it is possible that Paul employs a double entendre with his language about sobriety. They are to avoid alcoholic excess *and* to be sound-minded.

■ **7** The apostle supports this twofold injunction with a proverb: **Those who sleep, sleep at night, and those who get drunk, get drunk at night**. Night was the normal time for sleeping, but also for drinking parties. Daytime drunkenness was exceptional, and a cause for shame (Isa 5:11; Acts 2:15; 2 Pet 2:13; Sirach 31:28 warns that wine drinking is a good thing only "at the proper time and in moderation" [NRSV]). Believers' lives should reflect that they "do not belong to the night" (1 Thess 5:5) and things associated with it. The notorious Dionysiac celebrations held in Thessalonica on some evenings may be among the shameful events Paul had in mind (Brocke 2001, 128-29). Drunkenness and sexual promiscuity were common and popular features of banqueting in that culture (Winter 2001, 76-109).

Surely Paul expects his readers to reject literal intoxication. But we can't imagine that he wants them literally to give up sleeping because they are "children of the day" (vv 5, 8). His language is poetic, about Christians living in constant awareness that they belong to the new age (Wanamaker 1990, 185; see John Chrysostom, *Hom. 1 Thess.* 9.3).

■ **8** Paul issues a second call to be **sober** (*nēphōmen*), insisting that Christians can become sound-minded by living in **faith, love,** and **hope**. The reason for this has to do again with their identity: **since we belong to the day**. Believers live in preparedness now for the kingdom they anticipate. They are like soldiers on duty who cannot sleep at their post. And the Christian soldier must be properly "armed" with Christ's virtues.

Here, the military imagery of the Lord's return in 4:15-17 reechoes in the imagery of the believer's preparation to welcome him. Paul repeats the triad of faith, love, and hope, reiterating the importance of these virtues (→ 1 Thess 1:2-3). They represent the foundation of Christianity.

Christians should ***put on*** these virtues as though donning pieces of armor (v 8). The imagery seems inspired by Isa 59:17. There God as Israel's divine warrior-protector will arise to bring justice. Both passages mention the same two pieces of armor; both link the **helmet** with **salvation.**

Paul squeezes three virtues onto two pieces of armor, following his OT source. He anticipates here the call in Eph 5:1 to be "imitators of God" (ESV, NASB, NET, NRSV) and the further development of the divine armor theme in Eph 6:10-17.

Contemporary philosophy, especially by Cynics, employed military metaphors to describe the virtuous lives of those who pursue wisdom. "Virtue is a weapon that cannot be taken away" wrote Antisthenes (ca. 400 BC; Diogenes Laertius, *Lives* 6.12-13; see Philo, *Leg.* 3.155; *Somn.* 1.103; and Malherbe 2000, 297-98; 1989, 91-119). Thus, it should not surprise us that Paul uses military imagery to describe unwarlike traits. Greek-speaking audiences were accustomed to think of the struggle for virtue in this way.

Paul speaks of "fellow soldier[s]" (Phil 2:25; Phlm 2 [NRSV]), enduring campaign hardships (2 Tim 2:3-4), and apostolic "weapons" that "demolish strongholds" (2 Cor 10:3-6). He is like a prisoner of war for Christ (2 Cor 2:14). He urges believers to employ themselves as **weapons of righteousness** (Rom 6:13; see 2 Cor 6:7 and Eph 6:11-17). Unlike the philosophers, for Paul reason or virtue are not the principal armaments. Instead, Christians equip themselves with **faith, love,** and **hope** (→ 1 Thess 1:2-3).

Both **breastplate** and **helmet** are defensive armor, and both protect vital spots: a sharp blow to the chest or head without these would be fatal. Christian soldiers continue to live out their **work of faith and labor of love** (1:3). This safeguards them as they await the Lord's coming and witness to his kingdom. There is no need to look for reasons why Paul does not include other pieces of armor, or attach a particular significance to a protected body part. His point is in the metaphor of armor itself. For example, ancients did not widely realize that the brain was the organ of thought. So, it is doubtful Paul supposed that the helmet protected the thought life.

The **hope of salvation** appears last in Paul's list, giving it a place of emphasis. Hope was likely the weak point in the Thessalonians' armor. So Paul returns to the subject he began to address in 4:13: the Christian's ultimate fate, dead or alive (5:9-10).

Christian **hope** is not wishful thinking; it is an eager expectation of something we are sure of but have not yet seen. Its object is God's future **salvation** (from Isa 59:17). This is the completed work of God's restoration of his saints through Christ in resurrection life "with him" following the Parousia (v 10; 4:17). What believers have now is only the beginning, the promise of the finished work that is yet to appear.

■ **9** Christian hope arose from the conviction that **God did not appoint them to suffer wrath but to receive salvation through our Lord Jesus Christ.** Wrath is not God's "anger" in the human sense but is (→ 1 Thess 1:10) the execution of his justice on those who have not believed nor repented of their evil. The express purpose of the gospel is to deliver humanity from this end that we otherwise deserve. In this sense, **salvation** for Paul has a future aspect in the future vindication and resurrection of the saints.

Appoint translates the verb *tithēmi* (**set** or **place**). Elsewhere this describes assigning someone a position of responsibility (Judg 8:33; 2 Kgs 11:18; Acts 13:47; 1 Tim 1:12; 2:7; 2 Tim 1:11). Those who have faith in the Son of

God receive the honor of being set on track **to obtain salvation**. That is not their normal and natural destiny; it is available only as a gift of God's grace.

The language of appointment assures Paul's readers about God's saving purposes and good intentions for them. The concept of election and calling recurs throughout 1 and 2 Thessalonians (1 Thess 1:4; 2:12; 4:7; 2 Thess 1:11; 2:13-14). It emphasizes that the initiative in salvation always rests with God. It does not arise from our deserving it (Rom 5:6-10; 1 Cor 1:21-31).

Nevertheless, God calls for a human response to his gifts. After holding out the assurance of salvation (1 Thess 5:1-3), Paul urges these same believers to be spiritually, mentally, and ethically vigilant (vv 4-8, 11). This may explain why Paul says God appointed them to **obtain** (*peripoiēsis*; BDAG, 804) salvation, not simply, "appointed them to salvation." God expects a response of faith and love to his initiative of saving grace. And nothing here says that response is inevitable from the elect or impossible from others (Marshall 1983, 139-40; 2004, 443; Witherington 2006, 152).

Nothing here implies an unconditional guarantee that would allow Christians to live in defiance of God's will and expect no covenantal consequences (compare Jer 7:1-15; Gal 5:19-21; see Best 1986, 217). Such a smug sense of security was attacked by John the Baptist (Matt 3:9 ‖ Luke 3:8) and Jesus (Matt 8:11-12; Luke 13:26-30). We should also note that Paul does *not* speak of an election of people to wrath (Best 1986, 217; Marshall 1983, 140, and 2004, 443).

Why then does Paul say they are appointed? This promise is not for those hardened in their sin but for those who have "put on" the armor of faith, hope, and love (Witherington 2006, 152). It describes those who have decided for the gospel and are God's beloved, not an abstract set of "elect" people apart from that decision. It is a promise and assurance to Christians under assault by a hostile world that God has a destiny of life, joy, and salvation with the Son for them.

■ **10** The assurance of God's goodwill for our deliverance comes with the reminder that Jesus **died for us**. His death was the instrument of our deliverance. Final salvation comes **through our Lord** at the last day (v 9), because of what he has already done. Here Paul makes explicit the aspect of the gospel that was only implicit at 1:9. Here in seed form is the sacrificial theology of Romans: the death of Christ is **for us** (*hyper hēmōn*; i.e., to benefit us; see Rom 5:8; 1 Cor 8:11; 15:3; 2 Cor 5:14-15).

Paul describes the purpose of Christ's death: **So that, whether we are awake or asleep, we may live together with him** (→ 1 Thess 4:17). Paradoxically, his *death* brings all who believe *life* with him—that is, the eternal life of resurrection existence with the Father and Son and all the saints. This is a message even the weary Thessalonians may repeat to "encourage one another" (v 11).

Asleep here points not to moral stupor (→ 1 Thess 5:6-7) but to the sleep of death (→ 1 Thess 4:13, despite the different verb here, *katheudō*).

Thus, **awake** and **asleep** comprehends all believers, living and dead. All will be alive in Christ (see Mark 12:24-27 and parallels).

■ **11 Therefore**, on the basis of all that has been said about the guarantee of the Lord's return, the resurrection of the saints and their sharing life with Christ when he returns, and on the firm ground of God's love that provided for salvation, believers are called on to **encourage one another and build each other up**.

Encourage (*parakaleite*) occurs for the second time in this section of the letter (see 4:18). This ties together both halves of the eschatological encouragement/exhortation (4:13—5:11). Paul had no intention of offering a comprehensive exposition of Christian eschatology. The details were beyond human knowing or inconsequential. His interest was engendering hope, not encouraging fruitless speculation.

Encouragement here has the general sense of urging others to pursue a better course of action. It is to ***implore*** or ***exhort*** another to do the right thing. But it also frequently means "comfort" (Gen 24:67 LXX; 2 Sam 10:2; Isa 40:1). That they are to do this for **one another** (*allēlous*) gives the sense of a personal, one-on-one activity (as opposed to group teaching or preaching; see Malherbe [2000, 301]). Just as natural families take responsibility for supervising, teaching, consoling, correcting, and encouraging their members, so the church is called on to model family-like responsibility for one another.

To **build each other up** is a figure of speech taken from the construction of houses (*oikodomeite* [Luke 6:48]). **Build . . . up** (or ***edify***) describes what love does (1 Cor 8:1) and the proper functioning of spiritual gifts (1 Cor 14:3-19, 26). That is, those who love one another use their Spirit-given assets to strengthen, teach, console, and assist other believers toward maturity and fruitfulness. Paul specifies at least part of what he means by building up in his directions in 1 Thess 5:12-22 (Malherbe 2000, 301). Lest he seem to imply by his exhortation that they do *not* have any care for one another, Paul affirms their spiritual life by adding **just as in fact you are doing**. He shows his pastoral wisdom in his combination of praise, instruction, and admonishment.

FROM THE TEXT

Spiritual alertness. Christians are still called to stay spiritually awake, have sound minds, and make good judgments on a daily basis, with God's help. These are not accomplishments we can check off, like climbing a mountain. They are the way the journey of life is lived. We may live in a state of spiritual alertness as the Lord's soldiers using faith, love, and hope for our defensive armor.

How do contemporary Christians avoid falling "asleep" (1 Thess 5:6-7)? We have the Spirit, the presence of the living Christ with his church. We have scripture; we have prayer; we have the Lord's Supper to feast on Christ. We have the counsel of other believers; we have past experience to draw on (our own and that of other believers); we have writings from other saints in centuries past. We have reason.

Too often we disregard one or more of these assets. Christians should avail themselves of every resource God's grace has provided. Even if not all of them are equally authoritative, all are beneficial.

Christians' identity as children of light. In an age that is obsessed with defining personal identity, believers can know that they belong to God's future kingdom as "children of the day" (v 5). Their identity is not determined by their economic status or job title, by the house they live in, the car they drive, the clothes they wear, or the important people they know. Their worth is measured by the love the Lord Jesus demonstrated for them when he died to redeem them. This gives Christians courage to live boldly in this age with the confident hope of salvation. They know they serve the sovereign of the universe and their work for him "is not in vain" (1 Cor 15:58).

Final judgment and reassurance. Those who persist in faith in Christ should be assured that his return will mean deliverance from wrath for them. Christ died for them, and they belong to him. Those who have trusted other gods for salvation will be sorely disappointed when Christ returns.

In our day it is difficult to discuss God's judgment, because the spirit of our age is antithetical in general to the notion that God would condemn people for anything but the most heinous crimes. Yet the same Son of God who came to redeem humanity will also judge all humanity. Only he has the right to do that (Matt 25:31-46; John 5:22). His judgment will bring the ultimate loss for those who live in darkness, who have trusted in the idols of this world. The things they believed would bring them security will suddenly be destroyed along with the lives they knew.

Today's idols might include things such as financial security or a materialistic explanation for everything, which makes God superfluous. Or they might be one of the many self-created spiritualities that make people feel they are tapping into something transcendent without needing to listen to the word of the true and living God. All will face the risen Lord at his return. "Hell receives those who imagine themselves good; Jesus receives those who know themselves sinners" (Oden 1998, 450).

Living as God's people for the world's sake. Finally, there is another pressing reason for believers to live as children of the light today—for the sake of the world. Just as God had mercy on us, so he can have mercy on others. We have our part to play in this great drama, as the Lord's witnesses. But we will not be credible if we do not live sincerely as his children. The world needs us to live in faith and love, even though it does not know it (5:15). Our faithfulness may encourage others to believe the Lord's word and receive for themselves the blessed hope of life with him.

VI. THE COMMUNITY OF CHRIST: I THESSALONIANS 5:12-24

5:12-24

BEHIND THE TEXT

After 5:11 Paul's sentences begin to get shorter and shorter, and the subject matter changes quickly as he moves toward the conclusion of the letter. There are similarities between this passage and Rom 12: several verbal parallels exist, and both mention those **who are over you** (*proistamenous*).

Some scholars think Paul finished his letter with a list of standard ethical injunctions (e.g., Best 1986, 223). But there is evidence these exhortations have been adapted to the situation at Thessalonica. Nowhere else are believers cautioned against despising prophecy (v 20), nor are other churches warned about people living "disorderly" (*ataktous* [v 14]; LSJM, 267; see ASV, LEB; "unruly" [KJV, NASB, Phillips]; "undisciplined" [NET]). Fearfulness (v 14) and sanctification (v 23) are related directly to issues raised earlier in the letter (2:14; 4:13; 4:1-8). And personal retribution (5:15) would be a major temptation in this persecuted community. This is not to deny that some exhortations may reflect concerns common to early Christian congregations.

As to its structure, 5:12-22 returns to paraenesis with the same expression that began 4:1, "we ask you" (5:12). It is filled mostly with short sentences using imperatives (commands). The commands advise first about how the community should treat those doing ministry (vv 12-13), then how to deal with problem people of various sorts in the congregation (vv 14-15). This is followed by commands relating to spirituality in general, especially prophecy (vv 16-22). The body of the letter comes to a close with a prayer for the Thessalonians (vv 23-24).

IN THE TEXT

A. Respect Those Doing Ministry (5:12-13)

■ **12** The new section begins with a request using the same verb that began 4:1: **we ask you** [*erōtaō*], **brothers *and sisters***. Paul has finished explaining those things about Jesus' Parousia that are necessary to "comfort" and "encourage" them (4:13—5:11). Anticipating the Lord's return should motivate believers to live in a way that is ready to receive him when he comes (compare Mark 13:33-37). Paul moves into his final instructions on community life. As at 1 Thess 4:1, 13; and 5:1 he addresses the Thessalonians as **brothers and sisters**: they are God's family, and it is that identity he asks them to fulfill.

First, he asks them **to acknowledge those who work hard among you**. **Acknowledge** (*eidenai*), from the verb "know," has the sense "recognize them for who they are" (as in Ignatius: "It is good to *recognize* God and the bishop"†; Ign. *Smyrn.* 9.1; compare 1 Cor 16:18).

Work (*kopiōntas*) elsewhere refers to Christian ministry (Rom 6:6, 12; 1 Cor 15:10; 16:16; Gal 4:11; Phil 2:16; compare 1 Thess 1:3; 3:5). We cannot assume that the ministry Paul commends as **work** was only that of deacons (as opposed to pastors/elders; mistakenly, Lightfoot 1957, 79). His language is too vague. For Christians, all ministry is service, according to the example and teaching of the Lord himself (Mark 10:42-44). Paul names two activities of these Christian workers: **care for you in the Lord** and **admonish you**.

First, caring is often considered some form of leadership. It translates a participle from *proistēmi*, meaning "lead or govern"; "support, give aid, care for"; or "protect" (LSJM, 1482-83; Reicke 1968, 6:700-703; BDAG, 870). In Rom 12:8 it appears among a series of gifts describing compassionate ministry rather than leadership (compare 1 Tim 3:5).

The related term *prostatis* is used in secular Greek for a female *patron*; in Rom 16:2 Paul suggests Phoebe, his "benefactor," has a ministry of caring for and protecting others (see *1 Clem.* 36.1; 61.3; Green 2002, 250; Witherington 2006, 160; Furnish 2007, 114-15). From their resources these patrons provide the homes where the church meets and other material goods (e.g., food for the Lord's Supper, aid for the unemployed). Although the existence of formal client relations is not proven (Walters 1996; Willis 1996), in ancient Mediterranean society those who lent the use of their homes and bestowed goods on the community would automatically acquire a certain status and authority.

Paul qualifies these caregivers' duties as **in the Lord**: this, not the wealth or social status, gives them their authority. They lead out of their relationship with the risen Christ who transforms, distributes gifts, and directs his church (see 1 Cor 12:18-27; Eph 4:11-16).

Second, the other ministry these Christian workers perform is to **admonish** (*nouthetountas*). They warn and remind people of what they should do. The emphasis is on influencing the will to change behavior (BDAG, 679; Selter 1999; Best 1986, 226). Within the home, it was the duty of fathers to **admonish** their children, to ensure they grow up avoiding evil. Within the larger society, it was typically older persons or social superiors who admonished their younger or social inferiors (1 Sam 3:13; Job 30:1; 1 Cor 4:14). God admonishes the wise person or the righteous (Wis 11:10; *Pss. Sol.* 13:9). And there was a long tradition of "soul care" among philosophers, who admonished their disciples (Malherbe 2000, 314-15).

Elsewhere Paul encourages the whole church to **admonish** one another (Rom 15:14; Col 3:16; 1 Thess 5:14). Here it is the special responsibility of certain leaders in the congregation. Some modern people think of admonition as intrusive. But the ancients considered it a normal aspect of family and other social relations. It was not just for "bad" people but was also given to those making progress in the moral life, to help them do even better (Malherbe 2000, 314).

It seems doubtful that Paul describes several different kinds of leaders (workers, caregivers, admonishers). He probably describes generally what all these workers do. Leadership was not tightly defined or specialized at this point; circumstances did not permit that luxury. In the early church, leaders arose spontaneously and charismatically in many Greek-speaking Christian communities (e.g., Rom 12:3-8; 1 Cor 12:4-11; 16:15-16). Titles and offices were not as important as the *functions* carried out by believers. Organization was still fairly informal.

■ **13** Paul asks the rest of the Christians at Thessalonica to **hold** these Christian servants **in the highest regard in love because of their work**. To hold in regard (*hēgeisthai*) was "to think of," as in "esteem." He couples this with a term meaning "to the greatest degree."

As with v 12, it is not for normal cultural reasons these leaders are to be honored. They are to be loved for the sake of their work on behalf of the kingdom of God (see 1:3). **Work** is their ministry activity in general. Beyond that, we cannot specify: it could be intellectual activity such as teaching and admonishing (v 12; Rom 12:7-8; 1 Cor 12:8, 28), or it could involve physical resources such as giving to those in need (Rom 12:8). It is likely that then, as in later ages, different people carried out different tasks.

Even in a society where admonishing others was accepted, there was the danger that misunderstanding, hurt feelings, and enmity could arise. Realizing the risk, Paul urges the community to accept this spiritual guidance with **love**, and he commands them to **live in peace with each other**.

To be at peace is deliberately to set aside hostility and jealousy. Both those who give correction and those who receive it need to beware of stubbornness. The **peace** of this community would be under constant threat from external opposition and internal friction.

Externally, believers were suffering (1:6) for their adherence to a minority faith that challenged the very foundations of the gods of the empire and the city. It could not help but provoke conflict from family, neighbors, business associates, and others. It must have been wearying for believers to face verbal and physical abuse, economic and social discrimination. Some deaths may have resulted, intentionally or not, from persecution (2:14-15; 4:13). Many people must have come to the worship gatherings with nerves frayed.

Internally, this was a community more diverse than anything usually seen in Macedonian society. Here mingled free and slave, aristocrat and craftsman, women and men, Macedonians, Greeks, Romans, Egyptians, and Jews. It was diverse in every way. God's gospel of grace, love, and forgiveness had brought them together. But they were not instantly perfect. Friction was bound to occur. It was imperative that Christians not add more to the woes the world was heaping upon them. Their meetings needed to be places of refuge, love, and restoration.

The **peace** command here has in mind primarily Christians' relations with each other. Bassler has noted that peace is a major theme of this letter, both opening (1:1) and closing (5:23) it (1994, 72-85).

B. Caring for Difficult People (5:14-15)

■ 14 And we urge you, brothers and sisters, warn those who are *disorderly*. Some patristic commentators saw the **brothers** here as the leaders doing the disciplining (John Chrysostom, *Hom. 1 Thess.* 10; see Best 1986, 230). There is no evidence, however, that Paul has turned from talking to the whole church in v 12 to address leaders alone here. These are general exhortations for the body of Christ, even if leaders are doing this more than others.

The word translated *disorderly* is *ataktous* (NIV: **idle and disruptive**, from *taxis*, "order"). The *ataktoi* are people who are undisciplined, disorderly, or insubordinate to superiors (BDAG, 148; see LSJM, 267). Many commentators think Paul refers to the problem mentioned earlier concerning those who needed to be encouraged to work (4:11). Hence, they suggest the meaning "loafers" or "lazy" (Best 1986, 230; Bruce 1982, 122; Marshall 1983, 150-51). This is reinforced in 2 Thess 3:6, 11, where Paul orders those living *ataktōs* ("lazily") to work for their food in imitation of the apostles' example.

But if the problem in Thessalonica simply concerned a failure to work, there were plainer words for "lazy" in Greek that Paul might have used (Malherbe 2000, 317). *Ataktos* points to some problem with attitude, a failure to accept the order of church, society, or the law (see *T. Naph.* 2:8-9; 3:2-3; → 2 Thess 3:6; Behind the Text for 2 Thess 3:6-15, below).

The *ataktoi* may have been voluntarily unemployed. But Paul's term suggests that the problem was larger than that. Jewett proposed that the congregation be understood as a millenarian movement (1986, 161-78): some members of the congregation manifested ecstatic behavior, dropped out of society, and stopped working. They were radicals who thought the millennium was already dawning, the Lord's Parousia was near, and normal rules no longer applied to them—whether for work or sex (ibid., 172-78). But the issue of overly realized eschatology is only raised explicitly in 2 Thessalonians. And there, Paul never links it to ethical issues. In fact, if apocalyptic fever were the problem it would be strange for Paul to urge that they comfort one another with talk of the Parousia (4:18; 5:11)!

Other interpreters see here a reference to the patronage system: some members chose to live as clients, dependent on others. They are "disorderly" because they chose to ignore the apostles' instructions to mind their own business and be self-supporting (→ 1 Thess 4:11-12; Winter 1994, 48-51; Green 2002, 253; → Behind the Text for 1 Thess 4:9-12).

Encourage the disheartened (*oligopsychos*, lit. "small-souled"). Such persons are fearful or feel inadequate or discouraged (Bruce 1982, 123; Malherbe 2000, 318). They may well have been those who were broken-spirited over persecution, or despondent about the fate of their loved ones who had died. Paul had addressed them in 4:13—5.11. Some may have felt inadequate to defend the gospel in dialogue with synagogue elders or pagan intellectuals. All needed to be consoled and reminded of what they have in Christ.

Paul also asks them to **help the weak** (*asthenēs*). The Greek term may refer to those struggling with physical weakness, sickness, mental problems, or moral failures. In Rom 5:6 it describes sinful humanity before its rescue by Christ. Sin disables people, just as surely as illness does. Paul says the Spirit helps believers "in our *weakness*" (*astheneiai* [Rom 8:26])—in our lack of knowledge and spiritual fortitude.

Paul calls the Thessalonians to spiritual friendship here. Instead of adopting a self-centered, survivalist mentality, he urges them to support the spiritually weak. Presumably this would include showing a welcoming and loving spirit, prayer for them, counsel, and instruction (Rom 15:7, 14; Gal 6:1-2; Col 3:13, 16; 1 Thess 5:17).

Some assume the **weak** must be the "weak in faith" (as in Rom 14:1-23), those overly scrupulous about meat that had been offered previously in pagan worship (see 1 Cor 8:7-13; Best 1986, 231; Bruce 1982, 123). But there is no evidence for this narrow definition here.

Another possibility is that **weak** refers to the powerless social status of some within the community (as in 1 Cor 1:26-27, referring to slaves and freedmen; Green 2002, 254). This is possible, but the other terms in the list address issues of character and function (with the possible exception of the *proistamenous* in v 12). It seems unlikely that Paul shifted to issues of wealth and status here. So it seems best to take **weak** here in the most general sense of those especially needing soul care.

The next command is for the community to **be patient [*makrothymeite*] with everyone**. Patience is one of God's great attributes (Exod 34:6; Num 14:18), celebrated in both OT (Pss 86:15; 103:8; Joel 2:13; Nah 1:3) and NT (Rom 2:4; 2 Pet 3:9). It restrains his wrath and reflects his mercy. As a trait of wise people, *makrothymia* describes them as slow to become angry (Prov 16:32; 19:11; Sir 29:8). Patience is not mere passivity; it is the ability to control oneself and to show grace to others (see Matt 18:26).

Patience is a fruit of Spirit (Gal 5:22). God's people don it at conversion like baptismal robes, as essential for Christian community (Col 3:12). Those who love others are patient (1 Cor 13:4).

Pagan writers also admired patience, though the term *makrothymia* is rare. Plutarch's *Lives* frequently holds up examples of noble characters who are self-controlled, slow to take offense, and even forgive former enemies. In *How to Profit by One's Enemies* he recommends one should welcome abuse from enemies with "gentleness and forbearance," because they will be quicker to tell the truth about faults than friends will (*Inim. util.* 90B, F).

As with the command to "peace" (v 13), the text seems to have in mind primarily relations with other Christians. Yet the true practice of patience could hardly be kept from spilling over to the non-Christians who persecute them. This becomes the subject of the next sentence.

■ **15** The final exhortation about social aspects of community life is a prohibition on retaliation: **Make sure that nobody pays back wrong for wrong**. Jesus prohibited retaliation and called for love of enemies (Matt 5:39-42, 44; Luke 6:27-29, 35). That is the most likely inspiration for Paul's rule here. Jewish literature offers mixed advice about retribution. Some texts counsel forbearance (Prov 20:22; 25:21-22; Sir 28:1-7); others celebrate vengeance (Esth 8:11-13; 9:1-17; Ps 137:8-9; 1 Macc 2:42-47, 68; 4Q169 III-IV, 1-3).

Paul doesn't say who or how the church will **make sure that nobody** retaliates against persecutors. Would they employ private admonition (1 Thess 5:14)? Would they meet and try to shame any who wanted to take revenge into complying (Matt 18:15-17)? Would they ostracize wrongdoers (Matt 18:17; 1 Cor 5:1-5, 11)? Or is this simply a general command for all to watch themselves? We must remember that there were as yet no hard-and-fast boundaries between clergy and laity. Everyone was responsible to help make these social ideals realities.

The apostle offered as a Christian alternative to retaliation: **always strive to do what is good for each other and for everyone else**. He may here echo Jesus' golden rule (Matt 7:12; Luke 6:31) and his call to love. Versions of the golden rule are found around the world prior to Christianity, including in Buddhism and Judaism. But all the other versions are formulated in the *negative*: *Don't* do to others what you don't want done to yourself. Jesus' rule is the only known positive version, which calls for constructive activism: "*Do* to others what you would have them do to you" (Matt 7:12). Paul's positive call to **pursue good** (*to agathon diōkete*) and prohibition of vengeance resemble the same two teachings in Jesus' Sermon on the Mount/Plain (Matt 5—7; Luke 6:17-49).

Strive/*pursue* is the same verb used for a hunter seeking out game. Paul asks his converts to give attention to the affairs around them and actively chase after and do God's good will (Rom 12:2) as a spiritual discipline. The **good** (*agathon*) includes things such as justice, mercy, truthfulness, and faithfulness. This virtue is to be practiced not only with other Christians but with **everyone else**, even persecutors. Living the gospel is never easy.

C. Preserve a Life of Worship (5:16-22)

BEHIND THE TEXT

In the following verses Paul dashes off a series of short, staccato sentences. Each has a command for the church. He gives the impression that his speech is speeding up, as if he is in a hurry to finish the letter or squeeze as much into the last bit of papyrus that he can manage.

Some commentators think Paul just throws in a series of all-purpose maxims. It is true that he mentions the need to rejoice and to pray elsewhere (e.g., Eph 6:18; Phil 3:1; 4:6; Col 4:3; 2 Thess 3:1). But the command to "pray continually" is rare in Paul's letters—only here in 1 Thess 5:17 and in Eph 6:18. His instructions about prophecy (1 Thess 5:19-22) appear to be specific to this community's situation. The apostle is not tossing off trite slogans, as if they were theological bumper stickers. He has the good of a specific community in mind. Of course, some of their needs are similar to those of other young Christians. That does not make them any less real or relevant.

This subsection of the letter appears to be about *worship* in the broadest sense. Worship may happen when Christians gather in one of their houses, where someone prophesies (among other things, vv 19-22). Or it may occur as they work in their shops, cultivating an awareness of God as they "pray continually" (v 17). Worship is about being open to God at every moment.

Paul urges the Thessalonians to be open to the leading of the Spirit and to hold on to that which is "good" (vv 19-22). This leads directly and naturally into his closing prayer for their sanctification (vv 23-24). This is also about being wholly and continually open to God.

It is possible to understand the Greek present imperatives (commands) of vv 19-20 as indicating expected, future, habitual behavior (Bruce 1982, 125; Malherbe 2000, 331; Witherington 2006, 168). In this case, Paul is not correcting a problem, but simply offering good general advice.

However, several factors about the rhetoric of this passage, the context of the letter, and the cultural context of Thessalonica suggest otherwise. It is better to understand these commands as not only advocating habitual action but also implying that they are to cease doing something they have been doing. The reasons are as follows:

(a) Paul gives not one but *five* imperatives in a row relating to prophecy and charismatic phenomena in worship (vv 19-22). This seems a bit much for a passing reference to worship.

(b) "Do not treat . . . with contempt" (*mē exoutheneite* [v 20]) is extremely strong language. This implies there was a problem at the church. Paul could simply have said, "Do not reject" or "Listen to the prophets" (compare 2 Chr 36:16 LXX).

(c) Early Christianity was a charismatic movement. Thus, it seems surprising that Paul would have cautioned against *not* receiving a prophetic message. The closest thing to this in his letters is 1 Cor 14:39 ("Do not forbid speaking in tongues"). But Paul offers this warning only because of his prior *lengthy correction* of glossolalia. He wants to avoid the opposite extreme—extinguishing the gift. If the analogy stands, it implies some people at Thessalonica have been engaged in correcting prophecy/prophets.

(d) The commands in 1 Thess 5:21-22 urge readers to "test them all [prophecies]; hold on to what is good" and "reject every kind of evil." These are more than good general advice. In this context they add to the impression that there were problems with questionable prophetic utterances.

The unfortunate response of some may have been extreme: instead of thoughtful evaluation, total rejection of the phenomenon. Paul urges assessment and gives them permission to "reject" a so-called word of the Spirit (or other manifestation of the Spirit), if it turns out to be "evil."

(e) Were the charismatic prophets who had created these problems the same as the *atakoi*, the "idle and disruptive" (v 14)? Were they not working and disturbing the peace of the church or others (4:11)?

If so, we know that the situation became worse, and Paul had to address this at length in 2 Thess 3:6-12. The troublemakers may have justified their behavior partly on the grounds that they were Christ's prophets. This would also help explain Paul's rhetoric about apostolic work in this letter.

(f) We know that by the time Paul wrote 2 Thessalonians, false teaching about Christ's return was attributed in part to false prophecy (2 Thess 2:2). He will call on the church to ground its certainty in the knowledge of his past teaching, including 1 Thessalonians (2 Thess 2:15).

Yet already in 1 Thessalonians there are hints that the assemblies are confused about the end times (1 Thess 4:13, 15). And 5:1, "about times and dates we do not need to write to you," might be designed to discourage date setting. Was it false prophecies about the Lord's return that some Thessalonians rejected (Morris 1991, 177; Williams 1992, 101; Gaventa 1998, 84; Malherbe 2000, 335)?

(*g*) Prophecies may well have been treated "with contempt" because of the *manner* of prophecy. For most of these Macedonian Christians, the only models of "inspiration" they had ever seen prior to Paul would have been in the context of pagan cults.

It is not likely that early Christians would have blindly copied pagan ceremonies and imported them into their worship meetings. But contextualization of the gospel had already been going on since the church in Antioch began a mission to Gentiles, later baptized by Jerusalem (Acts 11:20-21; 15:1-35). It would not be surprising if, after the apostles left Thessalonica and new people entered the community, the manner in which they discerned the activity of the Spirit changed. Some believers leaned toward ecstatic, outrageous behavior as a sign of the Spirit's presence. They may have even facilitated this with wine used at the meetings, as had been done in Dionysiac ceremonies. It is striking how Paul twice calls on the church to "be . . . sober" as "children of the day" and not to "get drunk" like the children of "the night" (5:5-7).

Why does he pick this characteristic specifically? Why not speak about truth-telling or chastity (as earlier) or humility or other virtues? If this scenario is close to what happened, one can see why Paul might ask them to live "a *quiet* life" and seek "the *respect* of outsiders" rather than raving in Bacchic fashion (4:11). We know that at Corinth both drunkenness and inappropriate emphasis on nonsensical ecstatic speech occurred (1 Cor 11:21; 14:2, 6-17). It would be easy to imagine something similar beginning at Thessalonica, some wanting their new God to be as impressive as the old cults in the moving of Spirit and prophecy. So they model prophetic movements on what they know. Only unlike Corinth, this movement is opposed by a majority within the church, probably including the leadership itself (Wanamaker 1990, 202).

IN THE TEXT

■ **16 Rejoice always** begins the series of brief commands having to do with worship. As part of a triad of injunctions (vv 16-18), we know that the "rejoicing" Paul commands here is not self-centered or generic—he is not simply saying "be happy."

Joy is both a gift of the Spirit (Gal 5:22) and our response to the Spirit, the Son, and the Father for the loving embrace that sweeps us into the kingdom of God (Matt 13:44; Luke 15:10; 24:52-53; John 15:11). In Paul's letters rejoicing is often associated with conversion and the life of faith (Rom 15:13; 2 Cor 1:24; Phil 1:25; 1 Thess 1:6; 2:19, 20; 3:9).

Always should not be understood as "for everything." Many things in this life are disappointing, sorrowful, and evil. And Christian love does not rejoice at evil (1 Cor 13:6). The call to be joyful is a call to faith. We should remember at all times to whom we belong, what our future is with God, and what the risen Christ has promised us (see 1 Thess 5:9-10).

■ **17 Pray continually**, taken literally, seems an impossible command. So **continually** might be best understood (→ 1 Thess 1:2-3) as praying "often." We "should always pray and not give up," as Jesus exhorted his disciples (Luke 18:1). The business of work, the sorrow of grief, conflicts with family and society over their new faith—all these should drive believers to pray at every opportunity. They may cultivate an awareness of their heavenly Father wherever they are and remember his grace to them.

■ **18** The third instruction for worship is to **give thanks in all circumstances**. There is no word for **circumstances** in Greek. But this seems to be the intention of the expression *in all things*. Paul does *not* recommend that we give thanks *for* everything, no matter how evil it is. He has expressed anguish in this letter over things such as their suffering and his inability to return to them.

Believers can **give thanks** regardless, for the ground of their thanksgiving is God himself and what he has done for the world in Jesus Christ. He is the God who triumphs in spite of human evil. He has redeemed his people, sent his Spirit, and safeguarded their future with himself beyond death (5:9-10).

Paul adds a motivation: **this is God's will for you in Christ Jesus**. It is his will—it pleases him and fulfills his good plans—that we worship and acknowledge him. This is not because God is selfish but because it makes humans whole. And God is worthy of worship. This probably refers to all three injunctions: be joyful, pray, and give thanks (Green 2002, 260). It is not entirely clear how **in Christ Jesus** clarifies **God's will**. It could mean, "God's will for Christians"—those who are in Christ. Or, it could mean that this is what God intends and makes possible for his people *through* Jesus Christ (Marshall 1983, 156). Certainly Jesus taught these things and modeled the life of joy, prayer, and thankfulness (Woolsey 1997, 97). The reference to **God's will** echoes 4:3, enclosing almost all of the paraenesis of the letter in an inclusio. The other major term at 4:3, "sanctification," will occur in verbal form in the prayer of 5:23.

■ **19** Paul next advises on prophecy (vv 19-22). This was apparently a common event at early Christian worship gatherings (Acts 11:27; 13:1; 21:8-10; 1 Cor 12:28; 14:1, 5; 3 John 5-10). Prophets offered exhortation, comfort, teaching, words of conviction and correction, and occasionally prediction (see Acts 11:27-28; 13:2; 15:32; 21:10-11; 1 Cor 14:3-6). Some were local community members who prophesied on an ad hoc basis. Some traveled from place to place, speaking more regularly. Prophets apparently continued to function in this way into the early second century (see *Did.* 11).

It seems best to understand the five imperatives (commands) of vv 19-20 as all clarifying the theme of the use of charismata in worship, particularly prophecy. This is better than seeing vv 21-22 as generic advice. If they belong together, we can better interpret Paul's words and the situation at Thessalonica.

The first two prohibitions (vv 19-20) seem to stand in parallel. One who does not **quench the Spirit** allows the inspiration of the Spirit to operate freely within oneself and others.

■ **20** One might "extinguish the fire" of the Spirit speaking to the church by treating the **prophecies** of others **with contempt** (v 20). The Spirit and prophecy are intimately associated (see 1 Cor 12:7-11; 2 Pet 1:21; Rev 1:10; 2:7). When the author of 1 John 4:1 enjoins readers to "test the *spirits*," he is speaking about testing the genuineness of a prophet's claim to speak by divine inspiration. There may have been **contempt** for prophets who were drunk or who imitated pagan-style mantics. Or abuses may have led to some skeptically rejecting the whole enterprise (→ Behind the Text for 1 Thess 5:16-22, above). This prohibition is about one's response to prophecy in community worship (rather than one's own gifting). Paul urges the Thessalonians to be open to the voice of the Spirit to guide, correct, and comfort them through the words of the prophets (1 Cor 14:3, 24-25).

The commands in 1 Thess 5:21-22 reinforce the impression given by our survey of the world (→ Behind the Text for 5:16-22, above) that Paul here offers advice on how to deal with real problems in Thessalonica. Given that early Christianity as a whole was a charismatic movement, it seems surprising that Paul would have to correct opposition or skepticism toward prophecy at this early date. What would have led to this problem? The three injunctions in vv 21-22 probably give us a clue.

■ **21** Paul's counterpoint—***But test everything; hold tight to what is good***—could be a proverb applicable to any church. But here, immediately after his caution about "the Spirit" and prophecy, it appears to be a counterbalance. The "contempt" (v 20) of the cautious is an overreaction to the excesses of others in the church. Instead of correcting the problem, they rejected prophecy altogether.

The apostle acknowledges that criticism is necessary (1 Cor 14:29; 1 John 4:1)—**Test them all**. To **test** prophetic messages presumes there might be something **good** to retain. But to "treat prophecies with contempt" (1 Thess 5:20) is to condemn without a hearing.

What critical assessments could apply to prophecies? We have a few clues in this and other letters:

- the fragments of early creeds and affirmations of core beliefs (1 Cor 15:1-11; 1 Thess 1:9-10; 4:6, 15-17; 5:2-10; 2 Thess 1:5-10)
- polemical statements relating the new covenant to the Law (Gal 3:1—4:7)
- Paul's ethical teaching (1 Thess 4:1-12) grounded in the OT and common apostolic tradition (1 Cor 15:11)

They could use such material to gauge the veracity and usefulness of prophecies (see 1 Cor 14:29). Whatever accords with apostolic teaching is **good**. So they are to **hold on to** it (*katechete*)—accept it and put it into practice.

■ **22 Reject every kind of evil,** like v 21, has a generic quality to it. But within Paul's treatment of the problems with prophecy, **evil** must serve as an adjective: **Reject every kind of evil *prophecy*.** This fits his usage elsewhere (2 Cor 9:8; Gal 1:4; Eph 4:29; 1 Tim 6:4; 2 Tim 4:18; 2 Thess 2:17; Bruce 1982, 126; Fee 2009, 223). This translation closely links vv 21 and 22: ***Cling to the good to be found in prophecies; reject the evil sort.***

What was *evil* about prophecy, or what led the one party to treat prophecy with contempt? Suggestions focus on the *content* of the prophecy, the *manner* of prophecy, or the skeptical philosophical *perspective* of the overly cautious ones. One guess was that the prophets demanded money in the Spirit from the church elders (Frame 1912, 204). But the call to **test everything** (v 21) seems to be coupled with evidence of problems in understanding Jesus' return (4:13-15; → 2 Thess 2:1-3). Some recent interpreters identify the problem as excessively enthusiastic and false prophecy about the second coming (Jewett 1986, 101; Morris 1991, 177; Williams 1992, 101).

Had the cautious faction imbibed the jaundiced perspective on prophecy of Cicero and the Epicureans (so Green 2002, 263)? Was the basic controversy more about an unhealthy emphasis some had put on charismatic gifts, especially expressions of ecstatic prophecy? Had this produced a reaction by other believers who refused to accept the supernatural moving of the Spirit (so Marshall 1983, 157-58; Richard 1995, 279)? Did the ecstatic behavior of Christian prophets mimic the bizarre practices of their former pagan cults and mystery rites (so Best 1986, 239)? Did alcohol contribute to this? Had they used their alleged Spirit-inspiration to challenge the patronal leadership (so Jewett 1986, 101-5)?

The evidence of 1 Thessalonians is too slim to allow certainty beyond this:

- Problems did exist with eschatology. They got only worse with the help of false prophecies (→ 2 Thess 2:2).
- First Thessalonians 5:19-20 points to a church divided over its acceptance of prophecy or other charismatic phenomena.
- Paul encourages them to persevere in listening to the Spirit, to cling to the good and reject evil sorts of prophecy (or every sort of evil).
- Serious problems with the prophecies had to be overcome.

Pagan Models of Inspiration

For most of these Macedonian Christians, the only models of "inspiration" they had ever experienced prior to Paul would have been in the context of pagan cults. At Thessalonica the cults devoted to Dionysus and Cybele claimed to grant divine possession or inspiration to certain devotees.

Dionysus was associated with wine, harvest, sexual license, and alcohol-induced ecstasy. He represents the inversion of social order. His festivals were like an ancient Mardi Gras, full of excess in alcohol and lust. In artwork his female worshippers, called *maenads*, are portrayed as dancing or leaping in a raving ecstasy, oblivious to their surroundings, with hair and garments flying. Sometimes they are shown swinging their own infants round by one leg over their shoulders or being chased by mythical male creatures.

The priests of Cybele were a bizarre identity-shifting lot in other ways. They shaved their heads, wore women's makeup, jewelry, and colorful robes, deliberately looking effeminate. They paraded with musical instruments (cymbals, horns, and flutes) and chanted songs as they danced themselves into a frenzy. The priests showed their devotion by emasculating themselves in honor of the goddess. Cybele's worship had spread from Anatolia across Macedonia and into Italy by Paul's day (on both cults see: Edson 1948, 160-80, 189-201; Ferguson 1970, 26-31, 104-6; MacMullen 1981, 16, 21, 24; Burkert 1985, 109-11, 161-67; Easterling and Muir 1985, 118-21; Beard, North, and Price 1998, 1:95-97, 162-66, 261; Brocke 2001, 117-29).

In addition, there were independent seers who claimed the ability to undergo divine possession, whether through magic or other attachment to a deity, and were willing to sell their services, as the NT bears witness (Acts 8:9; 13:6-7; 16:16).

If these were the only models for "inspiration," it is not surprising if problems should arise over prophecy and whether or not to accept it, despite the positive examples the apostles left. Some of these problems may have been with the content of what was taught, but just as easily there may have been issues with how certain people behaved (or encouraged others to behave) while believing themselves possessed by the Holy Spirit.

Paul uses the strongest language anywhere in the NT to urge the Thessalonians not to despise prophecy and to guide their reception of it. Some may have assimilated Christianity to the religious inspiration they knew from their pagan pasts. Others reacted in the opposite way. They not only distanced themselves from paganism but also came down harshly on the first group. They may have been overly concerned not to arouse more political trouble with the Roman authorities.

D. Paul's Pastoral Prayer (5:23-24)

BEHIND THE TEXT

Paul's pastoral prayer for the Thessalonian church brings the paraenetic section and the body of the letter as a whole to a close. It reintroduces the theme of sanctification raised at 4:3 with literary bookends (an inclusio). Also reviewed from earlier in the letter are the Spirit, peace, the Lord's return (*parousia*), their calling, and, of course, God and Jesus as Lord.

Rhetorically, the prayer functions as a kind of peroratio, or summarizing conclusion. It is incomplete, however, because that is not its sole function (against Wanamaker 1990, 205). Paul reports a prayer he genuinely prays, using an old, formal style with the Greek optative verb form (the "wish mood"). For us it would be like someone using "King James" English. For similar prayers see Gen 27:28; 28:3-4; Pss 12:3; 67:7; Tob 5:17; Jdt 10:8; Wis 7:15.

Plato (late fifth—early fourth century BC) espoused various tripartite descriptions of humanity. In addition to the material body, the soul was the *rational* element that ruled. It was made up of *nous* (the mind), *thymos* (an *irrational appetite*—driving things such as hunger and lust), and *pathos* (passion, with sensitivities such as honor or courage). The good and just person was the one whose reasoning capacity could keep all the parts in balance, like a charioteer handling difficult horses (*Resp.* 439A-D, 440E, 441E, 443C-D; *Phaedr.* 246A-B, 248A-E, 253C-254E; see also Zakopoulos 1975, 59-66). By Paul's day, the Middle Platonists had revised this into a bipartite soul theory: a *rational* soul and an *irrational* soul (Dillon 1977, 174, 194, 291-92). This had become part of popular philosophy and was found in the Jewish writer Philo of Alexandria.

IN THE TEXT

■ **23** Paul circles around again to his people's holiness for the third time in this letter. He had prayed earlier for God to make them "blameless and holy" at the Parousia (1 Thess 3:13). And his paraenesis opened with "God's will" for them to "be sanctified" (4:3). Now again he prays for their entire sanctification.

He calls on **the God of peace** (5:23; compare Rom 15:33; 16:20; 2 Cor 13:11; Phil 4:9) to do what he alone can do. God is the one who can bring ultimate **peace**, the *shalom* of the messianic age when righteousness will reign on earth (Isa 32:16-18; Mic 4:1-5). God's peace is about people being in right relationship with him and with one another. The wicked are said to have no peace (Isa 57:19-21). The community longed for **peace** in the midst of difficulties they had both internally (1 Thess 5:12-14) and externally (1:6; 2:14; 5:14). So **peace** is a fitting epithet for the God who sanctifies.

The term **may** goes with **sanctify** to express in English that this reports a prayer (→ 3:11-13). To **sanctify** is to devote wholly to God. It implies that the people who are so devoted will take on the character of the God to whom they belong (→ 4:3). Earlier Paul had urged that those who belong to God also live to please God. Now the prayer recognizes the necessity for God to do the gracious work of sanctifying.

In one sense the Thessalonian believers are already holy, for they are God's people by faith. This is the meaning of **holy people** (*hagioi*; or "saints" [ESV, KJV, NASB, NRSV]; Rom 1:7; Eph 1:1; Phil 1:1; 1 Tim 5:10). But this prayer recognizes that this "positional" holiness is only the starting point, or the urgent incentive, for a continual turning to God with the whole self.

Paul prays that **God** will **sanctify** them *completely* (NIV: **through and through**). He uses an unusual term to emphasize that the sanctifying process occurs throughout the whole person (BDAG, 704; Bruce 1982, 129; Malherbe 2000, 338). He then elaborates on what this sanctification entails. He prays that their **whole spirit, soul and body** may **be kept blameless** at the Lord's return.

Whole (*holoklēron*) means something that is complete and undamaged. It was associated with physical health in ancient papyri letters (Wis 15:3; Jas 1:4; BDAG, 703; Green 2002, 268). For a second time Paul indicates that God's sanctifying and guarding work for believers is intended to comprehend the entirety of our humanity.

The prayer to **be kept** [*tērētheiē*] **blameless at the coming** presumes that judgment accompanies Christ's return (see Matt 25:31-46; 2 Cor 5:10). A favorable verdict will require God's sanctifying grace. In Greek **blameless** is actually an adverb (*amemptōs*), **blamelessly**.

Paul uses the "divine passive," **be kept**, to imply that God graciously acts to effect our sanctification (compare Eph 5:26-27). Canonical echoes suggest that believers may become like the great heroes of the faith: the adjective **blameless** (*amemptos*) in the LXX describes Abraham, Job, and Aaron (Gen 17:1; Job 1:1, 8; 2:3; Wis 10:5; 18:21).

Does **kept** mean "preserved as **blameless** beforehand up until his coming" (i.e., as something that begins now)? Or "**kept blameless** at the moment of his coming (by the grace of Christ's forgiveness)" only when the second coming occurs? Paul could easily have said, "kept blameless *until* the parousia" (using *mechri*, *heōs*, or *eis*). But he says **at the coming** (*en tē parousia*; Marshall 1983, 161).

5:23

The aorist tense of **kept** describes a simple action, rather than emphasizing an ongoing process. Along with the passive voice, this points to an action by God at the time of Christ's appearing. Nevertheless, the full prayer implies a previous process in believers' lives: The *sanctifying* **through and through** happens in the present age (see 1 Thess 3:12-13; 4:3) to prepare them for Christ's Parousia (Marshall 1983, 161).

It seems doubtful that Paul thought people were made up of three parts, one material (the **body** [*sōma*]) and two immaterial (the **soul** [*psychē*] and the **spirit** [*pneuma*]; → Behind the Text for 1 Thess 5:23-24, above). This tripartite division is found nowhere else in Paul's letters or the NT. Elsewhere Paul normally uses two-part descriptions of humanity, often alternating terms: "body" and "spirit" (1 Cor 5:3; 7:34); "flesh" and "spirit" (1 Cor 5:5); flesh (NIV: **sinful nature**) and "mind" (Rom 7:25). And he may even use "soul" and "spirit" synonymously, according to some readings of Phil 1:27 (see Malherbe 2000, 339; Aquinas 1969, on 1 Thess 5:23). In some passages, he differentiates "spirit" and "mind" (1 Cor 14:14-19; compare Rom 7:23).

Paul and other early Christians seem uninterested in mapping the human self as precisely or consistently as did the Platonists (Malherbe 2000, 339). For instance, Jesus' great commandment in Mark 12:30—to love God with all our heart, soul, mind, and strength—does not require a four-part theory of personhood. Both Mark 12:30 and 1 Thess 5:23 merely evoke a comprehensive picture of all that humans are.

Paul's tripartite language may sound like first-century philosophical anthropology. He may borrow that language for some local reason, but he is no Platonist. Platonists disparaged the body as an impediment to the soul, a prison they hoped to escape after death (Plato, *Phaed.* 82E-83C, 84A; *Crat.* 400B-C). Such thinking was later linked to Christian ideas in Gnosticism. Gnostics exalted the soul but despised the body. They even denied that Jesus had a real body, really died, or was raised bodily.

For Paul, believers' bodies are holy to God. Bodily existence can glorify God and is an indispensable part of being a redeemed human (1 Cor 6:19-20; 1 Thess 4:3-8). The body will be raised when the Lord returns. The kingdom of God is not for bodiless souls but for embodied souls.

In biblical writers, the term "soul" generally referred to the life force within individuals. To have soul was to be alive (as opposed to being a dead corpse, an unanimated body; Acts 20:10; 1 Cor 15:45). Hence, to lose one's soul (*psychē*) is to "die" (Mark 10:45; Luke 12:20; Rom 11:3). Jesus urged his generation to repent, follow him, and save their *psychē* by entering God's kingdom. The *psychē* was more valuable than anything in this world (Mark 8:34-37). The Bible also uses "soul" to describe the seat of the interior life—thought, feelings, will—the essential self (Matt 11:29; 2 Cor 1:23; Eph 6:6; see Dihle et al. 1974).

Some interpreters think "spirit" indicates an aspect of the self where humanity and God intersect by means of the Holy Spirit. *Pneuma* describes both the human and divine spirit (Fee 1994, 66). This is helpful, especially in 1 and 2 Corinthians. But it does not negate the observation that Paul's anthropological categories are fluid and overlap. The main thrust of 1 Thess 5:23 is not a lesson on anthropology. Paul uses **spirit, soul and body** to emphasize the totality of God's work (so Tertullian, *Res.* 47). God's sanctification affects all of the Christian's capacities—physical, mental, emotional, and spiritual.

Paul prays that God will **sanctify** the Thessalonians in every aspect of their humanity in this present age. And he prays that throughout their life's journey, God will ***preserve them blamelessly***, keeping them holy and wholly his until Jesus' return. Sanctification enables him to achieve his saving purposes in us: the Lord "died for us" so that we might not "suffer wrath but . . . receive salvation through our Lord Jesus Christ" and "live together with him" (5:10, 9).

■ **24** Paul gives a word of assurance for this far-reaching prayer. It is possible because **the one who calls you is faithful, and he will do it**. It is in God's hands, this miracle that leads from calling to sanctification to presenting the believer blameless before his throne.

Calls is a present-tense verb in Greek, meaning in this case an activity that habitually goes on. God is by nature the one who constantly looks for the lost (Matt 18:10-14; Luke 15:4-32; 19:10), who constantly invites and reinvites our participation in his life (see Oord and Lodahl 2005, 138). Paul has broken out of the prayer language to address the congregation directly again.

At the beginning of the letter Paul praised the Thessalonians' **work of faith** (1:3). Now he reminds them that *God* has a faithful work he does. He asks them to trust God to keep his promise to do it. The very sending of the Son on our behalf, his death and resurrection, are God's pledge that he is committed to rescue and sanctify the lost who turn to him in faith (1 Thess 1:10; 5:10).

FROM THE TEXT

The wide range of issues addressed in 5:12-24 calls for an equally wide set of suggestions (and questions) as we seek to implement this teaching as God's word for our time.

Leadership and communal discipline. Paul urges believers to honor church leadership, calling for communal discipline of problem members. This seems to reflect an early stage in church development. There is a mix of formal structure and Spirit-driven charismatic gifts.

Some emerging patterns of leadership by elders and some worship practices come from the synagogue, passed on by Jewish apostles and believers. Later letters describe some people as leading worship functions because they have a specific "gift" from the Spirit, not due to appointment or training (Rom 12:6-8; 1 Cor 14:26).

Here, Paul describes the Thessalonian leaders as those who "work hard among" them, caring for and admonishing them (1 Thess 5:12). It is not that they are lacking spiritual gifts. But this community valued service (compare Phil 2:29-30; 4:14-18).

Paul's familial language used throughout this letter indicates that he expected the Christian community to behave like a self-governing family. Families have structure and leadership, even if they do not have "offices." And families are concerned for one another's well-being. In healthy families, brothers, sisters, aunts, and uncles, as well as parents all share in the task of encouraging the dispirited or chiding those who misbehave.

In the family context, it is understood that correction is done out of love for the offender. And it is also clear—or can be made clear—that what one person does affects the welfare of all and the reputation of all in the family. Paul's vision of ethics is a *communal* ethic. And his view of spiritual discipline and growth is also communal. It is not simply "do what is good" but "do what is good *for each other and for everyone else*" (1 Thess 5:15). He does not simply tell the idle to shape up; he tells the community to "warn" them (v 14).

Could this familial context for encouragement, correction, and growth be recovered and adapted to the contemporary church? Without it, correction and admonition become not a normal but an abnormal thing. It must be administered by a professional (a pastor, district superintendent, bishop, etc.). The Western bent toward individualism and subjectivism in religion makes it difficult for people to interpret correction as anything other than somebody *else's* subjective will imposed upon them.

Recovering the familial atmosphere of the early Christian house churches, with their intimacy and oversight of one another's lives, was originally one of the functions of John Wesley's class meetings. In these small-group meetings members reported weekly on their spiritual condition and struggles. "Advice or reproof was given as need required, quarrels were made up, misunderstandings removed: and after an hour or two spent in this labour of love, they concluded with prayer and thanksgiving" (Snyder 1980, 55).

Small groups in more recent church practice similarly foster spiritual growth and fellowship. But rarely since the early Methodist days have they asked adherents to be as soul-baring and open to group admonishment or encouragement on a regular basis. This sense of group accountability and family dynamics, however, still exists within churches in traditional societies in places like sub-Saharan Africa and Central America. It remains to be seen whether the same is possible in churches within cultures dominated by the modern model of the nuclear family.

A life of constant prayer and thanksgiving. Across the centuries, some Christians have attempted to apply Paul's "pray continually" command (5:17) in a literal way. One method has been to use short prayers such as, "Lord, have mercy on me, a sinner" (see Luke 18:3). This really works well only if one is doing things that don't require significant concentration. Another method is known from Brother Lawrence's classic, *The Practice of the Presence of God*. He cultivated what he called a "conversation" with God, which lasted all day long. He continued his prayer time into his kitchen duties in the monastery where he worked. His were not always spoken prayers. He attempted to sustain an active awareness that all of life is lived in the presence of, and as an offering to, the triune God.

Unceasing prayer requires no single technique. The important thing is that it should not be like a AAA card, just to be taken out in emergencies. Prayer needs to be the breath of life always.

Gratitude is one of the most basic elements of worship. It is implicit in the harvest and fellowship offerings of the OT, which acknowledge God as the source of the earth's produce that feeds us. It is expressed in the blessings we say over meals. It may be felt wordlessly by a parent when a child returns safely from a trip. Some can find thankfulness just in being able to rise in the morning and have a place to live and food to eat.

Christians give God thanks amid all life's events and circumstances (1 Thess 5:18). Doing so recognizes that God remains Creator and Redeemer no matter what happens to us. He triumphs for us over sin and death (Rom 8:31-39; 1 Cor 15:57; 2 Cor 9:15). He has made believers heirs of his kingdom through Christ (Col 1:12-13). We can rejoice and give thanks that God continues to be at work making known his life-giving gospel until Christ returns. He remains the glorious God always. And his people can always pray, as the Book of Common Prayer puts it:

> Give us that due sense of all thy mercies, that our hearts may be unfeignedly thankful; and that we show forth thy praise, not only with our lips, but in our lives, by giving up our selves to thy service, and by walking before thee in holiness and righteousness all our days; through Jesus Christ our Lord. (1979, 59)

Embrace the work of the Spirit. There is evidence that Christian prophecy, like OT prophecy, was meant to address the specific situation of the audience with a word of encouragement or correction from God (Acts 21:10-11; 1 Cor 14:3, 24-25, 31). Prophets were accountable to the church to maintain apostolic doctrine and give trustworthy messages. And the church was responsible to test them—to assess their truth (1 Cor 14:29; 1 John 4:1-3).

A number of interpreters throughout Christian history have understood "prophecy" as expounding a biblical text or teaching doctrine (Ambrosiaster, Augustine, Aquinas, Calvin; see Thiselton 2011, 165-68). Hence, today some believe the task of preaching has subsumed this gift. True, good preaching may function prophetically, by God's grace. But should we narrowly confine prophetic speaking to the work of pastors and evangelists as they preach from the pulpit?

Like Corinth and Thessalonica, contemporary churches have divided on this issue. Charismatic churches too often promote movings of the Spirit without sufficient discernment, inviting abuse. Noncharismatic churches, in reaction, block all noninstitutional expressions of the Spirit. Neither have formal procedures for evaluating prophecy.

We should remember that Paul urged the church not to quash the gift of prophecy. But he also recognized the need to test everything spoken in the Spirit's name (→ 1 Thess 5:19-20 for tests that may have been employed). Some theological traditions believe that all miraculous gifts, including prophecy, ceased with the end of the apostolic age and the completion of Scripture. But nothing in the NT suggests that the gifts and working of the Spirit were to be temporary. Christ promised to be spiritually present with his disciples until the end of the age (Matt 28:20; John 20:22; Rom 8:9-10).

The Spirit and prophecy should never be seen as in competition with Scripture. Nor are they a substitute for it. The Spirit continues to lead, give insight, and convict the church throughout all ages. "The church is under the reign of the Spirit, not the reverse" (Pinnock 1996, 131). We continue to experience prophetic guidance through the wise word spoken at a critical time, through spiritual leaders' writings, even in this age through email, blogs and tweets. God is not limited in how he may speak.

The sanctification of the whole self. In 1 Thess 4:3-8 sanctification describes how believers live in obedience to God's will. In 5:23-24 sanctification is God's gracious work making believers blameless for the Parousia. These two passages must always be held together in creative tension by Christians: only God by his grace can sanctify. And, because his grace is present, believers may, and so must, respond with joyful and willing obedience. That Paul prays for this should be a paradigm for our spirituality also.

Sanctification means to be made holy, belonging to God, and in a relationship of total devotion to God (→ 4:3). The prayer for God to sanctify believers *completely* requests that their relationship to God may touch every facet of their human personality. Paul repeats the same idea with emphasis on the eschatological goal in his prayer that their whole spirit, soul, and body may be kept blameless at Jesus' Parousia. To be blameless *then*, they must be made holy *now*.

Wesley emphasized that sanctification was a work of God's grace in the lives of believers, which begins at justification and continues until death. He understood sanctification principally as love for God and neighbor, which was the restoration of the image of God marred in the fall. In this he follows Paul, who conjoins his prayer for the Thessalonians' *love* with that for their *holiness* (1 Thess 3:12-13; see Eph 3:16-19).

Wesley also believed that "entire sanctification" was possible in this life. God's work could lead believers to have a purity of intention in which their actions wholly proceeded from love of God and neighbor (Dunning 1988, 464-65; Maddox 1994, 176, 187, 190). He did not understand this to suggest that they were either "perfect" or error-free, but only blame-free. Sanctification is never static. It is a *relationship* of love to God and the world that is always developing, always responding to new circumstances (Oord and Lodahl, 2005).

Greek Verbs and Sanctification

Some earlier holiness exegetes argued that the aorist tense of the verb "sanctify" in Paul's prayer indicated an action that was "punctiliar" or "instantaneous," and once and for all. Therefore, it was said, this verb supported the theological idea of instantaneous sanctification (see the history in Maddox 1981, 106).

These interpreters misunderstood the Greek grammars of the day. These spoke of the "punctiliar" as the way the writer *presented* the action, not the reality of the action itself. Modern studies in linguistics and Greek reject the "punctiliar" label altogether (Comrie 1976, 16-21; Porter 1989, 89-91, 107; Wallace 1996, 239-40).

A more adequate understanding of the aorist in 1 Thess 5:23 indicates only that Paul viewed the action of sanctification as a whole. Just as the simple past tense, "I walked," does not specify how long my walk took or if it was simple or complex, but it merely states that it happened.

Holiness exegetes were right to note Paul's interest in sanctification in this letter, and the significance of his prayer that it happen to the Christian through and through. Of course, this passage alone cannot validate all that Wesleyan and holiness theologians have claimed for sanctification. But it certainly does not contradict it.

In the fourth century Gregory of Nyssa spoke about sanctification in his *Great Catechism*. He warned that Christians deceived themselves to think that no change of life was necessary after baptism. "It is evident that when those evil features which mark our nature have been obliterated a change to a better state takes place." If the postbaptismal life continues on the same moral level as before, then that person must lack the gift of the Holy Spirit (*Or. catech. magn.* 40 [Schaff]).

Gregory quotes John 1:12 to remind his readers that those who receive Christ become children of God. As his children, we should share God's nature and "manifest in [ourselves] Him that begot [us]." This character of God is known from Scripture and given for our instruction. Finally he adds, "Know you not in what way man is 'made admirable'? In no other way than by becoming holy" (*Or. catech. magn.* 40 [Schaff]).

There has been a persistent tendency throughout Christian history toward spiritualities that are either anti-body or anti-intellectual. Some popular evangelical writings have been guilty of speaking as if it is good to love God with the "heart" but not the mind or reason. Such talk forgets that Jesus is Lord of *all* and has redeemed *all* by becoming human for us. The mind is *not* outside the realm of redemption and sanctification.

Thomas Aquinas commented on 1 Thess 5:23 that Paul's prayer for "spirit, soul and body" addresses the three elements involved in sin: reason, the "sensitive appetite," and bodily actions (Aquinas 1969, on 5:23). Just as there is no aspect of our humanness uninfected by sin, so there is no part that God does not want to reclaim through the incarnation, death, and resurrection of Christ. He does this through the gracious work of sanctification.

Even our bodies partake of sanctification. When Christians speak about leaving their "shells" behind and their "real" selves "going to heaven," such talk is closer to Platonism (or Gnosticism) than biblical Christianity. Our physical bodies will perish. But we are mistaken to think they are unimportant to God. We misinterpret Paul's talk about the sinful pull of "the flesh" to mean that our bodies are the source of sin. Rather, we should realize that the Creator of our bodies designed them to be part of his good creation.

The doctrine of the resurrection entails the belief that having a body is important to who we are with God forever. So our current bodies are important to the Lord also (1 Thess 4:4, 16). As Paul wrote in 1 Cor 6:13*b*: "The body . . . is not meant for sexual immorality but for the Lord, and the Lord for the body."

But the issue of bodily sanctification does not merely concern the avoidance of sexual sins. If we abuse our bodies with unwise food choices or with alcohol and drugs, we endanger not only our health but also our spiritual life. We are to be good stewards of what God has entrusted us. "Your body is a temple of the Holy Spirit within you . . . you were bought with a price; therefore glorify God in your body" (1 Cor 6:19-20 NRSV).

What can we do *physically* to honor God with our bodies? Positively, we can serve the sick, the elderly, the hungry, the helpless victims of injustice. We can work with integrity at our jobs. We can involve ourselves in acts of kindness, such as aid and development missions or compassionate ministry. The possibilities are endless. May Christ give us wisdom.

5. *Debates about soul-body relationship.* Paul's tripartite formula for the human person (spirit, soul, body) has reverberated throughout church history. Later Christians often read Paul's terms through a Platonist lens. Aquinas believed soul and spirit referred to different soul functions. He specifically denied that the church taught a two-part soul. But others, including Luther, used this verse, with Heb 4:12, to argue for a tripartite view of human beings (Aquinas 1969, on 5:23; Thiselton 2011, 169). The tendency persists in the confusion of biblical assumptions with Platonist notions of the soul as the true self, which survives death, leaving the body behind to "go to heaven" (Jenson 1999, 110).

For over half a century, biblical scholars have emphasized that the OT views humanity as a body-soul unity. The soul (*nephesh*) represents the whole person as a living being in relationship to God, not a separable part. People do not *have* souls, they *are* living souls (Dihle et al. 1974, 9:620; Green 2008, 6-9). Paul took this view for granted. For him the soul is the whole person (e.g., Rom 2:9; 13:1; 1 Cor 15:45; 1 Thess 2:8). It stands for one's "life" (Rom 11:3; Phil 2:30; Dunn 1998, 76).

In recent years some interpreters have attempted to combine this biblical anthropology with newer trends in philosophy and neuroscience. They propose a view of humans that is monistic. That is, there is not a soul separable from the body at death; the soul is really only an aspect of the physical human person that God has created. It dies with the body and will be raised with it at the resurrection (e.g., Edgar 2002; Green 2008, 179).

Some Christians continue to defend some form of Christian dualism. They strongly contend that the soul is separable from the body. They insist that it survives death in the conscious presence of God (Cooper 1989).

We must insist that whatever view of anthropology we find persuasive, no aspect of our humanity may be excluded from God's sanctifying work in our lives. We cannot lightly dismiss bodily sins as inconsequential. Nor can we exclude the intellect from God's call for us to be wholly his. The life of the resurrection encompasses all that it means to be redeemed human creatures (see Wright 2008).

VII. EPISTOLARY CLOSING: I THESSALONIANS 5:25-28

BEHIND THE TEXT

Estimates are that roughly only 10 percent of the Roman world in Paul's day was literate (Harris 1989, 328-30). Literacy was probably higher among Jewish men because of the important role of the written law in their faith. But there were few Jewish males among the Thessalonian Christians (→ Introduction). Letters were still considered "high tech" in Paul's day.

Most people managed their lives by learning what they needed using their memories. They got experts to read letters, official decrees, legal documents, and so forth, for them when necessary. We cannot assume rich people did all the reading. Some rich people were illiterate, while some soldiers, merchants, "middle class," and even poor people might be able to read (Luke 4:16-19; Acts 23:24-30; Harris 1989, 196-233, 329-30; Pomeroy 1984, 117-19; Millar 1993, 371). Still, Paul depended on the literate minority to communicate with his churches.

Sending a letter was expensive. In Paul's day the papyrus needed to write even a short letter like 1 Thessalonians would have cost him half a day's wages or more (Harris 1989, 195). Struggling to maintain himself financially, this sacrifice speaks volumes of Paul's love and concern for his converts.

Many manuscripts add "amen" after the last verse. But it is missing from a variety of early and later manuscripts from different parts of the empire and from multiple ancient translations. It was probably added under the influence of the liturgy (Metzger 1994, 566), as Paul's letters came to be used in other church settings alongside the OT Scriptures.

IN THE TEXT

■ **25** Immediately after his prayer for the Thessalonians and his reassurance that God would be faithful to complete their sanctification (1 Thess 5:23-24), Paul addresses the Thessalonians once again as his **brothers and sisters** in Christ (→ 1:4; 2:1, 9, 14, 17; 3:7; 4:1, 10, 13; 5:1, 4, 12, 14).

He urges them to **pray for** him and his companions (see 1:1). Some of the earliest Greek manuscripts include the word "also" (the evidence is evenly divided [Metzger 1994, 565]. It is omitted in the NIV and placed within brackets in Greek critical texts. If it is original, it emphasizes again that they are to imitate his example in intercessory prayer.

Paul shows his humanity: he genuinely needs and desires their prayers in his behalf. He knows full well that he, too, is utterly dependent upon God for the inner strength to face trials with faith, for his daily provisions, and for the success of his mission in spreading the gospel (2 Cor 1:8-11).

We can guess from earlier references in the letter what he might have included among his prayer requests: the ability to see the Thessalonians again and to continue to live in a manner that would glorify Christ to the world (Furnish 2007, 125).

■ **26** Paul also asks that they **greet all the brothers and sisters** [NIV: all God's people] **with a holy kiss.** Though some needed correction or strengthening (1 Thess 4:11-12; 5:14-15), every Christian was to receive this symbol of welcome in God's family. This seems to be equal to "greet *one another*" (Rom 16:16; 1 Cor 16:20; 2 Cor 13:12; Phil 4:21).

Kissing one another was the normal way that family members would **greet** or bid farewell to one another in both Jewish and Gentile societies (Gen 31:55; 33:4; Luke 15:20; *Jos. Asen.* 8:6; Plutarch, *Rom.* 1; Stählin 1974, 9:120 n. 56). Paul's request reinforced again his understanding of the church as a family.

In the ancient Mediterranean world then and in some parts still, friends often met and parted with kisses, whether men or women. Kissing served as a sign of respect, as when a student kissed a master on the hand or cheek. Even soldiers kissed each other as a greeting or out of respect (Suetonius, *Otho* 6; *Vit.* 7; Plutarch, *Fab.* 13).

It seems likely that for these first Christians kissing was not only between people of the same gender but between men and women. The practice probably imitated Mediterranean family and friendship practices. Later, the church restricted the "kiss of peace" to one's own gender, to prevent abuses (Bruce 1982, 134; Keener 2000; *Apos. Con.* 2.57.17).

Whether the kiss was restricted to the cheeks is uncertain. Some evidence suggests it was acceptable in some quarters to have relatives greet one another with a light kiss on the lips (a "peck"; see Keener 2000; Shogren 2012, 234 n. 3). In either case, Christians clearly distinguished the *holy* kiss of welcome from anything erotic.

■ **27** Paul suddenly shifts from the first-person plural to the singular. This may indicate that he took the letter from his scribe and signed it personally (see 2 Thess 3:17; Gal 6:11).

I charge you before the Lord is an oath formula that is difficult to translate. Loosely put it means, "I am calling you to account by the name of the Lord and with him as witness, that you must do this." Paul treats the letter as a substitute for his personal presence with them in the worship assembly.

Because most of the congregation was probably illiterate, it was vital that someone **read** the letter aloud. Rather than "to the church," he asks that it be read **to all the brothers and sisters**, perhaps in multiple house churches in and around Thessalonica. Reading it aloud put all the saints on equal ground in hearing the words of the apostles.

This practice perhaps prepared the way for the early Christian recognition of Paul's letters as Scripture (see 2 Pet 3:15-16). We know that in church assemblies, all were to benefit from hearing Scripture read to them (1 Tim 4:13). Public reading of Scripture insured that there was to be no special "insider information" controlled by a privileged few.

■ **28** Paul's final words pronounce a benediction upon his hearers. He invokes **the grace of our Lord Jesus Christ** upon the community that has just heard this letter read, in obedience to his command (v 27). It is one final reminder that God's loving initiative stands behind all Christians' spiritual successes.

The Thessalonians will need the continuing **grace** of Christ to maintain the witness of the gospel within a hostile society. And they will need God's **grace** and forgiveness to fill their hearts with love for one another as they work out what it means to live together as "the church in . . . God the Father and the Lord Jesus Christ" (1:1). Until believers are with the Lord forever in the glorious resurrection life (4:17; 5:10), his **grace** will be **with** them to redeem and guide them by his Spirit (4:8). Notice too that at the end of the letter Paul closes with Jesus' name and twofold title, the **Lord Jesus Christ** (→ 1:1; the fifth time in the letter).

Paul opened the letter with a wish for God's "grace and peace" (1:1). At its close he comes full circle, referring to these same two expressions of God's work among them (5:23, 28), and emphasizing the majesty of the church's Lord who is the wellspring of grace and renewal for them.

FROM THE TEXT

The grace of family love for the church. Even the plain business of concluding a letter is transformed in Paul's hands into an occasion of grace. He shows his humility and his own need for prayer in his request that the Thessalonians intercede for him and his coworkers (1 Thess 5:25). He doesn't merely sign off with the culturally standard "farewell." His letter closing is not like the abrupt endings found in many ancient letters.

Paul reports again (→ 1:2-3; 2:13; 3:11-13) his prayer for them. This prayer is a benediction requesting God to shower his grace upon the church (5:28). Not only does he bless them in this way, but also he orders them to demonstrate grace physically to one another with the family embrace (v 27).

Paul has just dealt in the letter with multiple issues that might have risked embarrassing, shaming, and even angering some in his Thessalonian audience. There was the risk that others might want to punish and exclude the offenders, instead of redeeming them.

This may explain why Paul insists at the end of his letter that *all* come onstage for the final act of the weekly drama of worship. The entire church worships the God of peace and the God of grace. The Christian assembly is to be a drama of forgiveness and of redemption.

Church is to be a family drama, familiar to many ancient Mediterranean homes with "black sheep" who are chastened and try to make a comeback. The difference in this "home" is that God is the *paterfamilias*. He has ordered the feast and the terms of mutual welcome: kiss your brother and sister (Luke 15:20, 32)! Too often our church services have lost entirely the sense of *family* that this first generation had, which Paul envisioned, and which Jesus taught.

The church today has become proficient at distributing information, at teaching, and sometimes at entertaining. We might be able to preserve orthodoxy through faithfulness to a liturgy or a creed (or maybe not). But how are we doing at being the family of God?

There is no need to disavow all of the good and useful innovations in today's church. But as the final words of this letter roll off my mouth, I am confronted with this question: Would I want to *literally embrace* the members of my congregation, as I would my extended family at a holiday party? If not, how is the church any more precious to me than a social club? How is it the body of Christ?

The high Christology of the grace-wish. The form of the final wish reflects Paul's high Christology. We expect a pious Jewish person to pray for *God's* grace upon someone. God is its source. But here Paul prays for grace from the risen *Jesus*.

Paul addressed Jesus with the title Lord, customarily reserved in Jewish prayers for God alone (→ 1:1). Alongside this, he casually refers to Jesus with the title Christ. Contrary to Jewish expectations, their "Messiah" is somehow one with the Lord God himself. Paul may have lacked the christological precision of the later creeds. But his clear assumptions about Jesus made them necessary.

COMMENTARY

2 THESSALONIANS

I. GREETING: 2 THESSALONIANS 1:1-2

IN THE TEXT

■ 1 Paul opens the second letter as he did the first. He mentions the same three senders: **Paul, Silas and Timothy**, the same **church**, and the same wishes for **grace and peace** (v 2; see 1 Thess 1:1). The same senders suggests a date close in time to the sending of the first letter, perhaps while Paul was still at Corinth (AD 50-51). He identifies the church again by its *people*, the **Thessalonians**, rather than its place (Thessalonica), and by its spiritual status—**in God** and *in* **the Lord Jesus Christ**. Here, however, Paul adds the personal pronoun **our** with **God**, giving this an extra note of intimacy.

■ 2 The Greeks claimed Zeus as their father; the Romans, Jupiter. This Christian assembly has as its Father the God who raised the **Lord Jesus** from the dead, the only **God** who can truly bring **grace and peace** to the world. Paul makes explicit in this letter that **grace and peace** come **from God the Father and the Lord Jesus Christ** (contrast 1 Thess 1:1; compare 1 Cor 1:3; Phil 1:2).

II. THANKSGIVING AND EXCURSUS ON DIVINE JUSTICE: 2 THESSALONIANS 1:3-12

BEHIND THE TEXT

As with 1 Thessalonians, the thanksgiving of the second letter begins with implicit praise for the Thessalonians' faith in the midst of difficult circumstances. Paul is grateful to God for their perseverance. But his focus quickly shifts to the persecuted people of faith and their persecutors in 2 Thess 1:4. This accelerates in vv 5-10 with references to God's judgment, Jesus' Parousia, and the apocalyptic punishment of the persecutors. Paul adds a report of a prayer for them in vv 11-12.

This introduction is difficult to untangle. It anticipates the subject of the letter—as all Paul's thanksgivings do—in its reference to suffering, persecution, and *parousia*. But in such a short letter, it not only anticipates but also *is* the subject. These verses make up almost a fourth of the epistle's content.

Paul is genuinely grateful that his brothers and sisters in Thessalonica have bravely withstood fearsome sufferings and maintained their faith. No one knew yet where these hostilities would lead, or when they might end. Would people be disinherited? Would women be divorced? Would Christians be pursued by angry mobs, beaten in the streets? Would they be tortured as possible traitors to Caesar?

The text is unclear about the extent of the Thessalonians' sufferings. But Paul apparently believed the situation was urgent enough to send another letter soon after the first. The vehemence of his emphasis on the divine judgment of their persecutors suggests that the situation was much more dire than mere verbal abuse or job losses.

Malherbe correctly notes that *consolation* is a primary function of the letter. Often overlooked, commentators too often focus almost exclusively on the letter's eschatology and its differences from 1 Thessalonians. But this letter is composed not simply to correct eschatological confusion. It is a pastoral brief designed to give emergency soul aid to people who are emotionally and physically shattered, socially alienated from their own culture, and outcasts from their families. As such, this portion of the letter has something in common with the pastoral care of refugees from Somalia or Christians living under persecution in Muslim or Communist countries.

IN THE TEXT

A. Thanksgiving (1:3-4)

■ **3** The thanksgiving in 1 Thessalonians praised the church for the evidence of the well-known triad of faith, hope, and love Timothy observed in his visit to Thessalonica (→ 1 Thess 1:2-3; 3:6). The second letter's thanksgiving mentions only **faith** and **love** as still outstanding. This should not be taken as an implicit insult, as if he expected them to compare the two letters. This is still genuine praise for the young church. Nevertheless, the prominence of that triad in the first letter and the problems with eschatology in this letter both point to the absence of "hope" here as a significant issue.

The Thessalonians' **faith** has withstood hardships. More importantly, it is even **growing more and more**. Normally, by **faith** Paul means not a set of doctrines but the active trust of believers in Christ and in the God who raised him from the dead (→ 1 Thess 1:2-3). **Faith** is never totally separable from a set of beliefs, however. But the growth here must not refer to increased doctrinal sophistication. It must mean some kind of maturation—responses to crises that evidenced greater trust in God.

Their hardships led to their **love . . . for one another . . . increasing**—in answer to Paul's prayers (1 Thess 3:12) and obedience to his exhortation (4:10). He goes out of his way to stress that ***every*** individual **one** of the Thessalonian believers was loving other Christians extravagantly.

■ **4** The amazing fortitude and piety of these Macedonians continue to impress the apostle: he and his companions **boast about** them **among God's churches**. The aspect of their **faith** they boast of is specifically faith that endures **persecutions** [*diōgmos*] **and trials** (*thlipsis*).

Paul had already praised the Thessalonians for their faith in the gospel "in spite of persecution" (*thlipsis* [1 Thess 1:6 NRSV]). He sent Timothy to console them because of those persecutions (*thlipsis* [1 Thess 3:3]; NIV: **trials**). Their **trials** (*thlipsis*) did not harden their hearts to the needs of others (2 Cor 8:2).

Just as the English "persecution" comes from "pursue," the image of a hunt, so it is with the Greek word *diōgmos*, "persecution" or a "chase," related to the verb for hunting. *Diōgmos* can have physical manifestations, as when the apostles were literally forced out of town (Acts 13:50; 14:19; 17:6-10). It can apply to the violence directed against the pursued Christians in Judea (Acts 8:1) or to the social problems experienced by those who accept the gospel (Matt 13:21; Mark 10:30). It may refer to political/legal action, as was involved at Thessalonica.

Trials (*thlipsis*) may not be significantly different from persecutions, although it emphasizes the subjective suffering of the Thessalonians (→ "What Was the Thessalonians' 'Affliction'?" sidebar at 1 Thess 1:6). They must have paid dearly—in their families, their neighborhood connections, work, politics, finances, and so forth, for leaving all the old gods and remaining faithful to the One Creator and his Son.

B. An Excursus on Suffering and God's Justice (1:5-10)

Sometimes in his letters Paul seems to make an "excursus"—a side trip to comment on or explain something he has raised in his writing—and then return to his main subject. Some such parentheses may appear to have only a tenuous link to the subject matter. But upon closer inspection most are carefully interwoven with the rhetoric and subject matter (e.g., Rom 5:13-14; 1 Cor 9:1-27; 13:1-13).

Second Thessalonians 1:5-10 appears to be an excursus on God's ultimate justice for Christians who are suffering and for their persecutors. It is prompted by the mention of the Thessalonians' great endurance of oppression (vv 3-4). Its function is not philosophical explanation but to console the suffering saints—to dispel any false sense of injustice raised by the false teaching about the Day of the Lord (2:2). For if the Day of the Lord had already arrived, God ought to have ended all such suffering (Bassler 1984, 508). Paul's language is influenced by the prophets (especially Isaiah, Daniel), Sirach, Jewish apocalyptic literature, and Jesus' teachings.

■ **5** The excursus begins abruptly, without even a sentence break from v 4 in Greek. Literally, it opens: ***evidence of the righteous judgment of God in***

order for you to be counted worthy of the kingdom of God, for which you are suffering. Several questions need to be answered to make sense of this.

First, *what* is the **evidence** (*endeigma*)? Most commentators agree it refers to something in the preceding sentence (except Witherington [2006, 192], who thinks it refers to what follows). Some take the **evidence** to be the Thessalonians' "perseverance and faith" as it endured "persecutions" (v 4; Lightfoot 1957, 100; Frame 1912, 226; Best 1986, 254-55).

Similarly, in Phil 1:27-28 Paul urges the Philippians to be unafraid of their opponents, "striving together as one for the faith of the gospel without being frightened in any way by those who oppose you. This is a sign to them that they will be destroyed, but that you will be saved." The word "sign" (*endeixis*) in Philippians is related to the word **evidence** here. In both passages the issues are faith challenged by opposition. In Philippians, enduring faith serves as evidence. Here the **evidence** points to **God's** just **judgment**.

Bassler proposed understanding the problems of this text through the matrix of the first-century Jewish theology of suffering (*Leidenstheologie*):
    (i) God's retributive justice, the principle of *ius talionis* (punishment in kind) by which evil must be punished;
    (ii) God's elect are chastised lightly by God in this age so they may be made worthy of resurrection life;
    (iii) The fate of the wicked is the reverse: They enjoy good fortune now, but will have affliction in the next world; and
    (iv) Consequently, the afflictions of the pious are a sign of God's approval and assurance of his justice. (1984, 505)

Several commentators have suggested that this might explain Paul's "evidence" remark: it is not the Thessalonians' faith, but their *suffering*, that is evidence that they are God's elect (Wanamaker 1990, 221-22; Green 2002, 284; Furnish 2007, 146-47).

There are several difficulties with interpreting this text through the lens of Jewish *Leidenstheologie*.
    1. It would entail a kind of supplemental atonement for sins by the righteous unknown elsewhere in Paul.
    2. The focus in 1 Thessalonians is on Christians' suffering for their *faith*, not for their sins.
    3. A predominantly Gentile congregation would not have known this doctrine. Paul could not expect these few words to conjure it up, unless it was part of his basic teachings, which seems doubtful.

There is some general overlap of traditions in the ideas that (*a*) the righteous may be expected to suffer *more* than the unrighteous in this life, and (*b*) there will be a reversal and justice in the next life. But the rationale for suffering and reversal are rather different in Paul and in *Leidenstheologie*.

Some interpreters note that the words "in all [*your*] persecutions and [*afflictions*] you are enduring" (v 4) are the last ones in Greek before the word **evi-**

dence. They believe only the suffering is the **evidence**. But word order is weak evidence in Greek. The topic of Paul's boast about the church is their "perseverance and faith." The term **evidence** is best understood as being in apposition to the entire preceding phrase—faith *in the midst of* persecutions (Lightfoot 1957, 100; Bruce 1982, 149; Malherbe 2000, 394). This makes the most sense of Paul's reference.

But how does the Thessalonians' endurance of suffering and persecution with faith prove **that God's judgment is right**/just? From a modern perspective, it seems to say only that God lets the wicked get away with evil and fails to reward the pious.

Judgment (*krisis*) may refer to God's present evaluation (1 Pet 4:17). This is supported by its being linked with the result that the Thessalonians are **counted worthy of the kingdom of God**. Jesus taught that his disciples ought to consider themselves "blessed" when they were persecuted and falsely accused because of their faith in him (Matt 5:11). Persecution for uncompromising faith proves that believers belong to God's kingdom. It also anticipates an even greater heavenly welcome from God: "Rejoice and be glad, because great is your reward in heaven" (v 12).

This view that *suffering on behalf of the kingdom and the name of Christ is an honor* that affirms one's status in the kingdom is also found in Acts 5:41; 1 Pet 4:13-14, 16; and Paul's "fool's speech" in 2 Cor 11:16-33; 12:10. Acts reports Paul's teaching that "it is through many persecutions that we must enter the kingdom of God" (Acts 14:22 NRSV; compare Rom 8:17-18).

Interpreting this oblique sentence then through this wider Christian tradition and Paul's teaching elsewhere might justify the paraphrase of 2 Thess 1:4-5: *Your display of endurance and faith in the midst of affliction and persecution is not only grounds for us to boast about you to other churches. It is evidence that God's decision to have accounted you worthy of the kingdom of God is righteous. You have shown how genuine your faith is and how worthy you are of the kingdom, by suffering on its behalf.*

God *accounts the Thessalonians worthy* because of their faithfulness to him and his Son. They have demonstrated their faith by being willing to witness to a hostile society and by standing their ground despite suffering for that witness. Their *suffering* and God's *judgment* are related. It is not that their suffering "earns" the kingdom; it *affirms* that they already belong to it. Their faith was evidenced by their actions. Verse 5 functions to give consolation. God's **judgment** tests and approves the Thessalonians' faith (Marshall 1983, 173; see 1 Pet 4:17-19).

■ **6** God will repay the Thessalonians' persecutors at the Parousia. His future reward to persecuted Christians will make the reversal complete (v 7a). Paul describes the setting for this great reversal in a fairly detailed description of the Parousia, with dire consequences for unbelievers (vv 7b-9) and bliss for believers (v 10).

Verse 6 begins with Greek *ei*, usually "if"; here **for**. It invites readers to make the obvious judgment that it *is* just for God to **pay back trouble to those who trouble you**. John Chrysostom said this rhetorical use of "if" (as **for**) was used with "indisputable" truths (*Hom. 2 Thess.* 2.3).

That God is a just Judge is an ancient theme in Scripture and other Jewish literature. It is implicit in the very giving of the Law to Israel. Paul does not seek here to prove this, he simply asserts it (see Gen 18:25; Deut 4:7-8; Pss 7:11; 9:8; Tob 3:2; 2 Macc 12:6; Luke 18:7-8; Rom 2:2; 7:22; 2 Tim 4:8).

The ancient law known as *lex talionis*, the repayment of evil with a corresponding punishment, is seen in the Pentateuch and the Prophets (Exod 21:23-27; Deut 19:21; Isa 3:11; Obad 15; Mic 2:1-5; 6:9-16). And it is even found in Jesus' teaching concerning divine judgment (Matt 6:15; 7:1; 18:32-35; Mark 8:38; Luke 6:37; 16:25; also Paul, 1 Cor 3:17). Though it is not for humans to carry out anymore (Matt 5:38-41). God alone is competent to pass just and appropriate judgment (John 8:50; Rom 2:6-8; 12:17-19; Col 3:25; presumed in many other passages on future judgment). And he has appointed Jesus Christ as Judge (Matt 25:31-46; John 5:22-23, 26-27; Acts 10:42; 17:31; Rom 2:16; 2 Cor 5:10; 2 Tim 4:1).

Hence, the same Greek word, *thlipsis*, names the Thessalonian Christians' "trials" (2 Thess 1:4) and the **trouble** their powerful persecutors will suffer at the judgment (v 6). A cognate verb (*thlibō*) describes both the Christians "who are troubled" (v 7) and the action of those **who trouble** them (v 6). This emphasizes how **God is just** to "repay" the Thessalonian Christians' oppressors with his retributive justice (compare Luke 16:23-25; 1 Cor 3:17; Rev 18:5-8). The verb **pay back** may echo the LXX of Isa 66:4 ("I will *repay* their sins"). God "repays" those who have committed injustice and refused to listen to him with retributive justice (Isa 59:17; Jer 25:14; 50:29; Hos 4:6-9). Jesus now stands in the role that God played in the OT Day of the Lord.

God's judgment and "paying back" have two sides, however. There is the negative side directed against injustice. But there is also a positive side, to reward God's faithful people, including the Thessalonian believers (2 Thess 1:7).

It is important to keep in mind that the purpose of this section is not to frighten unbelievers (it is not written to them), nor to harden believers against non-Christians. The purpose of vv 5-12 is the *consolation* of suffering Christians who are in a small minority in their society (→ Behind the Text for 2 Thess 1:3-12 and Excursus on Suffering and God's Justice, above). Like Jesus, Paul forbids Christians from taking vengeance (Rom 12:19, citing Deut 32:35; Col 3:25; 1 Thess 5:15) even while affirming God's ultimate judgment on the wicked. Paul wants to assure the Thessalonians that **God is just** and that he still cares about his people. The wicked *will* eventually face judgment if they do not repent. The certainty that God's future judgment will arrive, and that it will be appropriate, rests on his character.

So for Christians, teaching about divine retribution is never an excuse for violence, nor for enmity against opponents. The apostle does not want personal vengeance. But he is convinced the Last Judgment is real. It is coming in the future, and it will lead to eternal consequences, either damnation or blessedness. At present God offers grace: amnesty to any and all who will accept it. But people are accountable for how they live their lives in response to the gospel message and to God's people. Those who refuse grace will find they have only justice left to face on judgment day. To exclude judgment from the gospel would imply that God does not deeply value or take human lives seriously.

■ **7** Paul's consolation to his suffering Macedonian coverts assures them that present evils will end. He considers this from both sides: The wicked will be punished (2 Thess 1:6) and God will **give relief to you who are troubled**.

Relief points to the eschatological rest of the saints in the resurrection life of the messianic age. This reward of the righteous is a theme also found in Jewish apocalyptic texts (Furnish 2007, 147). **Relief** highlights how this discussion of eschatological reversal is meant to console the suffering.

You who are troubled (lit. ***being afflicted***) is a present participle in Greek; the Thessalonians are still undergoing persecution as Paul writes. The **relief** that comes with the Lord's return will benefit **us** apostles **as well**. They, too, experience deprivations and opposition of all sorts, even violence, due to their evangelism. As the Thessalonian believers have shared faith, suffering, and friendship with the apostles now, so they will together share the joy of Messiah's reign in peace. The reward of the righteous is not simply individualistic; it is to join all the saints.

Retribution and reward will begin **when the Lord Jesus is revealed from heaven . . . with his powerful angels**. The description of Jesus' return in vv 7*b*-8 parallels descriptions of the Day of the Lord in the OT and Jewish apocalyptic literature. There is one significant difference: in the OT it is Yahweh, the God of Israel, who is the expected Judge. Here it is Jesus who will visit the earth to "punish" the wicked (v 8).

The divine splendor and authority of Jesus are emphasized by calling him **Lord** (*kyrios*), the LXX translation for the title given to the God of Israel. Paul's further descriptors of the Lord's coming also underline his glory: **from heaven**, the angelic accompaniment (v 7), and the execution of divine justice (v 8).

Many OT texts speak of a coming of the Lord, but only a few speak of his being **revealed**. These normally refer either to prophetic speech or to the appearance of some saving action (1 Sam 2:27; 3:7, 21; Ps 98:2; Isa 52:10; 56:1). Here Paul emphasizes that judgment comes ***at the revelation*** [*apokalypsei*] ***of the Lord Jesus*** (NIV: when the Lord Jesus is revealed).

Some other NT texts also use *apokalypsis* for Jesus' return (1 Cor 1:7; 1 Pet 1:7, 13; 4:13; see the verbal form in Rom 2:5; 8:18-19; 1 Cor 3:13; 1 Pet 5:1). Paul often uses other terms, such as *parousia* (1 Cor 15:23; 1 Thess 2:19; 3:13; 4:15; 5:23; 2 Thess 2:1, 8). *Apokalypsis*, "uncovering" or "revelation," emphasizes the visual aspect of the coming. It may suggest the Jewish notion that the Messiah is already present but hidden with God until God reveals him at the end of time (Malherbe 2000, 399; *4 Ezra* 7:28; 13:26, 32; *1 En.* 48:6).

From heaven is not simply an indicator of travel direction, but a statement of Christ's present status and origin. As the place of God's throne, **heaven** represents the seat of God's cosmic rule. That the Lord Jesus is **revealed from heaven** is to say that his disclosure comes with the authority of the Creator of the universe. He is the self-revelation of the Creator, in the Son, in judgment. It also says that this is an act of **heaven**, that is, of God. Therefore, the lordship of Jesus does not usurp the rule of God. He is not a second or rival deity next to the Father; he is mysteriously one with him.

Jesus comes to earth in the manner of God. This is how God comes from Mount Sinai, accompanied by a retinue of thousands (Deut 33:2; Ps 68:17). This is how God arrives on judgment day, with "thousands upon thousands" of angels (Dan 7:10; Zech 14:5). Just as God "unleashed . . . a band of destroying angels" (Ps 78:49) against Egypt to free his people (see vv 49-51), so Jesus comes with a band of **angels**. Thus, **angels** here are probably to be understood as the awesome instruments of his wrath against the oppressors of his people and enemies of God (2 Thess 1:8-9; compare 1 Thess 5:2-3).

In 1 Thess 4:16 an "archangel" is associated with the Lord's coming for his saints and the resurrection of the dead. Here, in 2 Thess 1:7, ***angels of his power*** is probably a Hebraic way of saying **his powerful angels** (Bruce 1982, 150). Not a class of angels, they are merely the agents of God's might (Best 1986, 258; Wanamaker 1990, 226; Green 2002, 289). Jesus expected to be accompanied by angels at his return (Matt 16:27; 24:30-31; 25:31; Mark 8:38; 13:27).

The final description of Jesus' revelation is **in blazing fire** (2 Thess 1:7 in the NIV; v 8 in the ESV, GNT, HCSB, KJV, NET, and NRSV). The placement of this phrase makes it uncertain whether it describes Jesus' **revelation** (so most English translations), or how **he will punish** (HCSB, KJV, NET). The fire symbolizes both God's glorious presence and his judgment. Paul may allude to Isa 66:15-16, which connects God *coming* in judgment and *fire*. YHWH appears to Moses "in flames of fire" at his calling (Exod 3:2). Numerous other texts associate "flames of fire" with a theophany (Ps 29:7 [KJV, ESV, NASB, NRSV]; Isa 4:5; simply "fire" in Exod 19:18; 24:17; Deut 4:12, 15, 33). Or it can be a metaphor for destruction coming as a result of God's judgment (Isa 10:17; 29:5-6; 30:30; Jer 48:45; Lam 2:3; Sir 45:19).

Another text that influenced the apocalyptic thought of Paul, Jewish apocalyptic literature, and Jesus is the vision of Dan 7. This vision combines a theophany, a judgment scene, fire issuing from God's presence, and heavenly attendants (vv 9-11). These are all part of Paul's portrayal of Jesus' return here. In addition, vv 13-14 mention the coming of "a son of man . . . with the clouds of heaven."

This text is a template for Jesus' description of his victorious return in power and judgment (see esp. Matt 16:27; 24:30-31; 26:64; Mark 8:38; 13:26-27; 14:62; Luke 21:27; John 5:27). The early church believed that the hopes of Israel and the prophets and the dreams of the apocalyptists had come to fulfillment in Messiah Jesus. Their longing for deliverance had been met with a coming of grace and divine amnesty. But the day of reckoning, the Day of the Lord the prophets had spoken about, was not canceled. Paul expects Jesus to return bearing the shattering glory of God the Father, commanding the Father's servants and carrying out the Father's justice.

■ **8** After his description of the divine majesty of Jesus' Parousia, Paul turns to its dual purpose—negative and positive. He begins with its negative aspect, raising again the fate of the opponents of Christians at the Parousia. He sets judgment in a larger framework. The doomed are **those who do not know God and . . . [*those who*] do not obey the gospel of our Lord Jesus**.

Some commentators argue that there are two different groups here (Frame 1912, 233; Marshall 1983, 178), but this seems doubtful. In the OT and Jewish literature Gentiles are sometimes characterized as not knowing God (Ps 79:6; Jer 10:25). But Israel can be similarly described (Jer 4:22; Hos 4:1). Some identify those who **do not obey the gospel** as Jews. But Paul can describe all humanity in this way (Rom 11:30-32).

More likely, the two descriptions employ synonymous parallelism as a comprehensive identification of all those under divine condemnation (Wanamaker 1990, 227; Malherbe 2000, 401; Green 2002, 290-91). Paul's purpose is not sociological boundary-making, to distinguish those who are "in" from those who are "out." This is not a veiled threat for the church to stay in the bounds (against Wanamaker 1990, 227-28).

Paul's language moves the issue beyond personal offenses at the local level into a more universal context. Unlike 2 Thess 1:6, he makes no explicit mention in v 8 of the afflictions of Thessalonian Christians. As John Chrysostom observed, these people must be punished ultimately not on account of the Thessalonians but on account of God (*Hom. 2 Thess.* 2.3).

The apostle has in mind a judgment that is general, not local. In biblical parlance, whenever people are indicted for not knowing God, the issue is not simply lack of knowledge. They are culpable for deliberately rejecting whatever knowledge was available, whether in creation or divine revelation (Hos 4:1-10; Rom 1:18-32). It is only in this sense that they **do not know** God. The verb **know** here presumes its Hebrew sense of understanding and relationship (Jer 31:33-34).

Why did Paul not describe this group as those who "do not *believe* the gospel," given his stress on the importance of faith elsewhere? One could argue that to obey the gospel invitation *is* to believe in the one God and the Son whom he sent. Nevertheless, this sentence is a reminder that for Paul faith and obedience to God are not antithetical; each requires the other.

In 2 Thess 1:6 Paul had spoken of God paying back the Thessalonian persecutors at the judgment. In vv 7-8 he speaks of the **Lord Jesus** carrying out this judgment with the authority of God. Jesus assumes God's role as just Judge of all the earth (Deut 32:35; Isa 66:15; Ezek 25:14; Rom 12:19; Heb 10:30; compare Matt 25:31-46; Mark 8:38).

He will punish translates a Greek adverbial participle (lit. *inflicting punishment*). It continues the sentence that began in v 3 and concludes in v 10. *Ekdikēsis* (**punishment, vengeance**) occurs in OT texts about judgment day, the time when God will punish people for their sins, including Israel (Deut 32:35; Jer 46:10, 21 [26:10, 21 LXX]; 50:31 [27:31 LXX]; Hos 9:7; Sir 5:7; Schrenk 1964, 445).

Divine **punishment** is not an emotional vendetta but the administration of justice (→ 2 Thess 1:6; see Malherbe 2000, 400; BDAG, 301; Green 2002, 290). The word occurs in Isa 66:15, which apparently influenced Paul's language in 2 Thess 1:7-8 (→ 2 Thess 1:1). Paul had warned Christians in 1 Thess 4:6 that God is an "avenger" (*ekdikos*; ESV, GNT, NET, NASB, NRSV) for any kind of sexual immorality.

That some are worthy of divine justice does not authorize powerful Christians to take revenge themselves (→ 2 Thess 1:6; see 1 Thess 5:15). Christians are the power*less* here. Paul assures them that the powerful Lord Jesus can be trusted with their wounds and grievances. He will carry out perfect justice; he takes judgment out of imperfect human hands. He alone is qualified to decide whom and how to punish, and whom to save.

■ **9** Juridical language continues here in the description of the penalty exacted upon the unrighteous. Verse 8 of 2 Thess 1 borrows language from the OT. But the phrase **They will be punished** comes from secular Greek (not the LXX). The Thessalonian audience would have recognized this immediately (BAGD, 818; Malherbe 2000, 402). Paul reemphasizes that the frightening apocalyptic penalty of the doomed is the just consequence for their lives of stubborn resistance to the available knowledge of God (v 8), and, perhaps, retribution for persecuting the church (v 6).

The penalty of the unrighteous is **with everlasting destruction and shut out from the presence of the Lord**. Is this another example of synonymous parallelism (→ v 8)? Are these two ways of describing a single penalty? The second clause seems a clear corollary of the first; maybe its cause. To be in **the presence of the Lord** is blessedness—the destiny of believers (v 10; 1 Thess 4:17; 5:10; Rev 22:3-5).

Interpreters dispute the meaning of the phrase *olethron aiōnion*, **everlasting destruction / eternal ruin**. A few argue that it refers to (*a*) "a final and absolute destruction" or annihilation of the wicked, arguing that the adjective *eternal* refers to the effects of the destruction and that the destruction is total (Fudge 1984, 325, 333). Most commentators, however, understand the phrase to refer to (*b*) punishment that never ends. That they face ruin **shut out**

from the presence of the Lord forever implies their continued existence. The phrase "everlasting destruction" and similar expressions such as "eternal fire" and "eternal chastisement" (Matt 18:8; 25:41, 46; Jude 7) always appear in eschatological contexts.

Similar expressions appear in nearly contemporary Second Temple Jewish literature (*Pss. Sol.* 2:31-35; 15:12-13; 4 Macc 10:15; 12:11-12, 17-18; 1QS II, 15; V, 13; similarly *1 En.* 10:13-14; 62:1-11; 108:4-7). The Synoptic Gospels report that Jesus predicts "eternal fire" (Matt 18:8; 25:41), "fire [that] never goes out" (Mark 9:43-48; compare Luke 16:22-25), and "eternal punishment" for the doomed (Matt 25:46) in hell (Matt 5:22, 29, 30; Luke 12:5). Early rabbinic sources also mention eternal punishment for the wicked (*t. Sanh.* 13:4-5).

Modern Christians might prefer a commuted sentence or annihilation for the eternally damned. But we must not forget that the everlasting life of the redeemed in Christ's **presence** is paralleled by the everlasting woe of the lost *away from* the Father and the Son. Paul's theological heritage and the present literary context point to "eternal ruin" or "everlasting death" as unending (see Frame 1912, 234; Marshall 1983, 179; Malherbe 2000, 402; Green 2002, 291-93).

The wicked pay this penalty of destruction **shut out from** [*apo*] **the presence of the Lord.** They are forever banished from the Lord they refused to honor. The Greek preposition *apo* is usually taken to convey this directional meaning—*away from*. **Presence** translates the word for "face," a Hebrew idiom for being in proximity to a person.

Separation **from the presence of the Lord** with the following qualification, **and from the glory of his might**, seems to echo the terrifying theophany of the Creator God in Isa 2:10, 19, 21; now it is Jesus' coming. Isaiah counsels the wicked to "hide in the dust from the terror of the LORD, and from the glory of his majesty" (Isa 2:10 NRSV). Paul omits reference to the "fear of the LORD" (KJV).

Most commentators read the text in this directional sense. But *apo* might have a causative sense: destruction will *come from* **the presence of the Lord** because of **the glory of his might** (Quarles 1997; Green 2002, 293). Read this way, the punishment is not *absence* from God. The divine *presence* and glory are what destroys the wicked.

Glory (*doxa*) speaks of the unveiled, regal brilliance of the appearing of Jesus illuminated in divine splendor (2 Thess 1:7), equal to the one who descended on Sinai and whose presence is deadly to ordinary sinful humans (Exod 19:21, 24; 33:20). Christ has opened the way for those who obey the gospel to access God's presence (2 Cor 3:16-18; Eph 2:18; 3:12; Heb 9:11-14; 10:19-22). Specifically, it is the **glory of his might** [*power/strength*] (*ischys*). This emphasizes his ability to subdue and punish the wicked and to give "rest" with all that implies to God's faithful—the restoration of the world (Rom 8:18-23; Col 1:20).

This is why Christ is the "hope of glory" (Col 1:27). This power is anticipated in the present when it is at work in his apostles and servants as they preach the gospel (2 Cor 4:7). **The glory of his might** at once excludes the wicked from his **presence** and is the ultimate joy of the redeemed.

■ **10** To accentuate again (→ 2 Thess 1:6-7) the great eschatological reversal, the hour of doom for the rebellious and the oppressors of Christians is described as the time Christ comes to be adored by his people.

When he comes refers to the moment of his **revelation**, his *parousia* (v 7; see 1 Thess 4:15-17; 2 Thess 2:1). Paul uses two passive infinitives of purpose (**to be glorified** and **to be marveled**) to express this positive side of the Parousia. As with the Day of the Lord in the OT, Jesus' coming is not only for judgment but also brings ultimate salvation.

The **holy ones** (*hagioi*) here could refer to angels (as in Zech 14:5; 1 Thess 3:13 [→]; *1 En.* 1:9). But the heavenly hosts need not come to earth to glorify the Son; they do that constantly (Rev 4:8-11). It is equally unlikely that Paul speaks of OT saints vs. new covenant believers here. **Those who have believed** applies to both. Paul probably uses the term *hagioi* to refer to believers simply for stylistic variety. It allows him to emphasize two aspects of Christian identity as they greet their returning Lord: they are **holy**—devoted to and belonging to him. And they are redeemed because they **have believed** the gospel. This makes them the diametric opposite of those punished (→ 2 Thess 1:8).

That the returning Jesus will **be glorified in** (*en*) his people could be their subjective response: they give unending praise and honor to their Savior. Some interpreters read *en* as "by" (NRSV), showing that *the saints* are the *means* by which Christ will be glorified.

This could mean that the fact of their rescue, the grace shown to them, the marvelous changes worked in their lives, or the great deeds of love Christ did through them to the world, all contribute to the Son's glory (see Malherbe 2000, 404-5). If so, this is further praise of and comfort to the suffering church.

Jesus will also **be marveled at / *wondered at*** by those who have believed. Although the term *thaumazō* is rare in Paul—only here and in Gal 1:6, it is often used elsewhere in the NT to express human wonder at the miracles of God. God's deeds leave people dumbfounded (Matt 8:27; 9:33; 15:31; 21:20; Mark 5:20; Luke 1:63; 8:25; 9:43; 11:14). Sometimes people marvel at Jesus' speech (Mark 12:17; Luke 4:22). The disciples marvel when they see the resurrected Jesus (Luke 24:12, 41), in a scene that foreshadows the Parousia. Marvel suggests the overwhelming awe of worshipful adoration, perhaps bordering on sensory overload at the stunning revealing of the Son of God in all of his cosmic majesty.

Those who receive the Lord Jesus positively are characterized as **those who have believed**. They represent the polar opposite of those in v 8 "who do not know God and do not obey the gospel." Paul does not suggest that right living or morals are unimportant. Faith comprehensively describes the implications of one's trust commitment to the true and living God. It is the necessary foundation for a restored humanity.

Confession of the one God took primacy of place in Israel's Decalogue (Exod 20:3), in the Shema (Deut 6:4-5), and in Jesus' summary of the Scriptures' greatest commandment (Mark 12:29-31). Paul's analysis of the human condition in Romans traces the source of humanity's social and moral devastation to our idolatrous rejection of the Creator and choosing of substitutes (Rom 1:18-32). Faith is the necessary way back to God, modeled by Abraham. Since the first coming of Christ, faith's object is the hope of the ages, Jesus whose death and resurrection powerfully redeems (Gal 3:6-14; Rom 4:11-12, 24-25).

The final clause in v 10 is a parenthetical aside. **This includes you, because you believed our testimony to you** reassures the Thessalonians again that they stand with those who will be redeemed on that day. They will greet the returning Lord with joy. The NIV translation is actually a paraphrase. It treats the final clause of the sentence as a separate active sentence, to make it easier to read (see Lightfoot 1957, 105). It is (lit.) *because our testimony to you was believed*.

The spontaneity and awkwardness of this aside are good reasons to believe this is the genuine work of Paul and not an imitator (Wanamaker 1990, 231; Witherington 2006, 198). The use of an aorist (past tense) form of "believe" is genuine Pauline style, despite Paul's slim preference for present tenses of this verb (against Furnish 2007, 149). It is a complex aorist, emphasizing the completeness and the fact of their commitment to gospel truths (other aorists of "believe": Rom 3:2; 4:17, 18; 10:9; 1 Cor 3:5; 15:2, 11; Gal 2:16).

Our testimony is the same as **our gospel** (2 Thess 2:14; 1 Thess 1:5; 2 Cor 4:3; compare "our testimony about Christ" in 1 Cor 1:6; and "the testimony about our Lord" in 2 Tim 1:8). It is unclear why Paul switches from **gospel** (v 8) to **testimony** here. It may be merely for stylistic variation. Or the quasi-courtroom terminology may be prompted by the judgment theme of the Parousia. The Thessalonians stand with the acquitted. They will celebrate the great assize because they believed the **testimony** of the Lord's representatives, the apostles. They *put their trust in* (another meaning of **believed** [*episteuthē*]) the risen Christ and the gospel story that saves.

The very last words of this sentence in Greek, and this section, return to the thought of *when he comes to be glorified* and add *on that day*, which comes last for dramatic emphasis at the end of one very long sentence (vv 3-10 in Greek). All of this—an end to present suffering, future inbreaking glory of the Lord Jesus at his Parousia, punishment of injustice, the reward of the righteous—will climax *on that day*. The NIV moves these words to the start of v 10 for easier reading. "That day" is used in OT prophecy to refer to the Day of the Lord (Hos 2:16-20; Amos 8:9; 9:11; Zech 2:11); now it has become the Lord Jesus' Parousia (see Isa 2, esp. vv 12, 20).

C. Prayer (1:11-12)

Having started with a thanksgiving report, Paul returns to prayer to conclude his opening thoughts. He has prayed that the Thessalonians might be well prepared by God to encounter his returning Son. He will welcome them with rest and glorify them, and their lives will glorify him also. That is, he prays as in the previous letter that they might obtain salvation and live with him (1 Thess 5:9-10).

■ **11 With this in mind** introduces Paul's report of his prayer. The object of his request is that the Thessalonians might be able to greet Jesus joyfully among "his holy people," pointing back to v 10.

Paul prays first **that our God may make you worthy of his calling**. Adding the possessive **our** to **God** emphasizes the link between the apostle and his distant community, united in their allegiance to the true God, and new existence in him (compare 1 Thess 1:3; 2:2; 3:9, 11). As with 2 Thess 1:5, scholars debate whether the verb *axioō* means "make worthy" (Best 1986, 268; BAGD, 78; Malherbe 2000, 410) or "count as worthy." But the Greek lexicons and most recent commentators now agree that only the second meaning has good lexical support (LSJM, 171; BDAG, 94; Green 2002, 296; Witherington 2006, 200; Shogren 2012, 257). Hence, the sense is that **God may regard you as worthy of his calling and complete by his power every desire for goodness** and their faith-deeds. God's regarding is a relational act of grace, a response to their faith-life, which leads to empowerment for Christian living. It is like God's *crediting* Abraham with righteousness for his faith (Rom 4:3) or God justifying the ungodly (Rom 4:5; 1 Cor 6:11). In all these, the "indicative" of a new status, a new reality created by God's declaration, leads directly to the "imperative" to live out the implications of this gift.

Their **calling** refers to the time when the gospel reached them and summoned them to faith (1 Cor 1:26; Eph 4:1; *Herm. Mand.* 4.3.6; *Herm. Sim.* 8.11.1; compare Gal 1:6; 2 Thess 2:14). "Call" can refer to a friendly invitation to a social event (Matt 22:9; Luke 14:8, 13, 16; John 2:2) or an official summons for someone to appear (issued by a superior to an inferior, such as a master to his slave in Luke 19:13; by a king his generals in 1 Macc 1:6). A number of NT texts speak of a lifestyle of discipleship as the proper, grateful response to the divine calling. It is a holy (1 Thess 4:7) or worthy life (2:12; Eph 4:1), marked by godly virtues such as love, peace, and self-control (Gal 5:13; Col 3:15; 2 Pet 1:10). God continues to call people to the life of faith (on the present tense, → 1 Thess 5:24; see Gal 5:8).

Earlier Paul had noted (2 Thess 1:5) that their endurance and faith were evidence that God had already "counted [them] worthy of the kingdom." So why this prayer? From one perspective, no one is ever worthy of the invitation to the kingdom of God (Rom 3:9, 23-24). The sentence has the rhetorical effect of placing God in the position of the church's great heavenly patron. He has extended the summons-invitation to his kingdom and glory, with all its benefits (Col 1:13-14; 2 Thess 2:14). His benefits far outweigh anything that any aristocrat, even Caesar himself, can offer them: forgiveness of sins, reconciliation to one another and to God, the gift of the Spirit, and resurrection life after death.

Paul has also shown that the fear of God's enmity should be greater than the fear of any human political foe, whether Thessalonian politarchs or the Roman emperor. So as with the "citizenship" language of Philippians, the "calling" language here reminds them that they are under obligation to their divine patron. They belong to his kingdom, and their way of life must be shaped by the summons they have already received, which was both gift and demand. Continuing in their present path with faith and love will assure they have a glorious reception when Jesus returns. Paul has in mind not only the graciousness of God's salvation but also the moral life that grace grows. Verse 5 of 2 Thess 1 looks back to their past lives of faith and endurance; verses 11-12 look forward to future lives of faith that glorify Christ.

Paul further prays that God **may bring to fruition your every desire for goodness**. The Thessalonian believers' highest aspirations arose from the **goodness** (*agathōsynē*) that grows within believers as the fruit of the Spirit (Gal 5:22; Eph 5:9; Green 2002, 297; see Best 1986, 270; Malherbe 2000, 410-11).

This stands in parallel to another prayer, that God may fulfill **your every deed prompted by faith**. This is exactly what Paul had commended in 1 Thess 1:3. He refers not only to the activity of believing but also to the **work** (*ergon*) or **deeds** that true faith generates.

God wants believers to learn to desire what he desires. Even more, he wants us to be able to put into practice the purposes that arise out of his good presence with us and our faith in him. Paul realizes that we need divine help. It requires more than willpower to bring to completion what faith knows. So Paul has prayed that God may be at work with the Thessalonian believers **by his power**, which is another way of saying by his Holy Spirit (Rom 15:13; 1 Cor 2:4-5; 1 Thess 1:5). The Spirit who worked miracles and distributed spiritual gifts among the first Christians was also at work in the ordinary living of the faith. "God . . . works in you to will and to act in order to fulfill his good purpose" (Phil 2:13).

■ **12** The goal of this prayer comes in the purpose clause: **We pray this so that the name of our Lord Jesus may be glorified in you, and you in him**. To glorify Jesus' **name** is another way of saying that **Jesus is praised**. Expressing it this way may emphasize the focus on the reputation of the church's Lord in the midst of a conflict-ridden situation. Only a few Thessalonians had thus far acknowledged Jesus as **Lord**. Citing the glory of his **name** is also a reminder that **Jesus** was recited in prayer and worship as a divine name, alongside that of the Father (Rom 10:10-13; 1 Cor 1:2-3; 1 Thess 3:11), and in contrast to other deities worshipped in Thessalonica.

John's Gospel evidences a similar concern with the name of God the Father: Jesus claims to have made known God's name (John 17:6, 26) and prays that he may continue to glorify God's name (12:28).

The verb *doxazō* (**glorify**) has to do with increasing someone's honor or reputation. When God is its object, it is praise. When God has or gives glory, it refers to ineffable divine splendor. The passive verb (**be glorified**) may point to a prayer that non-Christians may praise the Lord on account of the lives of the Thessalonian Christians. More basically, it is a prayer that God will act to bring honor to his Son in and through the lives of believers (compare Isa 49:3; 2 Cor 8:23; Gal 1:24).

When Jesus is **glorified,** it is perceptible by others, whether or not they acknowledge it. And the process is mutual: not only is **Jesus** honored, but Paul prays that **you** believers may be honored **in him** also. Commentaries are divided over whether Paul is thinking primarily of something happening during the present lives of the Thessalonian believers or the eschatological glorification of believers as they come to share in Christ's glory at the resurrection. It seems more likely to point to the immediate present, since works of faith (v 11) will not be needed presumably at Christ's return. **In you** does not indicate the agent ("by") but the means: God is the glorifier, working through believers' lives.

Whether the second half of this prayer—**and you in him**—also happens in the present or in the eschatological future, is harder to say. Jesus' similar prayer in John 17 (vv 1, 4-5, 10, 21-23) uses the language of mutual glorification of Jesus by the Father and vice versa, and of Jesus by his disciples and vice versa, with "the world" as witness to this glorification.

In either case, Paul cannot end without the reminder that none of it occurs except **according to the grace of our God and the Lord Jesus Christ**. **Grace** occurs here for the first time in the Thessalonian letters, outside the opening greetings and closing formulas. **Grace** is God's freely and mercifully given benefits.

Mutual glorification, like justification, is a work that begins with God's initiative and is possible only because of his working. That Paul prays for **grace** implies that humans play a part in its effective operation (by asking for it, seeking God). Grace is needed for believers to make life choices that will bring Christ glory. By praying to this end, we anticipate God's grace will be at work in our lives.

The verse closes with an unusual reference to **our God and the Lord Jesus**. One article introduces both **God** and **Lord** in Greek. This grammatical construction often indicates that the two describe the same thing: *our God and Lord, Jesus Christ*. Taken this way, Paul would be calling Jesus God

(Marshall 1983, 184; Green 2002, 300; compare 2 Pet 1:11). Few other Pauline texts seem explicitly to identify Jesus with God (Rom 9:5; Titus 2:13). Since the expression "Lord Jesus (Christ)" often occurs as a set phrase without the article in Paul (Phil 3:20; 1 Thess 1:1; 4:1; 2 Thess 3:12), most commentators believe it is two formulas run together here and only appear as if they might be one (Best 1986, 272; Bruce 1982, 156-57; Malherbe 2000, 412; Witherington 2006, 201 n. 10).

FROM THE TEXT

Once again, the "Christian triad" of faith, love, and hope makes its appearance to show us the importance of these fundamental virtues (2 Thess 1:3; 1 Thess 1:3; 5:8). The first two are named as strengths that the Thessalonian Christians had which allowed them to survive and even bear spiritual fruit in the midst of a hostile society. The last virtue, hope, is implied in Paul's words of consolation to them about the certainty of Christ's future return for them and for all believers. Perhaps there are lessons here for Christians around the world today who live in increasingly hostile societies, even in the formerly Christian West. What we do for the Lord in this life is important, but it is not the end of all that we are. Nor can anyone measure our ultimate success by present prosperity, social standing, or apparent victory (or lack of it) over opponents. Our hope is to see the glory of Christ, to be accounted worthy by him more than any social media. Our hope is to bring honor to the Father and the Son through lives of faith, love, and hope, with the assistance of God's grace. In the face of severe suffering, Paul refuses to give in to the temptation to call for vengeance. Instead, he points to Christ's role as judge. And he calls on us to deliberately set the course of our lives so that God may powerfully enact *goodness* through us, to his glory. This is faith and love in action, miming Christ for a world that will not listen.

The Savior puts off the role of Judge as long as possible—until the end of the world. Multiple witnesses attest that he described his first coming as a rescue mission. "I have not come to call the righteous, but sinners" (Mark 2:17); "the Son of Man came to seek and to save the lost" (Luke 19:10); "I did not come to judge the world, but to save the world" (John 12:47).

Without divine grace, no one could be saved. But this era of amnesty will one day come to an end. Some misunderstand God's grace as a license to sin: they think if judgment does not fall immediately, God either approves of evil or does not care. Some use his mercy as an excuse to prop up their unbelief, thinking God should surely show himself more or punish sinners more in the present, if he were real. All such thinking will be exposed by the "shock and awe" of Jesus' second appearance on earth.

At the second coming, he *will* assume his designated role as Judge. He will appear not as the meek carpenter of Galilee but as the Son of God coming in divine glory, accompanied by angelic armies, with powers so unimaginable that they will make our most sophisticated nuclear weapons seem like stone axes by comparison.

This coming, however, will not be only to punish the wicked. Like the OT Day of the Lord, it has a positive side as well. For those who are in Christ, this day brings ultimate relief from suffering, the beginning of resurrection life, and the opening up of the grandeur of the messianic age (compare 1 Thess 4:13-18; 5:4, 8-10).

This text also highlights the notion of *wonder*. While Jesus' coming will terrify the wicked, the righteous will *adore* him. They will be lost in amazement. The interpreter who would properly make sense of this text today must pay attention to its original audience. Christians *suffering for their faith* are promised "relief" by the Lord Jesus at his return (2 Thess 1:4, 7).

Like certain lament psalms (58; 79:9-13; 94), parts of Exodus (3:7-8, 20; 6:5-6), and certain OT prophets (Isa 1:23-24; 3:13-15; 5:18-25; Mic 2:1-5; 3:9-12), Paul looks to God to exercise justice against the powerful wicked who oppress God's people.

Some may think it difficult to reconcile this picture of Jesus as cosmic Judge and punisher of evil with the Sermon on the Mount. Yet even in that sermon Jesus warned his audience to take steps to avoid hell (Matt 5:22-26, 29-30) and indicated he would have a role in judging that would involve the exclusion of some from the kingdom (7:21-23; compare Mark 8:35-38).

Jesus taught love for enemies and that his disciples were to forestall vengeance as human agents. But his instructions against taking vengeance do not suppose that retributive justice is wrong. They are predicated on the supposition that the task of justice is to be turned over to God. He alone is qualified to perform it.

This text reminds believers that Jesus will participate with the Father in bringing humanity to judgment, just as he had participated in redemption. Even today some Christians need to hear from Scripture that God cares about justice.

This text is certainly not intended to support any sort of Christian holy war against God's enemies. It is not about human vengeance. Nor is it intended to prop up a smug sense of election that would look with pleasure on the future destruction of non-Christians. It was not written to comfort Christians who enjoy political and economic comfort in the West. Rather, it ought to give us, if anything, sorrow for those who reject the Lord. John Chrysostom's comments on 2 Thess 1:9 are salutary here:

> Let us not rejoice at the punishment of others as being avenged, but as ourselves escaping from such punishment and vengeance. For what advantage is it to us when others are punished? Let us not, I beseech you, have such souls! (*Hom. 2 Thess.* 2.3).

Paul does not deal directly here with our modern question about the fate of the unevangelized. Here at 1:7-10, and again at 2:10-11, the letter's context tells us he is speaking of people who consciously, deliberately reject God's grace offered through Christ in the gospel, who oppose Christ's church, and who prefer false religion to the true God.

Paul's prayer that closes this section reminds us that faith is never an activity that can be confined to the mental sphere. God's *calling* to people through the gospel always entails a *lifestyle* that befits the character and the kingdom of the one who calls. Saving faith will naturally lead, like a tree bearing fruit, to choices that bring honor to Jesus in the public sphere and in our families. Sometimes these will be difficult and costly choices. But by the mighty working of God's grace, even small and frail lights set in dark places can become stars in the night.

III. ABOUT THE PAROUSIA AND THE MAN OF LAWLESSNESS: 2 THESSALONIANS 2:1-12

BEHIND THE TEXT

Here Paul comes to his primary motive for writing. Some Christians have confused and distressed the Thessalonian church. They have invoked the apostle's authority to teach that "the day of the Lord has already come" (v 2). What exactly they taught, or why, is not entirely clear. The simplest explanation may be that they misunderstood Paul's earlier letter, perhaps because of problems created by persecution (→ Introduction; → v 2, below).

Paul refutes their error by reminding them (v 5) of eschatological teaching he had delivered earlier. Paul considers this refutation only a "refresher," rather than a full account of the end times. This explains why some typical eschatological events are never mentioned and others only cryptically (v 6).

Another reason for the apostle's cautious language may be the political sensitivity of the topic. The prediction of a divine overthrow of a world ruler might well be taken as seditious. The dictator who was the Roman emperor also styled himself "son of god" on his coins. His subjects worshipped his predecessors in temples across the Mediterranean world.

The text is also difficult to read because it is not arranged in chronological order:

- Vv 1-2 introduce the problem.
- Vv 3-4 tell how the man of lawlessness will appear before the day of the Lord arrives.
- Vv 5-7 remind the Thessalonians of what is holding him back in the present.
- V 8 reminds them that the man of lawlessness will be destroyed by the Lord Jesus at his Parousia.
- But before the Parousia, vv 9-12 recount the coming of the man of lawlessness and the judgment on the unbelievers he will deceive.

Commentators are divided as to the main literary function of this section. The majority see it as Paul's refutation of the false teaching and his warning about the coming antichrist figure (so Bruce 1982, 166; Wanamaker 1990, 237, 242; Green 2002, 306; Witherington 2006, 2005-6). A few argue that the main purpose of this chapter is to *comfort* readers distressed by persecutions and fears that the Day of the Lord had passed them by (Malherbe 2000, 413-14; Fee 2009, 277; anticipated in Frame 1912, 242-43).

Paul draws on three main sources: OT Scripture (Daniel), Jewish apocalyptic traditions, and Jesus' teaching passed on through the church. Paul may also have depended on his own prophetic inspiration (see 2 Cor 12:2-4; 1 Tim 4:1-3). All these sources offer similar warnings about the perils of the end of history. It will be a time of great moral decline and apostasy; those faithful to God will be persecuted (Dan 7:21, 25; 8:23; 11:14, 32-34; *1 En.* 91:5-7; 93:9; *Jub.* 23:14-23; *4 Ezra* 14:16-18; 4Q174 II, 12; III, 7-9; IV, 1-4; 1QpHab II, 1-10; Matt 24:9-13; Mark 13:12-13; 2 Tim 3:1-9).

The end will come when a human attempts to exalt himself to divine status and usurp worldwide rule. Jesus also warned of false Christs (Dan 11:36-37; Matt 24:5, 11, 23-26; Mark 13:5-6, 21-22). This scenario is featured in the Gospels, Paul, 1—3 John, and in its most developed apocalyptic form in Revelation.

Some argue that the eschatology of 2 Thess 2:1-12 is so different from that of 1 Thessalonians that the second letter must be by someone other than Paul. First Thessalonians expects an imminent surprise return of Jesus (5:2); 2 Thess 2:1-12 offers signs that precede the end. The scenario of the "lawless one" is not even alluded to elsewhere in Paul. The letter appeals to unverifiable oral teaching (2:5) for support.

But this skeptical approach skews the evidence. First Thessalonians addresses the participation of the dead in the Parousia, not its timing. The remark about Jesus coming "like a thief in the night" will be a surprise for *unbelievers*, not Christians (1 Thess 5:2-4).

Although unique to Paul, much of 2 Thess 2:1-12 aligns fully with common early Christian apocalyptic teachings elsewhere in the NT (see Matt 24:4-24, 30, 33; Mark 13:5-6, 14-26, 29; 1 John 2:18; 4:3; Rev 13; 16:13-15; 19:19-20). It may seem inconsistent to have the end unpredictable and yet preceded with signs. Yet both ideas go together in the earliest Gospel traditions (Mark 13:4-37).

We are not dealing with a modern chronology. And the logic of apocalyptic literature is not Aristotelian. The "tension" between 1 and 2 Thessalonians echoes exactly the inner tension of Jesus' teaching. Nothing in 2 Thess 2:1-12 is incompatible with Pauline eschatology elsewhere.

Finally, it should be expected as normal that Paul would refer to his earlier oral teaching (compare 1 Cor 2:1-5; 15:1-2, 11; Gal 1:8; 1 Thess 2:11-12; 4:1, 11). In the ancient world the majority of learning was oral and most people in his Gentile churches were probably illiterate (Harris 1989, 326-30; Gamble 1995, 8-10). The letters represent only a fraction of Paul's actual teaching (as Fee 2009, 285) and often are corrective.

IN THE TEXT

■ **1-2** In 2 Thess 1:6-10, Paul comforts his audience by reflecting on the effects of Jesus' return. Only then does he attempt to correct their mistaken understanding of the present situation. Paul desires that they avoid the mental and emotional consequences of the false teaching about **the coming** [*parousias*] **of our Lord Jesus Christ**.

This is the same event Paul had just described in 1:7-10 and addressed earlier in 1 Thess 4:15-17. Christ's public return and the gathering of living saints, the resurrection of the faithful dead, and the final judgment are all aspects of a single event (see 2 Thess 1:8-9; 1 Thess 5:2-4). No scriptural evidence exists supporting the latter-day doctrine of two different returns, one to rapture the church and one to judge (→ "The Rapture Theory" sidebar at 1 Thess 4:17; → Behind the Text for 1 Thess 4:13-18).

Paul probably uses the full title for Jesus here to emphasize his majesty and glory: this is not the first or last time he combines the titles **Lord** and **Christ** in the Thessalonian letters (→ 1 Thess 1:1; 1:3; 4:16; 5:9, 23, 28; 2 Thess 1:1, 2, 12; 2:1, 14, 16; 3:6, 12, 18).

Christ's return includes God's people **being gathered to him**. This echoes the ancient hope of Israel that God would gather the Diaspora from the four corners of the earth, bringing them to the promised land. With the return from exile would come a spiritual revolution in their hearts to love and serve God (Ps 106:47; Isa 11:11-12; 27:12-13; 43:5-7; Jer 32:37-41; Ezek 11:17;

28:25-26; Tob 14:7; 2 Macc 1:27; 2:7-8, 18; *Pss. Sol.* 17:26-27; *T. Naph.* 8:3). Jesus interpreted this hope as fulfilled in the eschatological gathering of believers by God's angels at the end of the age (Matt 23:37; 24:31; Mark 13:27; Luke 13:34). In the first letter Paul described a taking up of all believers, dead and alive, to be with the Lord forever (1 Thess 4:17).

Paul again (→ 1 Thess 1:4; 2:1, 9, 14, 17; 4:1, 13; 5:1; 12; 2 Thess 1:3; 2:13, 15; 3:1, 13) appeals to his audience as **brothers and sisters**. This emphasizes the bond between them: they are God's family in Christ. Paul frequently uses this language to encourage his readers to remain faithful to the Christian lifestyle and teaching.

Paul does not say how he received news of the problem in Thessalonica. He expresses only his concern that they should **not . . . become easily unsettled or alarmed . . . that the day of the Lord has already come** (2 Thess 2:2). His words suggest that he is apprehensive for both sound doctrine and their emotional well-being.

Unsettled (*saleuthēnai*) appears in a phrase that means "to be shaken from [your] understanding." The verb describes the upheaval created by earthquakes or storm-tossed seas. The false teaching rocked the Thessalonians' understanding of reality. Theologically shaken, they are now **alarmed** (*throeisthai*), **emotionally disturbed**, because they were led to believe that the Day of the Lord had arrived. Yet here they were, unresurrected, persecuted, still needing a means of making a living, and without an appearance of Jesus. The consequences for the community's faith and practical affairs could be disastrous.

Paul mentions a few possible sources of this mistaken notion: (1) **A prophecy** (lit. *a spirit*). This refers to a message claiming the inspiration of the Spirit (see 1 John 4:1-3). **Prophecy** appears to have been a fairly regular part of early Christian gatherings (Acts 21:9-11; Rom 12:6; 1 Cor 14:26-32; 1 John 4:1; *Did.* 11.7-12). This would not be the first or last time human opinions have been mistaken for a message from God.

(2) It could have come as an oral utterance, **by word of mouth** (*logos*, a message of exhortation or interpretation of Scripture). Or (3) it could have come in written form, **by letter**.

Regardless of the medium, Paul denies responsibility for the message, the false **teaching allegedly from us** (*'hōs di' hēmōn*). This denial certainly applies to the **letter**. It may also apply to the teaching **word**, if somebody claimed Paul's authorization. It is unlikely that prophets would have claimed to speak for Paul. They considered their authority to come directly from the Spirit. But it is conceivable that some reported they *heard* a prophecy from Paul, and distorted it. But the expression here, *by a spirit*, suggests "live" prophecy.

Paul could imply that a letter was forged under his name. He denied authoring it. This would explain his drawing attention to his distinctive signature in 3:17 (so John Chrysostom, *Hom. 2 Thess.* 3.2; Bruce 1982, 164; Richard 1995, 325; Green 2002, 303).

On the other hand, *hōs* (**allegedly**) with the preposition *dia* (**from, by,** or **through**), normally refers to a means or instrument. Thus, Paul may only have denied that he was the *source* of their *misinterpretation* (of 1 Thessalonians, that is), not that he was the source of the letter itself (Best 1986, 278; Marshall 1983, 187; Fee 2009, 275).

It is possible that **allegedly by us** refers to what follows. Paul denied that the idea that the Day of the Lord was already present originated with the apostles (Fee 2009, 275). We might then read *hoti* (**that**) as *recitativum* (introducing direct speech), and translate vv 1-2: . . . ***we ask you, brothers and sisters, not to let your wits be easily rattled or become alarmed, whether by a prophecy, or by a teaching, or by a letter, as though it were through us, as some are saying: "The day of the Lord has arrived!"***

The misinterpreted **letter** could refer to 1 Thessalonians, in this scenario. Was it misunderstood and misinterpreted as it was passed around the Thessalonian churches? Were copies of it glossed with an "explanation" about **the day of the Lord**? This might explain Paul's need to verify his original letter (so Frame 1912, 247; Malherbe 2000, 353-56). It seems too soon for a forgery to have arisen, if Paul wrote 2 Thessalonians soon after 1 Thessalonians (so Best 1986, 279; Marshall 1983, 187).

How could the Thessalonian believers think that **the day of the Lord** had **already come** (2 Thess 2:2)? Paul's own theology had elements of "realized eschatology" that reflected the changed state of believers in Christ. These could easily have been misunderstood. For example, he claimed that believers are already "children of the day" and no longer belong to "the darkness," the power of Satan (1 Thess 5:5, 8). Believers are "raised with [Christ] through . . . faith" (Col 2:12; 3:1). They are clothed with Christ and live in the promised age of fulfillment, where social distinctions are nullified (Gal 3:27-29; 4:6). "The night is nearly over; the day is almost here" (Rom 13:12). We can only guess what Paul may have said at Thessalonica that his hearers misunderstood (2 Pet 3:15-16).

Eschatological confusion is also reported in 2 Tim 2:17-18. There some claim the resurrection has already occurred. Some interpreters think the Corinthians also espoused an unbalanced eschatology. Paul resorted to sarcasm about their illusions of already "reigning" with Christ (1 Cor 4:8). He reminds them of the divine order, in which believers are not yet resurrected (1 Cor 15:20-23, 46; e.g., Thiselton 1978).

One source of the Thessalonians' confused ideas could be gnostic spiritualizing of the idea of "resurrection." Later examples of this survive in which Jewish eschatological concepts about the world's end are morphed into timeless truths about the soul, using Hellenistic philosophy (see *Gos. Thom.* 52). But if this were the problem, a further timetable would hardly resolve it (2 Thess 2:3, 8; Best 1986, 276).

It is possible that someone led Paul's converts to regard their persecution as part of the "messianic woes," the harbinger of the last hour (Wanamaker 1990, 240). In the end, we simply don't have enough information to reconstruct fully their views or the causes that occasioned them.

We can only say for sure what the letter says: somehow they came to believe the **day** had begun (not necessarily a twenty-four-hour period). And they attributed their belief to the apostles. The effect of this teaching was chaos in the church. It countered what Paul believed was the plain sense of apostolic teaching (v 5). And it threw them into needless grief over their suffering and deaths. They mistakenly believed they were being unjustly deprived of the deliverance from these they had been led to expect (1:5-7; 1 Thess 4:13-14).

■ **3** Paul responds to the view that "the day of the Lord has already come" (v 2) with an apostolic order: **Don't let anyone deceive you in any way.** He debunks the false teaching as *deceit*, reminding them of eschatological events that must precede the **day**. Jesus (in Matt 24:4-8 ‖ Mark 13:5-8) warns of being deceived by mistaking certain events for signs that the end has arrived. Paul considers the deception no innocent mistake, but a deliberate distortion of the truth (*exapataō*, an intensified form of the verb "deceive").

The Thessalonians should reject this false doctrine in **any way** it arrives, even if someone claims the authority of the Holy Spirit or the apostle (v 2). Paul warns not to accept it from **anyone**. This does not imply ignorance of the source (against Best 1986, 280). His standard tactic is not to name his opponents. Paul knows the doctrine, its effects on the church, and that he is its supposed source—all this implies that he possesses some definite information.

The first event Paul mentions that must occur prior to the **day** of the Lord is **the rebellion** (*apostasia*). In secular Greek this designates a political revolution. In the LXX it can also mean rebellion against God (Josh 22:22; 2 Chr 28:19; Jer 2:19). Most relevant to this text, and burned in the memory of Jews, was the *apostasy* of those who abandoned Judaism and God's Law during the reign of Antiochus IV Epiphanes (215—163 BC). At first renegade Jews committed apostasy to gain political favor, then to avoid persecution (168-167 BC; 1 Macc 1:15; 2:15). During Antiochus' reign Jews were forced to sacrifice publicly to the Greek gods to prove their loyalty, or face execution. Daniel says this ruler "will corrupt those who have violated the covenant" (11:32). This persecution became the prototype for expectations in later Jewish literature about the end times:

> After that in the seventh week an apostate generation shall arise; its deeds shall be many, and all of them criminal. (*1 En.* 93:9)

> For they all did evil and every mouth speaks of sin and all of their deeds are polluted and abominable . . . And they will pollute the holy of holies with their pollution and with the corruption of their contamination.

(*Jub.* 23:17, 21; see vv 14-21; 2 Esd 5:3-12; *1 En.* 91:5-7; *4 Ezra* 14:16-18; *2 Bar.* 41:3)

Jesus also expected a time of intense evil and apostasy to precede the world's end, including deception by false prophets and false Christs (Matt 24:11-12, 23-24; Mark 13:5-6, 19-22; Luke 21:8, 16-17; John 16:1-4). This is the tradition Paul seems to have in mind here.

Although *apostasia* can be translated "apostasy," Paul does not think of *Christians* turning away from the true God. He details the effect of the rebellion and the **man of lawlessness** on the world at large (2 Thess 2:4) and on "those who are perishing" (vv 10-12; 1 Cor 1:18). This is a general world **rebellion** against the true God and his moral law (1 Tim 4:1-2; 2 Tim 4:3-4; Jude 17-19; Rev 17:1-6; Frame 1912, 251; Malherbe 2000, 418; Witherington 2006, 216; Fee 2009, 281).

The sentence in Greek is an anacoluthon: it leaves out bits for the reader to fill in. It begins, literally: **Don't let anyone deceive you in any way, because unless the rebellion comes first and the man of lawlessness is revealed . . .** The NIV supplies **that day will not come** from the context (see ESV, KJV, NRSV, etc.). **First** seems to apply to both the **rebellion** and the **man of lawlessness** as preceding the **day** (Best 1986, 281; Wanamaker 1990, 243; Malherbe 2000, 418).

The **man of lawlessness** will be **revealed** at this future time (2 Thess 2:3*b*). Whether the **rebellion** leads to his rise, or he precipitates it, is not clear. Nowhere else in his letters does Paul mention this figure. That he will be **revealed** (*apokaluphthē* [vv 3*b*, 8]) hints that he is hidden now and suggests his pseudomessianic claim. For Jesus' coming is also a "revelation" (1:7; 1 Cor 1:7); they both have a *parousia* (2 Thess 2:8, 9).

Although we might be tempted to think from certain passages in Paul that **lawlessness** is a good thing (being free from law [Rom 3:20-26; 10:4; Gal 2:19-21; 3:23-25; 5:4]), it is not. **Lawlessness** (*anomia*) as a biblical synonym for sin is the opposite of righteousness (in Paul: Rom 4:7; 2 Cor 6:14; Titus 2:14; in the rest of the NT: Heb 1:9; 1 John 3:4). Jesus warned that those who practice *anomia* would be excluded from the kingdom of God (Matt 7:23; 13:41). In the OT and Judaism **lawlessness** is covenant-breaking sin (Exod 34:7, 9; Lev 16:21; Ezra 9:6-7, 13; Ps 31:1, 5).

Lawless ones have no regard for God or his people; they are sociopaths, rebels set on evil for their own gain (Pss 14:4; 35:2-4; 49:5-6; Isa 58:1-4; 59:3-6; Jer 16:18; see Isa 1:28; 9:13-21). The title **man of lawlessness** identifies him as the ultimate enemy of God and humanity, a person with no regard for what is right (confirmed in 2 Thess 2:9-10). Many later manuscripts interpretively read "man of sin" instead of **lawlessness** (replacing *anomia* with the more familiar *hamartia*; Metzger 1994, 567). But vv 7-8 presume the second title ("mystery of *lawlessness*" [ESV, HCSB, NASB, NRSV], "the *lawless one*").

The lawless one is the **son of destruction**. This Hebrew idiom means he is **doomed to destruction** (v 3b). The same term describes the betrayer of Jesus (John 17:12), reminding readers that his success will be short-lived; God will be victorious. He is the opposite of the "children of the day" (1 Thess 5:5), who inherit the kingdom of God.

■ 4 The full extent of his rebellion against God is seen here. He sets himself up to be worshipped, supplanting every supposed deity. *He will oppose and exalt himself over every so-called god*. Paul describes the lawless one echoing Dan 11:36, speaking of Antiochus IV: "He will exalt and magnify himself above every god and will say unheard-of things against the God of gods." Paul inserts *so-called* (*legomenon*) into Daniel's "every god" to imply that the deities of Mediterranean polytheism are mere human inventions compared to the one true God (see 1 Cor 8:5).

Antiochus took the throne name Epiphanes, which conveyed his self-portrayal as the "manifestation" of a god on earth. His brutal policy of enforced hellenization attempted to extinguish Judaism in his kingdom. He converted the Jerusalem temple into a temple of the Olympian Zeus and sacrificed a pig on its high altar (2 Macc 6:2-6). He outlawed all distinctively Jewish customs, rounded up and burned copies of the Law, and executed anyone caught keeping the Law (1 Macc 1:45-58). He did not explicitly insist that his subjects worship him. Nevertheless, like other arrogant, pretentious, and powerful enemy kings (Isa 14:13-14; Ezek 28:2), he became a biblical prototype for the great end-time enemy of God's people.

The lawless one **will exalt himself**, flaunting his pride and political power. Like Napoleon who insisted on crowning himself, the lawless one will promote himself. He will claim to be greater than any deity, using satanic miracles and power to deceive (2 Thess 2:8-12). **He will oppose** all religions because no rival can be tolerated and nothing else **worshiped**—no statue, site, or temple. His insanity will lead him eventually to **sit in God's temple, proclaiming himself to be God**. Paul calls him *the one who opposes* (*ho antikeimenos*), echoing the meaning of the Hebrew *Satan* (Zech 3:1; 1 Tim 5:14; *Mart. Pol.* 17.1; Best 1986, 285). He will seek to usurp completely the worship of God everywhere and in every manner possible.

Another precursor to this end-times figure is the Roman general Pompey. The Psalms of Solomon call him "the lawless one" and accuse him of massacring Jerusalem and leading people to paganism (17:11-20; Wanamaker 1990, 245). Pompey conducted a bloody assault on Jerusalem and shocked Jews by entering the most holy place of the temple. But Pompey never opposed the Jewish cult, and he had the support of a large faction of the populace (Josephus, *Ant.* 14.71-72; *J.W.* 1.152).

The Roman imperial cult evidenced many traits of the expected end-times apostasy. Paul may well have thought of it as a precursor to the lawless one. From Julius Caesar onward, dead emperors were deified. Living emperors were styled "son of God," because they had been adopted by their predecessors. This title appears on coins minted in Macedonia and Achaia. Outside Italy, people began to treat living emperors as divine, with inscriptions, temples, and priesthoods erected in their honor (Price 1997, 69). In Paul's day there were temples to Augustus at Thessalonica and Corinth (from where he wrote 1 Thessalonians; Pausanias, *Descr.* 2.3.1). Thessalonica issued coins with Julius Caesar on the obverse with the inscription *THEOS* ("god") and on the reverse Augustus. Other coins bore the goddess Roma. Macedonian coins from other cities proclaimed Augustus and other emperors "son of a god" (Edson 1940, 132; Head 1963, 52-53, 115). The iconography and propaganda of emperor worship were everywhere, even in the city markets.

The emperor Caligula ordered his image to be erected in the Jerusalem temple as an object of worship in AD 40 (Josephus, *Ant.* 18.261-309; Philo, *Legat.* 203-346). The plan was never executed, because he was assassinated before the orders were completed. This event, only a few years prior to the writing of 2 Thessalonians, perhaps comes closest to the description of the "man of lawlessness" here. Undoubtedly, it served as an example of the "mystery of lawlessness . . . already at work" (2:7 NASB, NRSV).

What **temple** [*naon*] does Paul have in mind as the locus of the evil one's proclamation? The term may be used of the innermost part of a temple: at Jerusalem, the most holy place (LSJM, 1160; Josephus, *J.W.* 1.152). Paul calls it **God's temple**, clearly referring to the Jerusalem temple. The blasphemous self-exaltation of a human to divine status precisely in *this* spot makes it a horrifying act of defiance.

2:4

Since the Jerusalem temple was destroyed in AD 70, this now seems an impossible prediction, calling for an alternate interpretation (so Wanamaker [1990, 248]: it "can no longer be understood as valid"). John Chrysostom understood it as referring to the church and the church's apostasy (*Hom. 2 Thess.* 3.2; Giblin 1967, 76-80). But the passage is about universal delusion (***over every so-called god*** [2:4, 9-12]), and Paul seems optimistic about these Christians (3:3-4; 1 Thess 5:4-10). When the apostle uses "temple" metaphorically elsewhere (1 Cor 3:16-17; 6:19; Eph 2:19-22), its figurative force is clear, but not here.

Perhaps Paul refers to the lawless one occupying the Jerusalem temple as a metaphor of his usurping the place of God (Bruce 1982, 169; Marshall 1983, 191; Richard 1995, 329). This has the advantage of retaining the reference to Jerusalem as a place but does not require the rebuilding of a temple. Could Paul have thought of it that way?

A recent creative option sees the **temple** as one devoted specially to the antichrist, similar to the imperial cult sites of Thessalonica (Green 2002, 312-13). But this does not seem to fully do justice to the biblical echoes of 2 Thess 2:3-4, nor might one think Paul would call such a site **God's temple**.

The best option seems to be that Paul envisions the "man of lawlessness" (v 3) enthroned as a deity in the Jerusalem temple, attempting to exalt himself even above the Creator. **Sits** cannot be literal, for there is no throne or image in that temple. The usurper will not dwell there. He merely will claim to be the god of that place (NIV: **sets himself up**). The ultimate enemy of God and of Christ's people will be like the arrogant and murderous Antiochus. His cult will be like an extreme version of the imperial cult already operating throughout the East (see Green 2002, 212-13; Witherington 2006, 218-19).

■ **5** The first half of Paul's response to the false teaching is rounded off with a mention of his earlier teaching. This is not new information to the Thessalonians. There may be a hint of annoyance in Paul's reminder of repeated instructions—**Don't you remember that I . . . used to tell you . . . ?** (compare 1 Cor 3:16; 5:6; 6:2-3, 9, 15-16, 19; 9:13, 24; Malherbe 2000, 421).

Here Paul switches to the first person, **I**, emphasizing his statement and identifying himself as the letter's principal author. In the two letters Paul repeatedly reminds them of his past behavior and teaching with the phrase "you know" (1 Thess 1:5; 2:1-2, 5, 11; 3:3-4; 4:2; 5:2; 2 Thess 3:7; and 3:10 [without "you know"]).

But we do not know. Many details of this passage must remain cryptic to modern readers. His mention of key events and players with enigmatic epithets allowed his first readers to fill in the blanks based on his previous instruction—**when I was with you**. We will never know what he leaves unsaid here. We were not there when Paul ministered among the Thessalonians.

Some people have thought it suspicious that Paul does not refer to 1 Thessalonians. But that letter did not address these issues. Paul refers to his original oral instruction to circumvent any sources of error (Malherbe 2000, 421). Oral instruction was the norm in antiquity. Most people were illiterate, so it is not surprising that Paul followed this cultural method (→ Behind the Text for 2 Thess 2:1-12, above).

■ **6-7** Paul addresses the present, reminding the Thessalonians why (**For** [v 7]) the day of the Lord cannot have already arrived. The man of lawlessness has something **holding him back** (v 6). The Thessalonians **know what** it is, so Paul never names it. The thing **holding . . . back** the usurper is neuter in v 6 (*to katechon*) but masculine in v 7 (*ho katechōn*). This may imply that it is somehow both impersonal and personal.

The main contextual meanings of the verb *katechō* here are: (1) to restrain or prevent the doing of something, or to hold back someone from going away; (2) to suppress something; (3) to possess as one's own; (4) gain possession of, be master of; control; (5) to possess a person, as a god does (LSJM, 926; BDAG, 532-33).

The meaning that makes the most sense of the evidence is "restrain." ***That which restrains*** (neuter in v 6) suppresses "the man of lawlessness" (v 3) for this purpose: **so that** [*eis to*] **that he may be revealed at the proper time.**

Restraint prevents him from appearing prematurely, ahead of God's plan. And "the one who now restrains it" (masculine in v 7 NRSV) at present will do so only "until" he "is removed" (NRSV; see Bruce 1982, 170-71).

The Identity of the Restrainer

Interpreters have speculated widely as to the identity of the restrainer:

(1) The Roman state and the emperor (Tertullian, *Res.* 24; followed by John Chrysostom, *Hom. 2 Thess.* 4.1; Bruce 1982, 172; Richard 1995, 338-40). Evidence for this includes Paul's positive assessment of government for restraining evil in God's design (Rom 13:1-7) and his supposedly happy experience with the Roman judicial system. It would also explain his reticence to name Rome as the power that must be removed one day.

The difficulty with this view is the plethora of implicit anti-imperial rhetoric throughout these letters. Paul replaces the imperial cult with the Lord Jesus Christ, and the benefits of empire with those of the kingdom of God. Even worse, the imperial cult seems to be a model for antichrist (Green 2002, 315; Witherington 2006, 209).

There is also the hermeneutical problem that in our time the empire has long since fallen. A modified version of this solution envisions a general restraint by civil government, with the masculine expression in v 7 being a literary personification (Lightfoot 1957, 114-15; Morris 1991, 227).

(2) Some suggest that Paul refers to God or his Holy Spirit. The force of v 6 and the personal agent of v 7 both restrain the rise of "the man of lawlessness" (v 3). Both oppose evil. Paul implies that this force/person facilitates God's plan for the final phase of history by first restraining "the lawless one" (v 8), then by allowing his rise. The word for "Spirit" (*pneuma*) is grammatically neuter in Greek. Nevertheless, he is sometimes referred to personally with masculine pronouns.

The passive "be revealed" points to God's agency in the unveiling (v 8; Malherbe 2000, 433-34). This fits Paul's confidence that God is ultimately in charge of history (1:6-10; Rom 8:31-39; 1 Cor 15:24-26). But it raises unanswerable questions. Why should Paul be so cryptic about naming God or the Spirit? Why would he speak of God "removing" himself from the midst of the world? There is no biblical evidence elsewhere that the Spirit will ever be taken from the world. Jesus does not retract his parting gift to the church. No one will be saved without the Spirit, even in times of tribulation. He will continue God's work of convicting the world until the end (Luke 24:49; John 16:7-11; 20:22; Acts 2:1-4, 32-33, 39; Rom 8:9-10).

(3) Some interpreters identify the preaching of the gospel as what restrains the man of lawlessness and the end. The one condition Jesus gave to delay the end's coming was the evangelization of all nations (Mark 13:10). In this view, Paul thought his preaching of the gospel would hold back (2 Thess 2:6) the antichrist until he died (Oscar Cullmann, cited in Marshall 1983, 198). But when Paul wrote, he expected to be among those greeting Jesus' Parousia (1 Thess 4:17). Did he really consider himself so pivotal in restraining global evil? In a twist on views (2) and (3), Powell argued 2:6-7 refers to the ministry of the Holy Spirit through the whole church, as the gospel is preached until the rapture (1997, 330-31).

(4) Some identify the restrainer as an angelic figure acting for God. He assists the preaching of the gospel until God decides to allow the lawless one's final manifestation (Marshall 1983, 199). Some identify him specifically as the archangel Michael, based on his role in Jewish and Christian apocalyptic texts. There he is the defender of God's people, heavenly warrior, and arch-opponent of Satan (Nicholl 2000, 27-53; 2004, 225-49; Witherington 2006, 210-12; Dan 12:1; *1 En.* 24:6; 10:11; 54:6; 1QM XVII, 5-8; *T. Isaac* 2.1; Jude 9; Rev 12:7-9).

(5) Some interpreters, however, see the restrainer (2 Thess 2:7) as aligned with the forces hostile to God. It is Satan or his minion (v 7) and an evil power (v 6) at work. They help prepare the way for the man of lawlessness. *Ho katechōn* (masculine in v 7) is variously understood as "the ruler," "occupier" (of this world; Frame 1912, 261; Best 1986, 301-2; Wanamaker 1990, 256-57 [the emperor]), or "the one who [demonically] possesses" (Green 2002, 316-18). And *to katechon* (neuter in v 6) is correspondingly "the hostile occupying power" or "the power that possesses" people and brings them under Satan's influence.

It seems self-defeating for Satan to put himself out of the way for the antichrist. And without further contextual signals it is difficult to read *katechō* with a very specific, infrequent meaning ("be possessed [by a deity]"), when its everyday use "restrain, hold down" makes good sense. This is reinforced by its antithesis in v 7, **till he is taken out of the way.**

A fully satisfactory answer to the question of the identity of the restrainer must take into account that its/his activity can be expressed as both impersonal agency and the activity of a person. The verb describing his activity frequently refers to the suppressing or holding back of something (see Phlm 13). The thing/person restraining must be opposed to the lawless one if his *removal* facilitates the hour of revelation. In fact "suppression" happens for the express purpose that the man of lawlessness not be revealed until his proper time (v 6). The neuter **restrainer** cannot be the same thing as the neuter "mystery of lawlessness" (v 7 ESV, HCSB, NASB, NRSV). The "mystery" prefigures the lawless one, while the **restrainer** opposes him.

Paul thinks of the **restraining thing/restrainer** as something already at work in his day—**now**. It was holding evil in check until the unknown moment when his time will come according to the divine plan. The apostle here agrees with apocalyptic literature in general: despite the rise of evil and chaos in the world, God is still in control, working his hidden plan (Malherbe 2000, 422-23, 432-34). This is to be a source of comfort to the church.

It is impossible to reach a more adequate solution due to the fragmentary nature of our information. Much can be said for the fourth theory (an angel of God). But it remains at best a conjecture.

Paul reminds the Thessalonians that they already have been instructed and **now you know what is holding him back** (v 6). **Now** could indicate that the restraining occurs in the present. More probably it claims only: ***And as for the present time, you know that which is restraining.***

The activity of God, restraining evil to allow the gospel to reach all nations, operates on a divine timetable. Its result (**so that**) is that the lawless one may be revealed *when it is his time*. Satan does not control the time, but God has assigned him a place in the unfolding of history (NIV: **at the proper time**). Even if Satan enjoys temporary success, it is only by God's permission, to test or punish a rebellious world (vv 11-12).

The term **revealed** (v 6) seems deliberately to echo the appearing of Jesus (1:7). So "the lawless one" (v 8) is a kind of antichrist (*anti-* meaning "instead of" as well as "against"). He has his own *parousia* (v 9), miracles, and supernatural power (vv 9-10). The lawless one's appearance, however, is not glorious like the Son's.

The language of **holding . . . back** and **revealed** does not necessarily imply that Paul thought of the lawless one as already alive and waiting in the wings. Paul's point is to prove to the Thessalonians that his time has not come yet.

But Jesus' church needs to be alert nonetheless, **for the *mystery* of lawlessness is already at work** (v 7). The term *mystery* (*to mysterion*), when used of the gospel, tells of ancient secrets now revealed in Christ. Christ himself is the "mystery" of God's reconciliation with us (Rom 16:25; 1 Cor 4:1; Eph 3:3-6; Col 1:27; 2:2; 4:3). Here *mystery* points to the way **lawlessness** is secretly at work in the world in rebellion against God. It prepares society for the coming of the "lawless one." It is only perceptible to people who have heard and accepted the gospel, who are guided by the Spirit and the apostles' teachings to discern it and avoid it.

Given the nature of evil, is **lawlessness** a *mystery* because it makes no sense? Evil is self-destructive, irrational, and perplexing. Although it is working, it will not launch the end prematurely, before God allows it. It cannot stop the church from witnessing to the gospel and the kingdom.

There is an agent of God at work at present, **the one who now holds it back**. This restraining activity allows this age of grace to continue. The gospel will be proclaimed to all nations. He **holds . . . back** not only the coming of antichrist but also the arrival of final judgment on the world. He is an expression of God's mercy and long-suffering patience (Rom 2:4; 2 Pet 3:9, 15).

The words **will continue to do so** are interpretively added in the NIV to help make sense of the sentence. This anonymous agent restrains **till he is taken out of the way** by God. The end will come when God decides the world has gone so far that his only remaining choice is to hand humanity over to its own twisted desires (2 Thess 2:7; compare Rom 1:20-31). No one has found a parallel to this concept of the "restrainer" in other NT or apocalyptic literature; it seems to be Paul's own contribution.

■ **8 And then**, when divine restraint is lifted and the peak of human rebellion against God arrives, **the lawless one will be revealed** (*apokaluptō*) to all (2 Thess 2:8*a*). The verb suggests a making public of something previously hidden. Satan will unveil his mouthpiece in a dark imitation of Jesus' revealing from heaven (1:7, same verb). This fraud is **lawless**, God's enemy (→ v 3).

We might expect Paul next to describe the evil reign of **the lawless one**. Instead he first reminds his readers that **the Lord Jesus will *destroy*** the usurper at **his coming**. The word of comfort to the persecuted and fearful is that God will triumph. Rhetorically, as in vv 3-4, Paul emphasizes the inevitable doom of Satan's ultimate weapon *before* describing his reign. His reign is limited. There is no need to dread the great power and deception he will wield (vv 10-11). Christ will be victorious.

Paul appears to have adapted this sentence from Isa 11:4, which speaks of a Spirit-endowed future king rising "from the stump of Jesse" (v 1) to reign over God's people: "He will strike the earth with the word of his mouth, and by the breath through his lips he will destroy the ungodly"† (LXX). Paul combines the parallel lines into one, perhaps influenced by Ps 33:6. Jesus is the promised Messiah of Isaiah's prophecy (note the theme of salvation in both Isa 11:5-9 and 2 Thess 2:13-14).

Paul employs the familiar synonymous parallelism of Psalms: **whom the Lord Jesus will *slay* with the breath of his mouth / and destroy by the splendor of his coming**. The verb **overthrow** (*anaireō*) in the NIV clearly means ***slay*** (Frankenmölle 1990, 81; BDAG, 64), since it stands in parallel with **destroy** (*katargeō*) in the next line. There is a certain poetic and prophetic irony here: **the lawless one**, the epitome of the forces that opposed and killed the Lord Jesus and his saints, will himself be destroyed by the appearance of Jesus (see Luke 22:2; Acts 2:23; 5:33; 9:23-24).

The word **Jesus** is omitted in some manuscripts. A wide geographic spread of texts include it, some quite early. So most interpreters include it, although the Greek critical texts put it in brackets, indicating uncertainty (Metzger 1994, 568). Clearly, **Lord** refers to Jesus with or without the word.

The **Lord's** power is so great compared to **the lawless one** that, like God, his **breath** (*pneuma*, **Spirit**) is all it takes to ***slay*** him. The imagery reminds readers of God's judgment on Pharaoh's army: "You blew with your breath [*pneuma*], and the sea covered them" (Exod 15:10 LXX; see 15:7-9; Job 4:8-9). It also hints of the Messiah's likeness to the Creator, who spoke the world into existence by his breath (Ps 33:6) and breathed the breath of life into Adam (Gen 2:7).

Paul also says Jesus will **destroy** him **by the splendor of his coming**. The verb **destroy** (*katargeō*) may be used to indicate that someone or something is abolished (BDAG, 525; LSJM, 908). It emphasizes the final termination of the lawless one's power.

The term for Jesus' **coming** is *parousia*, the majestic visit by a king to one of his cities (→ 1 Thess 4:15). **Splendor** translates *epiphaneia*, "appearing" or "manifestation." In pagan Greek it was often used for alleged *manifestations* of deities—in visions or in acts of divine power that saved one from illness or delivered one in battle (Bultmann and Lührmann 1974; Gärtner 1999; BDAG, 385; Green 2002, 320). In the LXX and Josephus, it describes appearances of Israel's God (2 Macc 2:21; 3:24; 12:22; 14:15; 15:27; 3 Macc 2:9; 5:8; Josephus, *Ant.* 2.339; 3.310). The term does not carry a hostile connotation, although it is associated with God's intervention (against Best 1986, 304; with Malherbe 2000, 424). Paul portrays Jesus' coming as like the sudden, unexpected but glorious appearance of God to intervene on behalf of his people.

Epiphaneia and *parousia* are not synonymous here, although "appearing" refers to the second coming in the Pastorals (1 Tim 6:14; 2 Tim 1:10; 4:1, 8; Titus 2:13). *Parousia* stresses the reality of Jesus' future presence, with echoes of *imperial* visits. *Epiphaneia* emphasizes the stunning *visual* impact of the glory of Christ's coming—his arrival to *rescue*. The phrase "by the *epiphaneia* of his *parousia*" could be paraphrased **by the glorious, saving manifestation that will happen at his royal coming.**

■ **9** Having described the end of **the lawless one**, Paul returns to where he left off at vv 4 and 8a. Only now does he describe the appearing and reign of the usurper. The result is a sharp contrast of two *parousias*: that of Jesus (v 8c) and the lawless one, whose **coming . . . will be in accordance with how Satan works**. Supernatural evil launches his rise to power.

In accordance with (*kata*) may mean either that his rise is *achieved by* the work of Satan or that it happens *in the manner* in which Satan works. In either case, we understand that satanic power lies behind the rise to power and prominence of **the lawless one**. Satan assists him **in every sort of power, signs and wonders of falsehood**. The usurper comes in a frighteningly convincing display that, when combined with his power to deceive (v 10a), completely captivates "those who are perishing" (v 10). Paul presents **the lawless one** as a false prophet with satanic backing. His powers seem to validate the lies that he tells to lead unbelievers away from the true God and his gospel.

Elsewhere in the NT, the word **power** (*dynamis*) in the plural refers to miracles (Acts 8:13; 19:11; Gal 3:5; Heb 2:4). The singular here, associated with **signs and wonders**, seems to have the same force (Acts 2:22; 2 Cor 12:12; Heb 2:4; Malherbe 2000, 245). God validated Moses as a prophet by "signs" (Exod 4:8-9, 28-30) and "wonders" (Deut 34:11). The plagues God sent on Egypt are his "signs and wonders" (Deut 4:34; 6:22; 7:19; 26:8). The ministries of Jesus (Mark 6:56; Luke 6:17-19; Acts 2:22) and of the apostles and evangelists (Acts 2:43; 4:30; 5:12; 6:8; 14:3; Rom 15:19) were marked by miracles, **signs and wonders** from the true God. The **all** modifying **power, signs**, and **wonders** must mean **all sorts of** (Malherbe 2000, 425). **The lawless one**'s evil deception of the world imitates and mocks the ministry of the Lord Jesus and the apostles. He presents himself as divine and attempts to validate his claim by his miracles.

Pseudos (lit. *of a lie*) follows the word **wonders** in Greek. The genitive case of *pseudos* could indicate that the source of **the lawless one**'s miracles is **deceit** (NIV: **that serve the lie**). Or, it could be meant adjectivally, referring to **deceptive signs and wonders** (Furnish 2007, 158). In either case, it does not mean they are false miracles. Satan has his own powers, although they serve deceit and death (see 2 Cor 11:13-15; 2 Thess 2:10-12). An apparent parallel in Revelation refers to a beast given power (*dynamis*) from the dragon, Satan, to rule and be worshipped by the world (Rev 13:1-8). Another beast is given dark power to do great and miraculous signs and deceive the people (Rev 13:11-14).

The picture of **the lawless one** as an antichrist is now complete: he takes over the temple (2 Thess 2:4); he has his own revelation and parousia (vv 7-8), just as Jesus does (1:7; 2:8). He is supported by a supernatural evil power (v 9), the opposite of God's power working through Jesus. And he practices deceit on the world, which contributes to the destruction of those who believe him (vv 10-11). He is a consummate fraud, whereas Jesus spoke truth to the world so that those who believed him might be saved and have life (Luke 19:10; John 3:11-16; 8:31-32).

■ **10** The sentence concludes that began in 2 Thess 2:9: The parousia of the lawless one is characterized by **all the ways that wickedness deceives those who are perishing** (lit. *every sort of deception of wickedness*). He is creative and multifaceted in communicating his lies. **Wickedness** may indicate the source of his deception (as NIV), or it may simply characterize the deception as "wicked" (NRSV). He is the star pupil of "the father of lies" (John 8:44) and disinformation. Evil always lies about what it can offer and about what its cost is.

Satanic *deception* fools only **those who are perishing**. These vulnerable people are **perishing** because they have rejected the gospel. That is, they **refused to love the truth** and do not know Christ or God (see 1 Cor 1:18; 2 Cor 2:15; 4:3; the gospel is described as the "truth" in Rom 15:8; 2 Cor 4:2-3; Gal 2:5, 14; Eph 1:13; Col 1:5; 1 Tim 3:15; Titus 1:1). Truth here is not abstract information about the nature of the world, but the gospel. It gives a trustworthy way to know God and to **be saved**, that is, rescued from God's final judgment on sin and offered new life in Messiah's kingdom (1 Thess 1:10; 5:9-10). But people will prefer lies to the truth. Their choices progressively lead them (present participle) to ultimate ruin. This process can be reversed only by repentance and faith in Christ.

Paul does not suggest that the **perishing** are predestined by God to destruction. Their own choices are responsible: **Because they *did not welcome* [*ou edexanto*] *love for the truth*,** they are on the road to ruin. The disciples of deception are unlike Paul's converts, who **welcomed** the gospel (*edexasthe* [1 Thess 1:6; 2:13]). They do not simply reject the truth, **they refused to love the truth.** They rejected God's offer of salvation. They prefer darkness over light and hate the true God. Had they shown **love** for the gospel and the one who stands behind it, it would have led to their being **saved** from judgment (see Mark 12:29-30).

■ **11 God** judges those who believe the lawless one. His divine judgment is that he abandons them to become prisoners of their disastrous choices. He deprives them of the power of discrimination. Since they hated the truth, he leaves them incapable of choosing it.

What **God sends** the perishing is an ***operation of delusion*** or a ***deluding influence*** (BDAG, 335). This is not just the moral law of nature; God actively intervenes. There are a number of OT precedents, in which God even sends lying spirits to deceive rebellious kings (2 Sam 24:1; 1 Kgs 22:19-23; 1 Chr 21:1).

They do not reject "the truth" (v 10) because God has deluded them or predestined them to damnation. God punishes them for their choices (vv 10 and 12). Paul's point here resembles his description of God handing over rebellious humanity to its own sinful desires in Rom 1:21-32 (also Ps 81:11-12). And following the exodus, when Israel refused to enter the promised land, its desire became its punishment: they were banished from Canaan for a generation (Num 13:31—14:4, 26-35).

The present tense verb **sends** has futuristic sense, referring to people at the time of the lawless one's parousia. Nevertheless, it had clear implications for Paul's own day and the "mystery of lawlessness" (2 Thess 2:7 ESV, HCSB, NASB, NRSV) already operating among the persecutors of Christians at Thessalonica. It is hard not to hear a generalized truth as a secondary reference, particularly in light of the **all** here.

The result (**so that**) of the **delusion** is that **they will believe the lie**. Paul thinks of that most heinous lie, the lawless one's claim to deity and demand for worship (v 4). It is the anti-truth: in place of the true God and his Messiah who saves, they worship a deceiver who will only bring disaster.

■ **12** The final result for **all . . . who . . . have not believed the truth** about the true God and have chosen a false god and a false religion is **that** they **will be condemned** (*krithōsin*). This verb means "to be judged," with the overtone of the resulting verdict (Best 1986, 309).

To emphasize the rebelliousness of their lost condition, Paul gives the corollary to their lack of belief: they have **delighted in wickedness.** *Eudokeō* means to take pleasure in something, or to give one's willing consent (→ 1:11; Christians **delight in goodness** [*eudokian agathosunēs*]). God desires that all may receive his grace, amnesty, and restoration through Christ (2 Cor 5:14, 19-21; 1 Tim 2:4). But it is also his will that those who reject grace face judgment.

FROM THE TEXT

We should allow Paul's opening plea in this section to sink in to the church: do not become "unsettled or alarmed" about the coming of the day of the Lord (2:2). Some ministries make a living off of scaring their adherents into believing that the rise of antichrist, or the rapture, is just around the corner. They claim to be privy to God's timetable, ignoring Jesus' own warning about no one knowing when it would occur (Matt 24:36; Mark 13:32-33; Luke 12:40).

Paul's purpose in speaking about the rise of "the man of lawlessness" (2 Thess 2:3) or "the lawless one" (vv 8, 9) was *not* to give date-setters another peg on which to hang their imaginative system. Nor did he encourage people to guess at his identity ahead of time, as if it were possible to hack God's end-time software.

On the contrary, Paul describes the revelation of this antichrist-like figure as open: he is arrogant, satanically inspired, miracle-working, and demands worldwide worship. Believers won't have to guess who it is. The point is that when the end comes we will know it. We won't need clever prophets manipulating scripture promises and current events to convince us that the end has arrived.

For those who were still fearful for one reason or another, Paul holds out a simple promise. Those who love God and put their faith in his gospel will not be deceived. They already know the true Messiah of God; they will not listen to a false one. They have believed the truth of the gospel. They will not turn to the lawless one's lies, even if he has great political power and works wonders.

God is with his people whom he called through the preaching of the gospel. Paul urged the Thessalonians to remember what he had previously taught them as a safeguard. Let us also remember what we have been taught by God in Scripture and through the historic confessions of the church, and so have our hearts and minds firmly grounded.

Although the title "lawless one" is unique to Paul, his description clearly fits the role of a great end-times imposter and opponent of God mentioned in multiple NT texts. The church has come to call this final figure of evil the *antichrist*, a word found in the NT only in John's letters (1 John 2:18, 22; 4:3; 2 John 7). The term is fitting since Greek *anti-* can mean either "against" or "instead of," and antichrist is both *opposed* to the Son of God and a *pretender* to his glory.

The antichrist corresponds to the "false Christs" Jesus warned about (Matt 24:23-24; Mark 13:21-22) and the beast of Revelation (Rev 13:1-10). Like the lawless one, the beast is empowered by Satan, comes to world domination, and is worshipped by all. For Paul "the lawless one" is an anti-God, a self-made idol who lusts for total control over all humanity. He can brook no rival, not even the Creator. His audacity and powers of persuasion will be frightening. He will even employ miracles on his behalf. As Fee points out, Paul warns us that "signs and wonders can accompany falsehood as well as truth" (2009, 293). One knows the true God by the *truth* of his gospel and by the Spirit (2 Thess 2:10, 13; 1 Thess 1:5; 2:13).

Paul believed that the way was already being prepared in the present for the world to receive the deception of the lawless one. He called this deception the "mystery of lawlessness" (v 7 ESV, HCSB, NASB, NRSV). We have witnessed powerfully in the last century examples of this mystery. From the megalomania of Hitler and his death camps, to the bloody communist dictatorships that sought to wipe out all religion from their countries and replace it with cultic devotion to the ruler and the state. Down to today ruler cults, genocide, and persecutions continue. General R. Dallaire's report about his meeting with Hutu militia leaders in Rwanda in 1993 is haunting. As the commander of UN peacekeeping forces, he attempted to end the slaughtering of Tutsis. He arranged to meet the militia leaders responsible:

> As I was looking at them and shaking their hands I noticed some blood spots still on them [from the people they had freshly killed]. And all of a sudden they disappeared from being human. . . . I literally was talking with evil, personified . . . the devil. That [expletive] had come on earth, in that paradise, and literally taken over. (Frontline 2004)

In such events we may have a glimpse of how *lawlessness* will reign supreme in the lawless one: the antichrist will respect neither God nor people, nor have any righteousness nor mercy. To believe this does not excuse humans from responsibility for their actions. But it does acknowledge there are other sinister forces at work.

The message of this apocalyptic perspective is that, in the end, there is no neutral position with regard to God. Either one believes in him and finds life, or one rejects him and ends up serving forces that will destroy life (Rom 6:16-22; Matt 12:30 ‖ Luke 11:23; John 3:20-21; 1 John 2:15-17; 5:12). And for those who choose Jesus, he will bring in a victory that will sweep away every power of wickedness in an instant. This adds to believers' *hope* for the ultimate renewal of the world, giving us courage to live now in anticipation of that future day, even when it may seem that evil is ascendant.

The notion that God brings to judgment those who refuse the gospel, and even hardens them in their rejection, seems bizarre and unacceptable to many modern Americans. Some people are used to thinking of God like a Santa Claus in the sky who never says no to anyone and who would never really condemn anyone. But what recourse is there to the one who rejects the Creator of life and the Lord of resurrection? As C. S. Lewis so memorably put it, "There are only two kinds of people in the end: those who say to God, 'Thy will be done,' and those to whom God says, in the end, '*Thy* will be done.' All that are in Hell, choose it" (1996, 72). No one is condemned for not *knowing* the truth. Condemnation comes to those who do not *want* the truth. Our life decisions matter. The first one to fall under the mighty judgment of the returning Christ at his Parousia will be the master of rebellion, "the lawless one" (2 Thess 2:8).

IV. THE THESSALONIANS STAND IN CONTRAST TO THE DECEIVED: THANKSGIVING, EXHORTATION, PRAYER: 2 THESSALONIANS 2:13-17

BEHIND THE TEXT

Paul does not leave his readers hanging with a future scenario in which Satan's emissary is victorious, deceiving those who rejected God's truth (2 Thess 2:4-12). The last word is always one of God's victory in Christ for his people (2:8*b*; 1 Cor 15:26, 51-57; Rev 21:1-7).

Moral instruction often proceeds by means of contrast. Here, Paul contrasts the fate of the Thessalonians with that of the perishing (2 Thess 2:10-11). This served to ease anxieties about the false eschatology (v 2). In a manner reminiscent of 1 Thess 5:4-10, Paul reassures his readers that the awful judgment awaiting rebellious humanity will not fall on them. They know this because God *loves* them, *chose* them, and *called* them to eternal salvation (2 Thess 2:13-14).

This reassurance and exhortation takes the unexpected form of celebration and worship. It is the second instance of reported prayer in the letter (see 1:11-12). A thanksgiving report (vv 13-14) assures them they can know they are chosen and called because they responded in faith to the gospel message and experienced the Spirit's sanctifying presence. Then comes a short exhortation in the form of a command to hang on to the apostolic teaching (v 15). Paul closes with a prayer for their strengthening (vv 16-17).

IN THE TEXT

A. Paul's Confidence in Thessalonian Christians (2:13-15)

■ 13 Paul contrasts vividly the condition of the Thessalonian believers with that of the perishing (→ 2 Thess 2:10-11). He uses the literary device of a thanksgiving prayer report, the second in the letter: **But we ought always to thank God for you, brothers and sisters** (2:13; 1:3; see 1 Thess 1:2).

Paul often uses thanksgivings to express important things about his audience (Rom 1:8; 1 Cor 1:4-9; Phil 1:3-6; Col 1:3-6; 1 Thess 1:2; 2:13; Phlm 4-6) or to reflect on an important aspect of God's saving work in the world (1 Cor 15:57; 2 Cor 2:14-16; 9:15). They allow him at once to draw attention to things that should be said, while praising God as the source of these blessings.

The leading epithet for the church, **loved by the Lord**, stands as a sign of blessing in contrast to the previous paragraph. Paul's expression echoes the blessing on Benjamin from Deut 33:12 (Malherbe 2000, 436; Fee 2009, 299). The devotees of "the lawless one" refused to love the truth, and face judgment for their obstinacy (2 Thess 2:10, 12).

The **Lord** here refers to Jesus, as is usual in Paul and especially 1 and 2 Thessalonians (Best 1986, 311; Marshall 1983, 206; Fee 2009, 300; e.g., 1 Thess 1:1, 3, 6, 8; 2:15, 19; 3:11-13; 4:1-2, 15-17; 5:2, 9; 2 Thess 1:1-2, 7-9, 12; 2:1-2, 8, 13, 14, 16; 3:1, 6, 12). Hence, Paul again mentions **God** in the next phrase, to make his reference clear. **Loved** may recall God's gracious offer of salvation to the world in the reconciling death and resurrection of Christ (2:16; Rom 5:8; "love of Christ" [John 3:16; 2 Cor 5:14]).

The basis for thanks is **because God chose you** [→ 1 Thess 1:4] **as firstfruits to be saved**. This echoes the OT statement that the Lord (Yahweh) chose Israel only because he *loved* her and was keeping his covenant with the patriarchs (Deut 7:7-8). Only here the **Lord** who loves is now Jesus.

Some Greek manuscripts here have **firstfruits** (*aparchēn*) and others *from the beginning* (*ap' archēs*). Paul does not normally express **beginning** in this way. He usually uses the term *archē* for "ruler" or "authority" (Rom 8:38; 1 Cor 15:24; Eph 1:21; Col 1:16).

Some interpreters insist that he refers to the pretemporal origins of God's choice to comfort the troubled believers. They claim that **firstfruits** makes no sense, because (*a*) the Thessalonians were not the first to be converted in Macedonia, the Philippians were; (*b*) Paul can't mean the first ones saved locally either, because he addresses the entire church (Best 1986, 313-14; Richard 1995, 356; Furnish 2007, 163). But Paul never says they are **firstfruits** of Macedonia. They were the first converts of Thessalonica, the capital of Macedonia.

The offering of **firstfruits** in the worship of Israel involved the consecration of the entire harvest that is to come to Yahweh. Returning to him the earliest ripened fruit expressed trust in him as provider and God of the covenant (Deut 26:1-11).

That the Thessalonians are **firstfruits** complements their choosing (v 3), which is *inclusive, not exclusive*. The choosing of Abraham had in view the blessing of all nations (Gen 12:3). God chose Israel to be "a kingdom of priests" so that they would mediate the knowledge of him to the nations (Exod 19:6). So his choice of these Macedonian Christians as **firstfruits** led to the evangelism of others (1 Thess 1:7) and implies there is a greater harvest yet to come.

This fits the inclusive sense of election. The goal of this choosing by God is for people **to be saved** (or *for salvation*, *eis sōtērian*). Paul probably has in mind their ultimate "deliverance" (another meaning of *sōtēria*) on the Day of the Lord.

The twofold means God used to choose them is introduced with the preposition *en*, used instrumentally (**through**): ***through sanctification of the Spirit/spirit*** and **belief in the truth**. Grammatically the first could refer to either the human or Holy Spirit. Since **sanctification** is God's work, and **belief** is the expected human response, it seems best to see this as a balanced statement about the two sides of the process. Hence, *pneuma* here must refer to God's **Spirit**. In 1 Thessalonians Paul linked sanctification to the indwelling Holy Spirit (1 Thess 4:7-8; see 1 Cor 6:11). God the great Lover initiates, and his beloved respond.

The Thessalonian believers' holiness effected by God's **Spirit** stands in stark contrast to those who "delighted in wickedness" (v 12). And their **belief in the truth** (v 13) of the gospel contrasts with those who would not love the truth, preferred the deception of the lawless one, and are condemned by God to believe "the lie" (vv 10-12).

■ **14** Paul continues the sentence begun in v 13, beginning here with Greek expression *eis ho*, "to which [end]." The neuter "which" seems to refer generally to the whole salvation sequence just mentioned (Fee 2009, 303). God **called** the Thessalonians to salvation **through our gospel**. Paul does not speak of their choosing and calling in terms of some pretemporal divine decree. This is the language of religious experience framed in terms of the story of God's grace extended to them, in the context of Paul's mission preaching (as Fee 2009, 303): they believed, God sanctified them through his Spirit.

Our gospel is not a peculiar possession of Paul and his associates. It is the common Christian message he proclaimed. He merely distinguishes it from nonapostolic so-called gospels. It recalls both the message and moment of the Thessalonians' initial hearing of Paul's preaching. It is *in the proclamation* that they experienced the call to salvation. They heard the oral message; they responded in faith; they experienced the Spirit's sanctifying presence (vv 13-14; see also Gal 3:1-5). This dynamic experience of the living God (1 Thess 1:9) *is* their choosing. It reminds us once again that what drew people to Christianity was not simply superior doctrine but the real presence of the living God (1 Cor 12:7; 14:24-25; Rom 15:18-19; Gal 3:2-5; 1 Thess 1:5).

Paul looks ahead to the final goal of the salvation process for believers: *so* **that you might** *obtain* [*peripoiēsis*; BDAG, 804] **the glory of our Lord Jesus Christ. Glory** is the exalted state into which the resurrected Lord ascended (Acts 7:55; 1 Tim 3:16) and in which he will return (Matt 25:31; Mark 8:38 and parallel; 13:26 and parallel; Titus 2:13). It is the brilliant splendor and overwhelming power of God's presence that none dared face directly under the old covenant. Here Paul refers to the hope of a body "raised in glory" like Christ's, fit to share God's unveiled presence (Rom 5:2; 1 Cor 15:42-43; Phil 3:21; Col 3:4; compare 2 Cor 4:17).

For believers to **share in the glory** of Christ does not mean they become equal to him. They will receive what God has promised them: "his kingdom and glory" (→ 1 Thess 2:12). Their destiny is to participate in Christ's resurrection life and honor (Rom 8:17). Their future **glory** stands in marked contrast to the present dishonor they experienced from society (Green 2002, 328). Again, their fate is the opposite of those who are condemned and perish (2 Thess 2:10, 12), including their present persecutors.

The function of the passage is not to cause them to gloat over their opponents' impending disaster. It comforts the distressed church by reminding them that they are "at the center of [God's] saving purpose" (Malherbe 2000, 438).

■ **15 So then** introduces a concluding commandment on the basis of what has gone before: the refutation of the false teaching, the corrected scenario of how the Day of the Lord will dawn, and the knowledge that they have chosen the path to salvation, with God's calling.

In light of all God has done for them and will do for them, they must **stand firm** in their faith. This is the opposite of being "shaken" or "alarmed" (v 2; → 1 Thess 3:8; see 1 Cor 16:13; Gal 5:1; Phil 1:27; 4:1). The way they will do this is to **hold fast to the teachings** Paul **passed on to** them. He refers literally *to the traditions that you were taught*.

The word *traditions* sometimes has a negative connotation in the NT (Mark 7:8-9; Gal 1:14; Col 2:8). The Reformation's battle with Roman Catholicism left most Protestants with a deep suspicion of tradition. But some traditions are good. In the ancient social context in which Paul wrote, **teaching** was personal (not by books). Learning was done by committing things to memory. *Traditions* here is simply the normal way *all* learning was passed on from master to disciple, including Jesus' teaching. So the *traditions* of the apostles are good and *must* be kept if Christianity is to be preserved faithful to its Lord (1 Cor 11:23; 15:1-2, 11; Gal 1:8-9; see Acts 1:21-22; 1 John 1:1-3).

Traditions refer here to Paul's teachings, given to the church **whether by word of mouth** when he was with them personally **or by letter**. The **letter** likely refers to our 1 Thessalonians. Trust in these two sources will bypass whatever the cause of their misunderstandings and bad teaching may be.

The omission of **spirit** from the list here (compared to 2:2 [→]) should not to be taken as a criticism of prophetic utterances (against Hughes 1989, 56-57; Richard 1995, 359; Furnish 2007, 168). Paul gives a list of "approved" traditions. He apparently did not use prophecy as his normal mode of teaching with them. He recommends it in other letters (Rom 12:6; 1 Cor 12:10, 28; 14:5, 31; 1 Thess 5:19-21). This may suggest, however, that he suspected some additions or alterations had been made to his teaching by prophecy that had not been tested as he required (→ 1 Thess 5:20).

B. Prayer (2:16-17)

■ **16-17** In line with Paul's view that no human service to God is accomplished without divine assistance, he seals this section by praying for his people. This prayer opens like that in 1 Thess 3:11-13, except that Jesus is placed first here. Amazing for what it says about Paul's Christology is that the prayer is directed to *both* **God** and **the Lord Jesus Christ** together (2 Thess 2:16; → 1 Thess 3:11). Also, the main verbs (**encourage, strengthen**) are *singular*, with *both* Jesus and God as their subject (for secular instances of this, see Smyth 1984, 265). They act as one. Paul does not argue for any particular status of Jesus here; he simply *assumes* that Christians may *pray to the risen Christ* alongside God. The fact that such exalted treatment of Jesus never appears to be the subject of controversy between Paul and Judean Christians, even at this early date (unlike food laws and circumcision) is fatal to theories that Christianity only began to regard Jesus as divine when it moved into the Greco-Roman world. Paul has inherited this exalted Christology as an apostolic commonplace.

In keeping with the theme of consolation, Paul expands on the appellation of God as the Christians' **Father** (→ 2 Thess 1:1; 1 Thess 1:1). God is addressed as the one who **loved us** believers **and by his grace gave us eternal encouragement and good hope** (v 16). **Loved** and **gave** may allude to the sending of Christ, supremely demonstrating God's love and establishing his grace for believing humanity. Just as love for God and neighbor is to be the supreme imperative for disciples of Jesus (Mark 12:29-31; Rom 13:8-10), so in the NT love supremely describes the character of God.

God's **everlasting comfort** (BDAG, 766) may point to the unending life of glory with the Father and Son awaiting believers at Christ's return, ending present suffering (compare Rom 8:17; 1 Thess 4:17-18; 5:9-11). Or possibly Paul meant *aiōnian* as "unending" in the sense that God the Father is ever present, gives comfort and counsel that never ceases. An example is this prayer itself that he would **encourage** their **hearts** in the face of persecution and false teaching (2 Thess 2:17; Marshall 1983, 211; Witherington 2006, 239).

The **good hope** (v 16) God has given is the promise of redemption, resurrection, and reception into his kingdom. This may have been some "local color" adapted by Paul. The phrase in some pagan religions referred to life after death (Best 1986, 321). These things describe *who* the God is that Paul prays to.

The actual prayer request reflects the concerns of the foregoing verses. He asks God to **encourage** their **hearts** (v 17), which would protect them from being "alarmed" (v 2) by misunderstanding their situation or by persecution. And Paul prays for God to **strengthen** them **in every good deed and word** (v 17). The main verbs of the prayer (**may . . . encourage . . . and strengthen**) are cast in a formal, liturgical way (the optative mood; → 1 Thess 3:11-13). The **heart** (→ 1 Thess 2:4; 3:13) includes all the mental faculties: he prays for all their thought and will, all desires and emotions, and especially moral decision-making (Green 2002, 333). Not only does Paul seek to give comfort, but he wishes for God to do so, which will be more effective. Encouraging fits with the letter's theme of *comfort* to the Thessalonians, which is another way to translate the verb *parakaleō* (**encourage**). *Stērizō*, **strengthen,** has to do not with physical prowess, but with stability—setting something up and establishing it, such as a city or one's footing (LSJM, 1644; BDAG, 945). As a metaphor, it speaks of the Lord Jesus and God working to help believers become mature in their faith in every way: understanding, speaking, and living it out (compare Luke 22:32; 1 Pet 5:10). Thus strengthened, they will be "firmly grounded."

Although a few readers may feel the prayer for divine grounding in good deeds leans toward a "works-righteousness" inconsistent with Paul's theology of justification by faith, this is not really so. For Paul faith was "as much the basis for and means to right living as it was for and to being 'righteoused'" (Dunn 1998, 642; see 634-42, 649-58, 668-69; Rom 6:4; Gal 5:22-25; Phil 1:11; Col 1:9-10). Faith expressed in doing **good** is the opposite of delighting in unrighteousness (2 Thess 2:12). And faith firmly grounded in the good **word** is the opposite of the perishing who prefer lies (2:10-11). A good tree will bear good fruit (Matt 7:18), and so will those with saving faith.

Deed and word is probably a hendiadys expressing the totality of life, behavior, and speech of God's beloved (as Luke 24:19; Rom 15:18; Col 3:17).

There is a play on the identical description of the gospel as a **word** (*logos*; e.g., Rom 10:17; 1 Cor 15:2; 2 Cor 4:2; Eph 1:13; Phil 1:14; Col 4:3; 1 Thess 1:8; 2:13; 2 Thess 3:1; 2 Tim 4:2; Titus 1:3). The gospel message that made possible their salvation is the **good . . . word** upon which their lives are grounded. The good word should result in Christians producing good *words* that spread truth and heal the world.

FROM THE TEXT

God's calling and choosing. This prayerful reassurance of the Thessalonians' calling leaps off the page to address one of the perennial questions for Christians. How do people know they are *saved*? Or how do I know I am one of the "elect"? Although this passage doesn't give a comprehensive essay on the issue, Paul does suggest a basic answer.

Calling comes through the proclaimed word of the gospel, the good news that God sent his Son to us, that he died and rose again for our justification and sanctification, that he reigns as Lord, and that he is coming again. And the mystery is that at the moment weak human messengers present this, *God is presenting this to the world* (2 Cor 4:7). If you hear this, you are called; it is that simple. It is your choice to respond.

Christians do not agree on whether people are equally free to respond. Wesleyans believe that with the preaching of the gospel, God is at work to give every sinful listener the ability to choose to respond with faith. Those who believe the truth are, by definition, the elect (2 Thess 1:10-11; 2:13-14). Those who refuse it are perishing (2:10).

The Spirit is a necessary element in the Christian life. Here, as in 1 Thess 4:8, the Spirit is associated with holiness, a life devoted to God and lived in love (2 Thess 2:13; see 1:3; 3:5). These are the only evidences of election Paul gives. Can we also say, I have believed the gospel and have the Spirit, therefore, I am God's elect, God loves me?

Calling and sanctification. Paul's prayer also reminds us that *election* brings humans into a process of being made holy (sanctification) by the Spirit, living out God' will, not being complacent. This is not an exclusively Wesleyan idea. Even Calvin remarked, "Election has as its goal holiness of life" (1960b 3.23.12).

The purpose of our calling. God's loving *purpose* in calling us is that we might obtain resurrection *glory* with Christ. Although Wesleyans believe that it is *possible* to fall away from grace and to lose one's place in the kingdom (1 Cor 10:1-12; Heb 6:4-6), it is not the Father's *will* that we reject him. We need to remember that it is God's passionate desire to save that put the three persons of the Holy Trinity to work on our behalf. And God continues to be at work with believers to sanctify, guide, correct, and comfort his beloved so they might reach their goal.

Stand firm. How necessary that command is today also! Although the challenges may be different, God's people around the globe still face pressures of the same sorts the Thessalonians did. We still face conflicts with cultural values; conflicts with common religious ideas; opposition from society to basic Christian beliefs; and even physical violence. God's calling entails a call to be his witnesses in and to a fallen world. In order to be effective witnesses and bring God's healing to broken lives, the church needs to be faithful to the gospel it received. The church still has the testimony of the apostles, their faithful *tradition*, in the NT scriptures. And the church still has the Spirit as grace-giver and guide.

God is with us. That is the essence of Paul's prayer for them, and for us. The thanksgiving and prayer are a proto-Trinitarian conception of God's loving, saving, sanctifying work in us.

V. REQUEST FOR PRAYER: 2 THESSALONIANS 3:1-5

BEHIND THE TEXT

Here Paul introduces the last and most delicate subject of the letter (3:6-15): the issue of those who rejected his previous instructions about working. He does this indirectly, by first asking for prayer for himself and his coworkers (vv 1-2). He shows his humility as he lays bare his needs.

The prayer again reminds the Thessalonians of the apostles' exemplary lives (1 Thess 1:6; 2:9-14; 4:11). His request for the gospel to be "*honored*" (2 Thess 3:1) hints at the shortcomings of the "idle" (v 6). Paul does not dwell long on himself. He expresses confidence in the Lord's work in the community (v 3) and in their obedience (v 4). His praise anticipates his command to them in v 6.

He returns to his prayer for his audience (v 5) before directly attacking the problem of work and idleness. The Thessalonians and the apostles are bound to one another in a circle of prayer, in which each invokes the Lord's presence and aid for the other.

This passage functions much like a *captatio benevolentiae*—the praise of an audience at the beginning of a speech designed to gain their good will (Fee 2009, 311). As such, it prepares for the moral exhortation following in vv 6-15.

IN THE TEXT

■ **1 As for other matters** (*loipos*) often introduces a new section in Paul's letters (Phil 3:1; 1 Thess 4:1) or their conclusion (2 Cor 13:11; Gal 6:17; Eph 6:10). Direct address of his audience as **brothers and sisters** also frequently appears at the start of new sections (1 Thess 2:1, 17; 4:1, 13; 5:1, 12; 2 Thess 1:3; 2:1, 13; 3:6). So this seems to begin the final segment of the letter (Marshall 1983, 212; Green 2002, 334; Fee 2009, 312-13), calling for the translation ***Finally*** (so ESV, NASB, NRSV).

Paul prepares for the difficult task of correcting those who ignored his previous instructions (1 Thess 4:11-12; 5:14). He first makes himself vulnerable, acknowledging that he, too, faces opposition and needs divine assistance, just as they do. Paul urges the community to seek God's help for his apostolic commission. The need for mutual prayer support binds apostle and community together in the Spirit.

Paul's first prayer request is **that the message of the Lord may spread rapidly and be honored**. The **message of the Lord** refers to the gospel teaching about Jesus (→ 1 Thess 1:8; 2 Thess 1:8). **Honored** (*doxazētai*) here characterizes the human response to the gospel. When people either accept it as God's truth or witness the good work of God in believers' lives, they will praise the **message** and the **Lord** who made it possible.

In preparation for his exhortations to follow in vv 6-15, Paul's prayer for honor may also hint that the behavior of the "idle and disruptive" (v 6) dishonors the community and its Lord. They shame their fictive family. Paul implicitly invites them to imitate the apostles' ideal of Christian living and evangelism. It was this sincere lifestyle, along with the activity of the Spirit, that caused the gospel to **be honored** by the Thessalonians (→ 1 Thess 1:5; 2:9-13). The phrase **just as it was with you** indirectly reminds them of how their initial response to the gospel continued its spread from them outward after the apostles left (1 Thess 1:8). Paul wants the evangelistic success he had at Thessalonica to be replicated elsewhere.

Spread rapidly translates the verb **run**. This athletic metaphor pictures the gospel message racing unhindered to victory. As people welcome the gospel, it is **honored** like the winner of a race (compare 1 Cor 9:24; Gal 2:2; 5:7;

Phil 2:16; 2 Tim 4:7; Marshall 1983, 213; Witherington, 2006, 241; Fee 2009, 313-14; see also Ps 147:15—"his word runs swiftly").

■ **2** Paul's second request for prayer is **that we may be delivered from wicked and evil people**. Human evil must not be allowed to hinder Paul and his companions as they preach the gospel. This continues the thought of allowing the gospel to "spread rapidly" (v 1). Paul's person and message were bound up together, because he was appointed by the risen Jesus as the Lord's apostle (Gal 1:1, 11-12). The success of his ambassadorial role in the face of opposition (see 2 Cor 5:20; 4:1-6) honored Christ.

Wicked translates *atopōn*, literally those who are *out of place*. It refers to people who behave inappropriately, in an improper or evil fashion (BDAG, 149). It is often paired with the "lawless" in the LXX (Best 1986, 325).

Evil (*ponērōn*) indicates people who are morally degenerate, deliberately bad. In secular Greek, it had associations with social disorder, lower-class status, and moral evil (Harder 1968, 547-49). In biblical Greek it refers to the depraved and evil in general (Gen 13:13; Matt 7:11) or specifically to those opposed to God (Amos 5:14; Matt 12:34; 13:49).

Paul is not praying to be separated from the evil in general, or else there would be no evangelism! But he does not want the advance of the gospel thwarted by those who reject the gospel and seek to make trouble for Paul and his companions. Perhaps his request echoes Isa 25:4 in the LXX, "You will deliver them from evil men."

The explanation **for not everyone has faith** credits the **evil** of his opponents to their rejection of the gospel. **Faith** means the subjective trust in God (Best 1986, 326; Malherbe 2000, 444; Green 2002, 336). There is no reason to suppose that Paul presumes the hyper-Calvinist view that God predestined some to salvation and others to reprobation.

Several commentators have sought to locate the historical context of Paul's opposition. Clearly, he has non-Christians in mind. Most piece together remarks about opposition by Jews in 1 Thess 2:14-16 with the story of the trial at Corinth sponsored by synagogue opponents (Acts 18:12-17; Marshall 1983, 214; Witherington 2006, 241; Fee 2009, 316). Certainly, Paul may reflect on this situation. But the language here is so general that it could easily refer to Gentile or Jewish opponents in virtually any city Paul visited (see Best 1986, 326).

■ **3** Prayers in the Psalms are often accompanied by statements of confidence and trust in the God of Israel (Pss 6:9-10; 10:14, 16-18; 12:7; 35:10). Paul follows this model here. But instead of expressing confidence in God's work for the apostles, Paul returns to his concern for the Thessalonians. He contrasts the wicked who lack "faith" (*pistis* [v 2]) with the **Lord**, who **is faithful** (*pistos*; Fee 2009, 318).

In the OT, being **faithful** is one of God's primary covenant-keeping qualities. It binds him to Israel and assures his people that he is reliable (Deut 7:9; 32:4; Ps 145:13; Isa 49:7). In Christ God proved he can be trusted to be faithful in the new covenant (1 Cor 1:9): **He will strengthen and protect you from the evil one.**

This expression of trust seems to echo the Lord's Prayer: "deliver us from the evil one" (Matt 6:13). Paul shows knowledge of Jesus' teachings elsewhere (see Rom 13:9; 1 Cor 7:10; 11:23-25; Gal 4:6). Paul is confident that his previous prayers for the Thessalonians will be answered: God will strengthen them "in every good deed and word" (2 Thess 2:17; see 1 Thess 3:2, 13). This is not a promise of protection from suffering or harm, for Paul had warned that persecution would follow their commitment to Christ (→ 1 Thess 3:3-4; 2 Thess 1:4-7).

False teaching was the topic Paul just dealt with (2:9-10). So we may surmise that he believed God would **protect** (*phylaxei*) them from deception. He would not allow them to be fatally misled. God's truth and his Spirit's aid would "guard" (3:3 NRSV) them (see 2:13; 1 Thess 1:5-6; 2:13). Elsewhere Paul speaks of God's assistance in temptation (1 Cor 10:13) and the role of the Spirit indwelling believers and overcoming the power of the flesh (Rom 8:1-14). Jesus taught his disciples to have confidence in God's protection (Luke 11:5-13; 18:1-7; 22:32).

The term for **evil one** is the same word (*ponēros*) used for "evil people" in the plural in 2 Thess 3:2. Satan is the **evil one** above all others, the instigator of error that leads to death (2:9-10; John 8:44; 2 Cor 4:3-4; compare Matt 13:19, 38; Eph 6:16; 1 John 2:13). But Christians need not fear him, if they trust God (2 Thess 2:13-14).

■ **4** Paul praises the Thessalonians by expressing his **confidence in the Lord that** they **are doing and will continue to do the things we command.** Paul's assurance was **in the Lord** as evidenced in God's saving history with the community and his gracious presence with them (v 3).

Paul does not specify what commands they are keeping. We might assume generally from the Thessalonian letters and his other letters that they would include:

- instructions on meeting together regularly and worship (1 Thess 5:19-22; see 1 Cor 11:20, 23-34; 14:26-40);
- arranging charity for the needy (2 Thess 3:6-15; see Rom 12:8; 2 Cor 8:1-15; 9:12; 1 Tim 5:3-16);
- personal and community ethics that please the Lord, especially about love and sexual purity (1 Thess 4:2-8; 2 Thess 1:3), work (1 Thess 2:9-12; 4:11-12; 2 Thess 3:6-12), and pursuing peace (1 Thess 5:15; 2 Thess 3:16);
- withdrawing from indigenous religions and their practices (1 Thess 1:9-10; compare 1 Cor 8:4-13; 10:1-22);
- preserving and passing on right teaching (2 Thess 2:15; see 1 Thess 1:8; compare Gal 1:6-9).

Paul's praise of their obedience surely helped gain his audience's attention and favor. His thanksgivings or praise typically precede instruction and correction, as here (1 Cor 1:4-7; Phil 4:1; Col 1:4-5; 1 Thess 1:2-3, 6-10; 3:6-10 with 4:1-8). He generally looks for something positive to say about his churches, even deeply troubled ones. Although this may serve a rhetorical function, it is not insincere. Paul nurtures their best traits. Because the majority of the Thessalonians trust and obey the apostles, he is able to give them directions concerning those who ignored his earlier teaching (→ 2 Thess 3:6-15).

■ **5** Paul closes this introduction to his final admonition with another prayer for the Thessalonians (→ 2:16-17; a report, 1:11-12). Like the other prayers in 1 and 2 Thessalonians, it uses the formal optative mood of the verb (reflected in **may**; → 1 Thess 3:11).

This reflects an unusual prayer for Paul, in that he petitions the risen Jesus. Other benedictions and prayers address both Father and Son (e.g., Rom 1:7; 1 Cor 1:3; 2 Cor 1:2; Gal 1:3; 1 Thess 3:11-13; 2 Thess 1:2; 2:16-17; 2 Tim 1:2), or God alone (e.g., Rom 15:5-6, 13, 33; 1 Thess 5:23; Col 1:2). That **Lord** refers to Jesus here seems clear from the previous prayer addressed to "our *Lord* Jesus Christ himself and God our Father" (2:16). **Lord** is Paul's standard title for Jesus.

Already in 1 Thess 3:11 Paul joined Jesus' name with that of the Creator God in prayer in an astounding christological affirmation. Here he demonstrates his exalted view of Christ by petitioning the community's risen **Lord** independently. The risen Christ carries out the work of the Father within the Spirit-endowed community. We have here the seeds of Trinitarian faith, the equality of and differentiation between Father and Son. Paul is unconcerned about technical questions that would come later, such as the precise nature of the Father-Son relationship. What is important here is that the church not only look to Jesus as teacher and prophet but also look to Jesus in prayer, as **Lord**. And mysteriously this does not supplant the Father; it is to his glory (Phil 2:11).

The divine work Paul petitions Jesus to perform is twofold: First, that he may **direct** the Thessalonians' **hearts into God's love**. Paul used the verb **direct** (*kateuthunō*) in the prayer of 1 Thess 3:11-13. There its more literal sense refers to Paul's longed-for return visit to Macedonia.

The expression "direct the heart" to God occurs several times in the LXX (2 Chr 12:14; 19:3; 20:33; Sir 49:3; 51:20; Best 1986, 329), where it describes a devotion to the Lord that is resolved to keep covenant (compare David's prayer in 1 Chr 29:18 [Fee 2009, 322]; and the admonition to Israel in Ps 78:8 [Gupta 2008, 180-83]).

The heart is the center of thinking and reasoning (→ 2 Thess 2:16-17). It is the place where moral decisions are made in biblical thinking and where loyalty is determined. Paul prays for God's assistance not merely to *feel* the right things but to *think* and *will* in ways consistent with **God's love**.

The expression *love of God* is as ambiguous in Greek as in English: Is it God's love for us? Our love for God? Or is it a divine sort of love? In Paul *love of God* typically refers to God's love (Rom 5:5; 8:39; 2 Cor 13:13), so nearly all commentators prefer the first sense here. This would reinforce statements about God's love already made in 2 Thess 2:13 and 16.

One might have expected from the context a prayer for the Thessalonians to love God. How would reliance on **God's love** cohere with the Lord's desire to "strengthen . . . and guard" them (v 3 NRSV)? And how does this prepare for the immediately following moral exhortation (vv 6-15)?

The answer is that Paul understood God's love to be a generating force for renewal within believers. It occasioned the plan of salvation and the sending of the Son to die for the world while we were sinners and enemies of God (Rom 5:6-11). Knowing this leads believers to live in an attitude of praise, assurance, and gratitude. It strengthens them to face moral struggles and persecution with hope and courage. It gives them a model to imitate (Matt 5:44-48; Eph 5:1-2; 1 John 4:7-11). Thus, Paul urged his audience to remember **God's love** and to express it, with the help of the Holy Spirit who communicates that love existentially to believers (Rom 5:5; see 1 Cor 13:13; Gal 4:6).

The profound experience of God's love gives a unique quality to the new covenant in Jesus Christ. It is not just another set of rules; it is to know the living God and his love. This experience is transformative, generating in turn a corresponding love within believers. "God's love" and "love towards God" are interwoven and combined here (Lightfoot 1957, 128).

A similar grammatical ambiguity affects the second divine work Paul prays for: that the **Lord direct** their **hearts** to the *perseverance of Christ*. The KJV understood it as an objective genitive, "the patient waiting for Christ" by the Thessalonians. But in parallel with the earlier phrase, it is better understood as **Christ's perseverance** (e.g., Best 1986, 330; Malherbe 2000, 447; Green 2002, 340).

Perseverance (*hypomonēn*) refers to endurance under pressure, remaining steady in faith despite persecution (Rom 5:3-4; 1 Thess 1:3; 2 Thess 1:4). It implies holding on without yielding, hence "steadfastness" (NRSV). The earthly Jesus' steadfastness in obeying the Father is the model for believers. He endured opposition and mockery, and even unjust trials and death, yet stood firm in the Father's will. He lived among sinners and witnessed to them, just as the Thessalonians are called to do. And as with God's love, Christ's type of steadfastness is not only available for contemplation but also available to be imparted to the Christian. It is part of what God does as he strengthens believers through his grace and the indwelling Holy Spirit.

FROM THE TEXT

Paul's selfless love for Christ is shown in his prayer request: he desires above all that the message of the gospel might spread with success and glory to its Lord (3:1-2). Do we care too much about our own honor? Do we pray about getting diplomas, better jobs, better clothes, better cars? Do we seek to be admired by people at church, at work, and elsewhere? Paul's example invites us to consider whether, and how much, we care about *Christ's* honor and whether *his* name is advertised by our lives in a way that brings "good publicity" to the gospel.

If we are to represent the gospel well, we must join our hearts together in the risen Christ and receive his strengthening, protection, love, and endurance. Prayer prepares us to hear the word of encouragement and the word of correction. Only *after* we have experienced God's gift of love, which transforms us (Rom 12:1-2; Col 3:1-3), may we seriously think about the challenging task of living as God's people. Knowing we are loved by God enables us to love others, to be salt and light to a fallen world (Matt 5:13-16). Paul teaches us to be confident that the Lord will be with us in this task.

VI. EXHORTATION: 2 THESSALONIANS 3:6-15

BEHIND THE TEXT

The disorderly in Thessalonica. In the first letter Paul reminded the Thessalonians of the importance of supporting themselves by working, being independent, and living "a quiet life" (1 Thess 4:11-12). There he referred to people he labeled as "disorderly" (*ataktous*; NIV: "those who are idle" [5:14]). Now we hear more about this issue, which seems only to have gotten worse.

Paul reminds them that he specifically taught about working when he was with them (2 Thess 3:6, 10). The *ataktoi* ignored his oral teaching and the admonition of the first letter. Their defiance calls for a sharper response: the church is to withdraw support from them and refuse to provide them food. This discipline is intended to shame them into securing their own support (vv 6, 10-12, 14).

The perception of the disorderly in ancient Rome. Rome was a military dictatorship, a vast empire stretching from Spain to Syria and Egypt. Its rule was sustained by conquest and occupation. Rome counted on the pacification and "Romanization" of its provinces to maintain law and order and keep income flowing toward the capital (Wengst 1987, 7-40).

The senatorial Roman provinces—such as Macedonia—were only lightly defended so the empire could commit troops more heavily in the contested border regions. Macedonia had in Paul's day only recently become a senatorial province (AD 44), considered more "safe" and stable for the empire. But Rome always took any threats to the social order seriously. Its much-vaunted peace and Roman law and order rested on the constant threat of violence from a superior force (Wengst 1987, 9-24; compare the shrine to "Necessity and Force" carved into the Acrocorinth by the Romans [Pausanias, *Descr.* 2.4.6]).

If Thessalonian society began to brand the Christians as *ataktōs*, it would mean that they would be perceived as not simply lazy but as a *dangerous* sect. This is an accusation the church had to fight already (Acts 17:6-9); it didn't need its own members stirring it up again.

Why disorderly Christians existed. One probable cause for the misbehavior of the "disorderly" in Thessalonica was explored in connection with 1 Thess 4:11-12 and 5:14 (→). With the supplemental information in 2 Thessalonians, we may consider the issue again:

1. Eschatological enthusiasm was once the preferred explanation. But Paul implies that the origins of this problem preceded his writing of both letters. Certainly the problems preceded the heresy of 2 Thess 2:2. When he was first in the city he instructed them on the necessity of self-support (2 Thess 3:10). In the first letter, he encouraged them to think of the Lord's return as a time of resurrection and rescue for believers, without imagining it would worsen apocalyptic fever. Within 2 Thessalonians no explicit link is ever made between the problems of the disorderly (*ataktoi*) and Christ's return. Nothing beyond speculation indicates that excessive preoccupation with the end was the reason some stopped working.

2. Could some Thessalonians have taken up itinerant evangelism and claimed the apostolic rule of support? Did they think that if they proclaimed the gospel they should be financed (Matt 10:10; Luke 10:7; 1 Cor 9:4-14; Jewett 1986, 105)? Did Paul try to prevent such a misinterpretation in 1 Thess 2:7-12 (see 2 Thess 3:7-9)? If the *ataktoi* tried to justify their support as Christian workers, Paul's emphasis on his example of self-support despite his apostolic right in 3:8-9 has an explanation.

3. Did irresponsible believers who refused to work receive support from patrons, as in the common Roman patron-client system? In this patronage culture, lesser citizens (*clients*) got food, financial support, recommendations, and other perquisites from their *patron*. In exchange,

the *clients* supported them politically, voted for them, supported their cause in legal disputes, and otherwise contributed to the patron's honor by forming a conspicuous following (see Saller 1982; Winter 1994, 41-60; Green 2002, 208-13; Witherington 2006, 118, 122-23).

Although a commendable investigation of the culture, there are weaknesses to this theory (→ Behind the Text for 1 Thess 4:9-12). The most serious of these is that patrons rarely supplied sufficient financial support to enable clients not to work or supply part of their own incomes. It is doubtful that any Thessalonian Christians were among the über-wealthy, who could afford to be so extravagant with their clients. And it is equally unlikely that any of them were among the class of clients who might attract such support. No pagan Thessalonian patron would lend serious support to those who denounced the city's deities and the imperial cult. Nevertheless, the values of the patronage culture may have contributed to the church's dilemma, by fostering hope for support by others and glamorizing it.

4. The simplest explanation (and the one accepted here) is that the disorderly were abusing the church's common fund. Charity was a sacred obligation, explaining the reticence of the majority to practice more critical oversight of the fund. The practice of almsgiving has deep roots in Judaism and the church. Giving to the poor by sharing harvests, tithing, and no-interest loans was commanded in Israel's covenant legislation (Lev 19:9-10; 23:22; Deut 14:28-29; 15:7-8, 11).

God's preferential concern for the needy is expressed in the proverb, "Whoever is kind to the poor lends to the LORD" (Prov 19:17; see Ps 68:5; Isa 3:14-15; Amos 8:4-6). Deeds of charity are one of three things by which the world is sustained, according to Simeon the Just (*m. 'Abot* 2:1). In ancient Judaism almsgiving is "lending to God," and it delivers from death (Tob 4:6-11, 16-17; *Sib. Or.* 2.80). It is like a thank offering in the temple; it even atones for sin (Sir 3:30; 35:4).

Jewish writers elaborate on the OT, reminding readers to assist widows, orphans, and the poor. They chide them not to be stingy or turn away from a request (Philo, *Virt.* 17; Tob 4:6-11, 16-17; Sir 3:30—4:10, 31; 7:10, 32-36; 29:8-13; *2 En.* 63:2; Josephus, *Ant.* 4.8.21).

In synagogues, charity was regularly pledged and collected, often on the Sabbath. Either the charity collectors or the *hazzan* had charge of taking the money, sometimes approaching people in the market and at home when special needs arose (Levine 2000, 372-73; Safrai 1995, 191-92). These charity funds were stored in the synagogue, as attested in a third-century inscription from a Macedonian synagogue at Stobi, about one hundred miles north of Thessalonica (Levine 2000, 252). Falling below a certain income level qualified the poor for food aid or access to other charitable assistance (*m. Pe'ah* 8:7-8; Levine 2000, 373).

The obligation to give alms is assumed in Jesus' teaching, with universal application: "Give to everyone who asks you" (Luke 6:30; see Matt 5:42; 6:1-4; Acts 20:35). Jesus interpreted his ministry as good news to the poor (Matt 11:2-6; Luke 4:18-21). He warned of eternal damnation to those who refused to share with the needy (Matt 25:31-46; Luke 16:20-31; compare *Barn.* 20.1-2; *Apoc. Pet.* 9; *Vis. Ezra* 27-32).

It is not surprising that Christians adopted the practice of almsgiving without debate. They practiced it from the first in an organized way. The first time we hear of it, it is already established and needing midcourse corrections (Acts 6:1; 2 Thess 3:11-13). It was the "one thing" the Jerusalem leaders asked of Paul (Gal 2:10). Second-century Christian writers regarded care for the needy as a command from Jesus, part of living the "way" (*Did.* 1.4-6; 4.5-8; *1 Clem.* 38.2; *Barn.* 19.8; *Herm. Mand.* 8.10; Aristides, *Apol.* 15).

Such generosity was bound to be abused by some. There are warnings elsewhere to the community about potential spongers: "Let him work and eat" is the instruction about prophets who stay too long in one place (*Did.* 12.1-5). And there are warnings to those who accept charity under false pretenses (*Herm. Mand.* 2.5). The tension between giving generously, as Christ commanded, and critical evaluation of needs is clear in *Did.* 1.5-6: "Give to everyone who asks you, and do not refuse. . . . But about this it was also said: Let your alms sweat in your palms, until you know to whom you should give."†

Early Christians took up voluntary offerings, which were held in a common fund and distributed by trusted persons to those in need, following the synagogue model (1 Tim 5:9-11, 16; *Barn.* 19.8; *1 Clem.* 38.2; Justin, *1 Apol.* 13, 67; Tertullian, *Apol.* 39.5-6). They spoke of this as sharing their goods in common. What was distributed was often not money but food or other necessaries (Acts 6:1).

We do not know who was entrusted with this duty at Thessalonica or how people made their claim on the common fund. Later, deacons were associated with charitable distributions. Paul mentions this office in a letter to another Macedonian city (Phil 1:1). In 1 Tim 5:3-16, Paul orders the church at Ephesus to deny alms to widows who have family to support them or are young enough to remarry (1 Tim 5:11, 14-16).

Paul directs his exhortation in 2 Thessalonians at some who are not working to earn their own support, but instead are living off of the church's generosity (3:6, 10-12; see the counterexample in vv 7-8). This is not a recent problem, but has been ongoing since Paul was first with them in person (v 10).

The reason the church continued to "enable" these people may be the same found in the *Didache*—conflicting authoritative traditions. Some assume they are entitled to the church's generosity. Others believe they are obligated to share their goods without question to those in need. That abuse of the church's charity crops up repeatedly in the literature of early Christianity indicates that it was a common problem.

IN THE TEXT

■ **6** Paul moves into his final exhortation directly and forcefully: **We command you, brothers and sisters** are the first words of this sentence in Greek. Command (*parangellō*) also means to ***direct*** or ***instruct*** but implies an order from a superior. A directive **in the name of *our* Lord Jesus Christ** comes with his authority. Paul represents the risen Lord as his commissioned apostle.

This rare use of the **name** formula reminds readers of their baptism, administered **in the name** of Jesus (Matt 28:19; Acts 2:38; 8:16; 10:48; 19:5; see 1 Cor 1:15). The only other example of Paul making a request in this way is 1 Cor 1:10 (which also appeals to their baptism [v 13]). But why should the *obedient* members of the community be especially reminded of their baptismal relationship to the Lord rather than the *disobedient* members (v 12)?

Specifically, Paul orders the obedient members of the Thessalonian church **to keep away from every *brother or sister who lives irresponsibly, and not according to the tradition that they received from us.*** The roots of this problem seem to be in an abuse of the church's common fund (→ Behind the Text for 2 Thess 3:6-15, above).

In the first letter, Paul reminded his audience that he had previously directed them on working and living quietly during his founding visit to Thessalonica (1 Thess 4:11). Here, Paul describes the troublemakers as ***walking*** in a way he describes as *ataktōs*, **idle and disruptive** (2 Thess 3:6).

The word **idle** makes us think of people doing nothing. But the Greek adverb *ataktōs* and its related terms in antiquity always implied violating societal norms—insubordinate, disorderly, irresponsible, or immoral conduct (LSJM, 267; LSJM Supplement, 58; BDAG, 148; Milligan 1908, 152-54; Malherbe 2000, 317; Witherington 2006, 162; Fee 2009, 209-10 and n. 18; see 1 Thess 5:14). The verbal form describes people stirring up riots, or soldiers behaving in an undisciplined way ("painting the town red," we might say; LSJM, 267). In 3 Macc 1:19 *ataktōs* describes the immodest and chaotic rush of Jewish brides into the streets in protest, over the fear that Pharaoh Ptolemy IV was about to enter the temple in Jerusalem.

The problem then is not that these people are simply "loafers." There are better words Paul could have chosen to express that, and *ataktōs* almost never means this (BDAG, 148; Malherbe 2000, 317; Fee 2009, 209). Modern readers must think of the ancient Roman sociopolitical context (→ Behind the Text for 2 Thess 3:6-15, above). Today, we think of "disruptive" persons as antisocial "jerks." At worst, they do something to get themselves arrested on minor charges. In Paul's day, they threatened the Roman peace and risked severe reaction from the state.

To protect the witness of the church to society, Paul urged the church to **keep away** from *believers who live irresponsibly*. The church needs to demonstrate to its neighbors, and make plain to disciples, that its teaching is not endorsing the disruptive, disorderly behavior of these confused believers. Facilitating repentance for these people from their disordered lifestyle is another reason Paul calls for withdrawing from them (*stellesthai*, middle voice: to **hold oneself aloof from** or **shun**; see v 14). This is the only way to stop "enabling" them, to prevent them from taking support (compare the more severe discipline of excommunication in 1 Cor 5:3-5). The offenders are not to be considered outsiders. The obedient majority should "warn them" as brothers (2 Thess 3:15), still part of the body of Christ.

Paul emphasizes that the irresponsible idle have actively ignored the teaching he passed on to them by example, admonition, and letter. This is what Paul calls **the tradition** they **received from us** but fail to observe (v 6; → 2:15). It includes the example the apostles set by their behavior as well as their teaching (3:7-8), and they expected the Thessalonians to follow it. The verb **received** is used several times in Paul's letters to designate the passing on of apostolic teaching (1 Cor 11:23; 15:1-3; Gal 1:9; Phil 4:9; Col 2:6; 1 Thess 2:13; 4:1). (On the textual variant "they"/**you received**, see Metzger 1994, 569; Fee 2009, 326 n. 54.)

■ **7-8** Here Paul introduces a justification for the command to shun the disorderly (see v 6): **You yourselves know** (v 7) is emphatic, as if to say, "I shouldn't have to tell you this." They know that living *according to the tradition* (v 6) means they **ought to follow**, or *imitate*, the apostles (v 7). Paul introduced the theme of imitation in 1 Thess 1:6; 2:10-14 (→). There Paul spoke of himself as a model of working and holy love (2:9). Jesus called disciples to "follow" his way of life as well as his teachings (Matt 4:19-22; 16:24-26; Mark 8:34; Luke 14:25-27; John 1:43; 8:12; 10:27).

Paul's reminders to his readers of what they already know serve as a paraenetic device (e.g., 1 Thess 2:1-2, 10-11; 3:3; 5:2; 2 Thess 2:5-6). They function like a parent's words, "I don't need to tell you again to . . ." Shared truths connect writers with readers. **Ought** (Gk.: *dei* [3:7]) is sometimes an indirect way of speaking about God's will (1 Thess 4:1; Rom 8:26; 12:3; 1 Cor 8:2; 15:25, 53; 2 Cor 5:10; Eph 6:20; 1 Tim 3:15).

Paul details the example the apostles set—how he and his companions *did not live irresponsibly when* they *were with* the Thessalonians. *Live irresponsibly* translates *ētaktēsamen*, the verbal form of *ataktōs* (2 Thess 3:6): to behave in a disordered, irresponsible, or unethical way (Milligan 1908, 152-53; BDAG, 148). It occurs in some ancient apprentice contracts to indicate failure to perform duties (Milligan 1908, 152-53).

The NIV translation **not idle** (v 7) paraphrases Paul's meaning in light of the context. The apostle denies taking any food from the Thessalonians **without paying for it** while he was with them (v 8*a*). The expression **eat . . .**

food may be a metonymy referring more broadly to his room and board with Jason (Acts 17:5-7). Instead of receiving anything "as a gift" Paul and his companions worked hard at a trade to earn a living. Paul's example was the direct opposite of the *ataktoi*—the "idle and disruptive" (2 Thess 3:11).

The hardships Paul experienced supporting himself are emphasized by the word pairs: **laboring and toiling** and **night and day** (v 8). The first pair emphasizes the drudgery of manual labor. The second emphasizes the extraordinary length of his working days. A normal free man's working hours were limited to the daytime, but Paul worked at **night** also, adopting the hours of a slave. Perhaps he earned so little he had to work long hours (Hock 1980, 34-35). As a bivocational minister, leading worship and making pastoral visits were done after work (→ 1 Thess 2:9).

The description of the apostles' labor on behalf of the church resembles 1 Thess 2:9. The memory of his difficulties was vivid in Paul's mind. Like an adventurer retelling his story, his greatest challenges stand out and get retold repeatedly.

The purpose for this work was **so that** Paul **would not be a burden to any of** them (v 8*b*). He refused to take support from them, though it was his apostolic right (see 1 Cor 9:4-5, 11, 14; 2 Cor 11:7). This was his usual policy (2 Cor 11:9; 12:13-16; 1 Cor 9:18, 12, 15).

Paul's example was the opposite of living irresponsibly (2 Thess 3:7*b*), unmindful of the impact of selfish behavior on others. Instead, Christian love led Paul to a mission policy of self-support. This policy also helped protect the reputation of the gospel and its evangelists. For it was commonplace in antiquity to suspect traveling philosophers of being charlatans out to bilk people of their money. Quasi-religious personnel (fortune-tellers, prophets, magicians) not connected to a civic cult lived under a cloud of suspicion. Paul's choice, to live so as **not** to **burden** anyone, correlates with his prayer that the gospel be honored (→ 3:1).

■ **9** Paul reminds his audience again that his purpose in working was to offer **a model** lifestyle for them **to imitate** (see 1 Thess 2:9-12; 4:1). But first he denies that he had to work because he lacked the apostolic **right** to material support from the church. This sentence begins with an ellipsis—**. . . not because we do not have the right**. Most translations supply the implied reference to the apostles' work—**We did this**.

This is not a response to a challenge. It is merely part of Paul's rhetorical strategy aimed at the irresponsible (*ataktoi*) believers in Thessalonica. If the apostle Paul, who was entitled to **help** from the community, set them a **model . . . to imitate** of self-support by his own labor, how much more should other believers work?

If those who had stopped working were also evangelizing (→ Behind the Text for 2 Thess 3:6-15, above), they might have claimed the **right** to support because they were "workers" like Paul and his associates (Jewett 1986, 105;

Barclay 1993, 520-23, 528). Paul's reference to himself as a model would be even more significant. In either case, Paul practiced what he taught.

■ **10** Paul now reminds the Thessalonians of his teaching, the tradition they received. **When we were with you**, during his time evangelizing the city, **we gave you this rule: "The one who is unwilling to work shall not eat."** Note about this rule:

(*a*) It was given during Paul's initial visit. This implies that the problem with work *preceded* any eschatological errors (→ Behind the Text for 2 Thess 3:6-15, above). In fact, Paul uses an imperfect tense verb in Greek, suggesting repeated exhortations (compare the NASB ["we used to give you this order"] and the NET ["we used to give you this command"]).

(*b*) The order is addressed to the working majority, who contribute to the common fund for the needy. They believe Jesus' command compels them to give to those who ask, no matter what (→ Behind the Text for 2 Thess 3:6-15, above). The intent is to give apostolic sanction to abstain from giving support to the undeserving (see 1 Tim 5:3-16). That is, those who refuse to work **shall not eat** from the church's table or poor box. Paul does not intend to starve the disorderly. He says nothing about unruly nonworkers eating from their own household stores. In time, of course, the diminishing supplies of the unruly will force them to work.

(*c*) Paul's order designates the problem of the *ataktoi* as a failure of *will*. It is not directed at those who cannot work due to illness or disability. Frequently cited, alleged parallels from Greek and rabbinic literature are actually maxims. These have the character of wisdom teaching: If you don't work, you won't have anything to eat (Best 1986, 339). Paul's rule, however, is an ethical imperative *for the community of faith* to enforce: the person who refuses to work should be refused sustenance.

Perhaps Paul addresses a communal "tenement church," in which the poor pooled their resources for shared meals (Jewett 1993, 37-42). This theory captures well the potential for abuse that individuals do in lower-class communities when they "share" the goods of others without contributing anything themselves.

■ **11** Paul finally addresses the problem of **idle and disruptive** believers (lit. those walking idly, as in v 6 [→]). He speaks of them in the third person. ***For we hear that some are living among you irresponsibly, doing no work but meddling***. He continues to address the obedient majority. The report Paul repeats reminds them of his rule about who may eat from community assets (v 10). The information may have come from Timothy, a letter, or a visitor from Thessalonica. What Paul heard indicates:

Some Thessalonian Christians have stopped "work" (v 10), by which Paul means paid employment (not ministry; → v 8). This explains why some interpreters identify the *ataktoi* as "idlers." But the adverb *ataktōs* and its related terms always imply violating social norms—insubordinate, irresponsible, or immoral behavior (→ v 6 and Behind the Text for 2 Thess 3:6-15, above).

Their misconduct includes idleness, but to limit it to "loafing" misunderstands the seriousness of Paul's order. They have refused to follow apostolic tradition (v 6), despite multiple reminders. They have wrongly taken support from the community's common fund that should have gone to those with real needs (→ Behind the Text for 2 Thess 3:6-15, above). They have selfishly taken advantage of the sensitivities of their Christian brothers and sisters. The problem with the *ataktoi* is not merely what they have *not* done but what they *have* done—other sorts of socially unacceptable behavior.

The irresponsibility of the disorderly is further manifested in their **meddling** (*periergazomenous*). The Greek word is a play on the verb **working** (*ergazomenous*). The NIV captures well Paul's wordplay with **not busy . . . busybodies**. What exactly this involved is mostly speculation.

Did the slackers bother church leaders for handouts (so Frame 1912, 305)? Did they annoy others with unending blather about religion (so Best 1986, 340)? Were they obnoxious street evangelists who mercilessly berated pagans (so Barclay 1993, 522-23)? Did they spread false teachings about the end times (so Beale 2003, 252)? Some speculate that the *ataktoi* made themselves **busybodies** by their involvement in civic politics on behalf of their patrons, as opposed to living quietly (v 12, and 1 Thess 4:11; Winter 1994, 50-51; Green 2002, 351; Witherington 2006, 247-49). These theories may reveal more about interpreters than about the first century. Certainly Paul seems unconcerned that evangelism might be a social problem; he heartily endorses it and even revels in the backlash the gospel causes (see 1 Cor 1:18; 2:1-5; 2 Cor 4.5, 7-13; 1 Thess 1:8-10; 2:2, 9).

At the end of the day it is impossible to know what acting like **busybodies** involved, except that it included an abuse of the common fund. *Periergazomenous* and *ataktōs* suggest behavior that disrupts and interferes, instead of being constructive. It troubles the fellowship and shames it before the wider public.

■ 12 Paul comes close here to addressing the disruptive minority. He issues orders to them, but without the normal second-person address: **Such people we command and urge in the Lord Jesus Christ**. **Such people** is a way Paul typically refers anonymously to misbehaving believers or false brothers (Rom 16:18; 1 Cor 5:5, 11; 2 Cor 2:6, 7). The rhetorical effect of this third-person address is to treat them as though Paul is already "keeping away" from them, as he commanded the church to do in 2 Thess 3:6. The contrast with his address to the faithful brothers as "you" (second-person plural, v 13) is stark. Paul refuses to address the *ataktoi* in the second-person, as friends, because they have persistently defied his instructions on how to live.

In language echoing v 6, Paul invokes the authority of **the Lord Jesus Christ** for his **command** to the irresponsible, just as he had invoked Christ's authority for his word to the faithful. He emphasizes his authority as an apostle. If he meant to echo here the baptismal formula, the intent would be that the audience should remember their baptism and take seriously the call to identify with Christ and submit to him as Lord in their ensuing life. (On the meaning of Jesus' full title, used for the eighth time in the letter here, → 1 Thess 1:1.)

To **command** Paul adds **urge** (from *parakaleō*), imploring the disorderly to choose the right path, and showing his deep personal concern for them. His command/plea is for them *to work quietly and eat their own food*.

Quietly refers to working in a calm, well-ordered way (NIV: **settle down**). The term sometimes serves as the opposite of political activism in Greek literature, suggesting a focus on private concerns (see 1 Thess 4:11-12; Malherbe 1987, 96-101; Green 2002, 352). Some interpreters take this as evidence that the disruptive members were involved in local politics as clients on behalf of their patrons, who supplied them with **food** (Winter 1994, 48-57; Green 2002, 351-52; Witherington 2006, 247). (On the problems with this patronage hypothesis, → 1 Thess 4:9-12 and Behind the Text for 2 Thess 3:6-15, above.)

Taken with **meddling** and not working (v 11), the command to *work quietly* implies that the irresponsible behavior of the *ataktoi* has become a nuisance to both Christians and the wider community. They are injuring the reputation of the church and undermining the credibility of the gospel.

Paul's assessment critiques their dishonorable refusal to support themselves alongside their willingness to receive support from the funds of the church without justification. Whatever they do instead of work seems to be causing trouble.

They need to (lit.) *eat their own bread*, that is, support themselves and **earn the food they eat**. In other words, they should follow the apostles' example (vv 7-8), get work, and stop begging from others or taking from the church's common fund. Paul assumes that the recalcitrant are able to work.

■ **13** Returning to the working majority, Paul addresses them as **brothers and sisters**. This emphasizes their common bond as the context for another command: **Never tire of doing what is good** (*kalopoiountes*). Paul urges them not to become discouraged and **give up** (*mē enkakēsēte*).

Many translations prefer "doing . . . right" (e.g., NRSV) to **doing . . . good**, perhaps due to Protestant misgivings about good works. But Paul understands these to be the fruit of real faith and regeneration (Rom 7:21; 13:8-10; Gal 5:14; 6:9; Eph 2:10; 1 Thess 4:7, 9-10; see Matt 5:16; Mark 14:6; John 10:32).

But why does Paul use the word **good** here? Is it just a generic encouragement: "Don't slip like these others are doing"? Or is it intended to remind the majority to treat the idle minority well, as Christian love demands, despite their troublemaking (so John Chrysostom, *Hom. 2 Thess.* 5; Frame 1912, 308; Best 1986, 342-43)? Is Paul bolstering their courage to carry out the difficult task of discipline (3:6, 14-15)? Paul certainly does not want the church to overreact to this crisis by becoming cynical or cutting off support from the truly needy (Malherbe 2000, 458; Green 2002, 353; Witherington 2006, 255).

■ **14** Paul suspects that some of the minority will not listen to him. After all, they have maintained their disorderly behavior despite his personal instructions (v 10), previous letter (1 Thess 4:11-12), and the efforts of fellow believers to intervene (5:14).

So the church is to **take special note** of any recalcitrant believer **who does not obey our instruction in this letter.** The verb **note** can mean "write down." But here Paul is probably not thinking of a literal register. The believers as a group should identify and remember those who are irresponsible. The object of isolating these people is to shame them publicly, to separate from them (if necessary), and to bring them to repentance.

Do not associate (*mingle*) is a rare verb used of social interaction (see Hos 7:8; 1 Cor 5:9, 11). The NT elsewhere calls for the exclusion of unrepentant offenders from the church, sometimes after a community process (Matt 18:15-17; Rom 16:17; Titus 3:10). It is difficult to envision precisely how Paul intended this separation from the offenders was to occur. He will add immediately in 2 Thess 3:15 that they are "not" to be treated "as an enemy" but warned as "a fellow believer." At a minimum, it implies an end to normal social activities (shared visits and meals) and may mean exclusion from worship gatherings.

The main purpose of the exercise of this community discipline is **that they may feel ashamed** of not working, living irresponsibly, causing trouble to the community, and treating the apostles' teaching flippantly. This shaming action may seem odd or harsh to modern readers. But it was the normal approach to enforcing social norms in the ancient world. (It may not be so different from the way the media attempts to enforce political correctness today!) In ancient Mediterranean societies, a person's honor was derived from the group the person identified with. Respect and honor from that group was extremely important to a person's sense of self-worth (→ "Shame, Honor, and Biblical Holiness" sidebar at 1 Thess 3:13; see also Du Boulay 1974, 81, 83).

Paul recommends one of the most powerful behavior-modification motivators available. By withdrawing contact, the group withdraws honor and status from the offenders. These believers had already undergone a loss of honor when they became Christians, for their new beliefs clashed with the old order and set them apart from pagan society. Their new faith may have brought "shame" on them in the eyes of their families and former associates. It may have cost them political standing, social status, and perhaps even their livelihoods.

But at least they had a Christian family and a new kind of honor (or "righteousness") in Christ. Now they face exclusion from the Christian community. This would leave them with few or no options. John Chrysostom thought it was out of fear that this shame might cut offenders off from the community entirely and drive them to despair that Paul wrote v 15 (*Hom. 2 Thess.* 5).

■ **15** Anticipating the danger of driving off offenders, Paul adds two admonitions:

First, **do not regard them as an enemy**. Separation and shaming often led to animosity and political/legal recrimination (Green 2002, 356). The purpose of the corrective Paul advised is loving discipline in the interest of reform. It should not get out of hand or be carried out in a spiteful way.

Instead, the apostle urged, **warn them as you would a fellow believer**. This sentence regards offenders as still within the orbit of the body of Christ (contrast the cases of Matt 18:17; 1 Cor 5:3-5; Titus 3:10). Here some continuing contact must be envisaged in the term **warn/*admonish*** (*noutheteite*, Wis 11:10; 12:2; *Pss. Sol.* 13:9; Rom 15:14; 1 Cor 4:14; Col 3:16; 1 Thess 5:12, 14). The present imperative in Greek suggests an ongoing activity—***continue to admonish*** the offenders.

Any interpretation presents a problem for modern Western readers. What sort of context does Paul envision? How are the obedient majority not to ***mingle***, not to feed or support, and to shun these irresponsible believers (3:6, 10, 14)? How are they to do this and still regard them as brothers and ***admonish*** them about their misbehavior?

Most commentators agree that Paul forbids sharing the church's *agapē* meal that accompanied worship meetings. He almost certainly does not want obedient Christians mingling socially in their homes with the recalcitrant. But since there were no church buildings yet, how were offenders to be excluded from house church / tenement church gatherings?

Some interpreters think the admonishing must have involved an official action done in a worship setting. Does this imply that the offenders are present for worship (so Best 1986, 343-44)? But ancient interpreters took ***admonish as a brother*** to imply private conversations, such as one would inevitably have with family members (John Chrysostom, *Hom. 2 Thess.* 5; Marshall 1983, 229; see Malherbe 2000, 460).

How could such people be noted or "marked" (v 14; BDAG, 921), if they were not present? How could they be totally excluded and not also be regarded as enemies? Were they admitted to the assembly? Were they allowed to participate in the Lord's Supper? Did their shame consist in being forced to sit apart from the others *within* the gathering (like the penalty box in hockey? see Witherington 2006, 255-56).

Should we assume that those under this discipline were banned from attending worship gatherings or sharing in all communal meals—whether the *agapē* meal or the Lord's Supper—until they repented? Did admonishing happen on an informal/individual basis by ordinary members/community leaders outside of the assembly?

The normal result of extreme forms of discipline in ancient society would be to make offenders enemies. This explains Paul's special caution here (Green 2002, 356). But how were the Thessalonians to avoid this unintended reaction? Could they treat offenders as the erring part of their family under correction (as in "time-out"?).

Certainty is impossible. The text explicitly forbids all material support and calls for communal shaming of the unrepentant. But it may leave open the possibility that as a **brother or sister** there was still a place even for the *ataktos* within the community. The church could continue to chide them and urge them to reform, as they would errant family members. The discipline Paul calls for here certainly appears be less severe than that he requires in 1 Cor 5:1-5, 9—excommunication.

FROM THE TEXT

Paul's "tradition" turns out to be complex, a lived-out pattern of life (3:7-9) accompanied by oral instructions (v 10). It is important to see his instructions as grounded in the gospel, leading to principles such as love for neighbor, care for one's family, and being a person who brings *shalom* to the community.

This text raises interesting questions for modern Christians about three issues: church discipline, work, and charity. Our radically different social situations make direct applications challenging. For example, there is no longer only a single Christian group in any one city, listening to a single set of apostolic commands. People disciplined by one church may simply go down the road and join another.

Perhaps we might apply Paul's command to those who claim to have a Christian ministry but whose lifestyle is irresponsible or contradicts the gospel. We ought to distance ourselves from such ministries and certainly not support them financially. This would make it clear to all that we do not endorse such undisciplined behavior.

Paul challenges us to value work and self-sufficiency, and not only for the personal benefits they afford. Those who work can contribute to others who have legitimate needs and by their exemplary work give a positive gospel witness to society. This imitates the self-giving of Christ and his apostles.

The locus of charitable aid has shifted from Paul's day to ours. Then there was virtually no government assistance except for the bread dole in the city of Rome. All charity was private, whether from patrons, family, or others. Most of contemporary society's charitable functions in the West have shifted to government-managed welfare programs. Of course, this doesn't mean there are no needs to fill. Church food pantries seem to be well used and are constantly running low on supplies.

How are we to implement Paul's rules for contemporary church relief efforts? Should we demand proof of a person's inability to work before allowing them to take from the food pantry? Few are callous enough to do that. On the other hand, we should hesitate to distribute money from the church treasury without ensuring there is a legitimate need.

Some tried to apply Paul's rule in the political sphere, to shape public policy toward the poor and welfare in the nineteenth and twentieth centuries (Copeland 1994, 25-73). Such efforts were sometimes more punitive than reforming. How far may rules intended for a small religious group with limited resources be applied to the economy of a nation?

We must not misread Paul. He does not deny the obligation of the people of God to support needy individuals. His concern was only to prevent the church from wasting their few resources on those with no legitimate claim to need. Paul's command reminds Christians today not to enable people who can support themselves, who prefer to take from others by abuse, manipulation, or deceit.

But we must never forget that the text also *presumes* the goodness of charitable giving. The Christian community must assist those who *cannot* work. If Christ's people had not firmly believed in doing charity for their Lord, the problem Paul attempted to solve would never have arisen.

A similar debate continues today in the public square: Who is "worthy" of welfare? The heart of such debates are not about economics but about deeply held values about what people—or society—should be expected to do for others. This letter reminds us that giving is always risky and may invite "scammers." But Paul does not recommend an end to generosity as a solution.

VII. CLOSING: 2 THESSALONIANS 3:16-18

BEHIND THE TEXT

In the conclusion of Paul's letters, he leaves his final personal touch and his prayer-wish for the community. Like the benediction of worship services, the letter closing seems designed to send the reader off with a blessing and a final contemplation of the gracious character of God.

Ancient letters never closed with a signature as modern ones do. The author's name appeared at the start of a papyrus letter and on the outside address. So when Paul speaks of the "distinguishing mark" (*sēmeion*, "sign") in all his letters (3:17), what he must refer to is his handwriting (**this greeting in my own hand**). It was his way of showing he had personally sent the original. Ancient papyrus letters survive in which the authors closed in a different hand after a scribe had written the majority of the text (e.g., P.Oxy. 3067; Stowers 1986, 61, 72; Deissmann 1910, 153, 158; Green 2002, 359).

Some skeptics consider v 17 an effort by a forger to get his work accepted as Paul's (Richard 1995, 393-94; Gaventa 1998, 133; Furnish 2007, 182). But, in fact, Paul's closing conforms with known literary practices. It also suits the church's situation in Thessalonica. Their theological confusion needed a sure response (→ 2:2).

Paul apparently normally dictated his letters to a secretary, who did the actual writing (see Rom 16:22). On several occasions he mentions that he was personally adding something in his own handwriting (1 Cor 16:21; Gal 6:11; Col 4:18; Phlm 19). Such a personal addition would likely have been visible in the handwriting of the original autograph of 1 Thessalonians as well, beginning in 5:27 or 28.

The endings of Paul's letters vary in form and content. The only constant is a wish for grace to the readers. Neither 1 or 2 Thessalonians have greetings to or from specific people (nor do 2 Corinthians, Galatians, Ephesians, or Philippians). The literary effect of Paul's letter closings is to focus all attention on Paul's offering of Christ's peace, Christ's presence, and Christ's grace to the community of believers.

IN THE TEXT

A. Prayer-Wish (3:16)

■ 16 In closing Paul pronounces his final prayer blessing on the Thessalonian Christian community. The Greek optative mood (→ 2:16-17; 3:5; 1 Thess 3:11-13; 5:23) gives this a liturgical feel. The words **may the Lord . . . give you peace** echo the Aaronic blessing of Num 6:26.

Only here in the NT is Jesus called the **Lord of peace**, echoing God's title in 1 Thess 5:23 (also Rom 15:33; Phil 4:9). Paul may think of Jesus as the fulfillment of Isa 9:6—he is the Davidic "Prince of Peace." He often alludes to Isaiah in this letter (in 1:6 [Isa 66:4]; 1:8 [Isa 66:15-16]; 1:9 [Isa 2:10]; 2:8 [Isa 11:4]; 3:2 [Isa 25:4 LXX]).

Christ is **Lord of peace** in that he has made peace possible between God and humanity. On this basis reconciliation can happen between people as well. Paul prays that Christ **may . . . give** his hearers **peace**. This **peace** includes being reconciled to God by his grace, the fullness of salvation (Frame 1912, 311; Best 1986, 63-64, 346).

Many commentators see the apostle's mention of **peace** as directed toward the potential conflict that will surely come from confronting the disorderly. But we should not forget the wider context of the Thessalonians' lives, which included serious conflict with their non-Christian society (2 Thess 1:4-7; 1 Thess 1:6; 2:14; 3:3-4).

The prayer for **peace at all times and in every way** emphatically embraces their total situation. Paul expects the **peace** Christ makes possible to bring overall well-being—improved relations between believers and their neighbors and relief from their suffering (Green 2002, 357). Paul longs for the establishment of God's *shalom* in every aspect of their lives: political, economic, interpersonal, and religious (compare Green 2002, 357; Witherington 2006, 259).

Paul includes even the unruly *ataktoi* in this blessing, as he indicates with the word **all** in his closing wish: May **the Lord be with all of you**. This is similar to the ancient Israelite greeting found in Judg 6:12, Ruth 2:4, and Luke 1:28. There, the **Lord** stands for Yahweh, the God of Israel; here, for Jesus, the **Lord** of the new covenant (2 Thess 3:18; see 2 Cor 5:19; Marshall 1983, 231; Fee 2009, 341). This stunning christological statement functionally places the risen Jesus in the liturgical position of the Lord of the covenant, the source of blessing and peace. Jesus is the living divine presence among the community of faith. It is also reminiscent of Matt 1:22-23 and 28:20—Jesus is "Emmanuel," God with us. And he has promised to remain with his disciples throughout this age. The **Lord** is with the community especially through the mediation of the Holy Spirit, who indwells, gifts, and guides believers (Rom 8:9-11; 1 Cor 15:45; Gal 4:6). This is what they need for comfort and wisdom in their situation.

B. Autographic Conclusion (3:17)

■ **17** At the end of the letter Paul takes the letter from his scribe and scrawls his own note, **Greetings from Paul—in my own hand, which is *a* mark in every letter; this is how I write**. In several other letters he mentions adding a postscript in his own handwriting, and he may have done this elsewhere without remark, since this was conventional in antiquity (→ Behind the Text for 2 Thess 3:16-18, above). The difference in handwriting would have been obvious in the original autograph. Of course, it is not in printed Bibles.

Some think the expression **all my letters** (lit. *every letter*) strange, since this is only the second or third earliest letter we have from Paul. But the strangeness is due to our modern perspective. Paul was perhaps forty-six or fifty-seven years old when he wrote this (Murphy-O'Connor 1996, 2-4, 8). He had been a Christian for nearly two decades. He must have written many more letters than the church saw fit to canonize.

This is how I write refers to Paul's distinctive handwriting, not his literary style. It is similar to his remark in Gal 6:11. But why does Paul draw particular attention to the letter closing in his own handwriting? In 2 Thess 2:2 (→) he mentioned the possibility that false teaching may have been communicated by means of a letter he supposedly had written.

The false teachers probably distorted 1 Thessalonians, but Paul cannot rule out forgeries. His handwriting should serve as the **mark** that the original letter was actually from him. His explanation underlines the authority of the letter when it was read aloud in church, since most of its recipients could not read it (or appreciate the handwriting change). Paul wants them to *hear* the letter is from him. This was particularly necessary in a letter that called for difficult disciplinary measures (→ 3:6-15). It is noteworthy that three of the four other texts that draw specific attention to Paul's autograph also occur in letters that deal severely with moral issues or false doctrine (1 Cor 16:21; Gal 6:11; Col 4:18).

C. Benediction (3:18)

■ **18** The letter opened with a wish for "grace" (1:2) and closes with the same, as do all of Paul's letters (e.g., Rom 1:7; 16:20; 1 Cor 1:3; 16:23). Paul suggests by this that God's unmerited favor to believers is the beginning and end of everything (Matera 2012, 87). **Grace** gives encouragement and hope (→ 2 Thess 2:16) for believers' future in God's kingdom, because of what the Lord has done for believers in and through **our Lord Jesus Christ** (Rom 3:21-26; 5:2; Gal 2:20-21). This is the ninth time Paul uses this full title in 2 Thessalonians (→ 3:11).

For Paul **grace** is not only God's favor that freely grants forgiveness, acceptance, and entrance into his kingdom but also an ongoing force, God's saving activity through Christ that continually comes to believers, frees them from the bondage of sin, strengthens, equips, transforms, and calls them to service (e.g., Gal 2:9; 2 Cor 1:12; 12:9; Eph 4:7; Dunn 1998, 322). For Paul, it is at times hard to distinguish between the **grace of** [coming from, due to] the **Lord Jesus Christ**, and **grace** which *is* the very presence of the risen **Lord** among his people by way of the Holy Spirit (2 Cor 13:14; 2 Thess 3:16; 2 Tim 4:22). By adding **all** to his prayer, Paul indicates his desire to include even the disobedient in Thessalonica, urging them to embrace the restoring **grace** of the risen Jesus.

FROM THE TEXT

As the body of Christ, we can embrace Paul's prayers as for us today. Although we live in a different age, a different world, the risen Jesus is still the Lord of peace. We are groaning with the old creation, longing for that *shalom*, which will surpass all imagining. The peace Christ will bring will so transform the fabric of our existence that we can barely comprehend it with the label "glory" (→ 2:14). Until that final day, we both pray and trust that the Lord will be with us as we look to him in faith. It is his living presence among and within the faithful that makes this thing called "Christianity" meaningful.

In this in-between time of groaning and spiritual birthing, the foretaste of that eschatological peace begins to appear, as God's miracle. The peace that the world longs for is what Christ longs to give. By his grace his peace may come to sin-ravaged humanity; to lives damaged by personal assaults or addictions; to troubled families and broken marriages. His peace may come to labor and management relations fraught with bitterness.

We pray for his peace to overcome racial tensions; his peace for those suffering with apparently hopeless injuries and illness. Christian NGOs and other groups dare to hope for Christ's peace to break in even where there have been kidnappings, hostage-taking, war, and economic disasters.

Paul's prayer reminds us of how important it is at every stage of the Christian walk to pray for *grace*. This is not just for "beginners"! All that we have, all that we are, we owe to God. It is God's grace that opens people's ears to the gospel, that helps bring erring believers to repentance, bring embittered brothers and sisters to reconciliation, that opens hearts to the needy, that brings willing hearts to spiritual maturity. We don't understand the logic of it and cannot predict it ahead of time. But again and again God's people have witnessed his grace transform fallen humanity. May the grace of our Lord Jesus Christ be with us all!

www.ingramcontent.com/pod-product-compliance
Lightning Source LLC
Chambersburg PA
CBHW070303240426
43661CB00057B/2631